KT-500-820

The Unified
Modeling Language
User Guide

The Addison-Wesley Object Technology Series

Grady Booch, Ivar Jacobson, and James Rumbaugh, Series Editors

For more information check out the series web site [http://www.awl.com /cseng/otseries/] as well as the pages on each book [http://www.awl.com/cseng/I-S-B-N/] (I-S-B-N represents the actual ISBN, including dashes).

David Bellin and Susan Suchman Simone, *The CRC Card Book*, ISBN 0-201-89535-8

Robert V. Binder, *Testing Object-Oriented Systems: Models, Patterns, and Tools*, ISBN 0-201-80938-9

Bob Blakley, *CORBA Security: An Introduction to Safe Computing with Objects*, ISBN 0-201-32565-9

Grady Booch, *Object Solutions: Managing the Object-Oriented Project*, ISBN 0-8053-0594-7

Grady Booch, *Object-Oriented Analysis and Design with Applications, Second Edition*, ISBN 0-8053-5340-2

Grady Booch, James Rumbaugh, and Ivar Jacobson, *The Unified Modeling Language User Guide*, ISBN 0-201-57168-4

Don Box, *Essential COM*, ISBN 0-201-63446-5

Don Box, Keith Brown, Tim Ewald, and Chris Sells, *Effective COM: 50 Ways to Improve Your COM and MTS-based Applications*, ISBN 0-201-37968-6

Alistair Cockburn, *Surviving Object-Oriented Projects: A Manager's Guide*, ISBN 0-201-49834-0

Dave Collins, *Designing Object-Oriented User Interfaces*, ISBN 0-8053-5350-X

Jim Conallen, *Building Web Applications with UML*, ISBN 0-201-61577-0

Desmond Frances D'Souza and Alan Cameron Wills, *Objects, Components, and Frameworks with UML: The Catalysis Approach*, ISBN 0-201-31012-0

Bruce Powel Douglass, *Doing Hard Time: Developing Real-Time Systems with UML, Objects, Frameworks, and Patterns*, ISBN 0-201-49837-5

Bruce Powel Douglass, *Real-Time UML, Second Edition: Developing Efficient Objects for Embedded Systems*, ISBN 0-201-65784-8

Martin Fowler, *Analysis Patterns: Reusable Object Models*, ISBN 0-201-89542-0

Martin Fowler, Kent Beck, John Brant, William Opdyke, and Don Roberts, *Refactoring: Improving the Design of Existing Code*, ISBN 0-201-48567-2

Martin Fowler with Kendall Scott, *UML Distilled, Second Edition: A Brief Guide to the Standard Object Modeling Language*, ISBN 0-201-65783-X

Ian Gorton, *Enterprise Transaction Processing Systems: Putting the CORBA OTS, Encina++ and Orbix OTM to Work*, ISBN 0-201-39859-1

Peter Heinckiens, *Building Scalable Database Applications: Object-Oriented Design, Architectures, and Implementations*, ISBN 0-201-31013-9

Christine Hofmeister, Robert Nord, and Soni Dilip, *Applied Software Architecture*, ISBN 0-201-32571-3

Ivar Jacobson, Grady Booch, and James Rumbaugh, *The Unified Software Development Process*, ISBN 0-201-57169-2

Ivar Jacobson, Magnus Christerson, Patrik Jonsson, and Gunnar Overgaard, *Object-Oriented Software Engineering: A Use Case Driven Approach*, ISBN 0-201-54435-0

Ivar Jacobson, Maria Ericsson, and Agneta Jacobson, *The Object Advantage: Business Process Reengineering with Object Technology*, ISBN 0-201-42289-1

Ivar Jacobson, Martin Griss, and Patrik Jonsson, *Software Reuse: Architecture, Process and Organization for Business Success*, ISBN 0-201-92476-5

David Jordan, *C++ Object Databases: Programming with the ODMG Standard*, ISBN 0-201-63488-0

Philippe Kruchten, *The Rational Unified Process, An Introduction, Second Edition*, ISBN 0-201-70710-1

Wilf LaLonde, *Discovering Smalltalk*, ISBN 0-8053-2720-7

Dean Leffingwell and Don Widrig, *Managing Software Requirements: A Unified Approach*, ISBN 0-201-61593-2

Lockheed Martin Advanced Concepts Center and Rational Software Corporation, *Succeeding with the Booch and OMT Methods: A Practical Approach*, ISBN 0-8053-2279-5

Chris Marshall, *Enterprise Modeling with UML: Designing Successful Software through Business Analysis*, ISBN 0-201-43313-3

Thomas J. Mowbray and William A. Ruh, *Inside CORBA: Distributed Object Standards and Applications*, ISBN 0-201-89540-4

Bernd Oestereich, *Developing Software with UML: Object-Oriented Analysis and Design in Practice*, ISBN 0-201-39826-5

Meilir Page-Jones, *Fundamentals of Object-Oriented Design in UML*, ISBN 0-201-69946-X

Ira Pohl, *Object-Oriented Programming Using C++, Second Edition*, ISBN 0-201-89550-1

Rob Pooley and Perdita Stevens, *Using UML: Software Engineering with Objects and Components*, ISBN 0-201-36067-5

Terry Quatrani, *Visual Modeling with Rational Rose 2000 and UML*, ISBN 0-201-69961-3

Brent Rector and Chris Sells, *ATL Internals*, ISBN 0-201-69589-8

Paul R. Reed, Jr., *Developing Applications with Visual Basic and UML*, ISBN 0-201-61579-7

Doug Rosenberg with Kendall Scott, *Use Case Driven Object Modeling with UML: A Practical Approach*, ISBN 0-201-43289-7

Walker Royce, *Software Project Management: A Unified Framework*, ISBN 0-201-30958-0

William Ruh, Thomas Herron, and Paul Klinker, *IIOP Complete: Understanding CORBA and Middleware Interoperability*, ISBN 0-201-37925-2

James Rumbaugh, Ivar Jacobson, and Grady Booch, *The Unified Modeling Language Reference Manual*, ISBN 0-201-30998-X

Geri Schneider and Jason P. Winters, *Applying Use Cases: A Practical Guide*, ISBN 0-201-30981-5

Yen-Ping Shan and Ralph H. Earle, *Enterprise Computing with Objects: From Client/Server Environments to the Internet*, ISBN 0-201-32566-7

David N. Smith, *IBM Smalltalk: The Language*, ISBN 0-8053-0908-X

Daniel Tkach, Walter Fang, and Andrew So, *Visual Modeling Technique: Object Technology Using Visual Programming*, ISBN 0-8053-2574-3

Daniel Tkach and Richard Puttick, *Object Technology in Application Development, Second Edition*, ISBN 0-201-49833-2

Jos Warmer and Anneke Kleppe, *The Object Constraint Language: Precise Modeling with UML*, ISBN 0-201-37940-6

The Unified Modeling Language User Guide

Grady Booch
James Rumbaugh
Ivar Jacobson
Rational Software Corporation

ADDISON-WESLEY

An imprint of Addison Wesley Longman, Inc.

Reading, Massachusetts • Harlow, England • Menlo Park, California
Berkeley, California • Don Mills, Ontario • Sydney
Bonn • Amsterdam • Tokyo • Mexico City

Many of the designations used by manufacturers and sellers to distinguish their products are claimed as trademarks. Where those designations appear in this book and Addison Wesley Longman, Inc. was aware of a trademark claim, the designations have been printed in initial caps or all caps.

The authors and publisher have taken care in the preparation of this book, but make no expressed or implied warranty of any kind and assume no responsibility for errors or omissions. No liability is assumed for incidental or consequential damages in connection with or arising out of the use of the information or programs contained herein.

The publisher offers discounts on this book when ordered in quantity for special sales. For more information, please contact:

> AWL Direct Sales
> Addison Wesley Longman, Inc.
> One Jacob Way
> Reading, Massachusetts 01867
> (781) 944-3700

Visit AW on the Web: www.awl.com/cseng/

Library of Congress Cataloging-in-Publication Data
Booch, Grady.
    The unified modeling language user guide / Grady Booch, James Rumbaugh, and Ivar Jacobson.
        p. cm. -- (Addison-Wesley object technology series)
    Includes index.
    ISBN 0-201-57168-4
    1. Computer software--Development. 2. UML (Computer science) I. Rumbaugh, James. II. Jacobson, Ivar. III. Title. IV. Series.
    QA76.76.D47B655 1998.
    005.1'7--dc21   98-30436
                                                                                                CIP

Copyright © 1999 by Addison Wesley Longman, Inc.

All rights reserved. No part of this publication may be reproduced, stored in a retrieval system, or transmitted, in any form or by any means, electronic, mechanical, photocopying, recording, or otherwise, without the prior written permission of the publisher. Printed in the United States of America. Published simultaneously in Canada.

Photo Credits: The illustrations on pages 1, 203, and 341 are from *A Visual Dictionary of Architecture*, Francis Ching, © 1997 by Van Nostrand Reinhold. Adapted by permission of John Wiley & Sons, Inc. The illustrations on pages 45, 117, 275, and 429 are from *Architecture: Form, Space, and Order, Second Edition*, Francis Ching, © 1996 by Van Nostrand Reinhold. Adapted by permission of John Wiley & Sons, Inc.

Executive Editor: J. Carter Shanklin   Project Editor: Krysia Bebick
Editorial Assistant: Meg Tangirala   Production Manager: Sarah Weaver
Copy Editor: Arlene Richman   Compositor: Grady Booch
Cover Designer: Simone R. Payment

Text printed on recycled and acid-free paper.

ISBN 0201571684

6 7 8 9 1011 MA   03 02 01 00

6th Printing   April 2000

To my loving wife, Jan, and my goddaughter, Elyse,
both of whom make me whole.

—Grady Booch

CONTENTS

PREFACE

The Unified Modeling Language (UML) is a graphical language for visualizing, specifying, constructing, and documenting the artifacts of a software-intensive system. The UML gives you a standard way to write a system's blueprints, covering conceptual things, such as business processes and system functions, as well as concrete things, such as classes written in a specific programming language, database schemas, and reusable software components.

This book teaches you how to use the UML effectively.

Goals

In this book, you will

- Learn what the UML is, what it is not, and why the UML is relevant to the process of developing software-intensive systems
- Master the vocabulary, rules, and idioms of the UML and, in general, learn how to "speak" the language effectively
- Understand how to apply the UML to solve a number of common modeling problems

The user guide provides a reference to the use of specific UML features. However, it is not intended to be a comprehensive reference manual for the UML; that is the focus of another book, *The Unified Modeling Language Reference Manual* (Rumbaugh, Jacobson, Booch, Addison-Wesley, 1999).

The user guide describes a development process for use with the UML. However, it is not intended to provide a complete reference to that process; that is the focus of yet another book, *The Unified Software Development Process* (Jacobson, Booch, Rumbaugh, Addison-Wesley, 1999).

Finally, this book provides hints and tips for using the UML to solve a number of common modeling problems, but it does not teach you how to model. This is similar to a user guide for a programming language that teaches you how to use the language but does not teach you how to program.

Audience

The UML is applicable to anyone involved in the production, deployment, and maintenance of software. The user guide is primarily directed to members of the development team who create UML models. However, it is also suitable to those who read them, working together to understand, build, test, and release a software-intensive system. Although this encompasses almost every role in a software development organization, the user guide is especially relevant to analysts and end users (who specify the required structure and behavior of a system), architects (who design systems that satisfy those requirements), developers (who turn those architectures into executable code), quality assurance personnel (who verify and validate the system's structure and behavior), librarians (who create and catalogue components), and project and program managers (who generally wrestle with chaos, provide leadership and direction, and orchestrate the resources necessary to deliver a successful system).

The user guide assumes a basic knowledge of object-oriented concepts. Experience in an object-oriented programming language or method is helpful but not required.

How to Use This Book

For the developer approaching the UML for the first time, the user guide is best read linearly. You should pay particular attention to Chapter 2, which presents a conceptual model of the UML. All chapters are structured so that each builds upon the content of the previous one, thus lending itself to a linear progression.

For the experienced developer seeking answers to common modeling problems using the UML, this book can be read in any order. You should pay particular attention to the common modeling problems presented in each chapter.

Organization and Special Features

The user guide is organized into seven major sections:

- Section 1 Getting Started
- Section 2 Basic Structural Modeling
- Section 3 Advanced Structural Modeling
- Section 4 Basic Behavioral Modeling
- Section 5 Advanced Behavioral Modeling
- Section 6 Architectural Modeling
- Section 7 Wrapping Up

The user guide contains three appendices: a summary of the UML notation, a list of standard UML elements, and a summary of the Rational Unified Process. A glossary of common terms is also provided.

Each chapter addresses the use of a specific UML feature, and most are organized into the following four sections:

1. Getting Started
2. Terms and Concepts
3. Common Modeling Techniques
4. Hints and Tips

The third section introduces and then solves a set of common modeling problems. To make it easy for you to browse the guide in search of these use cases for the UML, each problem is identified by a distinct heading, as in the following example.

Modeling Architectural Patterns

Each chapter begins with a summary of the features it covers, as in the following example.

In this chapter

- Active objects, processes, and threads
- Modeling multiple flows of control
- Modeling interprocess communication
- Building thread-safe abstractions

Similarly, parenthetical comments and general guidance are set apart as notes, as in the following example.

> **Note:** You can specify more complex multiplicities by using a list, such as `0..1, 3..4, 6..*`, which would mean "any number of objects other than 2 or 5."

Components are discussed in Chapter 25.

The UML is semantically rich. Therefore, a presentation about one feature may naturally involve another. In such cases, cross references are provided in the left margin, as on this page.

Blue highlights are used in figures to distinguish text that explains a model from text that is part of the model itself. Code is distinguished by displaying it in a monospace font, as in `this example`.

A Brief History of the UML

Object-oriented modeling languages appeared sometime between the mid 1970s and the late 1980s as methodologists, faced with a new genre of object-oriented programming languages and increasingly complex applications, began to experiment with alternative approaches to analysis and design. The number of object-oriented methods increased from fewer than 10 to more than 50 during the period between 1989 and 1994. Many users of these methods had trouble finding a modeling language that met their needs completely, thus fueling the so-called method wars. Learning from experience, new generations of these methods began to appear, with a few clearly prominent methods emerging, most notably Booch, Jacobson's OOSE (Object-Oriented Software Engineering), and Rumbaugh's OMT (Object Modeling Technique). Other important methods included Fusion, Shlaer-Mellor, and Coad-Yourdon. Each of these was a complete method, although each was recognized as having strengths and weaknesses. In simple terms, the Booch method was particularly expressive during the design and construction phases of projects, OOSE provided excellent support for use cases as a way to drive requirements capture, analysis, and high-level design, and OMT-2 was most useful for analysis and data-intensive information systems. The behavioral component of many object-oriented methods, including the Booch method and OMT, was the language of statecharts, invented by David Harel. Prior to this object-oriented adoption, statecharts were used mainly in the realm of functional decomposition and structured analysis, and led to the development of executable models and tools that generated full running code.

A critical mass of ideas started to form by the mid 1990s, when Grady Booch (Rational Software Corporation), Ivar Jacobson (Objectory), and James Rumbaugh (General Electric) began to adopt ideas from each other's methods, which collectively were becoming recognized as the leading object-oriented methods worldwide. As the primary authors of the Booch, OOSE, and OMT methods, we were motivated to create a unified modeling language for three reasons. First, our methods were already evolving toward each other independently. It made sense to continue that evolution together rather than apart, eliminating the potential for any unnecessary and gratuitous differences that would further confuse users. Second, by unifying our methods, we could bring some stability to the object-oriented marketplace, allowing projects to settle on one mature modeling language and letting tool builders focus on delivering more useful features. Third, we expected that our collaboration would yield improvements for all three earlier methods, helping us to capture lessons learned and to address problems that none of our methods previously handled well.

As we began our unification, we established three goals for our work:

1. To model systems, from concept to executable artifact, using object-oriented techniques
2. To address the issues of scale inherent in complex, mission-critical systems
3. To create a modeling language usable by both humans and machines

Devising a language for use in object-oriented analysis and design is not unlike designing a programming language. First, we had to constrain the problem: Should the language encompass requirements specification? Should the language be sufficient to permit visual programming? Second, we had to strike a balance between expressiveness and simplicity. Too simple a language would limit the breadth of problems that could be solved; too complex a language would overwhelm the mortal developer. In the case of unifying existing methods, we also had to be sensitive to the installed base. Make too many changes, and we would confuse existing users; resist advancing the language, and we would miss the opportunity of engaging a much broader set of users and of making the language simpler. The UML definition strives to make the best trade-offs in each of these areas.

The UML effort started officially in October 1994, when Rumbaugh joined Booch at Rational. Our project's initial focus was the unification of the Booch and OMT methods, with a state machine model based on statecharts as its central behavioral component. The version 0.8 draft of the Unified Method (as it was then called) was released in October 1995. Around the same time, Jacobson joined Rational and the scope of the UML project was expanded to incorporate OOSE. Our efforts resulted in the release of the UML version 0.9 documents in June 1996. Throughout 1996, we invited and received feedback from the general software engineering community. Notable contributions were made by Harel and Eran Gery from I-Logix, with whom we collaborated during that period based on their 1995 work on an object-oriented variant of statecharts. During this time, it also became clear that many software organizations saw the UML as strategic to their business. We established a UML consortium, with several organizations willing to dedicate resources to work toward a strong and complete UML definition. Those partners contributing to the UML 1.0 definition included Digital Equipment Corporation, Hewlett-Packard, I-Logix, Intellicorp, IBM, ICON Computing, MCI Systemhouse, Microsoft, Oracle, Rational, Texas Instruments, and Unisys. This collaboration resulted in the UML 1.0, a modeling language that was well-defined, expressive, powerful, and applicable to a wide spectrum of problem domains. UML 1.0 was offered for standardization to the Object Management Group (OMG) in January 1997, in response to their request for proposal for a standard modeling language.

Between January 1997 and July 1997, the original group of partners was expanded to include virtually all of the other submitters and contributors of the original OMG response, including Andersen Consulting, Ericsson, ObjecTime Limited, Platinum Technology, PTech, Reich Technologies, Softeam, Sterling Software, and Taskon. A semantics task force was formed, led by Cris Kobryn of MCI Systemhouse and administered by Ed Eykholt of Rational, to formalize the UML specification and to integrate the UML with other standardization efforts. A revised version of the UML (version 1.1) was offered to the OMG for standardization in July 1997. In September 1997, this version was accepted by the OMG Analysis and Design Task Force (ADTF) and the OMG Architecture Board and then put up for vote by the entire OMG membership. UML 1.1 was adopted by the OMG on November 14, 1997.

Maintenance of the UML was then taken over by the OMG Revision Task Force (RTF), led by Cris Kobryn. The RTF released an editorial revision, UML 1.2, in June 1998. In the fall of 1999, the RTF released UML 1.3, which this user guide describes, providing some technical cleanup.

Acknowledgments

Grady Booch, Ivar Jacobson, and James Rumbaugh began the UML effort and throughout the project were its original designers, but the final product was a team effort among all the UML partners. Although all partners came with their own perspectives, areas of concern, and areas of interest, the overall result has benefited from the contributions of each of them and from the diversity of their experience and viewpoints.

The core UML team included

- Hewlett-Packard: Martin Griss
- I-Logix: Eran Gery, David Harel
- IBM: Steve Cook, Jos Warmer
- ICON Computing: Desmond D'Souza
- Intellicorp and James Martin and Company: James Odell
- MCI Systemhouse: Cris Kobryn, Joaquin Miller
- ObjecTime: John Hogg, Bran Selic
- Oracle: Guus Ramackers
- Platinum Technology: Dilhar DeSilva
- Rational Software: Grady Booch, Ed Eykholt, Ivar Jacobson, Gunnar Overgaard, Karin Palmkvist, James Rumbaugh
- Taskon: Trygve Reenskaugh
- Texas Instruments/Sterling Software: John Cheesman, Keith Short
- Unisys: Sridhar Iyengar, G.K. Khalsa

Cris Kobryn deserves a special acknowledgment for his leadership in directing the UML technical team during the development of UML 1.1, 1.2, and 1.3.

We also acknowledge the contributions, influence, and support of the following individuals. In some cases, individuals mentioned here have not formally endorsed the UML but are nonetheless appreciated for their influence: Jim Amsden, Hernan Astudillo, Colin Atkinson, Dave Bernstein, Philip Bernstein, Michael Blaha, Conrad Bock, Mike Bradley, Ray Buhr, Gary Cernosek, James Cerrato, Michael Jesse Chonoles, Magnus Christerson, Dai Clegg, Geoff Clemm, Peter Coad, Derek Coleman, Ward Cunningham, Raj Datta, Philippe Desfray, Mike Devlin, Bruce Douglass, Staffan Ehnebom, Maria Ericsson, Johannes Ernst, Don Firesmith, Martin Fowler, Adam Frankl, Eric Gamma, Dipayan Gangopadhyay, Garth Gullekson, David Harel (who invented the original concept of statechart diagrams), Rick Hargrove, Tim Harrison, Richard Helm, Brian Hendersen-Sellers, Michael Hirsch, Bob Hodges, Yves Holvoet, Jon Hopkins, John Hsia, Glenn Hughes, Ralph Johnson, Anneke Kleppe, Philippe Kruchten, Paul Kyzivat, Martin Lang, Grant Larsen, Reed Letsinger, Mary Loomis, Jeff MacKay, Joe Marasco, Robert Martin, Terri McDaniel, Jim McGee, Mike Meier, Randy Messer, Bertrand Meyer, Greg Meyers, Fred Mol, Luis Montero, Paul Moskowitz, Andy Moss, Jan Pachl, Paul Patrick, Woody Pidcock, Bill Premerlani, Jeff Price, Jerri Pries, Terry Quatrani, Mats Rahm, Rudolf Riess, Rich Reitman, Erick Rivas, Kenny Rubin, Jim Rye, Danny Sabbahr, Tom Schultz, Colin Scott, Ed Seidewitz, Keith Short, Gregson Sui, Jeff Sutherland, Dan Tasker, Andy Trice, Dave Tropeano, Dan Uhlar, John Vlissides,

Larry Wall, Paul Ward, Alan Willis, Rebecca Wirfs-Brock, Bryan Wood, Ed Yourdon, and Steve Zeigler.

The development of the UML was an open process, and via the OTUG (Object Technology User's Group) we received thousands of e-mail messages from all over the world. Although we cannot mention every submitter by name, we do thank all of them for their comments and suggestions. We really did read each message, and the UML is better because of this broad international feedback.

A special acknowledgment also goes to a small band of lab rats (Loud and Boisterous RATional Students) who participated in a user guide course led by Booch in early 1997, during which they offered excellent ideas and gave much constructive criticism that helped fine-tune the contents of this book: Hernan Astudillo, Robin Brown, Robert Bundy, Magnus Christerson, Adam Frankl, Nookiah Kolluru, Ron Krubek, Grant Larsen, Dean Leffingwell, Robert Martin, Mills Ripley, Hugo Sanchez, Geri Schneider, Tom Schultz, Andy Trice, Dan Uhlar, and Lloyd Williams. Thanks go to the madmen at Number Six Software and to the folks who provided a technical review of this book: Jack Carter, Tim Budd, Bruce Douglass, Martin Fowler, Cris Kobryn, Philippe Kruchten, Ron Lusk, Terry Quatrani, and David Rine.

For More Information

The most current information about the UML, including its formal specification, may be found on the Internet at *www.rational.com* and *www.omg.org*. The work of the revision task force may be found at *uml.shl.com*.

There are several electronic forums that are appropriate for general discussion about the UML, including the Internet news groups *comp.software-eng* and *comp.object* and the public mailing lists *otug@rational.com* and *uml-rtf@omg.org*.

Grady Booch
Lakewood, Colorado
September 1998
egb@rational.com

UNIFIED
MODELING
LANGUAGE

Section 1
GETTING STARTED

UNIFIED
MODELING
LANGUAGE

Chapter 1
WHY WE MODEL

A successful software organization is one that consistently deploys quality software that meets the needs of its users. An organization that can develop such software in a timely and predictable fashion, with an efficient and effective use of resources, both human and material, is one that has a sustainable business.

There's an important implication in this message: The primary product of a development team is not beautiful documents, world-class meetings, great slogans, or Pulitzer prize–winning lines of source code. Rather, it is good software that satisfies the evolving needs of its users and the business. Everything else is secondary.

Unfortunately, many software organizations confuse "secondary" with "irrelevant." To deploy software that satisfies its intended purpose, you have to meet and engage users in a disciplined fashion, to expose the real requirements of your system. To develop software of lasting quality, you have to craft a solid architectural foundation that's resilient to change. To develop software rapidly, efficiently, and effectively, with a minimum of software scrap and rework, you have to have the right people, the right tools, and the right focus. To do all this consistently and predictably, with an appreciation for the lifetime costs of the system, you must have a sound development process that can adapt to the changing needs of your business and technology.

Modeling is a central part of all the activities that lead up to the deployment of good software. We build models to communicate the desired structure and behavior of our system. We build models to visualize and control the system's architecture. We build models to better understand the system we are building, often exposing opportunities for simplification and reuse. We build models to manage risk.

The Importance of Modeling

If you want to build a dog house, you can pretty much start with a pile of lumber, some nails, and a few basic tools, such as a hammer, saw, and tape measure. In a few hours, with little prior planning, you'll likely end up with a dog house that's reasonably functional, and you can probably do it with no one else's help. As long as it's big enough and doesn't leak too much, your dog will be happy. If it doesn't work out, you can always start over, or get a less demanding dog.

If you want to build a house for your family, you can start with a pile of lumber, some nails, and a few basic tools, but it's going to take you a lot longer, and your family will certainly be more demanding than the dog. In this case, unless you've already done it a few dozen times before, you'll be better served by doing some detailed planning before you pound the first nail or lay the foundation. At the very least, you'll want to make some sketches of how you want the house to look. If you want to build a quality house that meets the needs of your family and of local building codes, you'll need to draw some blueprints as well, so that you can think through the intended use of the rooms and the practical details of lighting, heating, and plumbing. Given these plans, you can start to make reasonable estimates of the amount of time and materials this job will require. Although it is humanly possible to build a house yourself, you'll find it is much more efficient to work with others, possibly subcontracting out many key work products or buying pre-built materials. As long as you stay true to your plans and stay within the limitations of time and money, your family will most likely be satisfied. If it doesn't work out, you can't exactly get a new family, so it is best to set expectations early and manage change carefully.

If you want to build a high-rise office building, it would be infinitely stupid for you to start with a pile of lumber, some nails, and a few basic tools. Because you are probably using other people's money, they will demand to have input into the size, shape, and style of the building. Often, they will change their minds, even after you've started building. You will want to do extensive planning, because the cost of failure is high. You will be just a part of a much larger group responsible for developing and deploying the building, and so the team will need all sorts of blueprints and models to communicate with one another.

As long as you get the right people and the right tools and actively manage the process of transforming an architectural concept into reality, you will likely end up with a building that will satisfy its tenants. If you want to keep building buildings, then you will want to be certain to balance the desires of your tenants with the realities of building technology, and you will want to treat the rest of your team professionally, never placing them at any risk or driving them so hard that they burn out.

Curiously, a lot of software development organizations start out wanting to build high rises but approach the problem as if they were knocking out a dog house.

Sometimes, you get lucky. If you have the right people at the right moment and if all the planets align properly, then you might, just might, get your team to push out a software product that dazzles its users. Typically, however, you can't get all the right people (the right ones are often already overcommitted), it's never the right moment (yesterday would have been better), and the planets never seem to align (instead, they keep moving out of your control). Given the increasing demand to develop software in Internet time, development teams often fall back on the only thing they really know how to do well—pound out lines of code. Heroic programming efforts are legend in this industry, and it often seems that working harder is the proper reaction to any crisis in development. However, these are not necessarily the right lines of code, and some projects are of such a magnitude that even adding more hours to the work day is not enough to get the job done.

If you really want to build the software equivalent of a house or a high rise, the problem is more than just a matter of writing lots of software—in fact, the trick is in creating the right software and in figuring out how to write less software. This makes quality software development an issue of architecture and process and tools. Even so, many projects start out looking like dog houses but grow to the magnitude of a high rise simply because they are a victim of their own success. There comes a time when, if there was no consideration given to architecture, process, or tools, that the dog house, now grown into a high rise, collapses of its own weight. The collapse of a dog house may annoy your dog; the failure of a high rise will materially affect its tenants.

Unsuccessful software projects fail in their own unique ways, but all successful projects are alike in many ways. There are many elements that contribute to a successful software organization; one common thread is the use of modeling.

Modeling is a proven and well-accepted engineering technique. We build architectural models of houses and high rises to help their users visualize the final product. We may even build mathematical models in order to analyze the effects of winds or earthquakes on our buildings.

Modeling is not just a part of the building industry. It would be inconceivable to deploy a new aircraft or an automobile without first building models—from computer models to physical wind tunnel models to full-scale prototypes. New electrical devices, from microprocessors to telephone switching systems require some degree of modeling in order to better understand the system and to communicate those ideas to others. In the motion picture industry, story-boarding, which is a form of modeling, is central to any production. In the fields of sociology, economics, and business management, we build models so that we can validate our theories or try out new ones with minimal risk and cost.

What, then, is a model? Simply put,

> *A model is a simplification of reality.*

A model provides the blueprints of a system. Models may encompass detailed plans, as well as more general plans that give a 30,000-foot view of the system under consideration. A good model includes those elements that have broad effect and omits those minor elements that are not relevant to the given level of abstraction. Every system may be described from different aspects using different models, and each model is therefore a semantically closed abstraction of the system. A model may be structural, emphasizing the organization of the system, or it may be behavioral, emphasizing the dynamics of the system.

Why do we model? There is one fundamental reason.

> *We build models so that we can better understand the system we are developing.*

Through modeling, we achieve four aims.

How the UML addresses these four things is discussed in Chapter 2.

1. Models help us to visualize a system as it is or as we want it to be.
2. Models permit us to specify the structure or behavior of a system.
3. Models give us a template that guides us in constructing a system.
4. Models document the decisions we have made.

Modeling is not just for big systems. Even the software equivalent of a dog house can benefit from some modeling. However, it's definitely true that the larger and more complex the system, the more important modeling becomes, for one very simple reason:

> *We build models of complex systems because we cannot comprehend such a system in its entirety.*

There are limits to the human ability to understand complexity. Through modeling, we narrow the problem we are studying by focusing on only one aspect at a time. This is essentially the approach of "divide-and-conquer" that Edsger Dijkstra spoke of years ago: Attack a hard problem by dividing it into a series of smaller problems that you can solve. Furthermore, through modeling, we amplify the human intellect. A model properly chosen can enable the modeler to work at higher levels of abstraction.

Saying that one ought to model does not necessarily make it so. In fact, a number of studies suggest that most software organizations do little if any formal modeling. Plot the use of modeling against the complexity of a project, and you'll find that the simpler the project, the less likely it is that formal modeling will be used.

The operative word here is "formal." In reality, in even the simplest project, developers do some amount of modeling, albeit very informally. A developer might sketch out an idea on a blackboard or a scrap of paper in order to visualize a part of a system, or the team might use CRC cards to work through a scenario or the design of a mechanism. There's nothing wrong with any of these models. If it works, by all means use it. However, these informal models are often *ad hoc* and do not provide a common language that can easily be shared with others. Just as there exists a common language of blueprints for the construction industry, a common language for electrical engineering, and a common language for mathematical modeling, so too can a development organization benefit by using a common language for software modeling.

Every project can benefit from some modeling. Even in the realm of disposable software, where it's sometimes more effective to throw away inadequate software because of the productivity offered by visual programming languages, modeling can help the development team better visualize the plan of their system and allow them to develop more rapidly by helping them build the right thing. The more complex your project, the more likely it is that you will fail or that you will build the wrong thing if you do no modeling at all. All interesting and useful systems have a natural tendency to become more complex over time. So, although you might think you don't need to model today, as your system evolves you will regret that decision, after it is too late.

Principles of Modeling

The use of modeling has a rich history in all the engineering disciplines. That experience suggests four basic principles of modeling. First,

*The choice of what models to create has a profound influence
on how a problem is attacked and how a solution is shaped.*

In other words, choose your models well. The right models will brilliantly illuminate the most wicked development problems, offering insight that you simply could not gain otherwise; the wrong models will mislead you, causing you to focus on irrelevant issues.

Setting aside software for a moment, suppose you are trying to tackle a problem in quantum physics. Certain problems, such as the interaction of photons in time-space, are full of wonderfully hairy mathematics. Choose a different model than the calculus, and all of a sudden this inherent complexity becomes tractable. In this field, this is precisely the value of Feynmann diagrams, which provide a graphical rendering of a very complex problem. Similarly, in a totally different domain, suppose you are constructing a new building and you are concerned about how it might behave in high winds. If you build a physical model and then subject it to wind tunnel tests, you might learn some interesting things, although materials in the small don't flex exactly as they do in the large. Hence, if you build a mathematical model and then subject it to simulations, you will learn some different things, and you will also probably be able to play with more new scenarios than if you were using a physical model. By rigorously and continuously testing your models, you'll end up with a far higher level of confidence that the system you have modeled will, in fact, behave as you expect it to in the real world.

In software, the models you choose can greatly affect your world view. If you build a system through the eyes of a database developer, you will likely focus on entity-relationship models that push behavior into triggers and stored procedures. If you build a system through the eyes of a structured analyst, you will likely end up with models that are algorithmic-centric, with data flowing from process to process. If you build a system through the eyes of an object-oriented developer, you'll end up with a system whose architecture is centered around a sea of classes and the patterns of interaction that direct how those classes work together. Any of these approaches might be right for a given application and development culture, although experience suggests that the object-oriented view is superior in crafting resilient architectures, even for systems that might have a large database or computational element. That fact notwithstanding, the point is that each world view leads to a different kind of system, with different costs and benefits.

Second,

Every model may be expressed at different levels of precision.

If you are building a high rise, sometimes you need a 30,000-foot view—for instance, to help your investors visualize its look and feel. Other times, you need to get down to the level of the studs—for instance, when there's a tricky pipe run or an unusual structural element.

The same is true with software models. Sometimes, a quick and simple executable model of the user interface is exactly what you need; at other times, you have to get down and dirty with the bits, such as when you are specifying cross-system interfaces or wrestling with networking bottlenecks. In any case, the best kinds of models are those that let you choose your degree of detail, depending on who is doing the viewing and why they need to view it. An analyst or an end user will want to focus on issues of what; a developer will want to focus on issues of how. Both of these stakeholders will want to visualize a system at different levels of detail at different times.

Third,

> *The best models are connected to reality.*

A physical model of a building that doesn't respond in the same way as do real materials has only limited value; a mathematical model of an aircraft that assumes only ideal conditions and perfect manufacturing can mask some potentially fatal characteristics of the real aircraft. It's best to have models that have a clear connection to reality, and where that connection is weak, to know exactly how those models are divorced from the real world. All models simplify reality; the trick is to be sure that your simplifications don't mask any important details.

In software, the Achilles heel of structured analysis techniques is the fact that there is a basic disconnect between its analysis model and the system's design model. Failing to bridge this chasm causes the system as conceived and the system as built to diverge over time. In object-oriented systems, it is possible to connect all the nearly independent views of a system into one semantic whole.

Fourth,

> *No single model is sufficient. Every nontrivial system is best approached through a small set of nearly independent models.*

If you are constructing a building, there is no single set of blueprints that reveal all its details. At the very least, you'll need floor plans, elevations, electrical plans, heating plans, and plumbing plans.

The operative phrase here is "nearly independent." In this context, it means having models that can be built and studied separately but that are still interrelated. As in the case of a building, you can study electrical plans in isolation, but you can also see their mapping to the floor plan and perhaps even their interaction with the routing of pipes in the plumbing plan.

The five views of an architecture are discussed in Chapter 2.

The same is true of object-oriented software systems. To understand the architecture of such a system, you need several complementary and interlocking views: a use case view (exposing the requirements of the system), a design view (capturing the vocabulary of the problem space and the solution space), a process view (modeling the distribution of the system's processes and threads), an implementation view (addressing the physical realization of the system), and a deployment view (focusing on system engineering issues). Each of these views may have structural, as well as behavioral, aspects. Together, these views represent the blueprints of software.

Depending on the nature of the system, some models may be more important than others. For example, in data-intensive systems, models addressing static design views will dominate. In GUI-intensive systems, static and dynamic use case views are quite important. In hard real time systems, dynamic process views tend to be more important. Finally, in distributed systems, such as one finds in Web-intensive applications, implementation and deployment models are the most important.

Object-Oriented Modeling

Civil engineers build many kinds of models. Most commonly, there are structural models that help people visualize and specify parts of systems and the way those parts relate to one another. Depending on the most important business or engineering concerns, engineers might also build dynamic models—for instance, to help them to study the behavior of a structure in the presence of an earthquake. Each kind of model is organized differently, and each has its own focus.

In software, there are several ways to approach a model. The two most common ways are from an algorithmic perspective and from an object-oriented perspective.

The traditional view of software development takes an algorithmic perspective. In this approach, the main building block of all software is the procedure or function. This view leads developers to focus on issues of control and the decomposition of larger algorithms into smaller ones. There's nothing inherently evil about such a point of view except that it tends to yield brittle systems. As requirements change (and they will) and the system grows (and it will), systems built with an algorithmic focus turn out to be very hard to maintain.

The contemporary view of software development takes an object-oriented perspective. In this approach, the main building block of all software systems is the object or class. Simply put, an object is a thing, generally drawn from the vocabulary of the problem space or the solution space; a class is a description of a set of common objects. Every object has identity (you can name it or otherwise distinguish it from other objects), state (there's generally some data associated with it), and behavior (you can do things to the object, and it can do things to other objects, as well).

For example, consider a simple three-tier architecture for a billing system, involving a user interface, middleware, and a database. In the user interface, you will find concrete objects, such as buttons, menus, and dialog boxes. In the database, you will find concrete objects, such as tables representing entities from the problem domain, including customers, products, and orders. In the middle layer, you will find objects such as transactions and business rules, as well as higher-level views of problem entities, such as customers, products, and orders.

The object-oriented approach to software development is decidedly a part of the mainstream simply because it has proven to be of value in building systems in all sorts of problem domains and encompassing all degrees of size and complexity. Furthermore, most contemporary languages, operating systems, and tools are object-oriented in some fashion, giving greater cause to view the world in terms of objects. Object-oriented development provides the conceptual foundation for assembling systems out of components using technology such as Java Beans or COM+.

These questions are discussed in Chapter 2.

A number of consequences flow from the choice of viewing the world in an object-oriented fashion: What's the structure of a good object-oriented architecture? What artifacts should the project create? Who should create them? How should they be measured?

Visualizing, specifying, constructing, and documenting object-oriented systems is exactly the purpose of the Unified Modeling Language.

UNIFIED
MODELING
LANGUAGE

Chapter 2
INTRODUCING THE UML

In this chapter

- Overview of the UML
- Three steps to understanding the UML
- Software architecture
- The software development process

The Unified Modeling Language (UML) is a standard language for writing software blueprints. The UML may be used to visualize, specify, construct, and document the artifacts of a software-intensive system.

The UML is appropriate for modeling systems ranging from enterprise information systems to distributed Web-based applications and even to hard real time embedded systems. It is a very expressive language, addressing all the views needed to develop and then deploy such systems. Even though it is expressive, the UML is not difficult to understand and to use. Learning to apply the UML effectively starts with forming a conceptual model of the language, which requires learning three major elements: the UML's basic building blocks, the rules that dictate how these building blocks may be put together, and some common mechanisms that apply throughout the language.

The UML is only a language and so is just one part of a software development method. The UML is process independent, although optimally it should be used in a process that is use case driven, architecture-centric, iterative, and incremental.

An Overview of the UML

The UML is a language for

- Visualizing
- Specifying
- Constructing
- Documenting

the artifacts of a software-intensive system.

The UML Is a Language

A language provides a vocabulary and the rules for combining words in that vocabulary for the purpose of communication. A *modeling* language is a language whose vocabulary and rules focus on the conceptual and physical representation of a system. A modeling language such as the UML is thus a standard language for software blueprints.

The basic principles of modeling are discussed in Chapter 1.

Modeling yields an understanding of a system. No one model is ever sufficient. Rather, you often need multiple models that are connected to one another in order to understand anything but the most trivial system. For software-intensive systems, this requires a language that addresses the different views of a system's architecture as it evolves throughout the software development life cycle.

The vocabulary and rules of a language such as the UML tell you how to create and read well-formed models, but they don't tell you what models you should create and when you should create them. That's the role of the software development process. A well-defined process will guide you in deciding what artifacts to produce, what activities and what workers to use to create them and manage them, and how to use those artifacts to measure and control the project as a whole.

The UML Is a Language for Visualizing

For many programmers, the distance between thinking of an implementation and then pounding it out in code is close to zero. You think it, you code it. In fact, some things are best cast directly in code. Text is a wonderfully minimal and direct way to write expressions and algorithms.

In such cases, the programmer is still doing some modeling, albeit entirely mentally. He or she may even sketch out a few ideas on a white board or on a napkin. However, there are several problems with this. First, communicating those conceptual models to others is error-prone unless everyone involved speaks the same language. Typically, projects and organizations develop their own language, and it is difficult to understand what's going on if you are an outsider or new to the group. Second, there are some things about a software system you can't understand unless you build models that transcend the textual programming language. For example, the meaning of a class hierarchy can be inferred, but not directly grasped, by staring at the code for all the classes in the hierarchy. Similarly, the physical distribution and possible migration of the objects in a Web-based system can be inferred, but not directly grasped, by studying the system's code. Third, if the developer who cut the code never wrote down the models that are in his or her head, that information would be lost forever or, at best, only partially recreatable from the implementation, once that developer moved on.

Writing models in the UML addresses the third issue: An explicit model facilitates communication.

Some things are best modeled textually; others are best modeled graphically. Indeed, in all interesting systems, there are structures that transcend what can be represented in a programming language. The UML is such a graphical language. This addresses the second problem described earlier.

The complete semantics of the UML are discussed in The Unified Modeling Language Reference Manual.

The UML is more than just a bunch of graphical symbols. Rather, behind each symbol in the UML notation is a well-defined semantics. In this manner, one developer can write a model in the UML, and another developer, or even another tool, can interpret that model unambiguously. This addresses the first issue described earlier.

The UML Is a Language for Specifying

In this context, *specifying* means building models that are precise, unambiguous, and complete. In particular, the UML addresses the specification of all the important analysis, design, and implementation decisions that must be made in developing and deploying a software-intensive system.

The UML Is a Language for Constructing

The UML is not a visual programming language, but its models can be directly connected to a variety of programming languages. This means that it is possible to map from a model in the UML to a programming language such as Java, C++, or Visual Basic, or even to tables in a relational database or the persistent store of an object-oriented database. Things that are best expressed graphically are done so graphically in the UML, whereas things that are best expressed textually are done so in the programming language.

Modeling the structure of a system is discussed in Sections 2 and 3.

This mapping permits forward engineering: The generation of code from a UML model into a programming language. The reverse is also possible: You can reconstruct a model from an implementation back into the UML. Reverse engineering is not magic. Unless you encode that information in the implementation, information is lost when moving forward from models to code. Reverse engineering thus requires tool support with human intervention. Combining these two paths of forward code generation and reverse engineering yields round-trip engineering, meaning the ability to work in either a graphical or a textual view, while tools keep the two views consistent.

Modeling the behavior of a system is discussed in Sections 4 and 5.

In addition to this direct mapping, the UML is sufficiently expressive and unambiguous to permit the direct execution of models, the simulation of systems, and the instrumentation of running systems.

The UML Is a Language for Documenting

A healthy software organization produces all sorts of artifacts in addition to raw executable code. These artifacts include (but are not limited to)

- Requirements
- Architecture
- Design
- Source code
- Project plans
- Tests
- Prototypes
- Releases

Depending on the development culture, some of these artifacts are treated more or less formally than others. Such artifacts are not only the deliverables of a project, they are also critical in controlling, measuring, and communicating about a system during its development and after its deployment.

The UML addresses the documentation of a system's architecture and all of its details. The UML also provides a language for expressing requirements and for tests. Finally, the UML provides a language for modeling the activities of project planning and release management.

Where Can the UML Be Used?

The UML is intended primarily for software-intensive systems. It has been used effectively for such domains as

- Enterprise information systems
- Banking and financial services
- Telecommunications
- Transportation
- Defense/aerospace
- Retail
- Medical electronics
- Scientific
- Distributed Web-based services

The UML is not limited to modeling software. In fact, it is expressive enough to model nonsoftware systems, such as workflow in the legal system, the structure and behavior of a patient healthcare system, and the design of hardware.

A Conceptual Model of the UML

To understand the UML, you need to form a conceptual model of the language, and this requires learning three major elements: the UML's basic building blocks, the rules that dictate how those building blocks may be put together, and some common mechanisms that apply throughout the UML. Once you have grasped these ideas, you will be able to read UML models and create some basic ones. As you gain more experience in applying the UML, you can build on this conceptual model, using more advanced features of the language.

Building Blocks of the UML

The vocabulary of the UML encompasses three kinds of building blocks:

1. Things
2. Relationships
3. Diagrams

Things are the abstractions that are first-class citizens in a model; relationships tie these things together; diagrams group interesting collections of things.

Things in the UML There are four kinds of things in the UML:

1. Structural things
2. Behavioral things
3. Grouping things
4. Annotational things

These things are the basic object-oriented building blocks of the UML. You use them to write well-formed models.

Structural Things *Structural things* are the nouns of UML models. These are the mostly static parts of a model, representing elements that are either conceptual or physical. In all, there are seven kinds of structural things.

Classes are discussed in Chapters 4 and 9.

First, a *class* is a description of a set of objects that share the same attributes, operations, relationships, and semantics. A class implements one or more interfaces. Graphically, a class is rendered as a rectangle, usually including its name, attributes, and operations, as in Figure 2-1.

Window
origin
size
open()
close()
move()
display()

Figure 2-1: Classes

Interfaces are discussed in Chapter 11.

Second, an *interface* is a collection of operations that specify a service of a class or component. An interface therefore describes the externally visible behavior of that element. An interface might represent the complete behavior of a class or component or only a part of that behavior. An interface defines a set of operation specifications (that is, their signatures) but never a set of operation implementations. Graphically, an interface is rendered as a circle together with its name. An interface rarely stands alone. Rather, it is typically attached to the class or component that realizes the interface, as in Figure 2-2.

ISpelling

Figure 2-2: Interfaces

Collaborations are discussed in Chapter 27.

Third, a *collaboration* defines an interaction and is a society of roles and other elements that work together to provide some cooperative behavior that's bigger than the sum of all the elements. Therefore, collaborations have structural, as well as behavioral, dimensions. A given class might participate in several collaborations. These collaborations therefore represent the implementation of patterns that make up a system. Graphically, a collaboration is rendered as an ellipse with dashed lines, usually including only its name, as in Figure 2-3.

Figure 2-3: Collaborations

Use cases are discussed in Chapter 16.

Fourth, a *use case* is a description of set of sequence of actions that a system performs that yields an observable result of value to a particular actor. A use case is used to structure the behavioral things in a model. A use case is realized by a collaboration. Graphically, a use case is rendered as an ellipse with solid lines, usually including only its name, as in Figure 2-4.

Figure 2-4: Use Cases

The remaining three things—active classes, components, and nodes—are all class-like, meaning they also describe a set of objects that share the same attributes, operations, relationships, and semantics. However, these three are different enough and are necessary for modeling certain aspects of an object-oriented system, and so they warrant special treatment.

Active classes are discussed in Chapter 22.

Fifth, an *active class* is a class whose objects own one or more processes or threads and therefore can initiate control activity. An active class is just like a class except that its objects represent elements whose behavior is concurrent with other elements. Graphically, an active class is rendered just like a class, but with heavy lines, usually including its name, attributes, and operations, as in Figure 2-5.

The remaining two elements—component, and nodes—are also different. They represent physical things, whereas the previous five things represent conceptual or logical things.

Figure 2-5: Active Classes

Components are discussed in Chapter 25.

Sixth, a *component* is a physical and replaceable part of a system that conforms to and provides the realization of a set of interfaces. In a system, you'll encounter different kinds of deployment components, such as COM+ components or Java Beans, as well as components that are artifacts of the development process, such as source code files. A component typically represents the physical packaging of otherwise logical elements, such as classes, interfaces, and collaborations. Graphically, a component is rendered as a rectangle with tabs, usually including only its name, as in Figure 2-6.

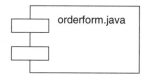

Figure 2-6: Components

Nodes are discussed in Chapter 26.

Seventh, a *node* is a physical element that exists at run time and represents a computational resource, generally having at least some memory and, often, processing capability. A set of components may reside on a node and may also migrate from node to node. Graphically, a node is rendered as a cube, usually including only its name, as in Figure 2-7.

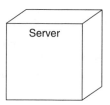

Figure 2-7: Nodes

These seven elements—classes, interfaces, collaborations, use cases, active classes, components, and nodes—are the basic structural things that you may include in a UML model. There are also variations on these seven, such as actors, signals, and utilities (kinds of classes), processes and threads (kinds of active classes), and applications, documents, files, libraries, pages, and tables (kinds of components).

Use cases, which are used to structure the behavioral things in a model, are discussed in Chapter 16; Interactions are discussed in Chapter 15.

Behavioral Things *Behavioral things* are the dynamic parts of UML models. These are the verbs of a model, representing behavior over time and space. In all, there are two primary kinds of behavioral things.

First, an *interaction* is a behavior that comprises a set of messages exchanged among a set of objects within a particular context to accomplish a specific purpose. The behavior of a society of objects or of an individual operation may be specified with an interaction. An interaction involves a number of other elements, including messages, action sequences (the behavior invoked by a message), and links (the connection between objects). Graphically, a message is rendered as a directed line, almost always including the name of its operation, as in Figure 2-8.

display

Figure 2-8: Messages

State machines are discussed in Chapter 21.

Second, a *state machine* is a behavior that specifies the sequences of states an object or an interaction goes through during its lifetime in response to events, together with its responses to those events. The behavior of an individual class or a collaboration of classes may be specified with a state machine. A state machine involves a number of other elements, including states, transitions (the flow from state to state), events (things that trigger a transition), and activities (the response to a transition). Graphically, a state is rendered as a rounded rectangle, usually including its name and its substates, if any, as in Figure 2-9.

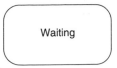

Waiting

Figure 2-9: States

These two elements—interactions and state machines—are the basic behavioral things that you may include in a UML model. Semantically, these elements are usually connected to various structural elements, primarily classes, collaborations, and objects.

Grouping Things *Grouping things* are the organizational parts of UML models. These are the boxes into which a model can be decomposed. In all, there is one primary kind of grouping thing, namely, packages.

Packages are discussed in Chapter 12.

A *package* is a general-purpose mechanism for organizing elements into groups. Structural things, behavioral things, and even other grouping things may be placed in a package. Unlike components (which exist at run time), a package is purely conceptual (meaning that it exists only at development time). Graphically, a package is rendered as a tabbed folder, usually including only its name and, sometimes, its contents, as in Figure 2-10.

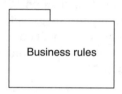

Business rules

Figure 2-10: Packages

Packages are the basic grouping things with which you may organize a UML model. There are also variations, such as frameworks, models, and subsystems (kinds of packages).

Notes are discussed in Chapter 6.

Annotational Things *Annotational things* are the explanatory parts of UML models. These are the comments you may apply to describe, illuminate, and remark about any element in a model. There is one primary kind of annotational thing, called a note. A *note* is simply a symbol for rendering constraints and comments attached to an element or a collection of elements. Graphically, a note is rendered as a rectangle with a dog-eared corner, together with a textual or graphical comment, as in Figure 2-11.

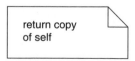

return copy
of self

Figure 2-11: Notes

This element is the one basic annotational thing you may include in a UML model. You'll typically use notes to adorn your diagrams with constraints or comments that are best expressed in informal or formal text. There are also variations on this element, such as requirements (which specify some desired behavior from the perspective of outside the model).

Relationships in the UML There are four kinds of relationships in the UML:

1. Dependency
2. Association
3. Generalization
4. Realization

These relationships are the basic relational building blocks of the UML. You use them to write well-formed models.

Dependencies are discussed in Chapters 5 and 10.

First, a *dependency* is a semantic relationship between two things in which a change to one thing (the independent thing) may affect the semantics of the other thing (the dependent thing). Graphically, a dependency is rendered as a dashed line, possibly directed, and occasionally including a label, as in Figure 2-12.

Figure 2-12: Dependencies

Associations are discussed in Chapters 5 and 10.

Second, an *association* is a structural relationship that describes a set of links, a link being a connection among objects. Aggregation is a special kind of association, representing a structural relationship between a whole and its parts. Graphically, an association is rendered as a solid line, possibly directed, occasionally including a label, and often containing other adornments, such as multiplicity and role names, as in Figure 2-13.

0..1	*
employer	employee

Figure 2-13: Associations

Generalizations are discussed in Chapters 5 and 10.

Third, a *generalization* is a specialization/generalization relationship in which objects of the specialized element (the child) are substitutable for objects of the generalized element (the parent). In this way, the child shares the structure and the behavior of the parent. Graphically, a generalization relationship is rendered as a solid line with a hollow arrowhead pointing to the parent, as in Figure 2-14.

Figure 2-14: Generalizations

Realizations
are discussed
in Chapter 10.

Fourth, a *realization* is a semantic relationship between classifiers, wherein one classifier specifies a contract that another classifier guarantees to carry out. You'll encounter realization relationships in two places: between interfaces and the classes or components that realize them, and between use cases and the collaborations that realize them. Graphically, a realization relationship is rendered as a cross between a generalization and a dependency relationship, as in Figure 2-15.

Figure 2-15: Realization

These four elements are the basic relational things you may include in a UML model. There are also variations on these four, such as refinement, trace, include, and extend (for dependencies).

The five views
of an architec-
ture are
discussed in
the following
section.

Diagrams in the UML A *diagram* is the graphical presentation of a set of elements, most often rendered as a connected graph of vertices (things) and arcs (relationships). You draw diagrams to visualize a system from different perspectives, so a diagram is a projection into a system. For all but the most trivial systems, a diagram represents an elided view of the elements that make up a system. The same element may appear in all diagrams, only a few diagrams (the most common case), or in no diagrams at all (a very rare case). In theory, a diagram may contain any combination of things and relationships. In practice, however, a small number of common combinations arise, which are consistent with the five most useful views that comprise the architecture of a software-intensive system. For this reason, the UML includes nine such diagrams:

1. Class diagram
2. Object diagram
3. Use case diagram
4. Sequence diagram
5. Collaboration diagram
6. Statechart diagram
7. Activity diagram
8. Component diagram
9. Deployment diagram

Class diagrams are discussed in Chapter 8.

A *class diagram* shows a set of classes, interfaces, and collaborations and their relationships. These diagrams are the most common diagram found in modeling object-oriented systems. Class diagrams address the static design view of a system. Class diagrams that include active classes address the static process view of a system.

Object diagrams are discussed in Chapter 14

An *object diagram* shows a set of objects and their relationships. Object diagrams represent static snapshots of instances of the things found in class diagrams. These diagrams address the static design view or static process view of a system as do class diagrams, but from the perspective of real or prototypical cases.

Use case diagrams are discussed in Chapter 17.

A *use case diagram* shows a set of use cases and actors (a special kind of class) and their relationships. Use case diagrams address the static use case view of a system. These diagrams are especially important in organizing and modeling the behaviors of a system.

Interaction diagrams are discussed in Chapter 18.

Both sequence diagrams and collaboration diagrams are kinds of interaction diagrams. An *interaction diagram* shows an interaction, consisting of a set of objects and their relationships, including the messages that may be dispatched among them. Interaction diagrams address the dynamic view of a system. A *sequence diagram* is an interaction diagram that emphasizes the time-ordering of messages; a *collaboration diagram* is an interaction diagram that emphasizes the structural organization of the objects that send and receive messages. Sequence diagrams and collaboration diagrams are isomorphic, meaning that you can take one and transform it into the other.

Statechart diagrams are discussed in Chapter 24.

A *statechart diagram* shows a state machine, consisting of states, transitions, events, and activities. Statechart diagrams address the dynamic view of a system. They are especially important in modeling the behavior of an interface, class, or collaboration and emphasize the event-ordered behavior of an object, which is especially useful in modeling reactive systems.

Activity diagrams are discussed in Chapter 19.

An *activity diagram* is a special kind of a statechart diagram that shows the flow from activity to activity within a system. Activity diagrams address the dynamic view of a system. They are especially important in modeling the function of a system and emphasize the flow of control among objects.

Component diagrams are discussed in Chapter 29.

A *component diagram* shows the organizations and dependencies among a set of components. Component diagrams address the static implementation view of a system. They are related to class diagrams in that a component typically maps to one or more classes, interfaces, or collaborations.

*Deployment
diagrams are
discussed in
Chapter 30.*

A *deployment diagram* shows the configuration of run-time processing nodes and the components that live on them. Deployment diagrams address the static deployment view of an architecture. They are related to component diagrams in that a node typically encloses one or more components.

This is not a closed list of diagrams. Tools may use the UML to provide other kinds of diagrams, although these nine are by far the most common you will encounter in practice.

Rules of the UML

The UML's building blocks can't simply be thrown together in a random fashion. Like any language, the UML has a number of rules that specify what a well-formed model should look like. A *well-formed model* is one that is semantically self-consistent and in harmony with all its related models.

The UML has semantic rules for

- Names   What you can call things, relationships, and diagrams
- Scope   The context that gives specific meaning to a name
- Visibility   How those names can be seen and used by others
- Integrity   How things properly and consistently relate to one another
- Execution What it means to run or simulate a dynamic model

Models built during the development of a software-intensive system tend to evolve and may be viewed by many stakeholders in different ways and at different times. For this reason, it is common for the development team to not only build models that are well-formed, but also to build models that are

- Elided   Certain elements are hidden to simplify the view
- Incomplete   Certain elements may be missing
- Inconsistent The integrity of the model is not guaranteed

These less-than-well-formed models are unavoidable as the details of a system unfold and churn during the software development life cycle. The rules of the UML encourage you—but do not force you—to address the most important analysis, design, and implementation questions that push such models to become well-formed over time.

Common Mechanisms in the UML

A building is made simpler and more harmonious by the conformance to a pattern of common features. A house may be built in the Victorian or French country style largely by using certain architectural patterns that define those styles. The same is true of the UML. It is made simpler by the presence of four common mechanisms that apply consistently throughout the language.

1. Specifications
2. Adornments
3. Common divisions
4. Extensibility mechanisms

Specifications The UML is more than just a graphical language. Rather, behind every part of its graphical notation there is a specification that provides a textual statement of the syntax and semantics of that building block. For example, behind a class icon is a specification that provides the full set of attributes, operations (including their full signatures), and behaviors that the class embodies; visually, that class icon might only show a small part of this specification. Furthermore, there might be another view of that class that presents a completely different set of parts yet is still consistent with the class's underlying specification. You use the UML's graphical notation to visualize a system; you use the UML's specification to state the system's details. Given this split, it's possible to build up a model incrementally by drawing diagrams and then adding semantics to the model's specifications, or directly by creating a specification, perhaps by reverse engineering an existing system, and then creating diagrams that are projections into those specifications.

The UML's specifications provide a semantic backplane that contains all the parts of all the models of a system, each part related to one another in a consistent fashion. The UML's diagrams are thus simply visual projections into that backplane, each diagram revealing a specific interesting aspect of the system.

Notes and other adornments are discussed in Chapter 6.

Adornments Most elements in the UML have a unique and direct graphical notation that provides a visual representation of the most important aspects of the element. For example, the notation for a class is intentionally designed to be easy to draw, because classes are the most common element found in modeling object-oriented systems. The class notation also exposes the most important aspects of a class, namely its name, attributes, and operations.

A class's specification may include other details, such as whether it is abstract or the visibility of its attributes and operations. Many of these details can be rendered as graphical or textual adornments to the class's basic rectangular notation. For example, Figure 2-16 shows a class, adorned to indicate that it is an abstract class with two public, one protected, and one private operation.

Figure 2-16: Adornments

Every element in the UML's notation starts with a basic symbol, to which can be added a variety of adornments specific to that symbol.

Common Divisions In modeling object-oriented systems, the world often gets divided in at least a couple of ways.

Objects are discussed in Chapter 13.

First, there is the division of class and object. A class is an abstraction; an object is one concrete manifestation of that abstraction. In the UML, you can model classes as well as objects, as shown in Figure 2-17.

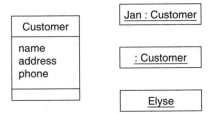

Figure 2-17: Classes And Objects

In this figure, there is one class, named Customer, together with three objects: Jan (which is marked explicitly as being a Customer object), : Customer (an anonymous Customer object), and Elyse (which in its specification is marked as being a kind of Customer object, although it's not shown explicitly here).

Almost every building block in the UML has this same kind of class/object dichotomy. For example, you can have use cases and use case instances, components and component instances, nodes and node instances, and so on. Graphically, the UML distinguishes an object by using the same symbol as its class and then simply underlying the object's name.

*Interfaces are
discussed in
Chapter 11.*

Second, there is the separation of interface and implementation. An interface declares a contract, and an implementation represents one concrete realization of that contract, responsible for faithfully carrying out the interface's complete semantics. In the UML, you can model both interfaces and their implementations, as shown in Figure 2-18.

Figure 2-18: Interfaces And Implementations

In this figure, there is one component named `spellingwizard.dll` that implements two interfaces, `IUnknown` and `ISpelling`.

Almost every building block in the UML has this same kind of interface/implementation dichotomy. For example, you can have use cases and the collaborations that realize them, as well as operations and the methods that implement them.

*The UML's
extensibility
mechanisms
are discussed
in Chapter 6.*

Extensibility Mechanisms The UML provides a standard language for writing software blueprints, but it is not possible for one closed language to ever be sufficient to express all possible nuances of all models across all domains across all time. For this reason, the UML is opened-ended, making it possible for you to extend the language in controlled ways. The UML's extensibility mechanisms include

- Stereotypes
- Tagged values
- Constraints

A *stereotype* extends the vocabulary of the UML, allowing you to create new kinds of building blocks that are derived from existing ones but that are specific to your problem. For example, if you are working in a programming language, such as Java or C++, you will often want to model exceptions. In these languages, exceptions are just classes, although they are treated in very special ways. Typically, you only want to allow them to be thrown and caught, nothing else. You can make exceptions first class citizens in your models—meaning that they are treated like basic building blocks—by marking them with an appropriate stereotype, as for the class `Overflow` in Figure 2-19.

A *tagged value* extends the properties of a UML building block, allowing you to create new information in that element's specification. For example, if you are working on a shrink-wrapped product that undergoes many releases over time, you often want to track the version and author of certain critical abstractions. Version and author are not primitive UML concepts. They can be added to any building block, such as a class, by introducing new tagged values to that building block. In Figure 2-19, for example, the class `EventQueue` is extended by marking its version and author explicitly.

A *constraint* extends the semantics of a UML building block, allowing you to add new rules or modify existing ones. For example, you might want to constrain the `EventQueue` class so that all additions are done in order. As Figure 2-19 shows, you can add a constraint that explicitly marks these for the operation `add`.

Figure 2-19: Extensibility Mechanisms

Collectively, these three extensibility mechanisms allow you to shape and grow the UML to your project's needs. These mechanisms also let the UML adapt to new software technology, such as the likely emergence of more powerful distributed programming languages. You can add new building blocks, modify the specification of existing ones, and even change their semantics. Naturally, it's important that you do so in controlled ways so that through these extensions, you remain true to the UML's purpose—the communication of information.

Architecture

The need for viewing complex systems from different perspectives is discussed in Chapter 1.

Visualizing, specifying, constructing, and documenting a software-intensive system demands that the system be viewed from a number of perspectives. Different stakeholders—end users, analysts, developers, system integrators, testers, technical writers, and project managers—each bring different agendas to a project, and each looks at that system in different ways at different times over the project's life. A system's architecture is perhaps the most important artifact that can be used to manage these different viewpoints and so control the iterative and incremental development of a system throughout its life cycle.

Architecture is the set of significant decisions about

- The organization of a software system
- The selection of the structural elements and their interfaces by which the system is composed
- Their behavior, as specified in the collaborations among those elements
- The composition of these structural and behavioral elements into progressively larger subsystems
- The architectural style that guides this organization: the static and dynamic elements and their interfaces, their collaborations, and their composition

Software architecture is not only concerned with structure and behavior, but also with usage, functionality, performance, resilience, reuse, comprehensibility, economic and technology constraints and trade-offs, and aesthetic concerns.

Modeling the architecture of a system is discussed in Chapter 31.

As Figure 2-20 illustrates, the architecture of a software-intensive system can best be described by five interlocking views. Each view is a projection into the organization and structure of the system, focused on a particular aspect of that system.

Figure 2-20: Modeling a System's Architecture

The *use case view* of a system encompasses the use cases that describe the behavior of the system as seen by its end users, analysts, and testers. This view doesn't really specify the organization of a software system. Rather, it exists to specify the forces that shape the system's architecture. With the UML, the static aspects of this view are captured in use case diagrams; the dynamic aspects of this view are captured in interaction diagrams, statechart diagrams, and activity diagrams.

The *design view* of a system encompasses the classes, interfaces, and collaborations that form the vocabulary of the problem and its solution. This view primarily supports the functional requirements of the system, meaning the services that the system should provide to its end users. With the UML, the static aspects of this view are captured in class diagrams and object diagrams; the dynamic aspects of this view are captured in interaction diagrams, statechart diagrams, and activity diagrams.

The *process view* of a system encompasses the threads and processes that form the system's concurrency and synchronization mechanisms. This view primarily addresses the performance, scalability, and throughput of the system. With the UML, the static and dynamic aspects of this view are captured in the same kinds of diagrams as for the design view, but with a focus on the active classes that represent these threads and processes.

The *implementation view* of a system encompasses the components and files that are used to assemble and release the physical system. This view primarily addresses the configuration management of the system's releases, made up of somewhat independent components and files that can be assembled in various ways to produce a running system. With the UML, the static aspects of this view are captured in component diagrams; the dynamic aspects of this view are captured in interaction diagrams, statechart diagrams, and activity diagrams.

The *deployment view* of a system encompasses the nodes that form the system's hardware topology on which the system executes. This view primarily addresses the distribution, delivery, and installation of the parts that make up the physical system. With the UML, the static aspects of this view are captured in deployment diagrams; the dynamic aspects of this view are captured in interaction diagrams, statechart diagrams, and activity diagrams.

Each of these five views can stand alone so that different stakeholders can focus on the issues of the system's architecture that most concern them. These five views also interact with one another—nodes in the deployment view hold components in the implementation view that, in turn, represent the physical realization of classes, interfaces, collaborations, and active classes from the design and process views. The UML permits you to express every one of these five views and their interactions.

Software Development Life Cycle

The Rational Unified Process is summarized in Appendix C; a more complete treatment of this process is discussed in The Unified Software Development Process.

The UML is largely process-independent, meaning that it is not tied to any particular software development life cycle. However, to get the most benefit from the UML, you should consider a process that is

- Use case driven
- Architecture-centric
- Iterative and incremental

Use case driven means that use cases are used as a primary artifact for establishing the desired behavior of the system, for verifying and validating the system's architecture, for testing, and for communicating among the stakeholders of the project.

Architecture-centric means that a system's architecture is used as a primary artifact for conceptualizing, constructing, managing, and evolving the system under development.

An *iterative process* is one that involves managing a stream of executable releases. An *incremental process* is one that involves the continuous integration of the system's architecture to produce these releases, with each new release embodying incremental improvements over the other. Together, an iterative and incremental process is *risk-driven*, meaning that each new release is focused on attacking and reducing the most significant risks to the success of the project.

This use case driven, architecture-centric, and iterative/incremental process can be broken into phases. A *phase* is the span of time between two major milestones of the process, when a well-defined set of objectives are met, artifacts are completed, and decisions are made whether to move into the next phase. As Figure 2-21 shows, there are four phases in the software development life cycle: inception, elaboration, construction, and transition. In the diagram, workflows are plotted against these phases, showing their varying degrees of focus over time.

Inception is the first phase of the process, when the seed idea for the development is brought up to the point of being—at least internally—sufficiently well-founded to warrant entering into the elaboration phase.

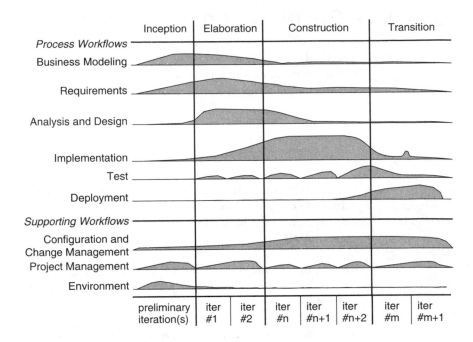

Figure 2-21: Software Development Life Cycle

Elaboration is the second phase of the process, when the product vision and its architecture are defined. In this phase, the system's requirements are articulated, prioritized, and baselined. A system's requirements may range from general vision statements to precise evaluation criteria, each specifying particular functional or nonfunctional behavior and each providing a basis for testing.

Construction is the third phase of the process, when the software is brought from an executable architectural baseline to being ready to be transitioned to the user community. Here also, the system's requirements and especially its evaluation criteria are constantly reexamined against the business needs of the project, and resources are allocated as appropriate to actively attack risks to the project.

Transition is the fourth phase of the process, when the software is turned into the hands of the user community. Rarely does the software development process end here, for even during this phase, the system is continuously improved, bugs are eradicated, and features that didn't make an earlier release are added.

One element that distinguishes this process and that cuts across all four phases is an iteration. An *iteration* is a distinct set of activities, with a baselined plan and evaluation criteria that result in a release, either internal or external. This means that the software development life cycle can be characterized as involving a continuous stream of executable releases of the system's architecture. It is this emphasis on architecture as an important artifact that drives the UML to focus on modeling the different views of a system's architecture.

Chapter 3
HELLO, WORLD!

In this chapter

- Classes and components
- Static models and dynamic models
- Connections among models
- Extending the UML

Brian Kernighan and Dennis Ritchie, the authors of the C programming language, point out that "the only way to learn a new programming language is by writing programs in it." The same is true of the UML. The only way to learn the UML is by writing models in it.

The first program many developers write when approaching a new programming language is a simple one, involving little more than printing the string "Hello, World!" This is a reasonable starting point, because mastering this trivial application provides some instant gratification. It also covers all the infrastructure needed to get something running.

This is where we begin with the UML. Modeling "Hello, World!" is about the simplest use of the UML you'll ever find. However, this application is deceptively easy because underneath it all there are some interesting mechanisms that make it work. These mechanisms can easily be modeled with the UML, providing a richer view of this simple application.

Key Abstractions

In Java, the applet for printing "Hello, World!" in a Web browser is quite simple:

```
import java.awt.Graphics;
class HelloWorld extends java.applet.Applet {
  public void paint (Graphics g) {
    g.drawString("Hello, World!", 10, 10);
  }
}
```

The first line of code:

```
import java.awt.Graphics;
```

makes the class `Graphics` directly available to the code that follows. The `java.awt` prefix specifies the Java package in which the class `Graphics` lives.

The second line of code:

```
class HelloWorld extends java.applet.Applet {
```

introduces a new class named `HelloWorld` and specifies that it is a kind of class just like `Applet`, which lives in the package `java.applet`.

The next three lines of code:

```
public void paint (Graphics g) {
  g.drawString("Hello, World!", 10, 10);
}
```

declare an operation named `paint`, whose implementation invokes another operation, named `drawString`, responsible for printing the string `"Hello, World!"` at the given coordinates. In the usual object-oriented fashion, `drawString` is an operation on a parameter named `g`, whose type is the class `Graphics`.

Classes are discussed in Chapters 4 and 9.

Modeling this application in the UML is straightforward. As Figure 3-1 shows, you can represent the class `HelloWorld` graphically as a rectangular icon. Its `paint` operation is shown here, as well, with all its formal parameters elided and its implementation specified in the attached note.

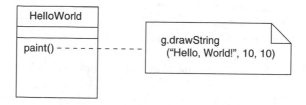

Figure 3-1: Key Abstractions for `HelloWorld`

Note: The UML is not a visual programming language, although, as the figure shows, the UML does allow— but does not require—a tight coupling to a variety of programming languages, such as Java. The UML is designed to allow models to be transformed into code and to allow code to be reengineered back into models. Some things are best written in the syntax of a textual programming language (for example, mathematical expressions); whereas, other things are best visualized graphically in the UML (for example, hierarchies of classes).

This class diagram captures the basics of the "Hello, World!" application, but it leaves out a number of things. As the preceding code specifies, two other classes—`Applet` and `Graphics`—are involved in this application and each is used in a different way. The class `Applet` is used as the parent of `HelloWorld`, and the class `Graphics` is used in the signature and implementation of one of its operations, `paint`. You can represent these classes and their different relationships to the class `HelloWorld` in a class diagram, as shown in Figure 3-2.

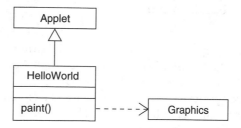

Figure 3-2: Immediate Neighbors Surrounding `HelloWorld`

Relationships are discussed in Chapters 5 and 10.

The `Applet` and `Graphics` classes are represented graphically as rectangular icons. No operations are shown for either of them, and so their icons are elided. The directed line with the hollow arrowhead from `HelloWorld` to `Applet` represents generalization, which in this case means that

HelloWorld is a child of Applet. The dashed directed line from HelloWorld to Graphics represents a dependency relationship, which means that HelloWorld uses Graphics.

This is not the end of the framework upon which HelloWorld is built. If you study the Java libraries for Applet and Graphics, you will discover that both of these classes are part of a larger hierarchy. Tracing just the classes that Applet extends and implements, you can generate another class diagram, shown in Figure 3-3.

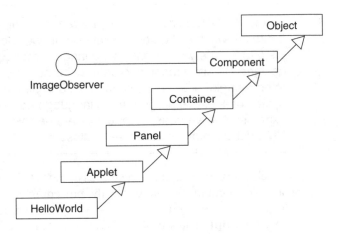

Figure 3-3: HelloWorld Inheritance Hierarchy

Note: This figure is a good example of a diagram generated by reverse engineering an existing system. Reverse engineering is the creation of a model from code.

This figure makes it clear that HelloWorld is just a leaf in a larger hierarchy of classes. HelloWorld is a child of Applet; Applet is a child of Panel; Panel is a child of Container; Container is a child of Component; and Component is a child of Object, which is the parent class of every class in Java. This model thus matches the Java library—each child extends some parent.

Interfaces are discussed in Chapter 11.

The relationship between ImageObserver and Component is a bit different, and the class diagram reflects this difference. In the Java library, ImageObserver is an interface, which, among other things, means that it has no implementation and instead requires that other classes implement it. As the figure shows, you can represent an interface in the UML as a circle. The fact that Component implements ImageObserver is represented by the solid line from the implementation (`Component`) to its interface (`ImageObserver`).

As these figures show, `HelloWorld` collaborates directly with only two classes (`Applet` and `Graphics`), and these two classes are but a small part of the larger library of predefined Java classes. To manage this large collection, Java organizes its interfaces and classes in a number of different packages. The root package in the Java environment is named, not surprisingly, `java`. Nested inside this package are several other packages, which contain other packages, interfaces, and classes. `Object` lives in the package `lang`, so its full path name is `java.lang.Object`. Similarly, `Panel`, `Container`, and `Component` live in `awt`; the class `Applet` lives in the package `applet`. The interface `ImageObserver` lives in the package `image`, which in turn lives in the package `awt`, so its full path name is the rather lengthy string `java.awt.image.ImageObserver`.

You can visualize this packaging in a class diagram, shown in Figure 3-4.

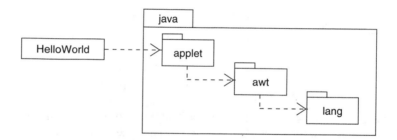

Figure 3-4: `HelloWorld` Packaging

Packages are discussed in Chapter 12.

As this figure shows, packages are represented in the UML as a tabbed folders. Packages may be nested, and the dashed directed lines represent dependencies among these packages. For example, `HelloWorld` depends on the package `java.applet`, and `java.applet` depends on the package `java.awt`.

Mechanisms

Patterns and frameworks are discussed in Chapter 28.

The hardest part of mastering a library as rich as Java's is learning how its parts work together. For example, how does `HelloWorld`'s `paint` operation get invoked? What operations must you use if you want to change the behavior of this applet, such as making it print the string in a different color? To answer these and other questions, you have to have a conceptual model of the way these classes work together dynamically.

Processes and threads are discussed in Chapter 22.

Studying the Java library reveals that `HelloWorld`'s `paint` operation is inherited from `Component`. This still begs the question of how this operation is invoked. The answer is that `paint` is called as part of running the thread that encloses the applet, as Figure 3-5 illustrates.

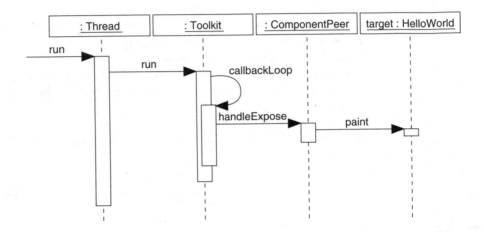

Figure 3-5: Painting Mechanism

Instances are discussed in Chapter 11.

This figure shows the collaboration of several objects, including one instance of the class `HelloWorld`. The other objects are a part of the Java environment and so, for the most part, live in the background of the applets you create. In the UML, instances are represented just like classes, but with their names underlined to distinguish them. The first three objects in this diagram are anonymous—they have no unique name. The `HelloWorld` object has a name (`target`) known by the `ComponentPeer` object.

Sequence diagrams are discussed in Chapter 18.

You can model the ordering of events using a sequence diagram, as in Figure 3-5. Here, the sequence begins by running the `Thread` object, which in turn calls the `Toolkit`'s `run` operation. The `Toolkit` object then calls one of its own operations (`callbackLoop`), which then calls the `ComponentPeer`'s `handleExpose` operation. The `ComponentPeer` object then calls its target's `paint` operation. The `ComponentPeer` object assumes that its target is a `Component`, but in this case, the target is actually a child of `Component` (namely, `HelloWorld`), and so `HelloWorld`'s `paint` operation is dispatched polymorphically.

Components

"Hello, World!" is implemented as an applet and so never stands alone but, rather, is typically a part of some Web page. The applet starts when its enclosing page is opened, triggered by some browser mechanism that runs the applet's `Thread` object. However, it's not the `HelloWorld` class that's directly a part of the Web page. Rather, it's a binary form of the class, created by a Java compiler that transforms the source code representing that class into a component that can be executed. This suggests a very different perspective of the system. Whereas all the earlier diagrams represented a logical view of the applet, what's going on here is a view of the applet's physical components.

Components are discussed in Chapter 25.

You can model this physical view using a component diagram, as in Figure 3-6.

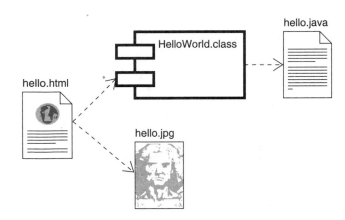

Figure 3-6: `HelloWorld` Components

Each of the icons in this figure represents a UML element in the implementation view of the system. The component called `hello.java` represents the source code for the logical class `HelloWorld`, so it is a file that may be manipulated by development environments and configuration management tools. This source code can be transformed into the binary applet `hello.class` by a Java compiler, making it suitable for execution by a computer's Java virtual machine.

The UML's extensibility mechanisms are discussed in Chapter 6.

The canonical icon for a component is a rectangle with two tabs. The binary applet `HelloWorld.class` is a variation of this basic symbol, with its lines made thicker, indicating that it is an executable component (just like an active class). The icon for the `hello.java` component has been replaced with a user-defined icon, representing a text file. The icon for the Web page hello.html has been similarly tailored by extending the UML's notation. As the figure indicates, this Web page has another component, hello.jpg, which is represented by a user-defined component icon, in this case providing a thumbnail sketch of the graphics image. Because these latter three components use user-defined graphical symbols, their names are placed outside the icon.

Note: The relationships among the class (HelloWorld), its source code (hello.java), and its object code (HelloWorld.class) are rarely modeled explicitly, although it is sometimes useful to do so to visualize the physical configuration of a system. On the other hand, it is common to visualize the organization of a Web-based system such as this by using component diagrams to model its pages and other executable components.

Section 2
BASIC STRUCTURAL
MODELING

UNIFIED
MODELING
LANGUAGE

Chapter 4
CLASSES

In this chapter

- Classes, attributes, operations, and responsibilities
- Modeling the vocabulary of a system
- Modeling the distribution of responsibilities in a system
- Modeling nonsoftware things
- Modeling primitive types
- Making quality abstractions

Classes are the most important building block of any object-oriented system. A class is a description of a set of objects that share the same attributes, operations, relationships, and semantics. A class implements one or more interfaces.

Advanced features of classes are discussed in Chapter 9.

You use classes to capture the vocabulary of the system you are developing. These classes may include abstractions that are part of the problem domain, as well as classes that make up an implementation. You can use classes to represent software things, hardware things, and even things that are purely conceptual.

Well-structured classes have crisp boundaries and form a part of a balanced distribution of responsibilities across the system.

Getting Started

Modeling a system involves identifying the things that are important to your particular view. These things form the vocabulary of the system you are modeling. For example, if you are building a house, things like walls, doors, windows, cabinets, and lights are some of the things that will be important to you as a home owner. Each of these things can be distinguished from the other.

Each of them also has a set of properties. Walls have a height and a width and are solid. Doors also have a height and a width and are solid, as well, but have the additional behavior that allows them to open in one direction. Windows are similar to doors in that both are openings that pass through walls, but windows and doors have slightly different properties. Windows are usually (but not always) designed so that you can look out of them instead of pass through them.

Individual walls, doors, and windows rarely exist in isolation, so you must also consider how specific instances of these things fit together. The things you identify and the relationships you choose to establish among them will be affected by how you expect to use the various rooms of your home, how you expect traffic to flow from room to room, and the general style and feel you want this arrangement to create.

Users will be concerned about different things. For example, the plumbers who help build your house will be interested in things like drains, traps, and vents. You, as a home owner, won't necessarily care about these things except insofar as they interact with the things in your view, such as where a drain might be placed in a floor or where a vent might intersect with the roof line.

Objects are discussed in Chapter 13. In the UML, all of these things are modeled as classes. A class is an abstraction of the things that are a part of your vocabulary. A class is not an individual object, but rather represents a whole set of objects. Thus, you may conceptually think of "wall" as a class of objects with certain common properties, such as height, length, thickness, load-bearing or not, and so on. You may also think of individual instances of wall, such as "the wall in the southwest corner of my study."

In software, many programming languages directly support the concept of a class. That's excellent, because it means that the abstractions you create can often be mapped directly to a programming language, even if these are abstractions of nonsoftware things, such as "customer," "trade," or "conversation."

The UML provides a graphical representation of class, as well, as Figure 4-1 shows. This notation permits you to visualize an abstraction apart from any specific programming language and in a way that lets you emphasize the most important parts of an abstraction: its name, attributes, and operations.

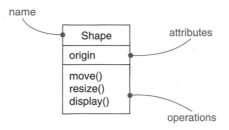

Figure 4-1: Classes

Terms and Concepts

A *class* is a description of a set of objects that share the same attributes, operations, relationships, and semantics. Graphically, a class is rendered as a rectangle.

Names

A class name must be unique within its enclosing package, as discussed in Chapter 12.

Every class must have a name that distinguishes it from other classes. A *name* is a textual string. That name alone is known as a *simple name*; a *path name* is the class name prefixed by the name of the package in which that class lives. A class may be drawn showing only its name, as Figure 4-2 shows.

Figure 4-2: Simple and Path Names

Note: A class name may be text consisting of any number of letters, numbers, and certain punctuation marks (except for marks such as the colon, which is used to separate a class name and the name of its enclosing package) and may continue over several lines. In practice, class names are short nouns or noun phrases drawn from the vocabulary of the system you are modeling. Typically, you capitalize the first letter of every word in a class name, as in `Customer` or `TemperatureSensor`.

Attributes

Attributes are related to the semantics of aggregation, as discussed in Chapter 10.

An *attribute* is a named property of a class that describes a range of values that instances of the property may hold. A class may have any number of attributes or no attributes at all. An attribute represents some property of the thing you are modeling that is shared by all objects of that class. For example, every wall has a height, width, and thickness; you might model your customers in such a way that each has a name, address, phone number, and date of birth. An attribute is therefore an abstraction of the kind of data or state an object of the class might encompass. At a given moment, an object of a class will have specific values for every one of its class's attributes. Graphically, attributes are listed in a compartment just below the class name. Attributes may be drawn showing only their names, as shown in Figure 4-3.

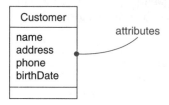

Figure 4-3: Attributes

Note: An attribute name may be text, just like a class name. In practice, an attribute name is a short noun or noun phrase that represents some property of its enclosing class. Typically, you capitalize the first letter of every word in an attribute name except the first letter, as in `name` or `loadBearing`.

You can specify other features of an attribute, such as marking it read-only or shared by all objects of the class, as discussed in Chapter 9.

You can further specify an attribute by stating its class and possibly a default initial value, as shown Figure 4-4.

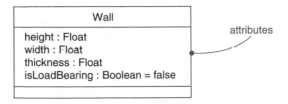

Figure 4-4: Attributes and Their Class

Operations

You can further specify the implementation of an operation by using a note, as described in Chapter 6, or by using an activity diagram, as discussed in Chapter 19.

An *operation* is the implementation of a service that can be requested from any object of the class to affect behavior. In other words, an operation is an abstraction of something you can do to an object and that is shared by all objects of that class. A class may have any number of operations or no operations at all. For example, in a windowing library such as the one found in Java's awt package, all objects of the class Rectangle can be moved, resized, or queried for their properties. Often (but not always), invoking an operation on an object changes the object's data or state. Graphically, operations are listed in a compartment just below the class attributes. Operations may be drawn showing only their names, as in Figure 4-5.

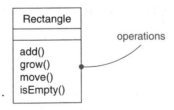

Figure 4-5: Operations

Note: An operation name may be text, just like a class name. In practice, an operation name is a short verb or verb phrase that represents some behavior of its enclosing class. Typically, you capitalize the first letter of every word in an operation name except the first letter, as in move or isEmpty.

*You can spec-
ify other
features of an
operation,
such as mark-
ing it polymor-
phic or
constant, or
specifying its
visibility, as
discussed in
Chapter 9.*

You can specify an operation by stating its signature, covering the name, type, and default value of all parameters and (in the case of functions) a return type, as shown in Figure 4-6.

Figure 4-6: Operations and Their Signatures

Organizing Attributes and Operations

When drawing a class, you don't have to show every attribute and every operation at once. In fact, in most cases, you can't (there are too many of them to put in one figure) and you probably shouldn't (only a subset of these attributes and operations are likely to be relevant to a specific view). For these reasons, you can elide a class, meaning that you can choose to show only some or none of a class's attributes and operations. An empty compartment doesn't necessarily mean there are no attributes or operations, just that you didn't choose to show them. You can explicitly specify that there are more attributes or properties than shown by ending each list with an ellipsis ("...").

*Stereotypes
are discussed
in Chapter 6.*

To better organize long lists of attributes and operations, you can also prefix each group with a descriptive category by using stereotypes, as shown in Figure 4-7.

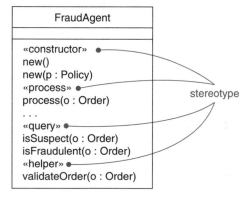

Figure 4-7: Stereotypes for Class Features

Responsibilities

Responsibilities are an example of a defined stereotype, as discussed in Chapter 6.

A *responsibility* is a contract or an obligation of a class. When you create a class, you are making a statement that all objects of that class have the same kind of state and the same kind of behavior. At a more abstract level, these corresponding attributes and operations are just the features by which the class's responsibilities are carried out. A `Wall` class is responsible for knowing about height, width, and thickness; a `FraudAgent` class, as you might find in a credit card application, is responsible for processing orders and determining if they are legitimate, suspect, or fraudulent; a `TemperatureSensor` class is responsible for measuring temperature and raising an alarm if the temperature reaches a certain point.

Modeling the semantics of a class is discussed in Chapter 9.

When you model classes, a good starting point is to specify the responsibilities of the things in your vocabulary. Techniques like CRC cards and use case-based analysis are especially helpful here. A class may have any number of responsibilities, although, in practice, every well-structured class has at least one responsibility and at most just a handful. As you refine your models, you will translate these responsibilities into a set of attributes and operations that best fulfill the class's responsibilities.

You can also draw the responsibilities of a class in a note, as discussed in Chapter 6.

Graphically, responsibilities can be drawn in a separate compartment at the bottom of the class icon, as shown in Figure 4-8.

Figure 4-8: Responsibilities

Note: Responsibilities are just free-form text. In practice, a single responsibility is written as a phrase, a sentence, or (at most) a short paragraph.

Other Features

Advanced class concepts are discussed in Chapter 9.

Attributes, operations, and responsibilities are the most common features you'll need when you create abstractions. In fact, for most models you build, the basic form of these three features will be all you need to convey the most important semantics of your classes. Sometimes, however, you'll need to visualize or specify other features, such as the visibility of individual attributes and operations; language-specific features of an operation, such as whether it is polymorphic or constant; or even the exceptions that objects of the class might produce or handle. These and many other features can be expressed in the UML, but they are treated as advanced concepts.

Interfaces are discussed in Chapter 11.

When you build models, you will soon discover that almost every abstraction you create is some kind of class. Sometimes, you will want to separate the implementation of a class from its specification, and this can be expressed in the UML by using interfaces.

Active classes, components, and nodes are discussed in Chapters 22, 24, and 26, respectively.

When you start building more complex models, you will also find yourself encountering the same kinds of classes over and over again, such as classes that represent concurrent processes and threads, or classes that represent physical things, such as applets, Java Beans, COM+ objects, files, Web pages, and hardware. Because these kinds of classes are so common and because they represent important architectural abstractions, the UML provides active classes (representing processes and threads), components (representing physical software components), and nodes (representing hardware devices).

Class diagrams are discussed in Chapter 8.

Finally, classes rarely stand alone. Rather, when you build models, you will typically focus on groups of classes that interact with one another. In the UML, these societies of classes form collaborations and are usually visualized in class diagrams.

Common Modeling Techniques

Modeling the Vocabulary of a System

You'll use classes most commonly to model abstractions that are drawn from the problem you are trying to solve or from the technology you are using to implement a solution to that problem. Each of these abstractions is a part of the vocabulary of your system, meaning that, together, they represent the things that are important to users and to implementers.

Use cases are discussed in Chapter 16.

For users, most abstractions are not that hard to identify because, typically, they are drawn from the things that users already use to describe their system. Techniques such as CRC cards and use case-based analysis are excellent ways to help users find these abstractions. For implementers, these abstractions are typically just the things in the technology that are parts of the solution.

To model the vocabulary of a system,

- Identify those things that users or implementers use to describe the problem or solution. Use CRC cards and use case-based analysis to help find these abstractions.
- For each abstraction, identify a set of responsibilities. Make sure that each class is crisply defined and that there is a good balance of responsibilities among all your classes.
- Provide the attributes and operations that are needed to carry out these responsibilities for each class.

Figure 4-9 shows a set of classes drawn from a retail system, including Customer, Order, and Product. This figure includes a few other related abstractions drawn from the vocabulary of the problem, such as Shipment (used to track orders), Invoice (used to bill orders), and Warehouse (where products are located prior to shipment). There is also one solution-related abstraction, Transaction, which applies to orders and shipments.

Figure 4-9: Modeling the Vocabulary of a System

Packages are discussed in Chapter 12.

As your models get larger, many of the classes you find will tend to cluster together in groups that are conceptually and semantically related. In the UML, you can use packages to model these clusters of classes.

Modeling behavior is discussed in Sections 4 and 5.

Most of your models will rarely be completely static. Instead, most abstractions in your system's vocabulary will interact with one another in dynamic ways. In the UML, there are a number of ways to model this dynamic behavior.

Modeling the Distribution of Responsibilities in a System

Once you start modeling more than just a handful of classes, you will want to be sure that your abstractions provide a balanced set of responsibilities. What this means is that you don't want any one class to be too big or too small. Each class should do one thing well. If you abstract classes that are too big, you'll find that your models are hard to change and are not very reusable. If you abstract classes that are too small, you'll end up with many more abstractions than you can reasonably manage or understand. You can use the UML to help you visualize and specify this balance of responsibilities.

To model the distribution of responsibilities in a system,

- Identify a set of classes that work together closely to carry out some behavior.
- Identify a set of responsibilities for each of these classes.
- Look at this set of classes as a whole, split classes that have too many responsibilities into smaller abstractions, collapse tiny classes that have trivial responsibilities into larger ones, and reallocate responsibilities so that each abstraction reasonably stands on its own.

Collaborations are discussed in Chapter 27.

- Consider the ways in which those classes collaborate with one another, and redistribute their responsibilities accordingly so that no class within a collaboration does too much or too little.

This set of classes forms a pattern, as discussed in Chapter 28.

For example, Figure 4-10 shows a set of classes drawn from Smalltalk, showing the distribution of responsibilities among `Model`, `View`, and `Controller` classes. Notice how all these classes work together such that no one class does too much or too little.

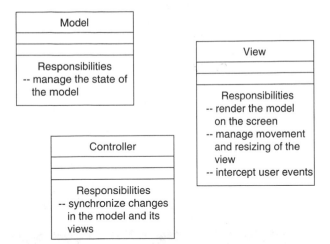

Figure 4-10: Modeling the Distribution of Responsibilities in a System

Modeling Nonsoftware Things

Sometimes, the things you model may never have an analog in software. For example, the people who send invoices and the robots that automatically package orders for shipping from a warehouse might be a part of the workflow you model in a retail system. Your application might not have any software that represents them (unlike customers in the example above, since your system will probably want to maintain information about them).

To model nonsoftware things,

Stereotypes are discussed in Chapter 6.

Nodes are discussed in Chapter 26.

- Model the thing you are abstracting as a class.
- If you want to distinguish these things from the UML's defined building blocks, create a new building block by using stereotypes to specify these new semantics and to give a distinctive visual cue.
- If the thing you are modeling is some kind of hardware that itself contains software, consider modeling it as a kind of node, as well, so that you can further expand on its structure.

Note: The UML is mainly intended for modeling software-intensive systems, although, in conjunction with textual hardware modeling languages, such as VHDL, the UML can be quite expressive for modeling hardware systems.

Things that are external to your system are often modeled as actors, as discussed in Chapter 16.

As Figure 4-11 shows, it's perfectly normal to abstract humans (like `AccountsReceivableAgent`) and hardware (like `Robot`) as classes, because each represents a set of objects with a common structure and a common behavior.

Figure 4-11: Modeling Nonsoftware Things

Modeling Primitive Types

Types are discussed in Chapter 11.

At the other extreme, the things you model may be drawn directly from the programming language you are using to implement a solution. Typically, these abstractions involve primitive types, such as integers, characters, strings, and even enumeration types, that you might create yourself.

To model primitive types,

Constraints are described in Chapter 6.

- Model the thing you are abstracting as a type or an enumeration, which is rendered using class notation with the appropriate stereotype.
- If you need to specify the range of values associated with this type, use constraints.

Types are discussed in Chapter 11.

As Figure 4-12 shows, these things can be modeled in the UML as types or enumerations, which are rendered just like classes but are explicitly marked via stereotypes. Things like integers (represented by the class `Int`) are modeled as types, and you can explicitly indicate the range of values these things can take on by using a constraint. Similarly, enumeration types, such as `Boolean` and `Status`, can be modeled as enumerations, with their individual values provided as attributes.

Note: Some languages, such as C and C++, let you set an equivalent integer value for an enumeration. You can model this in the UML by marking the attributes that denote an enumeration with a constant default initial value.

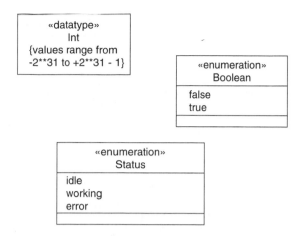

Figure 4-12: Modeling Primitive Types

Hints and Tips

When you model classes in the UML, remember that every class should map to some tangible or conceptual abstraction in the domain of the end user or the implementer. A well-structured class

- Provides a crisp abstraction of something drawn from the vocabulary of the problem domain or the solution domain.
- Embodies a small, well-defined set of responsibilities and carries them all out very well.
- Provides a clear separation of the abstraction's specification and its implementation.
- Is understandable and simple yet extensible and adaptable.

When you draw a class in the UML,

- Show only those properties of the class that are important to understanding the abstraction in its context.
- Organize long lists of attributes and operations by grouping them according to their category.
- Show related classes in the same class diagrams.

Chapter 5
RELATIONSHIPS

In this chapter

- Dependency, generalization, and association relationships
- Modeling simple dependencies
- Modeling single inheritance
- Modeling structural relationships
- Creating webs of relationships

When you build abstractions, you'll discover that very few of your classes stand alone. Instead, most of them collaborate with others in a number of ways. Therefore, when you model a system, not only must you identify the things that form the vocabulary of your system, you must also model how these things stand in relation to one another.

Advanced features of relationships are discussed in Chapter 10.

In object-oriented modeling, there are three kinds of relationships that are especially important: *dependencies*, which represent using relationships among classes (including refinement, trace, and bind relationships); *generalizations*, which link generalized classes to their specializations; and *associations*, which represent structural relationships among objects. Each of these relationships provides a different way of combining your abstractions.

Building webs of relationships is not unlike creating a balanced distribution of responsibilities among your classes. Over-engineer, and you'll end up with a tangled mess of relationships that make your model incomprehensible; under-engineer, and you'll have missed a lot of the richness of your system embodied in the way things collaborate.

Getting Started

If you are building a house, things like walls, doors, windows, cabinets, and lights will form part of your vocabulary. None of these things stands alone, however. Walls connect to other walls. Doors and windows are placed in walls to form openings for people and for light. Cabinets and lights are physically attached to walls and ceilings. You group walls, doors, windows, cabinets, and lights together to form higher-level things, such as rooms.

Not only will you find structural relationships among these things, you'll find other kinds of relationships, as well. For example, your house certainly has windows, but there are probably many kinds of windows. You might have large bay windows that don't open, as well as small kitchen windows that do. Some of your windows might open up and down; others, like patio windows, will slide left and right. Some windows have a single pane of glass; others have double. No matter their differences, there is some essential "window-ness" about each of them: Each is an opening in a wall, and each is designed to let in light, air, and sometimes, people.

In the UML, the ways that things can connect to one another, either logically or physically, are modeled as relationships. In object-oriented modeling, there are three kinds of relationships that are most important: dependencies, generalizations, and associations.

Dependencies are using relationships. For example, pipes depend on the water heater to heat the water they carry.

Generalizations connect generalized classes to more-specialized ones in what is known as subclass/superclass or child/parent relationships. For example, a bay window is a kind of window with large, fixed panes; a patio window is a kind of window with panes that open side to side.

Associations are structural relationships among instances. For example, rooms consist of walls and other things; walls themselves may have embedded doors and windows; pipes may pass through walls.

Other kinds of relationships, such as realization and refinement, are discussed in Chapter 10.

These three kinds of relationships cover most of the important ways in which things collaborate with one another. Not surprisingly, they also map well to the ways that are provided by most object-oriented programming languages to connect objects.

The UML provides a graphical representation for each of these kinds of relationships, as Figure 5-1 shows. This notation permits you to visualize relationships apart from any specific programming language, and in a way that lets you emphasize the most important parts of a relationship: its name, the things it connects, and its properties.

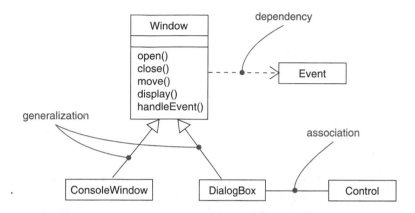

Figure 5-1: Relationships

Terms and Concepts

A *relationship* is a connection among things. In object-oriented modeling, the three most important relationships are dependencies, generalizations, and associations. Graphically, a relationship is rendered as a path, with different kinds of lines used to distinguish the kinds of relationships.

Dependency

A *dependency* is a using relationship that states that a change in specification of one thing (for example, class Event) may affect another thing that uses it (for example, class Window), but not necessarily the reverse. Graphically, a dependency is rendered as a dashed directed line, directed to the thing being depended on. Use dependencies when you want to show one thing using another.

Notes are discussed in Chapter 6; packages are discussed in Chapter 12.

Most often, you will use dependencies in the context of classes to show that one class uses another class as an argument in the signature of an operation; see Figure 5-2. This is very much a using relationship—if the used class changes, the operation of the other class may be affected, as well, because the used class may now present a different interface or behavior. In the UML you can also create dependencies among many other things, especially notes and packages.

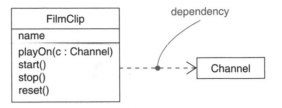

Figure 5-2: Dependencies

Different kinds of dependencies are discussed in Chapter 10; stereotypes are discussed in Chapter 6.

Note: A dependency can have a name, although names are rarely needed unless you have a model with many dependencies and you need to refer to or distinguish among dependencies. More commonly, you'll use stereotypes to distinguish different flavors of dependencies.

Generalization

A *generalization* is a relationship between a general thing (called the superclass or parent) and a more specific kind of that thing (called the subclass or child). Generalization is sometimes called an "is-a-kind-of" relationship: one thing (like the class `BayWindow`) is-a-kind-of a more general thing (for example, the class `Window`). Generalization means that objects of the child may be used anywhere the parent may appear, but not the reverse. In other words, generalization means that the child is substitutable for the parent. A child inherits the properties of its parents, especially their attributes and operations. Often—but not always—the child has attributes and operations in addition to those found in its parents. An operation of a child that has the same signature as an operation in a parent overrides the operation of the parent; this is known as polymorphism. Graphically, generalization is rendered as a solid directed line with a large open arrowhead, pointing to the parent, as shown in Figure 5-3. Use generalizations when you want to show parent/child relationships.

A class may have zero, one, or more parents. A class that has no parents and one or more children is called a root class or a base class. A class that has no children is called a leaf class. A class that has exactly one parent is said to use single inheritance; a class with more than one parent is said to use multiple inheritance.

*Packages are
discussed in
Chapter 12.*

Most often, you will use generalizations among classes and interfaces to show inheritance relationships. In the UML, you can also create generalizations among other things—most notably, packages.

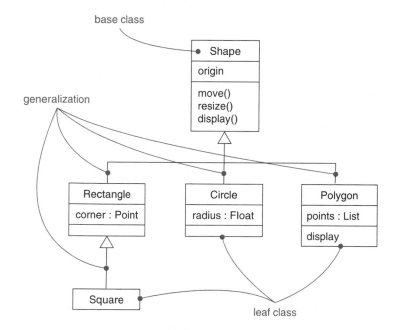

Figure 5-3: Generalization

Note: A generalization can have a name, although names are rarely needed unless you have a model with many generalizations and you need to refer to or discriminate among generalizations.

Association

*Associations
and dependen-
cies (but not
generalization
relationships)
may be
reflective, as
discussed in
Chapter 10.*

An *association* is a structural relationship that specifies that objects of one thing are connected to objects of another. Given an association connecting two classes, you can navigate from an object of one class to an object of the other class, and vice versa. It's quite legal to have both ends of an association circle back to the same class. This means that, given an object of the class, you can link to other objects of the same class. An association that connects exactly two classes is called a binary association. Although it's not as common, you can have associations that connect more than two classes; these are called n-ary associations. Graphically, an association is rendered as a solid line connecting the same or different classes. Use associations when you want to show structural relationships.

Beyond this basic form, there are four adornments that apply to associations.

Don't confuse
name
direction with
association
navigation, as
discussed in
Chapter 10.

Name An association can have a name, and you use that name to describe the nature of the relationship. So that there is no ambiguity about its meaning, you can give a direction to the name by providing a direction triangle that points in the direction you intend to read the name, as shown in Figure 5-4.

Figure 5-4: Association Names

Note: Although an association may have a name, you typically don't need to include one if you explicitly provide role names for the association, or if you have a model with many associations and you need to refer to or distinguish among associations. This is especially true when you have more than one association connecting the same classes.

Roles are
related to the
semantics of
interfaces, as
discussed in
Chapter 11.

Role When a class participates in an association, it has a specific role that it plays in that relationship; a role is just the face the class at the near end of the association presents to the class at the other end of the association. You can explicitly name the role a class plays in an association. In Figure 5-5, a Person playing the role of employee is associated with a Company playing the role of employer.

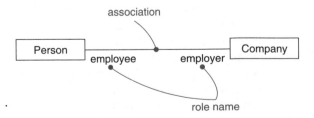

Figure 5-5: Roles

Note: The same class can play the same or different roles in other associations.

An instance of an association is called a link, as discussed in Chapter 15.

Multiplicity An association represents a structural relationship among objects. In many modeling situations, it's important for you to state how many objects may be connected across an instance of an association. This "how many" is called the multiplicity of an association's role, and is written as an expression that evaluates to a range of values or an explicit value as in Figure 5-6. When you state a multiplicity at one end of an association, you are specifying that, for each object of the class at the opposite end, there must be that many objects at the near end. You can show a multiplicity of exactly one (1), zero or one (0..1), many (0..*), or one or more (1..*). You can even state an exact number (for example, 3).

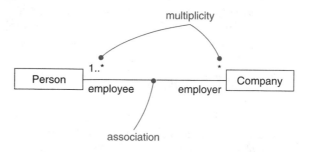

Figure 5-6: Multiplicity

Note: You can specify more complex multiplicities by using a list, such as 0..1, 3..4, 6..*, which would mean "any number of objects other than 2 or 5."

Aggregation has a number of important variations, as discussed in Chapter 10.

Aggregation A plain association between two classes represents a structural relationship between peers, meaning that both classes are conceptually at the same level, no one more important than the other. Sometimes, you will want to model a "whole/part" relationship, in which one class represents a larger thing (the "whole"), which consists of smaller things (the "parts"). This kind of relationship is called aggregation, which represents a "has-a" relationship, meaning that an object of the whole has objects of the part. Aggregation is really just a special kind of association and is specified by adorning a plain association with an open diamond at the whole end, as shown in Figure 5-7.

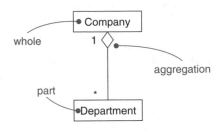

Figure 5-7: Aggregation

Note: The meaning of this simple form of aggregation is entirely conceptual. The open diamond distinguishes the "whole" from the "part," no more, no less. This means that simple aggregation does not change the meaning of navigation across the association between the whole and its parts, nor does it link the lifetimes of the whole and its parts.

Other Features

Advanced relationship concepts are discussed in Chapter 10.

Plain, unadorned dependencies, generalizations, and associations with names, multiplicities, and roles are the most common features you'll need when creating abstractions. In fact, for most of the models you build, the basic form of these three relationships will be all you need to convey the most important semantics of your relationships. Sometimes, however, you'll need to visualize or specify other features, such as composite aggregation, navigation, discriminants, association classes, and special kinds of dependencies and generalizations. These and many other features can be expressed in the UML, but they are treated as advanced concepts.

Class diagrams are discussed in Chapter 8.

Dependencies, generalization, and associations are all static things defined at the level of classes. In the UML, these relationships are usually visualized in class diagrams.

Links are discussed in Chapter 15; transitions are discussed in Chapter 21.

When you start modeling at the object level, and especially when you start working with dynamic collaborations of these objects, you'll encounter two other kinds of relationships—links (which are instances of associations representing connections among objects across which messages may be sent) and transitions (which are connections among states in a state machine).

Common Modeling Techniques

Modeling Simple Dependencies

The most common kind of dependency relationship is the connection between a class that only uses another class as a parameter to an operation.

To model this using relationship,

- Create a dependency pointing from the class with the operation to the class used as a parameter in the operation.

For example, Figure 5-8 shows a set of classes drawn from a system that manages the assignment of students and instructors to courses in a university. This figure shows a dependency from `CourseSchedule` to `Course`, because `Course` is used in both the `add` and `remove` operations of `CourseSchedule`.

If you provide the full signature of the operation as in this figure, you don't normally need to show the dependency, as well, because the use of the class is already explicit in the signature. However, you'll want to show this dependency sometimes, especially if you've elided operation signatures or if your model shows other relationships to the used class.

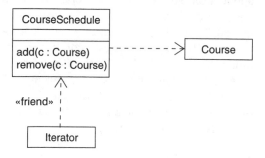

Figure 5-8: Dependency Relationships

Other relationship stereotypes are discussed in Chapter 10.

This figure shows one other dependency, this one not involving classes in operations but rather modeling a common C++ idiom. The dependency from `Iterator` shows that the `Iterator` uses the `CourseSchedule`; the `CourseSchedule` knows nothing about the `Iterator`. The dependency is marked with a stereotype, which specifies that this is not a plain dependency, but, rather, it represents a friend, as in C++.

Modeling Single Inheritance

In modeling the vocabulary of your system, you will often run across classes that are structurally or behaviorally similar to others. You could model each of these as distinct and unrelated abstractions. A better way would be to extract any common structural and behavioral features and place them in more-general classes from which the specialized ones inherit.

To model inheritance relationships,

- Given a set of classes, look for responsibilities, attributes, and operations that are common to two or more classes.
- Elevate these common responsibilities, attributes, and operations to a more general class. If necessary, create a new class to which you can assign these elements (but be careful about introducing too many levels).
- Specify that the more-specific classes inherit from the more-general class by placing a generalization relationship that is drawn from each specialized class to its more-general parent.

For example, Figure 5-9 shows a set of classes drawn from a trading application. You will find a generalization relationship from four classes—`CashAccount`, `Stock`, `Bond`, and `Property`—to the more-general class named `Security`. `Security` is the parent, and `CashAccount`, `Stock`, `Bond`, and `Property` are all children. Each of these specialized children is a kind of `Security`. You'll notice that `Security` includes two operations: `presentValue` and `history`. Because `Security` is their parent, `CashAccount`, `Stock`, `Bond`, and `Property` all inherit these two operations, and for that matter, any other attributes and operations of `Security` that may be elided in this figure.

Abstract classes and operations are discussed in Chapter 9.

You may notice that the names `Security` and `presentValue` are written a bit differently than others. There's a reason for this. When you build hierarchies as in the preceding figure, you often encounter nonleaf classes that are incomplete or are simply ones for which you don't want there to be any objects. Such classes are called *abstract*. You can specify a class as abstract in the UML by writing its name in italics, such as for the class `Security`. This convention applies to operations such `presentValue` and means that the given operation provides a signature but is otherwise incomplete and so must be implemented by some method at a lower level of abstraction. In fact, as the figure shows, all four of the immediate children of `Security` are concrete

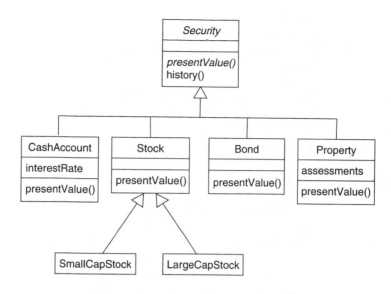

Figure 5-9: Inheritance Relationships

(meaning that they are nonabstract) and also provide a concrete implementation of the operation `presentValue`.

Your generalization/specialization hierarchies don't have to be limited to only two levels. In fact, as the figure shows, it is common to have more than two layers of inheritance. `SmallCapStock` and `LargeCapStock` are both children of `Stock`, which, in turn, is a child of `Security`. `Security` is therefore a base class because it has no parents. `SmallCapStock` and `LargeCapStock` are both leaf classes because they have no children. `Stock` has a parent as well as children, and so it is neither a root nor a leaf class.

Multiple inheritance is discussed in Chapter 10.

Although it is not shown here, you can also create classes that have more than one parent. This is called multiple inheritance and means that the given class has all the attributes, operations, and associations of all its parents.

Of course, there can be no cycles in an inheritance lattice; a given class cannot be its own parent.

Modeling Structural Relationships

When you model with dependencies or generalization relationships, you are modeling classes that represent different levels of importance or different levels of abstraction. Given a dependency between two classes, one class depends on another but the other class has no knowledge of the one. Given a generalization relationship between two classes, the child inherits from its parent but the parent has no specific knowledge of its children. In short, dependency and generalization relationships are one-sided.

Associations are, by default, bidirectional; you can limit their direction, as discussed in Chapter 10.

When you model with association relationships, you are modeling classes that are peers of one another. Given an association between two classes, both rely on the other in some way, and you can navigate in either direction. Whereas dependency is a using relationship and generalization is an is-a-kind-of relationship, an association specifies a structural path across which objects of the classes interact.

To model structural relationships,

- For each pair of classes, if you need to navigate from objects of one to objects of another, specify an association between the two. This is a data-driven view of associations.
- For each pair of classes, if objects of one class need to interact with objects of the other class other than as parameters to an operation, specify an association between the two. This is more of a behavior-driven view of associations.
- For each of these associations, specify a multiplicity (especially when the multiplicity is not *, which is the default), as well as role names (especially if it helps to explain the model).
- If one of the classes in an association is structurally or organizationally a whole compared with the classes at the other end that look like parts, mark this as an aggregation by adorning the association at the end near the whole.

Use cases are discussed in Chapter 16.

How do you know when objects of a given class must interact with objects of another class? The answer is that CRC cards and use case analysis help tremendously by forcing you to consider structural and behavioral scenarios. Where you find that two or more classes interact, specify an association.

Figure 5-10 shows a set of classes drawn from an information system for a school. Starting at the bottom left of this diagram, you will find the classes named `Student`, `Course`, and `Instructor`. There's an association between `Student` and `Course`, specifying that students attend courses. Furthermore, every student may attend any number of courses and every course may have any number of students.

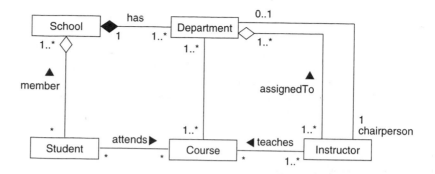

Figure 5-10: Structural Relationships

Similarly, you'll find an association between `Course` and `Instructor`, specifying that instructors teach courses. For every course there is at least one instructor and every instructor may teach zero or more courses.

The aggregation relationship between `School` *and* `Department` *is composite aggregation, as discussed in Chapter 10.*

The relationships between `School` and the classes `Student` and `Department` are a bit different. Here you'll see aggregation relationships. A school has zero or more students, each student may be a registered member of one or more schools, a school has one or more departments, each department belongs to exactly one school. You could leave off the aggregation adornments and use plain associations, but by specifying that `School` is a whole and that `Student` and `Department` are some of its parts, you make clear which one is organizationally superior to the other. Thus, schools are somewhat defined by the students and departments they have. Similarly, students and departments don't really stand alone outside the school to which they belong. Rather, they get some of their identity from their school.

You'll also see that there are two associations between `Department` and `Instructor`. One of these associations specifies that every instructor is assigned to one or more departments and that each department has one or more instructors. This is modeled as an aggregation because organizationally, departments are at a higher level in the school's structure than are instructors. The other association specifies that for every department, there is no more than one instructor who is the department chair. The way this model is specified, an instructor can be the chair of no more than one department and some instructors are not chairs of any department.

> **Note:** You may take exception to this model because it might not reflect your reality. Your school might not have departments. You might have chairs who are not instructors or you might even have students who are also instructors. That doesn't mean that the model here is wrong, it's just different. You cannot model in isolation, and every model like this depends on how you intend to use these models.

Hints and Tips

When you model relationships in the UML,

- Use dependencies only when the relationship you are modeling is not structural.
- Use generalization only when you have an "is-a-kind-of" relationship; multiple inheritance can often be replaced with aggregation.
- Beware of introducing cyclical generalization relationships.
- Keep your generalization relationships generally balanced; inheritance latices should not be too deep (more than five levels or so should be questioned) nor too wide (instead, look for the possibility of intermediate abstract classes).
- Use associations primarily where there are structural relationships among objects.

When you draw a relationship in the UML,

- Use either rectilinear or oblique lines consistently. Rectilinear lines give a visual cue that emphasizes the connections among related things all pointing to one common thing. Oblique lines are often more space-efficient in complex diagrams. Using both kinds of lines in the same diagram is useful for drawing attention to different groups of relationships.
- Avoid lines that cross.
- Show only those relationships that are necessary to understand a particular grouping of things. Superfluous relationships (especially redundant associations) should be elided.

UNIFIED
MODELING
LANGUAGE

Chapter 6
COMMON MECHANISMS

These common mechanisms are discussed in Chapter 2.

The UML is made simpler by the presence of four common mechanisms that apply consistently throughout the language: specifications, adornments, common divisions, and extensibility mechanisms. This chapter explains the use of two of these common mechanisms, adornments and extensibility mechanisms.

Notes are the most important kind of adornment that stands alone. A note is a graphical symbol for rendering constraints or comments attached to an element or a collection of elements. You use notes to attach information to a model, such as requirements, observations, reviews, and explanations.

The UML's extensibility mechanisms permit you to extend the language in controlled ways. These mechanisms include stereotypes, tagged values, and constraints. A stereotype extends the vocabulary of the UML, allowing you to create new kinds of building blocks that are derived from existing ones but that are specific to your problem. A tagged value extends the properties of a UML building block, allowing you to create new information in that element's specification. A constraint extends the semantics of a UML building block, allowing you to add new rules or modify existing ones. You use these mechanisms to tailor the UML to the specific needs of your domain and your development culture.

Getting Started

Sometimes, you just have to color outside the lines. For example, at a job site, an architect might scribble a few notes on the building's blueprints in order to communicate a subtle detail to the construction workers. In a recording studio, a composer might invent a new musical notation to represent some unusual effect she wants from a keyboard player. In both cases, there already exist well-defined languages—the language of structural blueprints and the language of musical notation—but, sometimes, you have to bend or extend those languages in controlled ways to communicate your intent.

Modeling is all about communication. The UML already gives you all the tools you need to visualize, specify, construct, and document the artifacts of a wide range of software-intensive systems. However, you might find circumstances in which you'll want to bend or extend the UML. This happens to human languages all the time (that's why new dictionaries get published every year), because no static language can ever be sufficient to cover everything you'll want to communicate for all time. When using a modeling language such as the UML, remember that you are doing so to communicate, and that means you'll want to stick to the core language unless there's compelling reason to deviate. When you find yourself needing to color outside the lines, you should do so only in controlled ways. Otherwise, you will make it impossible for anyone to understand what you've done.

Notes are the mechanism provided by the UML to let you capture arbitrary comments and constraints to help illuminate the models you've created. Notes may represent artifacts that play an important role in the software development life cycle, such as requirements, or they may simply represent free-form observations, reviews, or explanations.

The UML provides a graphical representation for comments and constraints, called a note, as Figure 6-1 shows. This notation permits you to visualize a comment directly. In conjunction with the proper tools, notes also give you a placeholder to link to or embed other documents.

Figure 6-1: Notes

Stereotypes, tagged values, and constraints are the mechanisms provided by the UML to let you add new building blocks, create new properties, and specify new semantics. For example, if you are modeling a network, you might want to have symbols for routers and hubs; you can use stereotyped nodes to make these things appear as primitive building blocks. Similarly, if you are part of your project's release team, responsible for assembling, testing, and then deploying releases, you might want to keep track of the version number and test results for each major subsystem. You can use tagged values to add this information to your models. Finally, if you are modeling hard real time systems, you might want to adorn your models with information about time budgets and deadlines; you can use constraints to capture these timing requirements.

The UML provides a textual representation for stereotypes, tagged values, and constraints, as Figure 6-2 shows. Stereotypes also let you introduce new graphical symbols so that you can provide visual cues to your models that speak the language of your domain and your development culture.

Figure 6-2: Stereotypes, Tagged Values, and Constraints

Terms and Concepts

A *note* is a graphical symbol for rendering constraints or comments attached to an element or a collection of elements. Graphically, a note is rendered as a rectangle with a dog-eared corner, together with a textual or graphical comment.

A *stereotype* is an extension of the vocabulary of the UML, allowing you to create new kinds of building blocks similar to existing ones but specific to your problem. Graphically, a stereotype is rendered as a name enclosed by guillemets and placed above the name of another element. As an option, the stereotyped element may be rendered by using a new icon associated with that stereotype.

A *tagged value* is an extension of the properties of a UML element, allowing you to create new information in that element's specification. Graphically, a tagged value is rendered as a string enclosed by brackets and placed below the name of another element.

A *constraint* is an extension of the semantics of a UML element, allowing you to add new rules or to modify existing ones. Graphically, a constraint is rendered as a string enclosed by brackets and placed near the associated element or connected to that element or elements by dependency relationships. As an alternative, you can render a constraint in a note.

Notes

A note that renders a comment has no semantic impact, meaning that its contents do not alter the meaning of the model to which it is attached. This is why notes are used to specify things like requirements, observations, reviews, and explanations, in addition to rendering constraints.

Notes may be attached to more than one element by using dependencies, as discussed in Chapter 5.

A note may contain any combination of text or graphics. If your implementation allows it, you can put a live URL inside a note, or even link to or embed another document. In this way, you can use the UML to organize all the artifacts you might generate or use during development, as Figure 6-3 illustrates.

Figure 6-3: Notes

Note: The UML specifies one standard stereotype that applies to notes—requirements. This stereotype names a common category of notes—those used to state some responsibility or obligation.

Other Adornments

The basic notation for an association, along with some of its adornments, are discussed in Chapters 5 and 10.

Adornments are textual or graphical items that are added to an element's basic notation and are used to visualize details from the element's specification. For example, the basic notation for an association is a line, but this may be adorned with such details as the role and multiplicity of each end. In using the UML, the general rule to follow is this: Start with the basic notation for each element and then add other adornments only as they are necessary to convey specific information that is important to your model.

Most adornments are rendered by placing text near the element of interest or by adding a graphic symbol to the basic notation. However, sometimes you'll want to adorn an element with more detail than can be accommodated by simple text or graphics. In the case of such things as classes, components, and nodes, you can add an extra compartment below the usual compartments to provide this information, as Figure 6-4 shows.

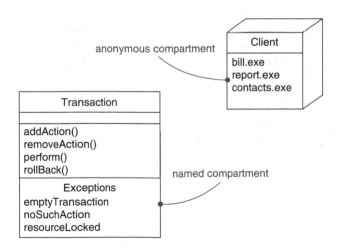

Figure 6-4: Extra Compartments

Note: Unless it's obvious by its content, it's good practice to name any extra compartment explicitly so that there is no confusion about its meaning. It's also good practice to use extra compartments sparingly, because if overused, they make diagrams cluttered.

Stereotypes

These four basic elements of the UML are discussed in Chapter 2.

The UML provides a language for structural things, behavioral things, grouping things, and notational things. These four basic kinds of things address the overwhelming majority of the systems you'll need to model. However, sometimes you'll want to introduce new things that speak the vocabulary of your domain and look like primitive building blocks.

The Rational Unified Process is summarized in Appendix C.

A stereotype is not the same as a parent class in a parent/child generalization relationship. Rather, you can think of a stereotype as a metatype, because each one creates the equivalent of a new class in the UML's metamodel. For example, if you are modeling a business process, you'll want to introduce things like workers, documents, and policies. Similarly, if you are following a development process, such as the Rational Unified Process, you'll want to model using boundary, control, and entity classes. This is where the real value of stereotypes comes in. When you stereotype an element such as a node or a class, you are in effect extending the UML by creating a new building block just like an existing one but with its own special properties (each stereotype may provide its own set of tagged values), semantics (each stereotype may provide its own constraints), and notation (each stereotype may provide its own icon).

In its simplest form, a stereotype is rendered as a name enclosed by guillemets (for example, «name») and placed above the name of another element. As a visual cue, you may define an icon for the stereotype and render that icon to the right of the name (if you are using the basic notation for the element) or use that icon as the basic symbol for the stereotyped item. All three of these approaches are illustrated in Figure 6-5.

The UML's defined stereotypes are discussed in Appendix B.

Note: When you define an icon for a stereotype, consider using color as an accent to provide a subtle visual cue (but use color sparingly). The UML lets you use any shape for such icons, and if your implementation permits it, these icons might appear as primitive tools so that users who create UML diagrams will have a palette of things that look basic to them and speak the vocabulary of their domain.

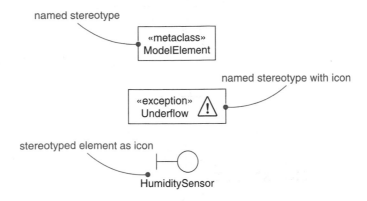

named stereotype

«metaclass»
ModelElement

named stereotype with icon

«exception»
Underflow

stereotyped element as icon

HumiditySensor

Figure 6-5: Stereotypes

Tagged Values

Every thing in the UML has its own set of properties: classes have names, attributes, and operations; associations have names and two or more ends (each with its own properties); and so on. With stereotypes, you can add new things to the UML; with tagged values, you can add new properties.

Attributes are discussed in Chapters 4 and 9.

You can define tags for existing elements of the UML, or you can define tags that apply to individual stereotypes so that everything with that stereotype has that tagged value. A tagged value is not the same as a class attribute. Rather, you can think of a tagged value as metadata because its value applies to the element itself, not its instances. For example, as Figure 6-6 shows, you might want to specify the number of processors installed on each kind of node in a deployment diagram, or you might want to require that every component be stereotyped as a library if it is intended to be deployed on a client or a server.

In its simplest form, a tagged value is rendered as a string enclosed by brackets and placed below the name of another element. That string includes a name (the tag), a separator (the symbol =), and a value (of the tag). You can specify just the value if its meaning is unambiguous, such as when the value is the name of enumeration.

The UML's defined tagged values are discussed in Appendix B.

Note: One of the most common uses of tagged values is to specify properties that are relevant to code generation or configuration management. For example, you can use tagged values to specify the programming language to which you map a particular class. Similarly, you can use tagged values to specify the author and version of a component.

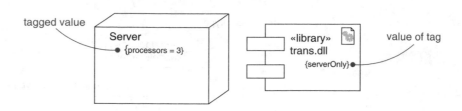

Figure 6-6: Tagged Values

Constraints

Time and
space
constraints,
commonly
used when
modeling real
time
systems, are
discussed in
Chapter 23.

Everything in the UML has its own semantics. Generalization implies the Liskov substitution principle, and multiple associations connected to one class denote distinct relationships. With constraints, you can add new semantics or change existing rules. A constraint specifies conditions that must be held true for the model to be well-formed. For example, as Figure 6-7 shows, you might want to specify that, across a given association, communication is encrypted. Similarly, you might want to specify that among a set of associations, only one is manifest at a time.

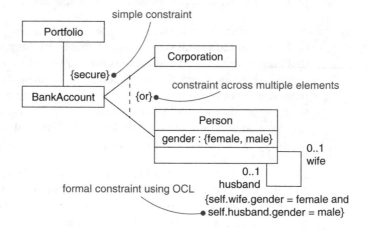

Figure 6-7: Constraint

The UML's
defined con-
straints are
discussed in
Appendix B.

Note: Constraints may be written as free-form text. If you want to specify your semantics more precisely, you can use the UML's Object Constraint Language (OCL), described further in *The Unified Modeling Language Reference Manual*.

Constraints may be attached to more than one element by using dependencies, as discussed in Chapter 5.

A constraint is rendered as a string enclosed by brackets and placed near the associated element. This notation is also used as an adornment to the basic notation of an element to visualize parts of an element's specification that have no graphical cue. For example, some properties of associations (order and changeability) are rendered using constraint notation.

Standard Elements

The UML's standard elements are summarized in Appendix B; classifiers are discussed in Chapter 9.

The UML defines a number of standard stereotypes for classifiers, components, relationships, and other modeling elements. There is one standard stereotype, mainly of interest to tool builders, that lets you model stereotypes themselves.

■ `stereotype`   Specifies that the classifier is a stereotype that may be applied to other elements

You'll use this stereotype when you want to explicitly model the stereotypes you've defined for your project.

The UML also specifies one standard tagged value that applies to all modeling elements.

■ `documentation`   Specifies a comment, description, or explanation of the element to which it is attached

You'll use this tagged value when you want to attach a comment directly to the specification of an element, such as a class.

Common Modeling Techniques

Modeling Comments

The most common purpose for which you'll use notes is to write down free-form observations, reviews, or explanations. By putting these comments directly in your models, your models can become a common repository for all the disparate artifacts you'll create during development. You can even use notes to visualize requirements and show how they tie explicitly to the parts of your model.

To model a comment,

- Put your comment as text in a note and place it adjacent to the element to which it refers. You can show a more explicit relationship by connecting a note to its elements using a dependency relationship.
- Remember that you can hide or make visible the elements of your model as you see fit. This means that you don't have to make your comments visible everywhere the elements to which it is attached are visible. Rather, expose your comments in your diagrams only insofar as you need to communicate that information in that context.
- If your comment is lengthy or involves something richer than plain text, consider putting your comment in an external document and linking or embedding that document in a note attached to your model.
- As your model evolves, keep those comments that record significant decisions that cannot be inferred from the model itself, and—unless they are of historic interest—discard the others.

Simple generalization is discussed in Chapter 5; advanced forms of generalization are discussed in Chapter 10.

For example, Figure 6-8 shows a model that's a work in progress of a class hierarchy, showing some requirements that shape the model, as well as some notes from a design review.

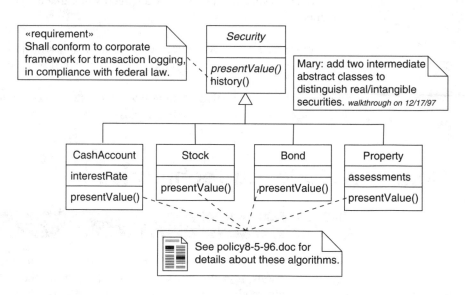

Figure 6-8: Modeling Comments

In this example, most of the comments are simple text (such as the note to Mary), but one of them (the note at the bottom of the diagram) provides a hyperlink to another document.

Modeling New Building Blocks

The UML's building blocks—classes, interfaces, collaborations, components, nodes, associations, and so on—are generic enough to address most of the things you'll want to model. However, if you want to extend your modeling vocabulary or give distinctive visual cues to certain kinds of abstractions that often appear in your domain, you need to use stereotypes.

To model new building blocks,

Building hierarchies of stereotypes is discussed in Chapter 10.

- Make sure there's not already a way to express what you want by using basic UML. If you have a common modeling problem, chances are there's already some standard stereotype that will do what you want.
- If you're convinced there's no other way to express these semantics, identify the primitive thing in the UML that's most like what you want to model (for example, class, interface, component, node, association, and so on) and define a new stereotype for that thing. Remember that you can define hierarchies of stereotypes so that you can have general kinds of stereotypes along with their specializations (but as with any hierarchy, use this sparingly).
- Specify the common properties and semantics that go beyond the basic element being stereotyped by defining a set of tagged values and constraints for the stereotype.
- If you want these stereotype elements to have a distinctive visual cue, define a new icon for the stereotype.

Instances are discussed in Chapter 13; roles are discussed in Chapter 11; activity diagrams are discussed in Chapter 19.

For example, suppose you are using activity diagrams to model a business process involving the flow of coaches and teams through a sporting event. In this context, it would make sense to visually distinguish coaches and teams from one another and from the other things in this domain, such as events and divisions. As Figure 6-9 shows, there are two things that stand out—Coach objects and Team objects. These are not just plain kinds of classes. Rather, they are now primitive building blocks that you can use in this context. You can create these new building blocks by defining a coach and team stereotype and applying them to UML's classes. In this figure, the anonymous instances called :Coach and :Team (the latter shown in various states—namely, unregistered, registered, and finished) appear using the icons associated with these stereotypes.

Figure 6-9: Modeling New Building Blocks.

Modeling New Properties

The basic properties of the UML's building blocks—attributes and operations for classes, the contents of packages, and so on—are generic enough to address most of the things you'll want to model. However, if you want to extend the properties of these basic building blocks (or the new building blocks you create using stereotypes), you need to use tagged values.

To model new properties,

- First, make sure there's not already a way to express what you want by using basic UML. If you have a common modeling problem, chances are that there's already some standard tagged value that will do what you want.
- If you're convinced there's no other way to express these semantics, add this new property to an individual element or a stereotype. The rules of generalization apply—tagged values defined for one kind of element apply to its children.

Subsystems are discussed in Chapter 31.

For example, suppose you want to tie the models you create to your project's configuration management system. Among other things, this means keeping track of the version number, current check in/check out status, and perhaps even the creation and modification dates of each subsystem. Because this is process-specific information, it is not a basic part of the UML, although you can add this information as tagged values. Furthermore, this information is not just a class attribute either. A subsystem's version number is part of its metadata, not part of the model.

Figure 6-10 shows four subsystems, each of which has been extended to include its version number and status. In the case of the `Billing` subsystem, one other tagged value is shown—the person who has currently checked out the subsystem.

Note: The values of tags such as `version` and `status` are things that can be set by tools. Rather than setting these values in your model by hand, you can use a development environment that integrates your configuration management tools with your modeling tools to maintain these values for you.

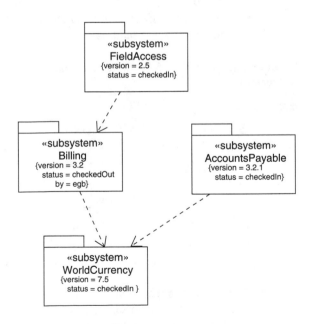

Figure 6-10: Modeling New Properties

Modeling New Semantics

When you create a model using the UML, you work within the rules the UML lays down. That's a good thing, because it means that you can communicate your intent without ambiguity to anyone else who knows how to read the UML. However, if you find yourself needing to express new semantics about which the UML is silent or that you need to modify the UML's rules, then you need to write a constraint.

To model new semantics,

- First, make sure there's not already a way to express what you want by using basic UML. If you have a common modeling problem, chances are that there's already some standard constraint that will do what you want.
- If you're convinced there's no other way to express these semantics, write your new semantics as text in a constraint and place it adjacent to the element to which it refers. You can show a more explicit relationship by connecting a constraint to its elements using a dependency relationship.
- If you need to specify your semantics more precisely and formally, write your new semantics using OCL.

For example, Figure 6-11 models a small part of a corporate human resources system.

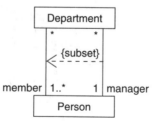

Figure 6-11: Modeling New Semantics

This diagram shows that each Person may be a member of zero or more Departments and that each Department must have at least one Person as a member. This diagram goes on to indicate that each Department must have exactly one Person as a manager and every Person may be the manager of zero or more Departments. All of these semantics can be expressed using simple UML. However, to assert that a manager must also be a member of the department is something that cuts across multiple associations and cannot be expressed using simple UML. To state this invariant, you have to write a constraint that shows the manager as a subset of the members of the Department, connecting the two associations and the constraint by a dependency from the subset to the superset.

Hints and Tips

When you adorn a model with notes,

- Use notes only for those requirements, observations, reviews, and explanations that you can't express simply or meaningfully using existing features of the UML.
- Use notes as a kind of electronic sticky note, to keep track of your work in progress.

When you draw notes,

- Don't clutter your models with large blocks of comments. Rather, if you really need a long comment, use notes as a placeholder to link to or embed a document that contains the full comment.

When you extend a model with stereotypes, tagged values, or constraints,

- Standardize on a small set of stereotypes, tagged values, and constraints to use on your project, and avoid letting individual developers create lots of new extensions.
- Chose short, meaningful names for your stereotypes and tagged values.
- Where precision can be relaxed, use free-form text for specifying constraints. If you need more rigor, use the OCL to write constraint expressions.

When you draw a stereotype, tagged value, or constraint,

- Use graphical stereotypes sparingly. You can totally change the basic notation of the UML with stereotypes, but in so doing, you'll make it impossible for anyone else to understand your models.
- Consider using simple color or shading for graphical stereotypes, as well as more complicated icons. Simple notations are generally the best, and even the most subtle visual cues can go a long way in communicating meaning.

UNIFIED
MODELING
LANGUAGE

Chapter 7
DIAGRAMS

Modeling is discussed in Chapter 1.

When you model something, you create a simplification of reality so that you can better understand the system you are developing. Using the UML, you build your models from basic building blocks, such as classes, interfaces, collaborations, components, nodes, dependencies, generalizations, and associations.

Diagrams are the means by which you view these building blocks. A diagram is a graphical presentation of a set of elements, most often rendered as a connected graph of vertices (things) and arcs (relationships). You use diagrams to visualize your system from different perspectives. Because no complex system can be understood in its entirety from only one perspective, the UML defines a number of diagrams so that you can focus on different aspects of your system independently.

Good diagrams make the system you are developing understandable and approachable. Choosing the right set of diagrams to model your system forces you to ask the right questions about your system and helps to illuminate the implications of your decisions.

91

Getting Started

When you work with an architect to design a house, you start with three things: a list of wants (such as "I want a house with three bedrooms" and "I want to pay no more than x"), a few simple sketches or pictures from other houses representing some of its key features (such as a picture of an entry with a circular staircase), and some general idea of style (such as "We'd like a French country look with hints of California coastal"). The job of the architect is to take these incomplete, ever-changing, and possibly contradictory requirements and turn them into a design.

To do that, the architect will probably start with a blueprint of a basic floor plan. This artifact provides a vehicle for you and your architect to visualize the final house, to specify details, and to document decisions. At each review, you'll want to make some changes, such as moving walls about, rearranging rooms, placing windows and doors. Early on, these blueprints change often. As the design matures and you become satisfied that you have a design that best fits all the constraints of form, function, time, and money, these blueprints will stabilize to the point at which they can be used for constructing your house. Even while your house is being built, you'll probably change some of these diagrams and create some new ones, as well.

Along the way, you'll want to see views of the house other than just the floor plan. For example, you'll want to see an elevation plan, showing the house from different sides. As you start specifying details so that the job can be meaningfully costed out, your architect will need to create electrical plans, plans for heating and ventilation, and plans for water and sewer connections. If your design requires some unusual feature (such as a long, unsupported span over the basement) or you have a feature that's important to you (such as the placement of a fireplace so that you can put a home theater near it), you and your architect will want to create some sketches that highlight those details.

The practice of creating diagrams to visualize systems from different perspectives is not limited to the construction industry. You'll find this in every engineering discipline involving the creation of complex systems, from civil engineering to aeronautical engineering, ship building, manufacturing, and software.

The five views of an architecture are discussed in Chapter 2.

In the context of software, there are five complementary views that are most important in visualizing, specifying, constructing, and documenting a software architecture: the use case view, the design view, the process view, the implementation view, and the deployment view. Each of these views involves structural modeling (modeling static things), as well as behavioral modeling (modeling dynamic things). Together, these different views capture the most important decisions about the system. Individually, each of these views lets you focus attention on one perspective of the system so that you can reason about your decisions with clarity.

Modeling the architecture of a system is discussed in Chapter 31.

When you view a software system from any perspective using the UML, you use diagrams to organize the elements of interest. The UML defines nine kinds of diagrams, which you can mix and match to assemble each view. For example, the static aspects of a system's implementation view might be visualized using component diagrams; the dynamic aspects of the same implementation view might be visualized using interaction diagrams. Similarly, the static aspects of a system's database might be visualized using class diagrams; its dynamic aspects might be visualized using collaboration diagrams.

Of course, you are not limited to these nine diagrams. In the UML, these nine are defined because they represent the most common packaging of viewed elements. To fit the needs of your project or organization, you can create your own kinds of diagrams to view UML elements in different ways.

This incremental and iterative process is summarized in Appendix C.

You'll use the UML's diagrams in two basic ways: to specify models from which you'll construct an executable system (forward engineering) and to reconstruct models from parts of an executable system (reverse engineering). Either way, just like a building architect, you'll tend to create your diagrams incrementally (crafting them one piece at a time) and iteratively (repeating the process of design a little, build a little).

Terms and Concepts

Systems, models, and views are discussed in Chapter 31.

A *system* is a collection of subsystems organized to accomplish a purpose and described by a set of models, possibly from different viewpoints. A *subsystem* is a grouping of elements, of which some constitute a specification of the behavior offered by the other contained elements. A *model* is a semantically closed abstraction of a system, meaning that it represents a complete and self-consistent simplification of reality, created in order to better understand the system. In the context of architecture, a *view* is a projection into the organization and structure of a system's model, focused on one aspect of that system. A *diagram* is the graphical presentation of a set of elements, most often rendered as a connected graph of vertices (things) and arcs (relationships).

To put it another way, a system represents the thing you are developing, viewed from different perspectives by different models, with those views presented in the form of diagrams.

A diagram is just a graphical projection into the elements that make up a system. For example, you might have several hundred classes in the design of a corporate human resources system. You could never visualize the structure or behavior of that system by staring at one large diagram containing all these classes and all their relationships. Instead, you'd want to create several diagrams, each focused on one view. For example, you might find one class diagram that includes classes, such as `Person`, `Department`, and `Office`, assembled to construct a database schema. You might find some of these same classes, along with other classes, in another diagram that presents an API that's used by client applications. You'd likely see some of these same classes mentioned in an interaction diagram, specifying the semantics of a transaction that reassigns a `Person` to a new `Department`.

As this example shows, the same thing in a system (such as the class `Person`) may appear multiple times in the same diagram or even in different diagrams. In each case, it's the same thing. Each diagram provides a view into the elements that make up the system.

In modeling real systems, no matter what the problem domain, you'll find yourself creating the same kinds of diagrams, because they represent common views into common models. Typically, you'll view the static parts of a system using one of the four following diagrams.

1. Class diagram
2. Object diagram
3. Component diagram
4. Deployment diagram

You'll often use five additional diagrams to view the dynamic parts of a system.

1. Use case diagram
2. Sequence diagram
3. Collaboration diagram
4. Statechart diagram
5. Activity diagram

The UML defines these nine kinds of diagrams.

Packages are discussed in Chapter 12.

Every diagram you create will most likely be one of these nine or occasionally of another kind, defined for your project or organization. Every diagram must have a name that's unique in its context so that you can refer to a specific diagram and distinguish one from another. For anything but the most trivial system, you'll want to organize your diagrams into packages.

You can project any combination of elements in the UML in the same diagram. For example, you might show both classes and objects in the same diagram (a common thing to do), or you might even show both classes and components in the same diagram (legal, but less common). Although there's nothing that prevents you from placing wildly disparate kinds of modeling elements in the same diagram, it's more common for you to have roughly the same kinds of things in one diagram. In fact, the UML's defined diagrams are named after the element you'll most often place in each. For example, if you want to visualize a set of classes and their relationships, you'll use a class diagram. Similarly, if you want to visualize a set of components, you'll use a component diagram.

Note: In practice, all the diagrams you'll create will be two-dimensional, meaning that they are just flat graphs of vertices and arcs that are drawn on a sheet of paper, a whiteboard, the back of an envelope, or on a computer display. The UML allows you to create three-dimensional diagrams, meaning that they are graphs with depth, allowing you to "swim" through a model. Some virtual reality research groups have already demonstrated this advanced use of the UML.

Structural Diagrams

The UML's four structural diagrams exist to visualize, specify, construct, and document the static aspects of a system. You can think of the static aspects of a system as representing its relatively stable skeleton and scaffolding. Just as the static aspects of a house encompass the existence and placement of such things as walls, doors, windows, pipes, wires, and vents, so too do the static aspects of a software system encompass the existence and placement of such things as classes, interfaces, collaborations, components, and nodes.

The UML's structural diagrams are roughly organized around the major groups of things you'll find when modeling a system.

1. Class diagram   Classes, interfaces, and collaborations
2. Object diagram   Objects
3. Component diagram   Components
4. Deployment diagram   Nodes

Class diagrams are discussed in Chapter 8.

Class Diagram A *class diagram* shows a set of classes, interfaces, and collaborations and their relationships. Class diagrams are the most common diagram found in modeling object-oriented systems. You use class diagrams to illustrate the static design view of a system. Class diagrams that include active classes are used to address the static process view of a system.

Object diagrams are discussed in Chapter 14

Object Diagram An *object diagram* shows a set of objects and their relationships. You use object diagrams to illustrate data structures, the static snapshots of instances of the things found in class diagrams. Object diagrams address the static design view or static process view of a system just as do class diagrams, but from the perspective of real or prototypical cases.

Component diagrams are discussed in Chapter 29.

Component Diagram A *component diagram* shows a set of components and their relationships. You use component diagrams to illustrate the static implementation view of a system. Component diagrams are related to class diagrams in that a component typically maps to one or more classes, interfaces, or collaborations.

Deployment diagrams are discussed in Chapter 30.

Deployment Diagram A *deployment diagram* shows a set of nodes and their relationships. You use deployment diagrams to illustrate the static deployment view of an architecture. Deployment diagrams are related to component diagrams in that a node typically encloses one or more components.

Note: There are some common variants of these four diagrams, named after their primary contents. For example, you might create a subsystem diagram to illustrate the structural decomposition of a system into subsystems. A subsystem diagram is just a class diagram that contains, primarily, subsystems.

Behavioral Diagrams

The UML's five behavioral diagrams are used to visualize, specify, construct, and document the dynamic aspects of a system. You can think of the dynamic aspects of a system as representing its changing parts. Just as the dynamic aspects of a house encompass airflow and traffic through the rooms of a house, so too do the dynamic aspects of a software system encompass such things as the flow of messages over time and the physical movement of components across a network.

The UML's behavioral diagrams are roughly organized around the major ways you can model the dynamics of a system.

1. Use case diagram	Organizes the behaviors of the system
2. Sequence diagram	Focused on the time ordering of messages
3. Collaboration diagram	Focused on the structural organization of objects that send and receive messages
4. Statechart diagram	Focused on the changing state of a system driven by events

5. Activity diagram   Focused on the flow of control from activity to activity

Use case diagrams are discussed in Chapter 17.

Use Case Diagram A *use case diagram* shows a set of use cases and actors (a special kind of class) and their relationships. You apply use case diagrams to illustrate the static use case view of a system. Use case diagrams are especially important in organizing and modeling the behaviors of a system.

The next two diagrams and the last two diagrams are semantically equivalent, which means that you can model the dynamics of a system using one kind of behavioral diagram and then transform it to another kind of diagram without loss of information. This lets you reason about different aspects of your system's dynamics. For example, you might want first to create a sequence diagram that illustrates the time ordering of messages and then turn that into a collaboration diagram so that you can develop the structural relationships among the classes whose objects participate in this collaboration (you can go from collaboration diagrams to sequence diagrams, as well). Similarly, you might want to start with a statechart diagram to illustrate the event-driven response of the system and then turn it into an activity diagram that focuses on the flow of control (you can also go from activity diagrams to statechart diagrams). The reason that the UML provides these semantically equivalent diagrams is that modeling the dynamics of a system is just plain hard, and often you must attack a wicked problem from more than one angle at the same time.

Interaction diagram is the collective name given to sequence diagrams and collaboration diagrams. All sequence diagrams and collaborations are interaction diagrams, and an interaction diagram is either a sequence diagram or a collaboration diagram.

Sequence diagrams are discussed in Chapter 18.

Sequence Diagram A *sequence diagram* is an interaction diagram that emphasizes the time ordering of messages. A sequence diagram shows a set of objects and the messages sent and received by those objects. The objects are typically named or anonymous instances of classes, but may also represent instances of other things, such as collaborations, components, and nodes. You use sequence diagrams to illustrate the dynamic view of a system.

Collaboration diagrams are discussed in Chapter 18.

Collaboration Diagram A *collaboration diagram* is an interaction diagram that emphasizes the structural organization of the objects that send and receive messages. A collaboration diagram shows a set of objects, links among those objects, and messages sent and received by those objects. The objects are typically named or anonymous instances of classes, but may also represent instances of other things, such as collaborations, components, and nodes. You use collaboration diagrams to illustrate the dynamic view of a system.

> **Note:** Sequence and collaboration diagrams are isomorphic, meaning that you can convert from one to the other without loss of information.

Statechart diagrams are discussed in Chapter 24.

Statechart Diagram A *statechart diagram* shows a state machine, consisting of states, transitions, events, and activities. You use statechart diagrams to illustrate the dynamic view of a system. They are especially important in modeling the behavior of an interface, class, or collaboration. Statechart diagrams emphasize the event-ordered behavior of an object, which is especially useful in modeling reactive systems.

Activity diagrams, a special case of statechart diagrams, are discussed in Chapter 19.

Activity Diagram An *activity diagram* shows the flow from activity to activity within a system. An activity shows a set of activities, the sequential or branching flow from activity to activity, and objects that act and are acted upon. You use activity diagrams to illustrate the dynamic view of a system. Activity diagrams are especially important in modeling the function of a system. Activity diagrams emphasize the flow of control among objects.

> **Note:** There are obvious practical limitations to illustrating something that's inherently dynamic (the behavior of a system) using diagrams (inherently static artifacts, especially when you draw them on a sheet of paper, a whiteboard, or the back of an envelope). Rendered on a computer display, there are opportunities for animating behavioral diagrams so that they either simulate an executable system or mirror the actual behavior of a system that's executing. The UML allows you to create dynamic diagrams and to use color or other visual cues to "run" the diagram. Some tools have already demonstrated this advanced use of the UML.

Common Modeling Techniques

Modeling Different Views of a System

When you model a system from different views, you are in effect constructing your system simultaneously from multiple dimensions. By choosing the right set of views, you set up a process that forces you to ask good questions about your system and to expose risks that need to be attacked. If you do a poor job of choosing these views or if you focus on one view at the expense of all others, you run the risk of hiding issues and deferring problems that will eventually destroy any chance of success.

To model a system from different views,

- Decide which views you need to best express the architecture of your system and to expose the technical risks to your project. The five views of an architecture described earlier are a good starting point.
- For each of these views, decide which artifacts you need to create to capture the essential details of that view. For the most part, these artifacts will consist of various UML diagrams.
- As part of your process planning, decide which of these diagrams you'll want to put under some sort of formal or semi-formal control. These are the diagrams for which you'll want to schedule reviews and to preserve as documentation for the project.
- Allow room for diagrams that are thrown away. Such transitory diagrams are still useful for exploring the implications of your decisions and for experimenting with changes.

For example, if you are modeling a simple monolithic application that runs on a single machine, you might need only the following handful of diagrams.

- Use case view   Use case diagrams
- Design view   Class diagrams (for structural modeling)
                         Interaction diagrams (for behavioral modeling)
- Process view   None required
- Implementation view   None required
- Deployment view   None required

If yours is a reactive system or if it focuses on process flow, you'll probably want to include statechart diagrams and activity diagrams, respectively, to model your system's behavior.

Similarly, if yours is a client/server system, you'll probably want to include component diagrams and deployment diagrams to model the physical details of your system.

Finally, if you are modeling a complex, distributed system, you'll need to employ the full range of the UML's diagrams in order to express the architecture of your system and the technical risks to your project, as in the following.

- Use case view   Use case diagrams
                         Activity diagrams (for behavioral modeling)
- Design view   Class diagrams (for structural modeling)
                         Interaction diagrams (for behavioral modeling)
                         Statechart diagrams (for behavioral modeling)

- Process view   Class diagrams (for structural modeling)
                        Interaction diagrams (for behavioral modeling)
- Implementation view   Component diagrams
- Deployment view   Deployment diagrams

Modeling Different Levels of Abstraction

Not only do you need to view a system from several angles, you'll also find
people involved in development who need the same view of the system but at
different levels of abstraction. For example, given a set of classes that capture
the vocabulary of your problem space, a programmer might want a detailed
view down to the level of each class's attributes, operations, and relationships.
On the other hand, an analyst who's walking through some use case scenarios
with an end user will likely want only a much elided view of these same
classes. In this context, the programmer is working at a lower level of abstraction and the analysis and end user are working at a higher level of abstraction,
but all are working from the same model. In fact, because diagrams are just a
graphical presentation of the elements that make up a model, you can create
several diagrams against the same model or different models, each hiding or
exposing different sets of these elements and each showing different levels of
detail.

Basically, there are two ways to model a system at different levels of abstraction: by presenting diagrams with different levels of detail against the same
model, or by creating models at different levels of abstraction with diagrams
that trace from one model to another.

To model a system at different levels of abstraction by presenting diagrams
with different levels of detail,

- Consider the needs of your readers, and start with a given model.
- If your reader is using the model to construct an implementation, she'll
  need diagrams that are at a lower level of abstraction, which means that
  they'll need to reveal a lot of detail. If she is using the model to present
  a conceptual model to an end user, she'll need diagrams that are at a
  higher level of abstraction, which means that they'll hide a lot of detail.
- Depending on where you land in this spectrum of low-to-high levels of
  abstraction, create a diagram at the right level of abstraction by hiding
  or revealing the following four categories of things from your model:
  1. *Building blocks and relationships*: Hide those that are not relevant to
     the intent of your diagram or the needs of your reader.
  2. *Adornments*: Reveal only the adornments of these building blocks
     and relationships that are essential to understanding your intent.

Messages are discussed in Chapter 15; transitions are discussed in Chapter 21; stereotypes are discussed in Chapter 6.

3. *Flow*: In the context of behavioral diagrams, expand only those messages or transitions that are essential to understanding your intent.
4. *Stereotypes*: In the context of stereotypes used to classify lists of things, such as attributes and operations, reveal only those stereotyped items that are essential to understanding your intent.

The main advantage of this approach is that you are always modeling from a common semantic repository. The main disadvantage of this approach is that changes from diagrams at one level of abstraction may make obsolete diagrams at a different level of abstraction.

To model a system at different levels of abstraction by creating models at different levels of abstraction,

Trace dependencies are discussed in Chapter 31.

- Consider the needs of your readers and decide on the level of abstraction that each should view, forming a separate model for each level.
- In general, populate your models that are at a high level of abstraction with simple abstractions and your models that are at a low level of abstraction with detailed abstractions. Establish trace dependencies among the related elements of different models.
- In practice, if you follow the five views of an architecture, there are four common situations you'll encounter when modeling a system at different levels of abstraction:

Use cases are discussed in Chapter 16; collaborations are discussed in Chapter 27; components are discussed in Chapter 25; nodes are discussed in Chapter 26.

1. *Use cases and their realization*: Use cases in a use case model will trace to collaborations in a design model.
2. *Collaborations and their realization*: Collaborations will trace to a society of classes that work together to carry out the collaboration.
3. *Components and their design*: Components in an implementation model will trace to the elements in a design model.
4. *Nodes and their components*: Nodes in a deployment model will trace to components in an implementation model.

The main advantage of the approach is that diagrams at different levels of abstraction remain more loosely coupled. This means that changes in one model will have less direct effect on other models. The main disadvantage of this approach is that you must spend resources to keep these models and their diagrams synchronized. This is especially true when your models parallel different phases of the software development life cycle, such as when you decide to maintain an analysis model separate from a design model.

Interaction diagrams are discussed in Chapter 18.

For example, suppose you are modeling a system for Web commerce—one of the main use cases of such a system would be for placing an order. If you're an analyst or an end user, you'd probably create some interaction diagrams at a high level of abstraction that show the action of placing an order, as in Figure 7-1.

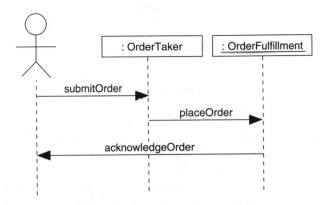

Figure 7-1: Interaction Diagram at a High Level of Abstraction

On the other hand, a programmer responsible for implementing this scenario would have to build on this diagram, expanding certain messages and adding other players in this interaction, as in Figure 7-2.

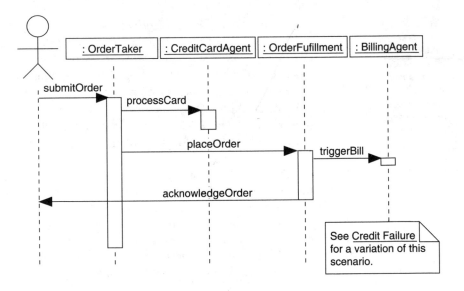

Figure 7-2: Interaction at a Low Level of Abstraction

Both of these diagrams work against the same model, but at different levels of detail. It's reasonable to have many diagrams such as these, especially if your tools make it easy to navigate from one diagram to another.

Modeling Complex Views

No matter how you break up your models, there are times when you'll find it necessary to create large and complex diagrams. For example, if you want to analyze the entire schema of a database encompassing 100 or more abstractions, it really is valuable to study a diagram showing all these classes and their associations. In so doing, you'll be able to see common patterns of collaboration. If you were to show this model at a higher level of abstraction by eliding some detail, you'd lose the information necessary to make these insights.

To model complex views,

- First, convince yourself there's no meaningful way to present this information at a higher level of abstraction, perhaps eliding some parts of the diagram and retaining the detail in other parts.

Packages are discussed in Chapter 12; collaborations are discussed in Chapter 27.

- If you've hidden as much detail as you can and your diagram is still complex, consider grouping some of the elements in packages or in higher level collaborations, then render only those packages or collaborations in your diagram.
- If your diagram is still complex, use notes and color as visual cues to draw the reader's attention to the points you want to make.
- If your diagram is still complex, print it in its entirety and hang it on a convenient large wall. You lose the interactivity an online version of the diagram brings, but you can step back from the diagram and study it for common patterns.

Hints and Tips

When you create a diagram,

- Remember that the purpose of a diagram in the UML is not to draw pretty pictures but, rather, to visualize, specify, construct, and document. Diagrams are a means to the end of deploying an executable system.
- Not all diagrams are meant to be preserved. Consider building up diagrams on the fly by querying the elements in your models, and use these diagrams to reason about your system as it is being built. Many of these

kinds of diagrams can be thrown away after they have served their purpose (but the semantics upon which they were created will remain as a part of the model).

- Avoid extraneous or redundant diagrams. They clutter your models.
- Reveal only enough detail in each diagram to address the issues for which it was intended. Extraneous information can distract the reader from the key point you're trying to make.
- On the other hand, don't make your diagrams minimalist unless you really need to present something at a very high level of abstraction. Oversimplification can hide details that are important to reasoning about your models.
- Keep a balance between the structural and behavioral diagrams in your system. Very few systems are totally static or totally dynamic.
- Don't make your diagrams too big (ones that run more than several printed pages are hard to navigate) or too small (consider joining several trivial diagrams into one).
- Give each diagram a meaningful name that clearly expresses its intent.
- Keep your diagrams organized. Group them into packages according to view.
- Don't obsess over the format of a diagram. Let tools help you.

A well-structured diagram

- Is focused on communicating one aspect of a system's view.
- Contains only those elements that are essential to understanding that aspect.
- Provides detail consistent with its level of abstraction (expose only those adornments that are essential to understanding).
- Is not so minimalist that it misinforms the reader about semantics that are important.

When you draw a diagram,

- Give it a name that communicates its purpose.
- Lay out its elements to minimize lines that cross.
- Organize its elements spatially so that things that are semantically close are laid out physically close.
- Use notes and color as visual cues to draw attention to important features of your diagram.

Chapter 8

CLASS DIAGRAMS

In this chapter

- Modeling simple collaborations
- Modeling a logical database schema
- Forward and reverse engineering

Class diagrams are the most common diagram found in modeling object-oriented systems. A class diagram shows a set of classes, interfaces, and collaborations and their relationships.

You use class diagrams to model the static design view of a system. For the most part, this involves modeling the vocabulary of the system, modeling collaborations, or modeling schemas. Class diagrams are also the foundation for a couple of related diagrams: component diagrams and deployment diagrams.

Class diagrams are important not only for visualizing, specifying, and documenting structural models, but also for constructing executable systems through forward and reverse engineering.

Getting Started

When you build a house, you start with a vocabulary that includes basic building blocks, such as walls, floors, windows, doors, ceilings, and joists. These things are largely structural (walls have height, width, and thickness), but they're also somewhat behavioral (different kinds of walls can support different loads, doors open and close, there are constraints on the span of a unsupported floor). In fact, you can't consider these structural and behavioral features independently. Rather, when you build your house, you must consider how they interact. The process of architecting your house thus involves assembling these things in a unique and pleasing manner intended to satisfy all your functional and nonfunctional requirements. The blueprints you create to visualize your house and to specify its details to your contractors for construction are, in effect, graphical presentations of these things and their relationships.

Building software has much the same characteristics except that, given the fluidity of software, you have the ability to define your own basic building blocks from scratch. With the UML, you use class diagrams to visualize the static aspects of these building blocks and their relationships and to specify their details for construction, as you can see in Figure 8-1.

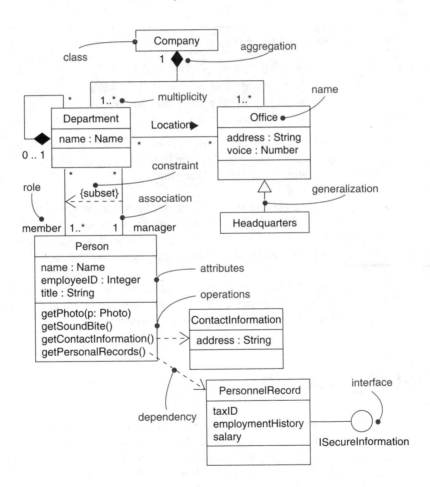

Figure 8-1: A Class Diagram

Terms and Concepts

A *class diagram* is a diagram that shows a set of classes, interfaces, and collaborations and their relationships. Graphically, a class diagram is a collection of vertices and arcs.

Common Properties

The general properties of diagrams are discussed in Chapter 7.

A class diagram is just a special kind of diagram and shares the same common properties as do all other diagrams— a name and graphical content that are a projection into a model. What distinguishes a class diagram from all other kinds of diagrams is its particular content.

Contents

Classes are discussed in Chapters 4 and 9; interfaces are discussed in Chapter 11; collaborations are discussed in Chapter 27; relationships are discussed in Chapters 5 and 10; packages are discussed in Chapter 12; subsystems are discussed in Chapter 31; instances are discussed in Chapter 13.

Class diagrams commonly contain the following things:

- Classes
- Interfaces
- Collaborations
- Dependency, generalization, and association relationships

Like all other diagrams, class diagrams may contain notes and constraints.

Class diagrams may also contain packages or subsystems, both of which are used to group elements of your model into larger chunks. Sometimes, you'll want to place instances in your class diagrams, as well, especially when you want to visualize the (possibly dynamic) type of an instance.

Note: Component diagrams and deployment diagrams are similar to class diagrams, except that instead of containing classes, they contain components and nodes, respectively.

Common Uses

Design views are discussed in Chapter 2.

You use class diagrams to model the static design view of a system. This view primarily supports the functional requirements of a system—the services the system should provide to its end users.

When you model the static design view of a system, you'll typically use class diagrams in one of three ways.

Modeling the vocabulary of a system is discussed in Chapter 4.

1. To model the vocabulary of a system

Modeling the vocabulary of a system involves making a decision about which abstractions are a part of the system under consideration and which fall outside its boundaries. You use class diagrams to specify these abstractions and their responsibilities.

Collaborations are discussed in Chapter 27.

2. To model simple collaborations

A collaboration is a society of classes, interfaces, and other elements that work together to provide some cooperative behavior that's bigger than the sum of all the elements. For example, when you're modeling the semantics of a transaction in a distributed system, you can't just stare at a single class to understand what's going on. Rather, these semantics are carried out by a set of classes that work together. You use class diagrams to visualize and specify this set of classes and their relationships.

Persistence is discussed in Chapter 23; modeling physical databases is discussed in Chapter 29.

3. To model a logical database schema

Think of a schema as the blueprint for the conceptual design of a database. In many domains, you'll want to store persistent information in a relational database or in an object-oriented database. You can model schemas for these databases using class diagrams.

Common Modeling Techniques

Modeling Simple Collaborations

No class stands alone. Rather, each works in collaboration with others to carry out some semantics greater than each individual. Therefore, in addition to capturing the vocabulary of your system, you'll also need to turn your attention to visualizing, specifying, constructing, and documenting the various ways these things in your vocabulary work together. You use class diagrams to represent such collaborations.

When you create a class diagram, you just model a part of the things and relationships that make up your system's design view. For this reason, each class diagram should focus on one collaboration at a time.

To model a collaboration,

Mechanisms such as this are often coupled to use cases, as discussed in Chapter 16; scenarios are threads through a use case, as discussed in Chapter 15.

- Identify the mechanism you'd like to model. A mechanism represents some function or behavior of the part of the system you are modeling that results from the interaction of a society of classes, interfaces, and other things.
- For each mechanism, identify the classes, interfaces, and other collaborations that participate in this collaboration. Identify the relationships among these things, as well.
- Use scenarios to walk through these things. Along the way, you'll discover parts of your model that were missing and parts that were just plain semantically wrong.
- Be sure to populate these elements with their contents. For classes, start with getting a good balance of responsibilities. Then, over time, turn these into concrete attributes and operations.

For example, Figure 8-2 shows a set of classes drawn from the implementation of an autonomous robot. The figure focuses on the classes involved in the mechanism for moving the robot along a path. You'll find one abstract class (`Motor`) with two concrete children, `SteeringMotor` and `MainMotor`. Both of these classes inherit the five operations of their parent, `Motor`. The two classes are, in turn, shown as parts of another class, `Driver`. The class `PathAgent` has a one-to-one association to `Driver` and a one-to-many association to `CollisionSensor`. No attributes or operations are shown for `PathAgent`, although its responsibilities are given.

There are many more classes involved in this system, but this diagram focuses only on those abstractions that are directly involved in moving the robot. You'll see some of these same classes in other diagrams. For example, although not shown here, the class `PathAgent` collaborates with at least two other classes (`Environment` and `GoalAgent`) in a higher-level mechanism for managing the conflicting goals the robot might have at a given moment. Similarly, also not shown here, the classes `CollisionSensor` and `Driver` (and its parts) collaborate with another class (`FaultAgent`) in a mechanism responsible for continuously checking the robot's hardware for errors. By focusing on each of these collaborations in different diagrams, you provide an understandable view of the system from several angles.

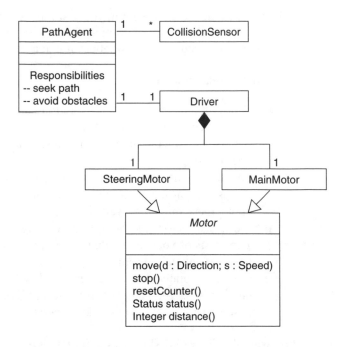

Figure 8-2: Modeling Simple Collaborations

Modeling a Logical Database Schema

Modeling the distribution and migration of persistent objects is discussed in Chapter 23; modeling physical databases is discussed in Chapter 29.

Many of the systems you'll model will have persistent objects, which means that they can be stored in a database for later retrieval. Most often, you'll use a relational database, an object-oriented database, or a hybrid object/relational database for persistent storage. The UML is well-suited to modeling logical database schemas, as well as physical databases themselves.

The UML's class diagrams are a superset of entity-relationship (E-R) diagrams, a common modeling tool for logical database design. Whereas classical E-R diagrams focus only on data, class diagrams go a step further by permitting the modeling of behavior, as well. In the physical database, these logical operations are generally turned into triggers or stored procedures.

To model a schema,

- Identify those classes in your model whose state must transcend the lifetime of their applications.

■ Create a class diagram that contains these classes and mark them as persistent (a standard tagged value). You can define your own set of tagged values to address database-specific details.

■ Expand the structural details of these classes. In general, this means specifying the details of their attributes and focusing on the associations and their cardinalities that structure these classes.

■ Watch for common patterns that complicate physical database design, such as cyclic associations, one-to-one associations, and n-ary associations. Where necessary, create intermediate abstractions to simplify your logical structure.

■ Consider also the behavior of these classes by expanding operations that are important for data access and data integrity. In general, to provide a better separation of concerns, business rules concerned with the manipulation of sets of these objects should be encapsulated in a layer above these persistent classes.

■ Where possible, use tools to help you transform your logical design into a physical design.

Stereotypes are discussed in Chapter 6.

Note: Logical database design is beyond the scope of this book. The focus here is simply to show how you can model schemas using the UML. In practice, you'll end up using stereotypes tuned to the kind of database (relational or object-oriented) you are using.

Figure 8-3 shows a set of classes drawn from an information system for a school. This figure expands upon an earlier class diagram, and you'll see the details of these classes revealed to a level sufficient to construct a physical database. Starting at the bottom-left of this diagram, you will find the classes named Student, Course, and Instructor. There's an association between Student and Course, specifying that students attend courses. Furthermore, every student may attend any number of courses and every course may have any number of students.

Modeling primitive types is discussed in Chapter 4; aggregation is discussed in Chapters 5 and 10.

All six of these classes are marked as persistent, indicating that their instances are intended to live in a database or some other form of persistent store. This diagram also exposes the attributes of all six of these classes. Notice that all the attributes are primitive types. When you are modeling a schema, you'll generally want to model the relationship to any nonprimitive types using an explicit aggregation rather than an attribute.

Two of these classes (School and Department) expose several operations for manipulating their parts. These operations are included because they are important to maintain data integrity (adding or removing a Department, for example, will have some rippling effects). There are many other operations that you might consider for these and the other classes, such as querying the prerequisites of a course before assigning a student. These are more business rules than they are operations for database integrity and so are best placed at a higher level of abstraction than this schema.

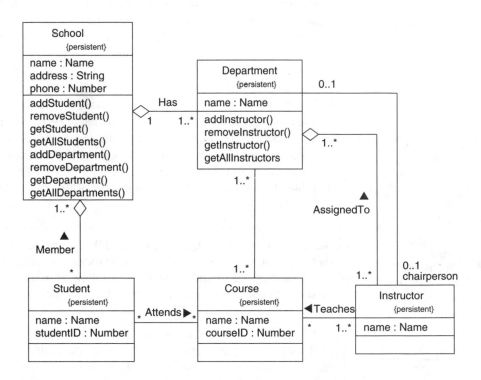

Figure 8-3: Modeling a Schema

Forward and Reverse Engineering

The importance of modeling is discussed in Chapter 1.

Modeling is important, but you have to remember that the primary product of a development team is software, not diagrams. Of course, the reason you create models is to predictably deliver at the right time the right software that satisfies the evolving goals of its users and the business. For this reason, it's important that the models you create and the implementations you deploy map to one another and do so in a way that minimizes or even eliminates the cost of keeping your models and your implementation in sync with one another.

Activity diagrams are discussed in Chapter 19.

For some uses of the UML, the models you create will never map to code. For example, if you are modeling a business process using activity diagrams, many of the activities you model will involve people, not computers. In other cases, you'll want to model systems whose parts are, from your level of abstraction, just a piece of hardware (although at another level of abstraction, it's a good bet that this hardware contains an embedded computer and software).

In most cases, though, the models you create will map to code. The UML does not specify a particular mapping to any object-oriented programming language, but the UML was designed with such mappings in mind. This is especially true for class diagrams, whose contents have a clear mapping to all the industrial-strength object-oriented languages, such as Java, C++, Smalltalk, Eiffel, Ada, ObjectPascal, and Forte. The UML was also designed to map to a variety of commercial object-based languages, such as Visual Basic.

<table>
<tr>
<td>Stereotypes and tagged values are discussed in Chapter 6.</td>
<td>Note: The mapping of the UML to specific implementation languages for forward and reverse engineering is beyond the scope of this book. In practice, you'll end up using stereotypes and tagged values tuned to the programming language you are using.</td>
</tr>
</table>

Forward engineering is the process of transforming a model into code through a mapping to an implementation language. Forward engineering results in a loss of information, because models written in the UML are semantically richer than any current object-oriented programming language. In fact, this is a major reason why you need models in addition to code. Structural features, such as collaborations, and behavioral features, such as interactions, can be visualized clearly in the UML, but not so clearly from raw code.

To forward engineer a class diagram,

- Identify the rules for mapping to your implementation language or languages of choice. This is something you'll want to do for your project or your organization as a whole.
- Depending on the semantics of the languages you choose, you may have to constrain your use of certain UML features. For example, the UML permits you to model multiple inheritance, but Smalltalk permits only single inheritance. You can either choose to prohibit developers from modeling with multiple inheritance (which makes your models language-dependent) or develop idioms that transform these richer features into the implementation language (which makes the mapping more complex).
- Use tagged values to specify your target language. You can do this at the level of individual classes if you need precise control. You can also do so at a higher level, such as with collaborations or packages.
- Use tools to forward engineer your models.

Patterns are discussed in Chapter 28.

Figure 8-4 illustrates a simple class diagram specifying an instantiation of the chain of responsibility pattern. This particular instantiation involves three classes: `Client`, `EventHandler`, and `GUIEventHandler`. `Client` and `EventHandler` are shown as abstract classes, whereas `GUIEventHandler` is concrete. `EventHandler` has the usual operation expected of this pattern (`handleRequest`), although two private attributes have been added for this instantiation.

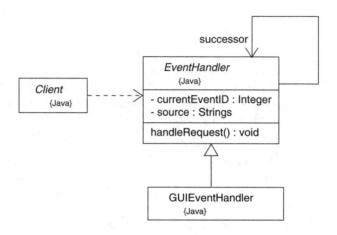

Figure 8-4: Forward Engineering

All of these classes specify a mapping to Java, as noted in their tagged value. Forward engineering the classes in this diagram to Java is straightforward, using a tool. Forward engineering the class `EventHandler` yields the following code.

```
public abstract class EventHandler {

    EventHandler successor;
    private Integer currentEventID;
    private String source;

    EventHandler() {}
    public void handleRequest() {}

}
```

Reverse engineering is the process of transforming code into a model through a mapping from a specific implementation language. Reverse engineering results in a flood of information, some of which is at a lower level of detail than you'll need to build useful models. At the same time, reverse engineering is incomplete. There is a loss of information when forward engineering models into code, and so you can't completely recreate a model from code unless your tools encode information in the source comments that goes beyond the semantics of the implementation language.

Figure 3-3 was created by reverse engineering part of the Java class library.

To reverse engineer a class diagram,

- Identify the rules for mapping from your implementation language or languages of choice. This is something you'll want to do for your project or your organization as a whole.
- Using a tool, point to the code you'd like to reverse engineer. Use your tool to generate a new model or modify an existing one that was previously forward engineered.
- Using your tool, create a class diagram by querying the model. For example, you might start with one or more classes, then expand the diagram by following specific relationships or other neighboring classes. Expose or hide details of the contents of this class diagram as necessary to communicate your intent.

Hints and Tips

When you create class diagrams in the UML, remember that every class diagram is just a graphical presentation of the static design view of a system. No single class diagram need capture everything about a system's design view. Collectively, all the class diagrams of a system represent the system's complete static design view; individually, each represents just one aspect.

A well-structured class diagram

- Is focused on communicating one aspect of a system's static design view.
- Contains only elements that are essential to understanding that aspect.
- Provides detail consistent with its level of abstraction, with only those adornments that are essential to understanding.
- Is not so minimalist that it misinforms the reader about important semantics.

When you draw a class diagram,

- Give it a name that communicates its purpose.
- Lay out its elements to minimize lines that cross.

- Organize its elements spatially so that things that are semantically close are laid out physically close.
- Use notes and color as visual cues to draw attention to important features of your diagram.
- Try not to show too many kinds of relationships. In general, one kind of relationship will tend to dominate each class diagram.

UNIFIED
MODELING
LANGUAGE

Section 3
ADVANCED STRUCTURAL
MODELING

UNIFIED
MODELING
LANGUAGE

Chapter 9

ADVANCED CLASSES

Classes are indeed the most important building block of any object-oriented system. However, classes are just one kind of an even more general building block in the UML—classifiers. A classifier is a mechanism that describes structural and behavioral features. Classifiers include classes, interfaces, datatypes, signals, components, nodes, use cases, and subsystems.

The basic properties of classes are discussed in Chapter 4.

Classifiers (and especially classes) have a number of advanced features beyond the simpler properties of attributes and operations described in the previous section: You can model multiplicity, visibility, signatures, polymorphism, and other characteristics. In the UML, you can model the semantics of a class so that you can state its meaning to whatever degree of formality you like.

In the UML, there are several kinds of classifiers and classes; it's important that you choose the one that best models your abstraction of the real world.

Getting Started

Architecture is discussed in Chapter 2.

When you build a house, at some point in the project you'll make an architectural decision about your building materials. Early on, it's sufficient to simply state wood, stone, or steel. That's a level of detail sufficient for you to move forward. The material you choose will be affected by the requirements of your project—steel and concrete would be a good choice if you are building in an area susceptible to hurricanes, for example. As you move forward, the material you choose will affect your design decisions that follow—choosing wood versus steel will affect the mass that can be supported, for example.

As your project continues, you'll have to refine these basic design decisions and add more detail sufficient for a structural engineer to validate the safety of the design and for a builder to proceed with construction. For example, you might have to specify not just wood, but wood of a certain grade that's been treated for resistance to insects.

Responsibilities are discussed in Chapter 6.

It's the same when you build software. Early in a project, it's sufficient to say that you'll include a `Customer` class that carries out certain responsibilities. As you refine your architecture and move to construction, you'll have to decide on a structure for the class (its attributes) and a behavior (its operations) that are sufficient and necessary to carry out those responsibilities. Finally, as you evolve to the executable system, you'll need to model details, such as the visibility of individual attributes and operations, the concurrency semantics of the class as a whole and its individual operations, and the interfaces the class realizes.

Forward and reverse engineering is discussed in Chapters 8, 14, 17, 18, 19, 24, 29, and 30.

The UML provides a representation for a number of advanced properties, as Figure 9-1 shows. This notation permits you to visualize, specify, construct, and document a class to any level of detail you wish, even sufficient to support forward and reverse engineering of models and code.

Figure 9-1: Advanced Classes

Terms and Concepts

A *classifier* is a mechanism that describes structural and behavioral features. Classifiers include classes, interfaces, datatypes, signals, components, nodes, use cases, and subsystems.

Classifiers

Modeling the vocabulary of a system is discussed in Chapter 4; the class/object dichotomy is discussed in Chapter 2.

When you model, you'll discover abstractions that represent things in the real world and things in your solution. For example, if you are building a Web-based ordering system, the vocabulary of your project will likely include a `Customer` class (representing people who order products) and a `Transaction` class (an implementation artifact, representing an atomic action). In the deployed system, you might have a `Pricing` component, with instances living on every client node. Each of these abstractions will have instances; separating the essence and the instance of the things in your world is an important part of modeling.

Instances are discussed in Chapter 13; packages are discussed in Chapter 12; generalization is discussed in Chapters 5 and 10; associations are discussed in Chapters 5 and 10; messages are discussed in Chapter 15; interfaces are discussed in Chapter 11; datatypes are discussed in Chapters 4 and 11; signals are discussed in Chapter 20; components are discussed in Chapter 25; nodes are discussed in Chapter 26; use cases are discussed in Chapter 16; subsystems are discussed in Chapter 31.

Some things in the UML don't have instances—for example, packages and generalization relationships. In general, those modeling elements that can have instances are called classifiers (associations and messages can have instances as well, but their instances are not quite the same as the instances of a class). Even more important, a classifier has structural features (in the form of attributes), as well as behavioral features (in the form of operations). Every instance of a given classifier shares the same features.

The most important kind of classifier in the UML is the class. A class is a description of a set of objects that share the same attributes, operations, relationships, and semantics. Classes are not the only kind of classifier, however. The UML provides a number of other kinds of classifiers to help you model.

- Interface   A collection of operations that are used to specify a service of a class or a component
- Datatype   A type whose values have no identity, including primitive built-in types (such as numbers and strings), as well as enumeration types (such as Boolean)
- Signal   The specification of an asynchronous stimulus communicated between instances
- Component   A physical and replaceable part of a system that conforms to and provides the realization of a set of interfaces
- Node   A physical element that exists at run time and that represents a computational resource, generally having at least some memory and often processing capability
- Use case   A description of a set of a sequence of actions, including variants, that a system performs that yields an observable result of value to a particular actor
- Subsystem   A grouping of elements of which some constitute a specification of the behavior offered by the other contained elements

For the most part, every kind of classifier has both structural and behavioral features (interfaces are the one exception; they may not have attributes). Furthermore, when you model with any of these classifiers, you may use all the advanced features described in this chapter to provide the level of detail you need to capture the meaning of the abstraction.

Graphically, the UML distinguishes among these different classifiers, as Figure 9-2 shows.

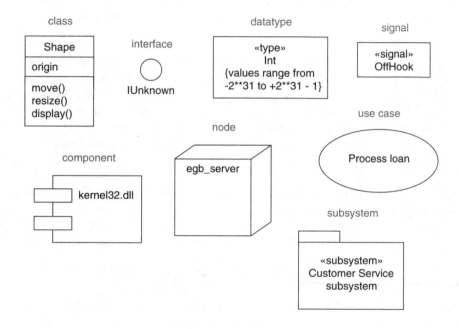

Figure 9-2: Classifiers

Note: A minimalist approach would have used one icon for all classifiers. That doesn't make sense because, for example, classes and components are very different abstractions (one is logical, the other physical), so having a distinctive visual cue was deemed important. Similarly, a maximal approach would have used different icons for each kind of classifier. That doesn't make sense either because, for example, classes and datatypes aren't that different. The design of the UML strikes a balance—those classifiers that are materially different from others have their own icon, and those that are not materially different use special keywords (such as `type`, `signal`, and `subsystem`).

Visibility

One of the most important details you can specify for a classifier's attributes and operations is its visibility. The visibility of a feature specifies whether it can be used by other classifiers. In the UML, you can specify any of three levels of visibility.

A classifier can see another classifier if it is in scope and if there is an explicit or implicit relationship to the target; relationships are discussed in Chapters 5 and 10; descendants come from generalization relationships, as discussed in Chapter 5; friendship allows a classifier to expose its private parts, as discussed in Chapter 10.

1. `public`   Any outside classifier with visibility to the given classifier can use the feature; specified by prepending the symbol +

2. `protected`   Any descendant of the classifier can use the feature; specified by prepending the symbol #

3. `private`   Only the classifier itself can use the feature; specified by prepending the symbol –

Figure 9-3 shows a mix of public, protected, and private figures for the class `Toolbar`.

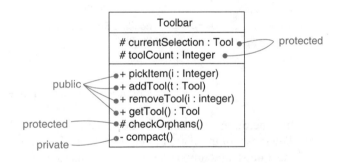

Figure 9-3: Visibility

When you specify the visibility of a classifier's features, you generally want to hide all its implementation details and expose only those features that are necessary to carry out the responsibilities of the abstraction. That's the very basis of information hiding, which is essential to building solid, resilient systems. If you don't explicitly adorn a feature with a visibility symbol, you can usually assume that it is public.

Note: The UML's visibility property matches the semantics common among most programming languages, including C++, Java, Ada, and Eiffel.

Scope

*Instances are
discussed in
Chapter 13.*

Another important detail you can specify for a classifier's attributes and operations is its owner scope. The owner scope of a feature specifies whether the
feature appears in each instance of the classifier or whether there is just a single instance of the feature for all instances of the classifier. In the UML, you
can specify two kinds of owner scope.

1. `instance`   Each instance of the classifier holds its own value for
the feature.
2. `classifier` There is just one value of the feature for all instances of
the classifier.

As Figure 9-4 (a simplification of the first figure) shows, a feature that is classifier scoped is rendered by underlining the feature's name. No adornment
means that the feature is instance scoped.

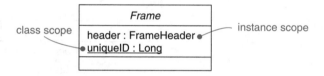

Figure 9-4: Owner Scope

In general, most features of the classifiers you model will be instance scoped.
The most common use of classifier scoped features is for private attributes that
must be shared among a set of instances (and with the guarantee that no other
instances have access to that attribute), such as for generating unique IDs
among all instances of a given classifier, and for operations that create
instances of the class.

Note: Classifier scoped maps to what C++ calls static attributes and
operations.

Abstract, Root, Leaf, and Polymorphic Elements

Generalization is discussed in Chapters 5 and 10; instances are discussed in Chapter 13.

You use generalization relationships to model a lattice of classes, with more-generalized abstractions at the top of the hierarchy and more-specific ones at the bottom. Within these hierarchies, it's common to specify that certain classes are abstract—meaning that they may not have any direct instances. In the UML, you specify that a class is abstract by writing its name in italics. For example, as Figure 9-5 shows, `Icon`, `RectangularIcon`, and `ArbitraryIcon` are all abstract classes. By contrast, a concrete class (such as `Button` and `OKButton`) is one that may have direct instances.

Whenever you use a class, you'll probably want to inherit features from other, more-general, classes, and have other, more-specific, classes inherit features from it. These are the normal semantics you get from classes in the UML. However, you can also specify that a class may have no children. Such an element is called a leaf class and is specified in the UML by writing the property `leaf` below the class's name. For example, in the figure, `OKButton` is a leaf class, so it may have no children.

Less common but still useful is the ability to specify that a class may have no parents. Such an element is called a root class, and is specified in the UML by writing the property `root` below the class's name. For example, in the figure, `Icon` is a root class. Especially when you have multiple, independent inheritance lattices, it's useful to designate the head of each hierarchy in this manner.

Messages are discussed in Chapter 15.

Operations have similar properties. Typically, an operation is polymorphic, which means that, in a hierarchy of classes, you can specify operations with the same signature at different points in the hierarchy. Ones in the child classes override the behavior of ones in the parent classes. When a message is dispatched at run time, the operation in the hierarchy that is invoked is chosen polymorphically—that is, a match is determined at run time according to the type of the object. For example, `display` and `isInside` are both polymorphic operations. Furthermore, the operation `Icon::display()` is abstract, meaning that it is incomplete and requires a child to supply an implementation of the operation. In the UML, you specify an abstract operation by writing its name in italics, just as you do for a class. By contrast, `Icon::getID()` is a leaf operation, so designated by the property `leaf`. This means that the operation is not polymorphic and may not be overridden.

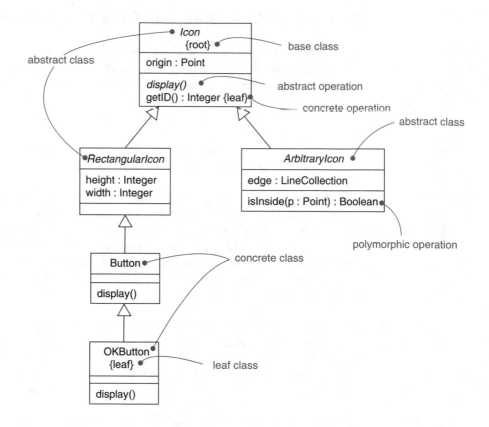

Figure 9-5: Abstract and Concrete Classes and Operations

Note: Abstract operations map to what C++ calls pure virtual operations; leaf operations in the UML map to C++ nonvirtual operations.

Multiplicity

Instances are discussed in Chapter 13.

Whenever you use a class, it's reasonable to assume that there may be any number of instances of that class (unless, of course, it is an abstract class and so it may not have any direct instances, although there may be any number of instances of its concrete children). Sometimes, though, you'll want to restrict the number of instances a class may have. Most often, you'll want to specify zero instances (in which case, the class is a utility class that exposes only class scoped attributes and operations), one instance (a singleton class), a specific number of instances, or many instances (the default case).

Multiplicity applies to associations, as well, as discussed in Chapters 5 and 10.

The number of instances a class may have is called its multiplicity. Multiplicity is a specification of the range of allowable cardinalities an entity may assume. In the UML, you can specify the multiplicity of a class by writing a multiplicity expression in the upper-right corner of the class icon. For example, in Figure 9-6, NetworkController is a singleton class. Similarly, there are exactly three instances of the class ControlRod in the system.

Attributes are related to the semantics of association, as discussed in Chapter 10.

Multiplicity applies to attributes, as well. You can specify the multiplicity of an attribute by writing a suitable expression in brackets just after the attribute name. For example, in the figure, there are two or more consolePort instances in the instance of NetworkController.

Figure 9-6: Multiplicity

Attributes

At the most abstract level, when you model a class's structural features (that is, its attributes), you simply write each attribute's name. That's usually enough information for the average reader to understand the intent of your model. As the previous sections have described, however, you can also specify the visibility, scope, and multiplicity of each attribute. There's still more. You can also specify the type, initial value, and changeability of each attribute.

You can also use stereotypes to designate sets of related attributes, such as housekeeping attributes, as discussed in Chapter 6.

In its full form, the syntax of an attribute in the UML is

```
[visibility] name [multiplicity] [: type]
    [= initial-value] [{property-string}]
```

For example, the following are all legal attribute declarations:

- origin   Name only
- + origin   Visibility and name
- origin : Point   Name and type
- head : *Item   Name and complex type
- name [0..1] : String   Name, multiplicity, and type

■ origin : Point = (0,0)   Name, type, and initial value
■ id : Integer {frozen}   Name and property

There are three defined properties that you can use with attributes.

1. changeable   There are no restrictions on modifying the attribute's value.
2. addOnly   For attributes with a multiplicity greater than one, additional values may be added, but once created, a value may not be removed or altered.
3. frozen   The attribute's value may not be changed after the object is initialized.

Unless otherwise specified, attributes are always changeable. You'll mainly want to use frozen when modeling constant or write-once attributes.

Note: The frozen property maps to const in C++.

Operations

Signals are discussed in Chapter 20.

At the most abstract level, when you model a class's behavioral features (that is, its operations and its signals), you will simply write each operation's name. That's usually enough information for the average reader to understand the intent of your model. As the previous sections have described, however, you can also specify the visibility and scope of each operation. There's still more: You can also specify the parameters, return type, concurrency semantics, and other properties of each operation. Collectively, the name of an operation plus its parameters (including its return type, if any) is called the operation's signature.

Note: The UML distinguishes between operation and method. An operation specifies a service that can be requested from any object of the class to affect behavior; a method is an implementation of an operation. Every nonabstract operation of a class must have a method, which supplies an executable algorithm as a body (generally designated in some programming language or structured text). In an inheritance lattice, there may be many methods for the same operation, and polymorphism selects which method in the hierarchy is dispatched during run time.

You can also use stereo-types to desig-nate sets of related opera-tions, such as helper func-tions, as discussed in Chapter 6.

In its full form, the syntax of an operation in the UML is

```
[visibility] name [(parameter-list)]
  [: return-type] [{property-string}]
```

For example, the following are all legal operation declarations:

- `display`   Name only
- `+ display`   Visibility and name
- `set(n : Name, s : String)`   Name and parameters
- `getID() : Integer`   Name and return type
- `restart() {guarded}`   Name and property

In an operation's signature, you may provide zero or more parameters, each of which follows the syntax

```
[direction] name : type [= default-value]
```

Direction may be any of the following values:

- `in`   An input parameter; may not be modified
- `out`   An output parameter; may be modified to communicate information to the caller
- `inout`   An input parameter; may be modified

In addition to the `leaf` property described earlier, there are four defined properties that you can use with operations.

1. `isQuery`   Execution of the operation leaves the state of the system unchanged. In other words, the operation is a pure function that has no side effects.
2. `sequential`   Callers must coordinate outside the object so that only one flow is in the object at a time. In the presence of multiple flows of control, the semantics and integrity of the object cannot be guaranteed.
3. `guarded`   The semantics and integrity of the object is guaranteed in the presence of multiple flows of control by sequentializing all calls to all of the object's guarded operations. In effect, exactly one operation at a time can be invoked on the object, reducing this to sequential semantics.
4. `concurrent`   The semantics and integrity of the object is guaranteed in the presence of multiple flows of control by treating the operation as atomic. Multiple calls from

concurrent flows of control may occur simultaneously to one object on any concurrent operation,
and all may proceed concurrently with correct
semantics; concurrent operations must be designed
so that they perform correctly in the case of a concurrent sequential or guarded operation on the same
object.

*Active object,
processes, and
threads are
discussed in
Chapter 22.*

The last three properties (`sequential`, `guarded`, `concurrent`) address
the concurrency semantics of an operation, properties that are relevant only in
the presence of active objects, processes, or threads.

Template Classes

A template is a parameterized element. In such languages as C++ and Ada, you
can write template classes, each of which defines a family of classes (you can
also write template functions, each of which defines a family of functions). A
template includes slots for classes, objects, and values, and these slots serve as
the template's parameters. You can't use a template directly; you have to
instantiate it first. Instantiation involves binding these formal template parameters to actual ones. For a template class, the result is a concrete class that can
be used just like any ordinary class.

The most common use of template classes is to specify containers that can be
instantiated for specific elements, making them type-safe. For example, the
following C++ code fragment declares a parameterized `Map` class.

```
template<class Item, class Value, int Buckets>
class Map {
public:
  virtual Boolean bind(const Item&, const Value&);
  virtual Boolean isBound(const Item&) const;
  ...
};
```

You might then instantiate this template to map `Customer` objects to `Order`
objects.

```
m : Map<Customer, Order, 3>;
```

*The basic
properties of
classes are
discussed in
Chapter 4.*

You can model template classes in the UML as well. As Figure 9-7 shows, you render a template class just as you do an ordinary class, but with an additional dashed box in the upper-right corner of the class icon, which lists the template parameters.

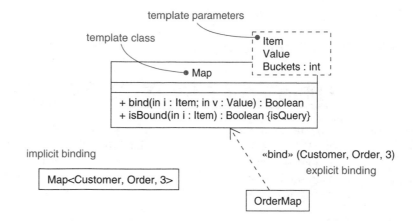

Figure 9-7: Template Classes

*Dependencies
are discussed
in Chapters 5
and 10; stereo-
types are
discussed in
Chapter 6.*

As the figure goes on to show, you can model the instantiation of a template class in two ways. First, you can do so implicitly, by declaring a class whose name provides the binding. Second, you can do so explicitly, by using a dependency stereotyped as `bind`, which specifies that the source instantiates the target template using the actual parameters.

Standard Elements

*The UML's
extensibility
mechanisms
are discussed
in Chapter 6;
interface, type,
and implemen-
tationClass are
discussed in
Chapter 11;
actors are
discussed in
Chapter 16;
signals are
discussed in
Chapter 20.*

All of the UML's extensibility mechanisms apply to classes. Most often, you'll use tagged values to extend class properties (such as specifying the version of a class) and stereotypes to specify new kinds of components (such as model-specific components).

The UML defines four standard stereotypes that apply to classes.

1. `metaclass`   Specifies a classifier whose objects are all classes
2. `powertype`   Specifies a classifier whose objects are the children of a given parent
3. `stereotype` Specifies that the classifier is a stereotype that may be applied to other elements
4. `utility`   Specifies a class whose attributes and operations are all class scoped

---

Note: A number of other standard stereotypes or keywords that apply to classes are discussed elsewhere: `interface`, `type`, `implementa-tionClass`, `actor`, `exception`, `signal`, `process`, **and** `thread`.

Common Modeling Techniques

Modeling the Semantics of a Class

The common uses of classes are discussed in Chapter 4.

The most common purpose for which you'll use classes is to model abstractions that are drawn from the problem you are trying to solve or from the technology you are using to implement a solution to that problem. Once you've identified those abstractions, the next thing you'll need to do is specify their semantics.

Modeling is discussed in Chapter 1; you can also model the semantics of an operation using an activity diagram, as discussed in Chapter 19.

In the UML, you have a wide spectrum of modeling possibilities at your disposal, ranging from the very informal (responsibilities) to the very formal (OCL, or Object Constraint Language). Given these choices, you must decide the level of detail that is appropriate to communicate the intent of your model. If the purpose of your model is to communicate with end users and domain experts, you'll tend to lean toward the less formal. If the purpose of your model is to support round-trip engineering, which flows between models and code, you'll tend to lean toward the more formal. If the purpose of your model is to rigorously and mathematically reason about your models and prove their correctness, you'll lean toward the very formal.

Note: Less formal does not mean less accurate. It means less complete and less detailed. Pragmatically, you'll want to strike a balance between informal and very formal. This means providing enough detail to support the creation of executable artifacts, but still hiding those details so that you do not overwhelm the reader of your models.

To model the semantics of a class, choose among the following possibilities, arranged from informal to formal.

Responsibili-ties are discussed in Chapter 4.

- Specify the responsibilities of the class. A responsibility is a contract or obligation of a type or class and is rendered in a note (stereotyped as `responsibility`) attached to the class, or in an extra compartment in the class icon.

Specifying the body of a method is discussed in Chapter 3; specifying the semantics of an operation is discussed in Chapter 19; state machines are discussed in Chapter 21; collaborations are discussed in Chapter 27.

- Specify the semantics of the class as a whole using structured text, rendered in a note (stereotyped as `semantics`) attached to the class.
- Specify the body of each method using structured text or a programming language, rendered in a note attached to the operation by a dependency relationship.
- Specify the pre- and postconditions of each operation, plus the invariants of the class as a whole, using structured text. These elements are rendered in notes (stereotyped as `precondition`, `postcondition`, and `invariant`) attached to the operation or class by a dependency relationship.
- Specify a state machine for the class. A state machine is a behavior that specifies the sequences of states an object goes through during its lifetime in response to events, together with its responses to those events.
- Specify a collaboration that represents the class. A collaboration is a society of roles and other elements that work together to provide some cooperative behavior that's bigger than the sum of all the elements. A collaboration has a structural part, as well as a dynamic part, so you can use collaborations to specify all dimensions of a class's semantics.

OCL is discussed in The Unified Modeling Language Reference Manual.

- Specify the pre- and postconditions of each operation, plus the invariants of the class as a whole, using a formal language such as OCL.

Pragmatically, you'll end up doing some combination of these approaches for the different abstractions in your system.

Note: When you specify the semantics of a class, keep in mind whether your intent is to specify what the class does or how it does it. Specifying the semantics of what a class does represents its public, outside view; specifying the semantics of how a class does it represents its private, inside view. You'll want to use a mixture of these two views, emphasizing the outside view for clients of the class and emphasizing the inside view for those who implement the class.

Hints and Tips

When you model classifiers in the UML, remember that there is a wide range of building blocks at your disposal, from interfaces to classes to components, and so on. You must choose the one that best fits your abstraction. A well-structured classifier

- Has both structural and behavioral aspects.

- Is tightly cohesive and loosely coupled.
- Exposes only those features necessary for clients to use the class, and hides all others.
- Is unambiguous in its intent and semantics.
- Is not so overly specified that it eliminates all degrees of freedom for its implementers.
- Is not so underspecified that it renders the meaning of the classifier ambiguous.

When you draw a classifier in the UML,

- Show only those properties of the classifier that are important to understand the abstraction in its context.
- Chose a stereotyped version that provides the best visual cue to the intent of the classifier.

UNIFIED
MODELING
LANGUAGE

Chapter 10
ADVANCED
RELATIONSHIPS

When you model the things that form the vocabulary of your system, you must also model how those things stand in relationship to one another. Relationships can be complex, however. Visualizing, specifying, constructing, and documenting webs of relationships require a number of advanced features.

The basic properties of relationships are discussed in Chapter 5; interfaces are discussed in Chapter 11; components are discussed in Chapter 25; use cases are discussed in Chapter 16; collaborations are discussed in Chapter 27.

Dependencies, generalizations, and associations are the three most important relational building blocks of the UML. These relationships have a number of properties beyond those described in the previous section. You can also model multiple inheritance, navigation, composition, refinement, and other characteristics. Using a fourth kind of relationship—realization—you can model the connection between an interface and a class or component, or between a use case and a collaboration. In the UML, you can model the semantics of relationships to any degree of formality.

Managing complex webs of relationships requires that you use the right relationships at the level of detail so that you neither under- nor over-engineer your system.

Getting Started

Use cases and scenarios are discussed in Chapter 16.

If you are building a house, deciding where to place each room in relation to others is a critical task. At one level of abstraction, you might decide to put the master bedroom on the main level, away from the front of the house. You might next think through common scenarios to help you reason about the use of this room arrangement. For example, consider bringing in groceries from the garage. It wouldn't make sense to walk from the garage through your bedroom to get to the kitchen, so that's an arrangement you'd reject.

You can form a fairly complete picture of your house's floor plan just by thinking through these basic relationships and use cases. However, that's not enough. You can end up with some real flaws in your design if you don't consider more-complex relationships.

For example, you might like the arrangement of rooms on each floor, but rooms on different floors might interact in unforeseen ways. Suppose you place your teenager daughter's room right above your bedroom. Now, suppose your teenager decides to learn how to play the drums. You'd clearly want to reject that floor plan, too.

Similarly, you have to consider how underlying mechanisms in the house might interact with your floor plan. For example, you'll increase the cost of construction if you don't arrange your rooms so that you have common walls in which to run pipes and drains.

Forward and reverse engineering are discussed in Chapters 8, 14, 17, 18, 19, 24, 29, and 30.

It's the same when you build software. Dependencies, generalizations, and associations are the most common relationships you'll encounter when modeling software-intensive systems. However, you need a number of advanced features of these relationships in order to capture the details of many systems—details that are important for you to consider so that you avoid real flaws in your design.

The UML provides a representation for a number of advanced properties, as Figure 10-1 shows. This notation permits you to visualize, specify, construct, and document webs of relationships to any level of detail you wish, even sufficient to support forward and reverse engineering of models and code.

Terms and Concepts

A *relationship* is a connection among things. In object-oriented modeling, the four most important relationships are dependencies, generalizations, associat-

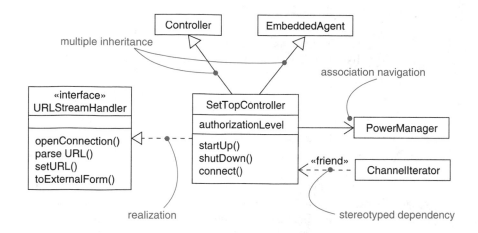

Figure 10-1: Advanced Relationships

tions, and realizations. Graphically, a relationship is rendered as a path, with different kinds of lines used to distinguish the different relationships.

Dependency

The basic properties of dependencies are discussed in Chapter 5.

A *dependency* is a using relationship, specifying that a change in the specification of one thing (for example, class SetTopController) may affect another thing that uses it (for example, class ChannelIterator), but not necessarily the reverse. Graphically, a dependency is rendered as a dashed line, directed to the thing that is depended on. Apply dependencies when you want to show one thing using another.

The UML's extensibility mechanisms are discussed in Chapter 6.

A plain, unadorned dependency relationship is sufficient for most of the using relationships you'll encounter. However, if you want to specify a shade of meaning, the UML defines a number of stereotypes that may be applied to dependency relationships. There are 17 such stereotypes, all of which can be organized into six groups.

Class diagrams are discussed in Chapter 8.

First, there are eight stereotypes that apply to dependency relationships among classes and objects in class diagrams.

  1. bind   Specifies that the source instantiates the target template using the given actual parameters

Templates and
bind depen-
dencies are
discussed in
Chapter 9.

You'll use `bind` when you want to model the details of template classes. For example, the relationship between a template container class and an instantiation of that class would be modeled as a `bind` dependency. Bind includes a list of actual arguments that map to the formal arguments of the template.

2. `derive`   Specifies that the source may be computed from the target

Attributes are
discussed in
Chapters 4
and 9; associa-
tions are
discussed in
Chapter 5 and
later in this
chapter.

You'll use `derive` when you want to model the relationship between two attributes or two associations, one of which is concrete and the other is conceptual. For example, a `Person` class might have the attribute `BirthDate` (which is concrete), as well as the attribute `Age` (which can be derived from `BirthDate`, so is not separately manifest in the class). You'd show the relationship between `Age` and `BirthDate` by using a `derive` dependency, showing `Age` derived from `BirthDate`.

3. `friend`   Specifies that the source is given special visibility into the target

Friend
dependencies
are discussed
in Chapter 5.

You'll use `friend` when you want to model relationships such as found with C++ friend classes.

4. `instanceOf`   Specifies that the source object is an instance of the target classifier

5. `instantiate`   Specifies that the source creates instances of the target

The
class/object
dichotomy is
discussed in
Chapter 2.

These last two stereotypes let you model class/object relationships explicitly. You'll use `instanceOf` when you want to model the relationship between a class and an object in the same diagram, or between a class and its metaclass. You'll use `instantiate` when you want to specify which element creates objects of another.

6. `powertype`   Specifies that the target is a powertype of the source; a powertype is a classifier whose objects are all the children of a given parent

Modeling
logical data-
bases is
discussed in
Chapter 8;
modeling
physical
databases is
discussed in
Chapter 29.

You'll use `powertype` when you want to model classes that cover other classes, such as you'll find when modeling databases.

7. `refine`   Specifies that the source is at a finer degree of abstraction than the target

You'll use `refine` when you want to model classes that are essentially the same but at different levels of abstraction. For example, during analysis, you might encounter a Customer class which, during design, you refine into a more detailed Customer class, complete with its implementation.

8. use		Specifies that the semantics of the source element depends on the semantics of the public part of the target

You'll apply use when you want to explicitly mark a dependency as a using relationship, in contrast to the shades of dependencies other stereotypes provide.

Packages are discussed in Chapter 12.

Continuing, there are two stereotypes that apply to dependency relationships among packages.

1. access		Specifies that the source package is granted the right to reference the elements of the target package
2. import		A kind of access that specifies that the public contents of the target package enter the flat namespace of the source, as if they had been declared in the source

You'll use access and import when you want to model the relationships among packages. Between two peer packages, the elements in one cannot reference the elements in the other unless there's an explicit access or import dependency. For example, suppose a target package T contains the class C. If you specify an access dependency from S to T, then the elements of S can reference C, using the fully qualified name T::C. If you specify an import dependency from S to T, then the elements of S can reference C using just its simple name.

Use cases are discussed in Chapter 16.

Two stereotypes apply to dependency relationships among use cases:

1. extend		Specifies that the target use case extends the behavior of the source
2. include		Specifies that the source use case explicitly incorporates the behavior of another use case at a location specified by the source

You'll use extend and include (and simple generalization) when you want to decompose use cases into reusable parts.

Interactions are discussed in Chapter 15.

You'll encounter three stereotypes when modeling interactions among objects.

1. become		Specifies that the target is the same object as the source but at a later point in time and with possibly different values, state, or roles

2. `call`   Specifies that the source operation invokes the target operation

3. `copy`   Specifies that the target object is an exact, but independent, copy of the source

Time and space are discussed in Chapter 23.

You'll use `become` and `copy` when you want to show the role, state, or attribute value of one object at different points in time or space. You'll use `call` when you want to model the calling dependencies among operations.

One stereotype you'll encounter in the context of state machines is

State machines are discussed in Chapter 21.

■ `send`   Specifies that the source operation sends the target event

You'll use `send` when you want to model an operation (such as found in the action associated with a state transition) dispatching a given event to a target object (which in turn might have an associated state machine). The `send` dependency in effect lets you tie independent state machines together.

Systems and models are discussed in Chapter 31.

Finally, one stereotype that you'll encounter in the context of organizing the elements of your system into subsystems and models is

The five views of an architecture are discussed in Chapter 2.

■ `trace`   Specifies that the target is an historical ancestor of the source

You'll use `trace` when you want to model the relationships among elements in different models. For example, in the context of a system's architecture, a use case in a use case model (representing a functional requirement) might trace to a package in the corresponding design model (representing the artifacts that realize that use case).

Note: Semantically, all relationships, including generalization, association, and realization, are kinds of dependencies. Generalization, association, and realization have enough important semantics about them that they warrant treatment as distinct kinds of relationships in the UML. The stereotypes listed above represent shades of dependencies, each of which has its own semantics, but each of which is not so semantically distant from plain dependencies to warrant treatment as distinct kinds of relationships. This is a judgment call on the part of the UML, but experience shows that this approach strikes a balance between highlighting the important kinds of relationships you'll encounter and not overwhelming the modeler with too many choices. You won't go wrong if you model generalization, association, and realization first, then view all other relationships as kinds of dependencies.

Generalization

The basic properties of generalizations are discussed in Chapter 5.

A *generalization* is a relationship between a general thing (called the super-class or parent) and a more specific kind of that thing (called the subclass or child). For example, you might encounter the general class Window with its more specific kind, MultiPaneWindow. With a generalization relationship from the child to the parent, the child (MultiPaneWindow) will inherit all the structure and behavior of the parent (Window). The child may even add new structure and behavior, or it may modify the behavior of the parent. In a generalization relationship, instances of the child may be used anywhere instances of the parent apply—meaning that the child is substitutable for the parent.

Most of the time, you'll find single inheritance sufficient. A class that has exactly one parent is said to use single inheritance. There are times, however, when multiple inheritance is better, and you can model those relationships, as well, in the UML. For example, Figure 10-2 shows a set of classes drawn from a financial services application. You see the class Asset with three children: BankAccount, RealEstate, and Security. Two of these children (BankAccount and Security) have their own children. For example, Stock and Bond are both children of Security.

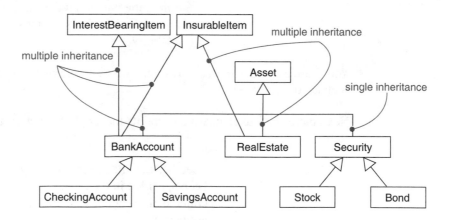

Figure 10-2: Multiple Inheritance

Two of these children (BankAccount and RealEstate) inherit from mul-tiple parents. RealEstate, for example, is a kind of Asset, as well as a kind of InsurableItem, and BankAccount is a kind of Asset, as well as a kind of InterestBearingItem and an InsurableItem.

Parents, such as InterestBearingItem and InsurableItem, are called mixins because they don't stand alone but, rather, are intended to be mixed in with other parents (such as Asset) to form children from these various bits of structure and behavior.

Note: Use multiple inheritance carefully. You'll run into problems if a child has multiple parents whose structure or behavior overlap. In fact, in most cases, multiple inheritance can be replaced by delegation, in which a child inherits from only one parent and then uses aggregation to obtain the structure and behavior of more subordinate parents. The main downside with this approach is that you lose the semantics of substitutability with these subordinate parents.

The UML's extensibility mechanisms are discussed in Chapter 6; the UML's defined stereotypes and constraints are discussed in Appendix B.

A plain, unadorned generalization relationship is sufficient for most of the inheritance relationships you'll encounter. However, if you want to specify a shade of meaning, the UML defines one stereotype and four constraints that may be applied to generalization relationships.

First, there is the one stereotype.

- implementation   Specifies that the child inherits the implementation of the parent but does not make public nor support its interfaces, thereby violating substitutability

You'll use implementation when you want to model private inheritance, such as found in C++.

Next, there are four standard constraints that apply to generalization relationships.

1. complete   Specifies that all children in the generalization have been specified in the model (although some may be elided in the diagram) and that no additional children are permitted
2. incomplete   Specifies that not all children in the generalization have been specified (even if some are elided) and that additional children are permitted

The general properties of diagrams are discussed in Chapter 7.

Unless otherwise stated, you can assume that any diagram shows only a partial view of an inheritance lattice and so is elided. However, elision is different from the completeness of a model. Specifically, you'll use the complete constraint when you want to show explicitly that you've fully specified a hierarchy in the model (although no one diagram may show that hierarchy); you'll use `incomplete` to show explicitly that you have not stated the full specification of the hierarchy in the model (although one diagram may show everything in the model).

3. `disjoint`   Specifies that objects of the parent may have no more than one of the children as a type
4. `overlapping`   Specifies that objects of the parent may have more than one of the children as a type

Types and interfaces are discussed in Chapter 11; interactions are discussed in Chapter 15.

These two constraints apply only in the context of multiple inheritance. You'll use `disjoint` and `overlapping` when you want to distinguish between static classification (`disjoint`) and dynamic classification (`overlapping`).

Note: In most cases, an object has one type at run time; that's a case of static classification. If an object can change its type during run time, that's a case of dynamic classification. Modeling dynamic classification is complex. But in the UML, you can use a combination of multiple inheritance (to show the potential types of an object) and types and interactions (to show the changing type of an object during run time).

Association

The basic properties of associations are discussed in Chapter 5.

An *association* is a structural relationship, specifying that objects of one thing are connected to objects of another. For example, a `Library` class might have a one-to-many association to a `Book` class, indicating that each `Book` instance is owned by one `Library` instance. Furthermore, given a `Book`, you can find its owning `Library`, and given a `Library`, you can navigate to all its `Books`. Graphically, an association is rendered as a solid line connecting the same or different classes. You use associations when you want to show structural relationships.

There are four basic adornments that apply to an association: a name, the role at each end of the association, the multiplicity at each end of the association, and aggregation. For advanced uses, there are a number of other properties you can use to model subtle details, such as navigation, qualification, and various flavors of aggregation.

Navigation Given a plain, unadorned association between two classes, such as `Book` and `Library`, it's possible to navigate from objects of one kind to objects of the other kind. Unless otherwise specified, navigation across an association is bidirectional. However, there are some circumstances in which you'll want to limit navigation to just one direction. For example, as Figure 10-3 shows, when modeling the services of an operating system, you'll find an association between User and Password objects. Given a User, you'll want to be able to find the corresponding Password objects; but given a Password, you don't want to be able to identify the corresponding User. You can explicitly represent the direction of navigation by adorning an association with an arrowhead pointing to the direction of traversal.

Note: Specifying a direction of traversal does not necessarily mean that you can't ever get from objects at one end of an association to objects at the other end. Rather, navigation is a statement of efficiency of traversal. For example, in the previous figure, it might still be possible to find the User objects associated with a Password through other associations that involve yet other classes not shown. Specifying that an association is navigable is a statement that, given an object at one end, you can easily and directly get to objects at the other end, usually because the source object stores some references to objects of the target.

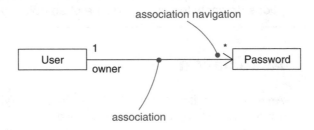

Figure 10-3: Navigation

Public, protected, and private visibility is discussed in Chapter 9.

Visibility Given an association between two classes, objects of one class can see and navigate to objects of the other, unless otherwise restricted by an explicit statement of navigation. However, there are circumstances in which you'll want to limit the visibility across that association relative to objects outside the association. For example, as Figure 10-4 shows, there is an association between UserGroup and User and another between User and Password. Given a User object, it's possible to identify its corresponding Password objects. However, a Password is private to a User, so it shouldn't be accessible from the outside (unless, of course, the User explicitly exposes access to the Password, perhaps through some public operation). Therefore, as the figure shows, given a UserGroup object, you can navigate to its User objects (and vice versa), but you cannot in turn see the User object's Password objects; they are private to the User. In the UML, you can specify three levels of visibility for an association end, just as you can for a class's features by appending a visibility symbol to a role name. Unless otherwise noted, the visibility of a role is public. Private visibility indicates that objects at that end are not accessible to any objects outside the association; protected visibility indicates that objects at that end are not accessible to any objects outside the association, except for children of the other end.

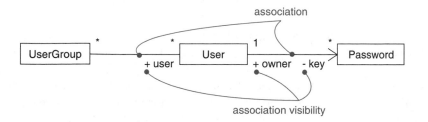

Figure 10-4: Visibility

Attributes are discussed in Chapters 4 and 9.

Qualification In the context of an association, one of the most common modeling idioms you'll encounter is the problem of lookup. Given an object at one end of an association, how do you identify an object or set of objects at the other end? For example, consider the problem of modeling a work desk at a manufacturing site at which returned items are processed to be fixed. As Figure 10-5 shows, you'd model an association between two classes, WorkDesk and ReturnedItem. In the context of the WorkDesk, you'd have a jobId that would identify a particular ReturnedItem. In that sense, jobId is an attribute of the association. It's not a feature of ReturnedItem because items really have no knowledge of things like repairs or jobs. Then, given an object of WorkDesk and given a particular value for jobId, you can navigate to zero or one objects of ReturnedItem. In the UML, you'd model this idiom using a qualifier, which is an association attribute whose values partition the set of objects related to an object across an association. You render a qualifier as a small rectangle attached to the end of an association, placing the attributes in the rectangle, as the figure shows. The source object, together with the values of the qualifier's attributes, yield a target object (if the target multiplicity is at most one) or a set of objects (if the target multiplicity is many).

Figure 10-5: Qualification

> **Note:** Qualifiers have some fairly deep semantics, and there are a number of complicated fringe cases in which you'll find them. However, most of the time, the circumstances for which you'll need qualifiers are pretty straightforward. If you can devise a lookup data structure at one end of an association (for example, a hash table or b-tree), then manifest that index as a qualifier. In most cases, the source end's multiplicity will be many and the target end's multiplicity will be `0..1`.

Roles are discussed in Chapter 4; interfaces are discussed in Chapter 11; classifiers are discussed in Chapter 9.

Interface Specifier An interface is a collection of operations that are used to specify a service of a class or a component; every class may realize many interfaces. Collectively, the interfaces realized by a class represent a complete specification of the behavior of that class. However, in the context of an association with another target class, a source class may choose to present only part of its face to the world. For example, in the vocabulary of a human resources system, a `Person` class may realize many interfaces: `IManager`, `IEmployee`, `IOfficer`, and so on. As Figure 10-6 shows, you can model the relationship between a supervisor and her workers with a one-to-many association, explicitly labeling the roles of this association as `supervisor` and `worker`. In the context of this association, a `Person` in the role of `supervisor` presents only the `IManager` face to the `worker`; a `Person` in the role of `worker` presents only the `IEmployee` face to the `supervisor`. As the figure shows, you can explicitly show the type of role using the syntax `rolename : iname`, where `iname` is some interface of the other classifier.

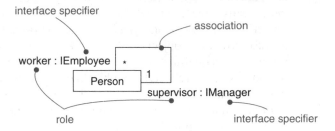

Figure 10-6: Interface Specifiers

Simple aggregation is discussed in Chapter 5.

Composition Aggregation turns out to be a simple concept with some fairly deep semantics. Simple aggregation is entirely conceptual and does nothing more than distinguish a "whole" from a "part." Simple aggregation does not change the meaning of navigation across the association between the whole and its parts, nor does it link the lifetimes of the whole and its parts.

An attribute is essentially a shorthand for composition; attributes are discussed in Chapters 4 and 9.

However, there is a variation of simple aggregation—composition—that does add some important semantics. Composition is a form of aggregation, with strong ownership and coincident lifetime as part of the whole. Parts with non-fixed multiplicity may be created after the composite itself, but once created they live and die with it. Such parts can also be explicitly removed before the death of the composite.

This means that, in a composite aggregation, an object may be a part of only one composite at a time. For example, in a windowing system, a `Frame` belongs to exactly one `Window`. This is in contrast to simple aggregation, in which a part may be shared by several wholes. For example, in the model of a house, a `Wall` may be a part of one or more `Room` objects.

In addition, in a composite aggregation, the whole is responsible for the disposition of its parts, which means that the composite must manage the creation and destruction of its parts. For example, when you create a `Frame` in a windowing system, you must attach it to an enclosing `Window`. Similarly, when you destroy the `Window`, the `Window` object must in turn destroy its `Frame` parts.

As Figure 10-7 shows, composition is really just a special kind of association and is specified by adorning a plain association with a filled diamond at the whole end.

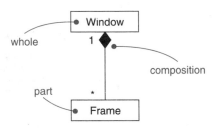

Figure 10-7: Composition

> **Note:** Alternately, you can show composition by nesting the symbols of the parts within the symbol of the composite. This form is most useful when you want to emphasize the relationships among the parts that apply only in the context of the whole.

Attributes are discussed in Chapters 4 and 9.

Association Classes In an association between two classes, the association itself might have properties. For example, in an employer/employee relationship between a `Company` and a `Person`, there is a `Job` that represents the properties of that relationship that apply to exactly one pairing of the `Person` and `Company`. It wouldn't be appropriate to model this situation with a `Company` to `Job` association together with a `Job` to `Person` association. That wouldn't tie a specific instance of the `Job` to the specific pairing of `Company` and `Person`.

In the UML, you'd model this as an association class, which is a modeling element that has both association and class properties. An association class can be seen as an association that also has class properties, or as a class that also has association properties. You render an association class as a class symbol attached by a dashed line to an association as in Figure 10-8.

Note: Sometimes you'll want to have the same properties for several different association classes. However, you can't attach an association class to more than one association, since an association class is the association itself. To achieve that effect, define a class (C) and then have each association class that needs those features inherit from C or use C as the type of an attribute.

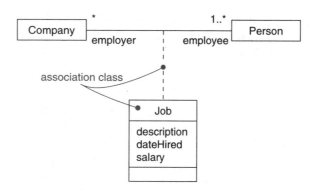

Figure 10-8: Association Classes

The UML's extensibility mechanisms are discussed in Chapter 6; the UML's defined stereotypes and constraints are discussed in Appendix B.

Constraints These simple and advanced properties of associations are sufficient for most of the structural relationships you'll encounter. However, if you want to specify a shade of meaning, the UML defines six constraints that may be applied to association relationships.

First, you can distinguish if the association is real or conceptual.

1. `implicit`　　Specifies that the relationship is not manifest but, rather, is only conceptual

For example, if you have an association between two base classes, you can specify that same association between two children of those base classes (because they inherit the relationships of the parent classes). You'd mark it as `implicit`, because it's not manifest separately but, rather, is implicit from the relationship that exists between the parent classes.

Second, you can specify that the objects at one end of an association (with a multiplicity greater than one) are ordered or unordered.

2. `ordered`   Specifies that the set of objects at one end of an association are in an explicit order

For example, in a `User/Password` association, the `Password`s associated with the `User` might be kept in a least-recently used order, and would be marked as `ordered`.

These change-ability properties apply to attributes, as well, as discussed in Chapter 9; links are discussed in Chapter 15.

Next, there are three properties, defined using constraint notation, that relate to the changeability of the instances of an association.

3. `changeable`   Links between objects may be added, removed, and changed freely
4. `addOnly`   New links may be added from an object on the opposite end of the association
5. `frozen`   A link, once added from an object on the opposite end of the association, may not be modified or deleted

Finally, there is one constraint for managing related sets of associations:

6. `xor`   Specifies that, over a set of associations, exactly one is manfest for each associated object

Realization

A *realization* is a semantic relationship between classifiers in which one classifier specifies a contract that another classifier guarantees to carry out. Graphically, a realization is rendered as a dashed directed line with a large open arrowhead pointing to the classifier that specifies the contract.

Realization is sufficiently different from dependency, generalization, and association relationships that it is treated as a separate kind of relationship. Semantically, realization is somewhat of a cross between dependency and generalization, and its notation is a combination of the notation for dependency and generalization. You'll use realization in two circumstances: in the context of interfaces and in the context of collaborations.

Interfaces are discussed in Chapter 11; classes are discussed in Chapters 4 and 9; components are discussed in Chapter 25; the five views of an architecture are discussed in Chapter 2.

Most of the time, you'll use realization to specify the relationship between an interface and the class or component that provides an operation or service for it. An interface is a collection of operations that are used to specify a service of a class or a component. Therefore, an interface specifies a contract that a class or component must carry out. An interface may be realized by many such classes or components, and a class or component may realize many interfaces. Perhaps the most interesting thing about interfaces is that they let you separate the specification of a contract (the interface itself) from its implementation (by a class or a component). Furthermore, interfaces span the logical and physical parts of a system's architecture. For example, as Figure 10-9 shows, a class (such as `AccountBusinessRules` in an order entry system) in a system's design view might realize a given interface (such as `IRuleAgent`). That same interface (`IRuleAgent`) might also be realized by a component (such as `acctrule.dll`) in the system's implementation view. Note that you can represent realization in two ways: in the canonical form (using the `interface` stereotype and the dashed directed line with a large open arrowhead) and in an elided form (using the interface lollipop notation).

Figure 10-9: Realization of an Interface

Use cases are discussed in Chapter 16; collaborations are discussed in Chapter 27.

You'll also use realization to specify the relationship between a use case and the collaboration that realizes that use case, as Figure 10-10 shows. In this circumstance, you'll almost always use the canonical form of realization.

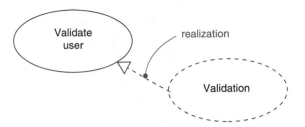

Figure 10-10: Realization of a Use Case

Note: When a class or a component realizes an interface, it means that clients can rely on the class or component to faithfully carry out the behavior specified by the interface. That means the class or component implements all the operations of the interface, responds to all its signals, and in all ways follows the protocol established by the interface for clients who use those operations or send those signals.

Common Modeling Techniques

Modeling Webs of Relationships

Modeling the vocabulary of a system and modeling the distribution of responsibilities in a system are discussed in Chapter 4.

When you model the vocabulary of a complex system, you may encounter dozens, if not hundreds or thousands, of classes, interfaces, components, nodes, and use cases. Establishing a crisp boundary around each of these abstractions is hard. Establishing the myriad of relationships among these abstractions is even harder: this requires you to form a balanced distribution of responsibilities in the system as a whole, with individual abstractions that are tightly cohesive and with relationships that are expressive, yet loosely coupled.

When you model these webs of relationships,

Use cases are discussed in Chapter 16.

- Don't begin in isolation. Apply use cases and scenarios to drive your discovery of the relationships among a set of abstractions.
- In general, start by modeling the structural relationships that are present. These reflect the static view of the system and are therefore fairly tangible.

- Next, identify opportunities for generalization/specialization relationships; use multiple inheritance sparingly.
- Only after completing the preceding steps should you look for dependencies; they generally represent more-subtle forms of semantic connection.
- For each kind of relationship, start with its basic form and apply advanced features only as absolutely necessary to express your intent.
- Remember that it is both undesirable and unnecessary to model all relationships among a set of abstractions in a single diagram or view. Rather, build up your system's relationships by considering different views on the system. Highlight interesting sets of relationships in individual diagrams.

The five views of an architecture are discussed in Chapter 2; the Rational Unified Process is summarized in Appendix C.

The key to successfully modeling complex webs of relationships is to do so in an incremental fashion. Build up relationships as you add to the structure of a system's architecture. Simplify those relationships as you discover opportunities for common mechanisms. At every release in your development process, assess the relationships among the key abstractions in your system.

Note: In practice—and especially if you are following an incremental and iterative development process—the relationships in your models will derive from explicit decisions by the modeler as well as from the reverse engineering of your implementation.

Hints and Tips

When you model advanced relationships in the UML, remember that there is a wide range of building blocks at your disposal, from simple associations to more-detailed properties of navigation, qualification, aggregation, and so on. You must choose the relationship and the details of that relationship to best fit your abstraction. A well-structured relationship

- Exposes only those features necessary for clients to use the relationship and hides all others.
- Is unambiguous in its intent and semantics.
- Is not so overly specified that it eliminates all degrees of freedom by its implementers.
- Is not so underspecified, that it renders the meaning of the relationship ambiguous.

When you draw a relationship in the UML,

- Show only those properties of the relationship that are important to understanding the abstraction in its context.
- Choose a stereotyped version that provides the best visual cue to the intent of the relationship.

Chapter 11

INTERFACES, TYPES, AND ROLES

In this chapter

- Interfaces, types, roles, and realization
- Modeling the seams in a system
- Modeling static and dynamic types
- Making interfaces understandable and approachable

Interfaces define a line between the specification of what an abstraction does and the implementation of how that abstraction does it. An interface is a collection of operations that are used to specify a service of a class or a component.

You use interfaces to visualize, specify, construct, and document the seams within your system. Types and roles provide a mechanism for you to model the static and dynamic conformance of an abstraction to an interface in a specific context.

A well-structured interface provides a clear separation between the outside view and the inside view of an abstraction, making it possible to understand and approach an abstraction without having to dive into the details of its implementation.

Getting Started

Designing houses is discussed in Chapter 1.

It wouldn't make a lot of sense to design a house that required you to rip up the foundations every time you needed to repaint the walls. Similarly, you wouldn't want to live in a place that required you to rewire the building whenever you needed to change a light bulb. The owner of a high rise wouldn't be thrilled to have to move doors or replace all electrical and phone jacks whenever a new tenant moved in.

Centuries of building experience have provided lots of pragmatic construction-related information to help builders avoid these obvious—and some not so obvious—problems that arise when a building grows and changes over time. In software terms, we call this designing with a clear separation of concerns. For example, in a well-structured building, the skin or facade of the structure can be modified or replaced without disturbing the rest of the building. Similarly, the furnishings inside a building can easily be moved about without changing the infrastructure. Services that run through the walls for electrical, heating, plumbing, and waste disposal facilities can be changed with some degree of scrap and rework, but you still don't have to rend the fabric of the building to do so.

Not only do standard building practices help you build buildings that can evolve over time, but there are many standard interfaces to which you can build, permitting you to use common, off-the-shelf components, whose use ultimately helps reduce the cost of construction and maintenance. For example, there are standard sizes for lumber, making it easy to build walls that are multiples of a common size. There are standard sizes doors and windows, which means that you don't have to hand-craft every opening in your building. There are even standards for electrical outlets and telephone plugs (although these vary from country to country) that make it easier for you to mix and match electronic equipment.

Frameworks are discussed in Chapter 28.

In software, it's important to build systems with a clear separation of concerns so that, as the system evolves, changes in one part of the system don't ripple through, rending other parts of the system. One important way of achieving this degree of separation is by specifying clear seams in your system, which draw a line between those parts that may change independently. Furthermore, by choosing the right interfaces, you can pick standard components, libraries, and frameworks to implement those interfaces, without having to build them yourself. As you discover better implementations, you can replace the old ones without disturbing their users.

Classes are discussed in Chapters 4 and 9; components are discussed in Chapter 25.

In the UML, you use interfaces to model the seams in a system. An interface is a collection of operations used to specify a service of a class or a component. By declaring an interface, you can state the desired behavior of an abstraction independent of an implementation of that abstraction. Clients can build against that interface, and you can build or buy any implementation of that interface, as long as the implementation satisfies the responsibilities and the contract denoted by the interface.

Packages are discussed in Chapter 12; subsystems are discussed in Chapter 31.

Many programming languages support the concept of interfaces, including Java and CORBA IDL. Interfaces are not only important for dividing the specification and the implementation of a class or component, but as you scale up to larger systems, you can use interfaces to specify the outside view of a package or subsystem.

Components are discussed in Chapter 25.

The UML provides a graphical representation for interfaces, as Figure 11-1 shows. This notation permits you to visualize the specification of an abstraction apart from any implementation.

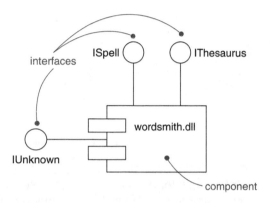

Figure 11-1: Interfaces

Terms and Concepts

An *interface* is a collection of operations that are used to specify a service of a class or a component. A *type* is a stereotype of a class used to specify a domain of objects, together with the operations (but not the methods) applicable to the object. A *role* is the behavior of an entity participating in a particular context. Graphically, an interface is rendered as a circle; in its expanded form, an interface may be rendered as a stereotyped class in order to expose its operations and other properties.

Use cases are discussed in Chapter 16; subsystems are discussed in Chapter 31.

Note: Interfaces may also be used to specify a contract for a use case or subsystem.

Names

An interface name must be unique within its enclosing package, as discussed in Chapter 12.

Every interface must have a name that distinguishes it from other interfaces. A *name* is a textual string. That name alone is known as a *simple name*; a *path name* is the interface name prefixed by the name of the package in which that interface lives. An interface may be drawn showing only its name, as in Figure 11-2:

Figure 11-2: Simple and Path Names

Note: An interface name may be text consisting of any number of letters, numbers, and certain punctuation marks (except for marks such as the colon, which is used to separate an interface name and the name of its enclosing package) and may continue over several lines. In practice, interface names are short nouns or noun phrases drawn from the vocabulary of the system you are modeling. To distinguish an interface from a class, consider prepending an I to every interface name, such as IUnknown and ISpelling. These same rules apply to types. To distinguish a type from an interface or a class, consider prepending a T to every type, such as TNatural and TCharacter.

Operations

Operations are discussed in Chapters 4 and 9; the UML's extensibility mechanisms are discussed in Chapter 6.

An interface is a named collection of operations used to specify a service of a class or of a component. Unlike classes or types, interfaces do not specify any structure (so they may not include any attributes), nor do they specify any implementation (so they may not include any methods, which provide the implementation of an operation). Like a class, an interface may have any number of operations. These operations may be adorned with visibility properties, concurrency properties, stereotypes, tagged values, and constraints.

When you visualize an interface in its normal form as a circle, by definition, you suppress the display of these operations. However, if it's important for your understanding of the current model, you can render an interface as a stereotyped class, listing its operations in the appropriate compartment. Operations may be drawn showing only their name, or they may be augmented to show their full signature and other properties, as in Figure 11-3.

Figure 11-3: Operations

Events are discussed in Chapter 20.

Note: You can also associate signals with an interface.

Relationships

Relationships are discussed in Chapters 5 and 10.

Like a class, an interface may participate in generalization, association, and dependency relationships. In addition, an interface may participate in realization relationships. Realization is a semantic relationship between two classifiers in which one classifier specifies a contract that another classifier guarantees to carry out.

An interface specifies a contract for a class or a component without dictating its implementation. A class or component may realize many interfaces. In so doing, it commits to carry out all these contracts faithfully, which means that it provides a set of methods that properly implement the operations defined in the interface. Similarly, a class or a component may depend on many interfaces. In so doing, it expects that these contracts will be honored by some set of components that realize them. This is why we say that an interface represents a seam in a system. An interface specifies a contract, and the client and the supplier on each side of the contract may change independently, as long as each fulfills its obligations to the contract.

As Figure 11-4 illustrates, you can show that an element realizes an interface in two ways. First, you can use the simple form in which the interface and its realization relationship are rendered as a lollipop sticking off to one side of a class or component. This form is useful when you simply want to expose the seams in your system. However, the limitation of this style is that you can't directly visualize the operations or signals provided by the interface. Second, you can use the expanded form in which you render an interface as a stereotyped class, which allows you to visualize its operations and other properties, and then draw a realization relationship from the classifier or component to the interface. In the UML, a realization relationship is rendered as a dashed directed line with a large open arrowhead pointing to the interface. This notation is a cross between generalization and dependency.

In both cases, you attach the class or component that builds on an interface with a dependency relationship from the element to the interface.

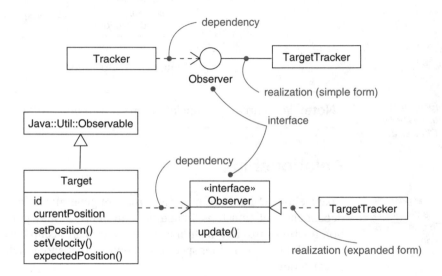

Figure 11-4: Realizations

Abstract classes are discussed in Chapter 4; components are discussed in Chapter 25.

Note: Interfaces are similar to abstract classes (for example, neither may have direct instances), but they are different enough to warrant being separate modeling elements in the UML. An abstract class may have attributes, but an interface may not. Furthermore, interfaces span model boundaries. The same interface may be realized by both a class (a logical abstraction) and a component (a physical abstraction that provides a manifestation of the class).

Understanding an Interface

Operations and their properties are discussed in Chapter 9; concurrency semantics are discussed in Chapter 23.

When you are handed an interface, the first thing you'll see is a set of operations that specify a service of a class or a component. Look a little deeper and you'll see the full signature of those operations, along with any of their special properties, such as visibility, scope, and concurrency semantics.

These properties are important, but for complex interfaces, they aren't enough to help you understand the semantics of the service they represent, much less know how to use those operations properly. In the absence of any other information, you'd have to dive into some abstraction that realizes the interface to figure out what each operation does and how those operations are meant to work together. However, that defeats the purpose of an interface, which is to provide a clear separation of concerns in a system.

Preconditions, postconditions, and invariants are discussed in Chapter 9; state machines are discussed in Chapter 21; collaborations are discussed in Chapter 27; OCL is discussed in Chapter 6.

In the UML, you can supply much more information to an interface in order to make it understandable and approachable. First, you may attach pre- and postconditions to each operation and invariants to the class or component as a whole. By doing this, a client who needs to use an interface will be able to understand what the interface does and how to use it, without having to dive into an implementation. If you need to be rigorous, you can use the UML's OCL to formally specify the semantics. Second, you can attach a state machine to the interface. You can use this state machine to specify the legal partial ordering of an interface's operations. Third, you can attach collaborations to the interface. You can use collaborations to specify the expected behavior of the interface through a series of interaction diagrams.

Types and Roles

A class may realize many interfaces. An instance of that class must therefore support all those interfaces, because an interface defines a contract, and any abstraction that conforms to that interface must, by definition, faithfully carry out that contract. Nonetheless, in a given context, an instance may present only one or more of its interfaces as relevant. In that case, each interface represents a role that the object plays. A role names a behavior of an entity participating in a particular context. Stated another way, a role is the face that an abstraction presents to the world.

Roles also play a part in collaborations, as discussed in Chapter 27.

For example, consider an instance of the class `Person`. Depending on the context, that `Person` instance may play the role of `Mother`, `Comforter`, `PayerOfBills`, `Employee`, `Customer`, `Manager`, `Pilot`, `Singer`, and so on. When an object plays a particular role, it presents a face to the world, and clients that interact with it expect a certain behavior depending on the role that it plays at the time. For example, an instance of Person in the role of Manager would present a different set of properties than if the instance were playing the role of Mother.

Associations are discussed in Chapters 5 and 10.

In the UML, you can specify a role an abstraction presents to another abstraction by adorning the name of an association end with a specific interface. For example, Figure 11-5 shows the interface Employee, whose definition includes three operations. There exists an association between the classes Person and Company in which context Person plays the role e, whose type is Employee. In a different association, the Person might present an entirely different face to the world. With this explicit type, the role the Person plays is more than just a name meaningful to the human reader of this diagram. In the UML, this means that the Person presents the role of Employee to the Company, and in that context, only the properties specified by Employee are visible and relevant to the Company.

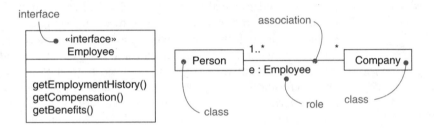

Figure 11-5: Roles

Class diagrams are discussed in Chapter 8; the become *stereotype is discussed in Chapter 13.*

A class diagram like this one is useful for modeling the static binding of an abstraction to its interface. You can model the dynamic binding of an abstraction to its interface by using the become stereotype in an interaction diagram, showing an object changing from one role to another.

If you want to formally model the semantics of an abstraction and its conformance to a specific interface, you'll want to use the defined stereotype type. Type is a stereotype of class, and you use it to specify a domain of objects, together with the operations (but not the methods) applicable to the objects of that type. The concept of type is closely related to that of interface, except that a type's definition may include attributes while an interface may not. If you want to show that an abstraction is statically typed, you'll want to use implementationClass, a stereotype of class that specifies a class whose instances are statically typed (unlike Person in the example above) and that defines the physical data structure and methods of an object as implemented in traditional programming languages.

> **Note:** For most uses, you may assume that type and interface are interchangeable.

Common Modeling Techniques

Modeling the Seams in a System

Components are discussed in Chapter 25; systems are discussed in Chapter 31.

The most common purpose for which you'll use interfaces is to model the seams in a system composed of software components, such as COM+ or Java Beans. You'll reuse some components from other systems or buy off the shelf; you will create others from scratch. In any case, you'll need to write glue code that weaves these components together. That requires you to understand the interfaces provided and relied on by each component.

Identifying the seams in a system involves identifying clear lines of demarcation in your architecture. On either side of those lines, you'll find components that may change independently, without affecting the components on the other side, as long as the components on both sides conform to the contract specified by that interface.

Patterns and frameworks are discussed in Chapter 28.

When you reuse a component from another system or when you buy it off the shelf, you'll probably be handed a set of operations with some minimal documentation about the meaning of each one. That's useful, but it's not sufficient. It's more important for you to understand the order in which to call each operation, and what underlying mechanisms the interface embodies. Unfortunately, given a poorly documented component, the best you can do is to build up, by trial and error, a conceptual model for how that interface works. You can then document your understanding by modeling that seam in the system using interfaces in the UML so that, later, you and others can approach that component more easily. Similarly, when you create your own component, you'll need to understand its context, which means specifying the interfaces it relies on to do its job, as well as the interfaces it presents to the world that others might build on.

> **Note:** Most component systems, such as COM+ and Enterprise Java Beans, provide for component introspection, meaning that you can programmatically query an interface to determine its operations. Doing so is the first step in understanding the nature of any under-documented component.

To model the seams in a system,

- Within the collection of classes and components in your system, draw a line around those that tend to be tightly coupled relative to other sets of classes and components.

Collaborations are discussed in Chapter 27.

- Refine your grouping by considering the impact of change. Classes or components that tend to change together should be grouped together as collaborations.
- Consider the operations and the signals that cross these boundaries, from instances of one set of classes or components to instances of other sets of classes and components.
- Package logically related sets of these operations and signals as interfaces.
- For each such collaboration in your system, identify the interfaces it relies on (imports) and those it provides to others (exports). You model the importing of interfaces by dependency relationships, and you model the exporting of interfaces by realization relationships.

Behavioral modeling is discussed in Sections 4 and 5.

- For each such interface in your system, document its dynamics by using pre- and postconditions for each operation, and use cases and state machines for the interface as a whole.

For example, Figure 11-6 shows the seams surrounding a component (the library ledger.dll) drawn from a financial system. This component realizes three interfaces: IUnknown, ILedger, and IReports. In this diagram, IUnknown is shown in its expanded form; the other two are shown in their simple form, as lollipops. These three interfaces are realized by ledger.dll and are exported to other components for them to build on.

Figure 11-6: Modeling the Seams in a System

As this diagram also shows, `ledger.dll` imports two interfaces, `IStreaming` and `ITransaction`, the latter of which is shown in its expanded form. These two interfaces are required by the `ledger.dll` component for its proper operation. Therefore, in a running system, you must supply components that realize these two interfaces. By identifying interfaces such as `ITransaction`, you've effectively decoupled the components on either side of the interface, permitting you to employ any component that conforms to that interface.

Use cases are discussed in Chapter 16.

Interfaces such as `ITransaction` are more than just a pile of operations. This particular interface makes some assumptions about the order in which its operations should be called. Although not shown here, you could attach use cases to this interface and enumerate the common ways you'd use it.

Modeling Static and Dynamic Types

Instances are discussed in Chapter 13.

Most object-oriented programming languages are statically typed, which means that the type of an object is bound at the time the object is created. Even so, that object will likely play different roles over time. This means that clients that use that object interact with the object through different sets of interfaces, representing interesting, possibly overlapping, sets of operations.

Class diagrams are discussed in Chapter 8.

Modeling the static nature of an object can be visualized in a class diagram. However, when you are modeling things like business objects, which naturally change their roles throughout a workflow, it's sometimes useful to explicitly model the dynamic nature of that object's type. In these circumstances, an object can gain and lose types during its life.

To model a dynamic type,

Associations and generalizations are discussed in Chapters 5 and 10.

- Specify the different possible types of that object by rendering each type as a class stereotyped as `type` (if the abstraction requires structure and behavior) or as `interface` (if the abstraction requires only behavior).
- Model all the roles the class of the object may take on at any point in time. You can do so in two ways:
  1. First, in a class diagram, explicitly type each role that the class plays in its association with other classes. Doing this specifies the face instances of that class put on in the context of the associated object.
  2. Second, also in a class diagram, specify the class-to-type relationships using generalization.

Interaction diagrams are discussed in Chapter 18.

- In an interaction diagram, properly render each instance of the dynamically typed class. Display the role of the instance in brackets below the object's name.

*Dependencies
are discussed
in Chapters 5
and 10.*

■ To show the change in role of an object, render the object once for each role it plays in the interaction, and connect these objects with a message stereotyped as `become`.

For example, Figure 11-7 shows the roles that instances of the class `Person` might play in the context of a human resources system.

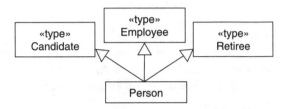

Figure 11-7: Modeling Static Types

This diagram specifies that instances of the `Person` class may be any of the three types—namely, `Candidate`, `Employee`, or `Retiree`.

Figure 11-8 shows the dynamic nature of a person's type. In this fragment of an interaction diagram, `p` (the `Person` object) changes its role from `Candidate` to `Employee`.

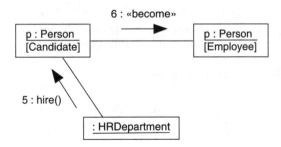

Figure 11-8: Modeling Dynamic Types

Hints and Tips

When you model an interface in the UML, remember that every interface should represent a seam in the system, separating specification from implementation. A well-structured interface

- Is simple yet complete, providing all the operations necessary yet sufficient to specify a single service.
- Is understandable, providing sufficient information to both use and realize the interface without having to examine an existing use or implementation.
- Is approachable, providing information to guide the user to its key properties without being overwhelmed by the details of a pile of operations.

When you draw an interface in the UML,

- Use the lollipop notation whenever you simply need to specify the presence of a seam in the system. Most of the time, you'll need this for components, not classes.
- Use the expanded form when you need to visualize the details of the service itself. Most of the time, you'll need this for specifying the seams in a system attached to a package or a subsystem.

UNIFIED
MODELING
LANGUAGE

Chapter 12
PACKAGES

Visualizing, specifying, constructing, and documenting large systems involves manipulating potentially large numbers of classes, interfaces, components, nodes, diagrams, and other elements. As you scale up to systems such as these, you will find it necessary to organize these things into larger chunks. In the UML, the package is a general purpose mechanism for organizing modeling elements into groups.

You use packages to arrange your modeling elements into larger chunks that you can manipulate as a group. You can control the visibility of these elements so that some things are visible outside the package while others are hidden. You can also use packages to present different views of your system's architecture.

Well-designed packages group elements that are semantically close and that tend to change together. Well-structured packages are therefore loosely coupled and very cohesive, with tightly controlled access to the package's contents.

Getting Started

The differences between building a dog house and building a high rise are discussed in Chapter 1.

Dog houses aren't complex: you have four walls, one of them with a dog-size hole, and a roof. When you build a dog house, you really need only a small pile of lumber. There's not a lot more structure than that.

Houses are more complex. Walls, ceilings, and floors come together in larger abstractions that we call rooms. Even these rooms are organized into larger chunks: the living area, the area for entertaining, and so on. These larger groups may not manifest themselves as anything to do with the physical house itself but may just be names we give to logically related rooms in the house, which we apply when we talk about how we'll use the house.

High rises are very complex. Not only are there elementary structures, such as walls, ceilings, and floors, but there are larger chunks, such as public areas, the retail wing, and office spaces. These chunks are probably grouped into even larger chunks, such as rental space and building service area. These larger chunks may have nothing to do with the final high rise itself but are simply artifacts we use to organize our plans for the high rise.

Every large system is layered in this way. In fact, about the only way you can understand a complex system is by chunking your abstractions into ever-larger groups. Most of these modest-size chunks (such as room) are, in their own right, class-like abstractions for which there are many instances. Most of these larger chunks are purely conceptual (such as retail wing), for which there are no real instances. They never manifest themselves in the physical system but, rather, exist for the sole purpose of understanding the system itself. These latter kinds of chunks have no identity in the deployed system; they have identity only in the model of the system.

Software architecture is discussed in Chapter 2; modeling the architecture of a system is discussed in Chapter 31.

In the UML, the chunks that organize a model are called packages. A package is a general-purpose mechanism for organizing elements into groups. Packages help you organize the elements in your models so that you can more easily understand them. Packages also let you control access to their contents so that you can control the seams in your system's architecture.

The UML provides a graphical representation of package, as Figure 12-1 shows. This notation permits you to visualize groups of elements that can be manipulated as a whole and in a way that lets you control the visibility of and access to individual elements.

Figure 12-1: Packages

Terms and Concepts

A *package* is a general-purpose mechanism for organizing elements into groups. Graphically, a package is rendered as a tabbed folder.

Names

A package name must be unique within its enclosing package.

Every package must have a name that distinguishes it from other packages. A *name* is a textual string. That name alone is known as a *simple name*; a *path name* is the package name prefixed by the name of the package in which that package lives, if any. A package is typically drawn showing only its name, as in Figure 12-2. Just as with classes, you may draw packages adorned with tagged values or with additional compartments to expose their details.

Figure 12-2: Simple and Extended Package

Note: A package name may be text consisting of any number of letters, numbers, and certain punctuation marks (except for marks such as the colon, which is used to separate a package name and the name of its enclosing package) and may continue over several lines. In practice, package names are short grouping nouns or noun phrases drawn from the vocabulary of the model.

Owned Elements

Composition is discussed in Chapter 10.

A package may own other elements, including classes, interfaces, components, nodes, collaborations, use cases, diagrams, and even other packages. Owning is a composite relationship, which means that the element is declared in the package. If the package is destroyed, the element is destroyed. Every element is uniquely owned by exactly one package.

A package forms a namespace, which means that elements of the same kind must be named uniquely within the context of its enclosing package. For example, you can't have two classes named Queue owned by the same package, but you can have a class named Queue in package P1 and another (and different) class named Queue in package P2. The classes P1::Queue and P2::Queue are, in fact, different classes and can be distinguished by their path names. Different kinds of elements may have the same name.

Elements of different kinds may have the same name within a package. Thus, you can have a class named Timer, as well as a component named Timer, within the same package. In practice, however, to avoid confusion, it's best to name elements uniquely for all kinds within a package.

Importing is discussed in a later section.

Packages may own other packages. This means that it's possible to decompose your models hierarchically. For example, you might have a class named Camera that lives in the package Vision that in turn lives in the package Sensors. The full name of this class is Sensors::Vision::Camera. In practice, it's best to avoid deeply nested packages. Two to three levels of nesting is about the limit that's manageable. More than nesting, you'll use importing to organize your packages.

These semantics of ownership make packages an important mechanism for dealing with scale. Without packages, you'd end up with large, flat models in which all elements would have to be named uniquely—an unmanageable situation, especially when you've brought in classes and other elements developed by multiple teams. Packages help you control the elements that compose your system as they evolve at different rates over time.

As Figure 12-3 shows, you can explicitly show the contents of a package either textually or graphically. Note that when you show these owned elements, you place the name of the package in the tab. In practice, you typically won't want to show the contents of packages this way. Instead, you'll use tools to zoom into the contents of a package.

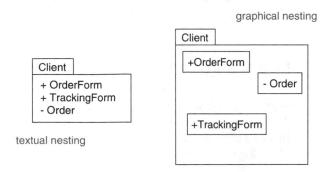

Figure 12-3: Owned Elements

Composition is discussed in Chapter 10.

Note: You can also display the contents of a package in tree form using a notation similar to composition (but with the symbol of a plus sign inside a circle instead of a solid diamond).

Visibility

Visibility is discussed in Chapter 9.

You can control the visibility of the elements owned by a package just as you can control the visibility of the attributes and operations owned by a class. Typically, an element owned by a package is public, which means that it is visible to the contents of any package that imports the element's enclosing package. Conversely, protected elements can only be seen by children, and private elements cannot be seen outside the package in which they are declared. In Figure 12-3, OrderForm is a public part of the package Client, and Order is a private part. A package that imports Client can see Order-Form, but it cannot see Order. As viewed from the outside, the fully qualified name of OrderForm would be Client::OrderForm.

You specify the visibility of an element owned by a package by prefixing the element's name with an appropriate visibility symbol. Public elements are rendered by prefixing their name with a + symbol, as for OrderForm in Figure 12-3. Collectively, the public parts of a package constitute the package's interface.

Inheritance of packages is discussed in a later section.

Just as with classes, you can designate an element as protected or private, rendered by prefixing the element's name with a # symbol and a – symbol, respectively. Protected elements are visible only to packages that inherit from another package; private elements are not visible outside the package at all.

Friend dependency relationships are discussed in Chapter 10.

Note: Packages that are friends to another may see all the elements of that package, no matter what their visibility.

Importing and Exporting

Suppose you have two classes named A and B sitting side by side. Because they are peers, A can see B and B can see A, so both can depend on the other. Just two classes makes for a trivial system, so you really don't need any kind of packaging.

Now, imagine having a few hundred such classes sitting side by side. There's no limit to the tangled web of relationships that you can weave. Furthermore, there's no way that you can understand such a large, unorganized group of classes. That's a very real problem for large systems—simple, unrestrained access does not scale up. For these situations, you need some kind of controlled packaging to organize your abstractions.

Dependency relationships are discussed in Chapter 5; the UML's extensibility mechanisms are discussed in Chapter 6.

So suppose that instead you put A in one package and B in another package, both packages sitting side by side. Suppose also that A and B are both declared as public parts of their respective packages. This is a very different situation. Although A and B are both public, neither can access the other because their enclosing packages form an opaque wall. However, if A's package imports B's package, A can now see B, although B cannot see A. Importing grants a one-way permission for the elements in one package to access the elements in another package. In the UML, you model an import relationship as a dependency adorned with the stereotype import. By packaging your abstractions into meaningful chunks and then controlling their access by importing, you can control the complexity of large numbers of abstractions.

Note: Actually, two stereotypes apply here—import and access—and both specify that the source package has access to the contents of the target. Import adds the contents of the target to the source's namespace, and so you don't have to qualify their names. This admits the possibility of name clashes which you must avoid to keep the model well-formed. Access does not add the contents of the target, and so you do have to qualify their names. Most of the time you'll use import.

Interfaces, an element often exported by packages, are discussed in Chapter 11.

The public parts of a package are called its exports. For example, in Figure 12-4, the package GUI exports two classes, Window and Form. EventHandler is not exported by GUI; EventHandler is a protected part of the package.

The parts that one package exports are visible only to the contents of those packages that explicitly import the package. In this example, Policies explicitly imports the package GUI. GUI::Window and GUI::Form are therefore made visible to the contents of the package Policies. However, GUI::EventHandler is not visible because it is protected. Because the package Server doesn't import GUI, the contents of Server don't have permission to access any of the contents of GUI. Similarly, the contents of GUI don't have permission to access any of the contents of Server.

Import and access dependencies are not transitive. In this example, Client imports Policies and Policies imports GUI, but Client does not by implication import GUI. Therefore, the contents of Client have access to the exports of Policies, but they do not have access to the exports of GUI. To gain access, Client would have to import GUI explicitly.

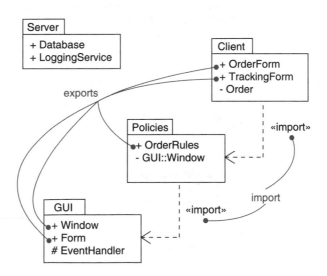

Figure 12-4: Importing and Exporting

Note: If an element is visible within a package, it is visible within all packages nested inside the package. Nested packages can see everything that their containing packages can see.

Generalization

Generalization is discussed in Chapters 5 and 10.

There are two kinds of relationships you can have between packages: import and access dependencies, used to import into one package elements exported from another, and generalizations, used to specify families of packages.

Generalization among packages is very much like generalization among classes. For example, in Figure 12-5, the package GUI is shown to export two classes (Window and Form) and one protected class (EventHandler). Two packages specialize the more general package GUI: WindowsGUI and MacGUI. These specialized packages inherit the public and protected elements of the more general package. But, just as in class inheritance, packages can replace more general elements and add new ones. For example, the package WindowsGUI inherits from GUI, so it includes the classes GUI::Window and GUI::EventHandler. In addition, WindowsGUI overrides one class (Form) and adds a new one (VBForm).

Packages involved in generalization relationships follow the same principle of substitutability as do classes. A specialized package (such as WindowsGUI) can be used anywhere a more general package (such as GUI) is used.

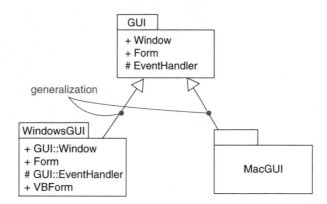

Figure 12-5 Generalization Among Packages

Standard Elements

The UML's extensibility mechanisms are discussed in Chapter 6.

All of the UML's extensibility mechanisms apply to packages. Most often, you'll use tagged values to add new package properties (such as specifying the author of a package) and stereotypes to specify new kinds of packages (such as packages that encapsulate operating system services).

The UML's standard elements are summarized in Appendix B.

The UML defines five standard stereotypes that apply to packages.

1. `facade`   Specifies a package that is only a view on some other package
2. `framework`   Specifies a package consisting mainly of patterns
3. `stub`   Specifies a package that serves as a proxy for the public contents of another package
4. `subsystem`   Specifies a package representing an independent part of the entire system being modeled
5. `system`   Specifies a package representing the entire system being modeled

Dependencies are discussed in Chapters 5 and 10.

The UML does not specify icons for any of these stereotypes. In addition to these five package stereotypes, you'll also use dependencies designated using the standard stereotype import.

Frameworks are discussed in Chapter 28; systems and subsystems are discussed in Chapter 31.

Most of these standard elements are discussed elsewhere, except for facade and stub. These two stereotypes help you to manage very large models. You use facades to provide elided views on otherwise complex packages. For example, your system might contain the package `BusinessModel`. You might want to expose a subset of its elements to one set of users (to show only those elements associated with customers), and another subset to a different set of users (to show only those elements associated with products). To do so, you would define facades, which import (and never own) only a subset of the elements in another package. You use stubs when you have tools that split apart a system into packages that you manipulate at different times and potentially in different places. For example, if you have a development team working in two locations, the team at one site would provide a stub for the packages the other team required. This strategy lets the teams work independently without disturbing each other's work, with the stub packages capturing the seams in the system that must be managed carefully.

Common Modeling Techniques

Modeling Groups of Elements

The most common purpose for which you'll use packages is to organize modeling elements into groups that you can name and manipulate as a set. If you are developing a trivial application, you won't need packages at all. All your abstractions will fit nicely into one package. For every other system, however, you'll find that many of your system's classes, interfaces, components, nodes, and even diagrams tend to naturally fall into groups. You model these groups as packages.

Systems and subsystems, which are similar to packages but have identity, are discussed in Chapter 31.

There is one important distinction between classes and packages: Classes are abstractions of things found in your problem or solution; packages are mechanisms you use to organize the things in your model. Packages have no identity (meaning that you can't have instances of packages, so they are invisible in the running system); classes do have identity (classes have instances, which are elements of a running system).

The five views of an architecture are discussed in Chapter 2.

Most of the time, you'll use packages to group the same basic kind of elements. For example, you might separate all the classes and their corresponding relationships from your system's design view into a series of packages, using the UML's import dependencies to control access among these packages. You might organize all the components in your system's implementation view in a similar fashion.

You can also use packages to group different kinds of elements. For example, for a system being developed by a geographically distributed team, you might use packages as your unit of configuration management, putting in them all the classes and diagrams that each team can check in and check out separately. In fact, it's common to use packages to group modeling elements and their associated diagrams.

To model groups of elements,

- Scan the modeling elements in a particular architectural view and look for clumps defined by elements that are conceptually or semantically close to one another.
- Surround each of these clumps in a package.
- For each package, distinguish which elements should be accessible outside the package. Mark them public, and all others protected or private. When in doubt, hide the element.
- Explicitly connect packages that build on others via import dependencies.
- In the case of families of packages, connect specialized packages to their more general part via generalizations.

For example, Figure 12-6 shows a set of packages that organize the classes in an information system's design view into a classic three-tier architecture. The elements in the package User Services provide the visual interface for presenting information and gathering data. The elements in the package Data Services maintain, access, and update data. The elements in the package Business Services bridge the elements in the other two packages and encompass all the classes and other elements that manage requests from the user to execute a business task, including business rules that dictate the policies for manipulating data.

In a trivial system, you could lump all your abstractions into one package. However, by organizing your classes and other elements of the system's design view into three packages, you not only make your model more understandable, but you can control access to the elements of your model by hiding some and exporting others.

---

*The documen-
tation tagged
value is
discussed in
Chapter 6.*

Note: When you render models such as these, you'll typically want to expose elements that are central to each package. To make clear the purpose of each package, you can also expose a documentation tagged value for each package.

Figure 12-6: Modeling Groups of Elements

Modeling Architectural Views

*The five views
of an architec-
ture are
discussed in
Chapter 2.*

Using packages to group related elements is important; you can't develop complex models without doing so. This approach works well for organizing related elements, such as classes, interfaces, components, nodes, and diagrams. As you consider the different views of a software system's architecture, you need even larger chunks. You can use packages to model the views of an architecture.

*Views are
related to
models, as
discussed in
Chapter 31.*

Remember that a view is a projection into the organization and structure of a system, focused on a particular aspect of that system. This definition has two implications. First, you can decompose a system into almost orthogonal packages, each of which addresses a set of architecturally significant decisions. For example, you might have a design view, a process view, an implementation view, a deployment view, and a use case view. Second, these packages own all the abstractions germane to that view. For example, all the components in your model would belong to the package that represents the implementation view.

Note: In this regard, packages as views are different from facades. Views own their elements; facades reference the elements that live in other packages. A given element may be owned by exactly one package, but the same element can be referenced by many facades.

To model architectural views,

- Identify the set of architectural views that are significant in the context of your problem. In practice, this typically includes a design view, a process view, an implementation view, a deployment view, and a use case view.
- Place the elements (and diagrams) that are necessary and sufficient to visualize, specify, construct, and document the semantics of each view into the appropriate package.
- As necessary, further group these elements into their own packages.
- There will typically be dependencies across the elements in different views. So, in general, let each view at the top of a system be open to all others at that level.

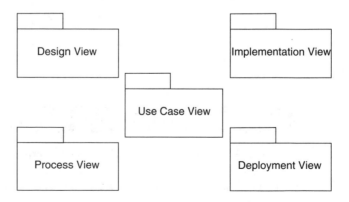

Figure 12-7: Modeling Architectural Views

Modeling systems is discussed in Chapter 31.

For example, Figure 12-7 illustrates a canonical top-level decomposition that's appropriate for even the most complex system you might encounter.

Hints and Tips

When you model packages in the UML, remember that they exist only to help you organize the elements of your model. If you have abstractions that manifest themselves as objects in the real system, don't use packages. Instead, use modeling elements such as classes or components. A well-structured package

- Is cohesive, providing a crisp boundary around a set of related elements.
- Is loosely coupled, exporting only those elements other packages really need to see, and importing only those elements necessary and sufficient for the elements in the package to do their job.
- Is not deeply nested, because there are limits to the human understanding of deeply nested structures.
- Owns a balanced set of contents; relative to one another in a system, packages should not be too large (split them up if necessary) or too small (combine elements that you manipulate as a group).

When you draw a package in the UML,

- Use the simple form of a package icon unless it's necessary for you to explicitly reveal the contents of that package.
- When you do reveal a package's contents, show only elements that are necessary to understand the meaning of that package in context.
- Especially if you are using packages to model things under configuration management, reveal the values of tags associated with versioning.

UNIFIED
MODELING
LANGUAGE

Chapter 13

INSTANCES

The terms "instance" and "object" are largely synonymous and so, for the most part, may be used interchangeably. An instance is a concrete manifestation of an abstraction to which a set of operations may be applied and which may have a state that stores the effects of the operation.

You use instances to model concrete or prototypical things that live in the real world. Almost every building block in the UML participates in this class/object dichotomy. For example, you can have use cases and use case instances, nodes and node instances, associations and association instances, and so on.

Getting Started

Suppose you've set out to build a house for your family. By saying "house" rather than "car," you've already begun to narrow the vocabulary of your solution space. House is an abstraction of "a permanent or semipermanent dwelling the purpose of which is to provide shelter." Car is "a mobile, powered vehicle the purpose of which is to transport people from place to place." As you work to reconcile the many competing requirements that shape your problem, you'll want to refine your abstraction of this house. For example, you might choose "a three bedroom house with a walkout basement," a kind of house, albeit a more specialized one.

When your builder finally hands you the keys to your house and you and your family walk through the front door, you are now dealing with something concrete and specific. It's no longer just a three bedroom house with a walkout, but it's "my three bedroom house with a walkout basement, located at 835 S. Moore Street." If you are terminally sentimental, you might even name your house something like Sanctuary or Our Money Pit.

There's a fundamental difference between a three bedroom house with a walkout basement and my three bedroom house named Sanctuary. The former is an abstraction representing a certain kind of house with various properties; the latter is a concrete instance of that abstraction, representing some thing that manifests itself in the real world, with real values for each of those properties.

An abstraction denotes the ideal essence of a thing; an instance denotes a concrete manifestation. You'll find this separation of abstraction and instance in everything you model. For a given abstraction, you can have innumerable instances. For a given instance, there is some abstraction that specifies the characteristics common to all such instances.

Classes are discussed in Chapters 4 and 9; components are discussed in Chapter 29; nodes are discussed in Chapter 26; use cases are discussed in Chapter 16.

In the UML, you can represent abstractions and their instances. Almost every building block in the UML—most notably classes, components, nodes, and use cases—may be modeled in terms of their essence or in terms of their instances. Most of the time, you'll work with them as abstractions. When you want to model concrete or prototypical manifestations, you'll need to work with their instances.

The UML provides a graphical representation for instances, as Figure 13-1 shows. This notation permits you to visualize named instances, as well as anonymous ones.

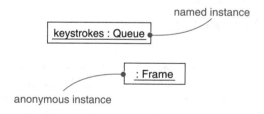

Figure 13-1: Instances

Terms and Concepts

The UML's class/object dichotomy is discussed in Chapter 2.

An *instance* is a concrete manifestation of an abstraction to which a set of operations can be applied and which has a state that stores the effects of the operations. *Instance* and *object* are largely synonymous. Graphically, an instance is rendered by underlining its name.

Associations are discussed in Chapters 5 and 10; links are discussed in Chapters 14 and 15.

Note: From common usage, the concrete manifestation of a class is called an object. Objects are instances of classes, so it's excruciatingly proper to say that all objects are instances, although some instances are not objects (for example, an instance of an association is really not an object, it's just an instance, also known as a link). Only power modelers will really care about this subtle distinction.

Abstractions and Instances

Classifiers are discussed in Chapter 9.

Instances don't stand alone; they are almost always tied to an abstraction. Most instances you'll model with the UML will be instances of classes (and these things are called objects), although you can have instances of other things, such as components, nodes, use cases, and associations. In the UML, an instance is easily distinguishable from an abstraction. To indicate an instance, you underline its name.

In a general sense, an object is something that takes up space in the real or conceptual world, and you can do things to it. For example, an instance of a node is typically a computer that physically sits in a room; an instance of a component takes up some space on the file system; an instance of a customer record consumes some amount of physical memory. Similarly, an instance of a flight envelope for an aircraft is something you can manipulate mathematically.

Abstract classes are discussed in Chapter 9; interfaces are discussed in Chapter 11.

You can use the UML to model these physical instances, but you can also model things that are not so concrete. For example, an abstract class, by definition, may not have any direct instances. However, you can model indirect instances of abstract classes in order to show the use of a prototypical instance of that abstract class. Literally, no such object might exist. But pragmatically, this instance lets you name one of any potential instances of concrete children of that abstract class. This same touch applies to interfaces. By their very definition, interfaces may not have any direct instances, but you can model a prototypical instance of an interface, representing one of any potential instances of concrete classes that realize that interface.

Object diagrams are discussed in Chapter 14; interaction diagrams are discussed in Chapter 18; activity diagrams are discussed in Chapter 19; dynamic typing is discussed in Chapter 11; classifiers are discussed in Chapter 9.

When you model instances, you'll place them in object diagrams (if you want to visualize their structural details) or in interaction and activity diagrams (if you want to visualize their participation in dynamic situations). Although typically not necessary, you can place objects in class diagrams if you want to explicitly show the relationship of an object to its abstraction.

The classifier of an instance is usually static. For example, once you create an instance of a class, its class won't change during the lifetime of that object. In some modeling situations and in some programming languages, however, it is possible to change the abstraction of an instance. For example, a `Caterpillar` object might become a `Butterfly` object. It's the same object, but of a different abstraction.

Note: During development, it's also possible for you to have instances with no associated classifier, which you can render as an object but with its abstraction name missing, as in Figure 13-2. You can introduce orphan objects such as these when you need to model very abstract behavior, although you must eventually tie such instances to an abstraction if you want to enforce any degree of semantics about the object.

Names

Operations are discussed in Chapters 4 and 9; components are discussed in Chapter 25; nodes are discussed in Chapter 26.

Every instance must have a name that distinguishes it from other instances within its context. Typically, an object lives within the context of an operation, a component, or a node. A *name* is a textual string, such as `t` and `myCustomer` in Figure 13-2. That name alone is known as a *simple name*. The abstraction of the instance may be a simple name (such as `Transaction`) or it may be a *path name* (such as `Multimedia::AudioStream`) which is the abstraction's name prefixed by the name of the package in which that abstraction lives.

When you explicitly name an object, you are really giving it a name (such as `t`) that's usable by a human. You can also simply name an object (such as `aCustomer`) and elide its abstraction if it's obvious in the given context. In many cases, however, the real name of an object is known only to the computer on which that object lives. In such cases, you can render an anonymous object (such as `: Multimedia::AudioStream`). Each occurrence of an anonymous object is considered distinct from all other occurrences. If you don't even know the object's associated abstraction, you must at least give it an explicit name (such as `agent :`).

You can use
stereotypes to
denote the
kind of
collection
represented by
a multiobject.
Stereotypes
are discussed
in Chapter 6.

Especially when you are modeling large collections of objects, it's clumsy to render the collection itself plus its individual instances. Instead, you can model multiobjects (such as : `keyCode`) as in Figure 13-2, representing a collection of anonymous objects.

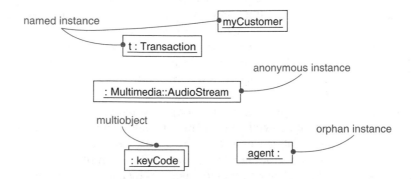

Figure 13-2: Named, Anonymous, Multiple, and Orphan Instances

Note: An instance name may be text consisting of any number of letters, numbers, and certain punctuation marks (except for marks such as the colon, which is used to separate the name of the instance from the name of its abstraction) and may continue over several lines. In practice, instance names are short nouns or noun phrases drawn from the vocabulary of the system you are modeling. Typically, you capitalize the first letter of all but the first word in an instance name, as in `t` or `myCustomer`.

Operations

Operations are
discussed in
Chapters 4
and 9; poly-
morphism is
discussed in
Chapter 9.

Not only is an object something that usually takes up space in the real world, it is also something you can do things to. The operations you can perform on an object are declared in the object's abstraction. For example, if the class `Transaction` defines the operation `commit`, then given the instance `t : Transaction`, you can write expressions such as `t.commit()`. The execution of this expression means that `t` (the object) is operated on by `commit` (the operation). Depending on the inheritance lattice associated with `Transaction`, this operation may or may not be invoked polymorphically.

State

Attributes are discussed in Chapter 4; interaction diagrams are discussed in Chapter 18. Another way to show the changing state of an individual object over time is via state machines, which are discussed in Chapter 21.

An object also has state, which in this sense encompasses all the (usually static) properties of the object plus the current (usually dynamic) values of each of these properties. These properties include the attributes of the object, as well as all its aggregate parts. An object's state is therefore dynamic. So when you visualize its state, you are really specifying the value of its state at a given moment in time and space. It's possible to show the changing state of an object by showing it multiple times in the same interaction diagram, but with each occurrence representing a different state.

When you operate on an object, you typically change its state; when you query an object, you don't change its state. For example, when you make an airline reservation (represented by the object r : Reservation), you might set the value of one of its attributes (for example, price = 395.75). If you change your reservation, perhaps by adding a new leg to your itinerary, then its state might change (for example, price = 1024.86).

As Figure 13-3 shows, you can use the UML to render the value of an object's attributes. For example, myCustomer is shown with the attribute id having the value "432-89-1783." In this case, id's type (SSN) is shown explicitly, although it can be elided (as for active = True), because its type can be found in the declaration of id in myCustomer's associated class.

You can associate a state machine with a class, which is especially useful when modeling event-driven systems or when modeling the lifetime of a class. In these cases, you can also show the state of this machine for a given object at a given time. For example, as Figure 13-3 shows, the object c (an instance of the class Phone) is indicated in the state WaitingForAnswer, a named state defined in the state machine for Phone.

Figure 13-3: Object State

> **Note:** Because an object may be in several states simultaneously, you can also show a list of its current states.

Other Features

Processes and threads are discussed in Chapter 22.

Processes and threads are an important element of a system's process view, so the UML provides a visual cue to distinguish elements that are active (those that are part of a process or thread and represent a root of a flow of control) from those that are passive. You can declare active classes that reify a process or thread, and in turn you can distinguish an instance of an active class, as in Figure 13-4.

Figure 13-4: Active Objects

Interaction diagrams are discussed in Chapter 18.

> **Note:** Most often, you'll use active objects in the context of interaction diagrams that model multiple flows of control. Each active object represents the root of a flow of control and may be used to name distinct flows.

Links are discussed in Chapters 14 and 15; class scoped attributes and operations are discussed in Chapter 9.

There are two other elements in the UML that may have instances. The first is a link. A link is a semantic connection among objects. An instance of an association is therefore a link. A link is rendered as a line, just like an association, but it can be distinguished from an association because links only connect objects. The second is a class-scoped attribute and operation. A class-scoped feature is in effect an object in the class that is shared by all instances of the class.

Standard Elements

The UML's extensibility mechanisms are discussed in Chapter 6.

All of the UML's extensibility mechanisms apply to objects. Usually, however, you don't stereotype an instance directly, nor do you give it its own tagged values. Instead, an object's stereotype and tagged values derive from the stereotype and tagged values of its associated abstraction. For example, as Figure 13-5 shows, you can explicitly indicate an object's stereotype, as well as its abstraction.

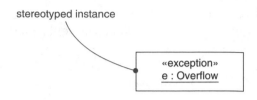

Figure 13-5: Stereotyped Objects

The UML's standard elements are summarized in Appendix B.

The UML defines two standard stereotypes that apply to the dependency relationships among objects and among classes:

1. `instanceOf`   Specifies that the client object is an instance of the supplier classifier
2. `instantiate`   Specifies that the client class creates instances of the supplier class

Become and copy are discussed in Chapter 18.

There are also two stereotypes related to objects that apply to messages and transitions:

1. `become`   Specifies that the client is the same object as the supplier, but at a later time and with possibly different values, state, or roles
2. `copy`   Specifies that the client object is an exact but independent copy of the supplier

Persistence is discussed in Chapter 29; interactions are discussed in Chapter 15.

The UML defines a standard constraint that applies to objects:

- `transient`   Specifies that an instance of the role is created during execution of the enclosing interaction but is destroyed before completion of execution

Common Modeling Techniques

Modeling Concrete Instances

When you model concrete instances, you are in effect visualizing things that live in the real world. You can't exactly see an instance of a `Customer` class, for example, unless that customer is standing beside you; in a debugger, you might be able to see a representation of that object, however.

Component diagrams are discussed in Chapter 29; deployment diagrams are discussed in Chapter 30; object diagrams are discussed in Chapter 14.

One of the things for which you'll use objects is to model concrete instances that exist in the real world. For example, if you want to model the topology of your organization's network, you'll use deployment diagrams containing instances of nodes. Similarly, if you want to model the components that live on the physical nodes in this network, you'll use component diagrams containing instances of the components. Finally, suppose you have a debugger connected to your running system; it can present the structural relationships among instances by rendering an object diagram.

To model concrete instances,

- Identify those instances necessary and sufficient to visualize, specify, construct, or document the problem you are modeling.
- Render these objects in the UML as instances. Where possible, give each object a name. If there is no meaningful name for the object, render it as an anonymous object.
- Expose the stereotype, tagged values, and attributes (with their values) of each instance necessary and sufficient to model your problem.
- Render these instances and their relationships in an object diagram or other diagram appropriate to the kind of the instance.

For example, Figure 13-6 shows an object diagram drawn from the execution of a credit card validation system, perhaps as seen by a debugger that's probing the running system. There is one multiobject, containing anonymous instances of the class Transaction. There are also two explicitly named objects—primaryAgent and current—both of which expose their class, although in different ways. The diagram also explicitly shows the current state of the object primaryAgent.

Note also the use of the dependency stereotyped as instanceOf, indicating the class of primaryAgent. Typically, you'll want to explicitly show these

Figure 13-6: Modeling Concrete Instances

class/object relationships only if you also intend to show relationships with other classes.

Modeling Prototypical Instances

*Interactions
are discussed
in Chapter 18.*

Perhaps the most important thing for which you'll use instances is to model the dynamic interactions among objects. When you model such interactions, you are generally not modeling concrete instances that exist in the real world. Instead, you are modeling conceptual objects that are essentially proxies or stand-ins for objects that will eventually act that way in the real world. These are prototypical objects and, therefore, are roles to which concrete instances conform. For example, if you want to model the ways objects in a windowing application react to a mouse event, you'd draw an interaction diagram containing prototypical instances of windows, events, and handlers.

Note: The semantic difference between concrete objects and prototypical objects is subtle and of relevance only to power modelers. As a typical user, you won't notice the difference at all. To be precise, however, the UML uses the term classifier role to denote a role to which instances conform, a subtle distinction that is context dependent. Concrete objects appear in static places, such as object diagrams, component diagrams, and deployment diagrams. Prototypical objects appear in such places as interaction diagrams and activity diagrams.

To model prototypical instances,

- Identify those prototypical instances necessary and sufficient to visualize, specify, construct, or document the problem you are modeling.
- Render these objects in the UML as instances. Where possible, give each object a name. If there is no meaningful name for the object, render it as an anonymous object.
- Expose the properties of each instance necessary and sufficient to model your problem.
- Render these instances and their relationships in an interaction diagram or an activity diagram.

*Interaction
diagrams are
discussed in
Chapter 15;
activity
diagrams are
discussed in
Chapter 19.*

Figure 13-7 shows an interaction diagram illustrating a partial scenario for initiating a phone call in the context of a switch. There are four prototypical objects: a (a CallingAgent), c (a Connection), and t1 and t2 (both instances of Terminal). All four of these objects are prototypical; all represent conceptual proxies for concrete objects that may exist in the real world.

Note: This example is a collaboration, which represents a society of roles and other elements that work together to provide some cooperative behavior that's bigger than the sum of all the elements. Collaborations have two aspects—one structural (representing the classifier roles and their relationships) and one dynamic (representing the interactions among those prototypical instances).

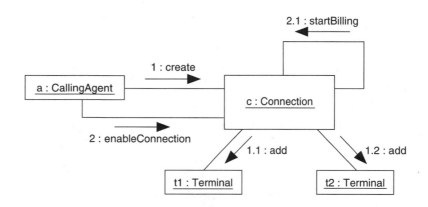

Figure 13-7: Modeling Prototypical Instances

Hints and Tips

When you model instances in the UML, remember that every instance should denote a concrete manifestation of some abstraction, typically a class, component, node, use case, or association. A well-structured instance

- Is explicitly associated with a specific abstraction.
- Has a unique name drawn from the vocabulary of the problem domain or the solution domain.

When you draw an instance in the UML,

- Render the name of the abstraction of which it is an instance unless it's obvious by context.
- Show the instance's stereotype, role, and state only as necessary to understand the object in its context.
- If visible, organize long lists of attributes and their values by grouping them according to their category.

UNIFIED
MODELING
LANGUAGE

Chapter 14
OBJECT DIAGRAMS

In this chapter
■ Modeling object structures
■ Forward and reverse engineering

Object diagrams model the instances of things contained in class diagrams. An object diagram shows a set of objects and their relationships at a point in time.

You use object diagrams to model the static design view or static process view of a system. This involves modeling a snapshot of the system at a moment in time and rendering a set of objects, their state, and their relationships.

Object diagrams are not only important for visualizing, specifying, and documenting structural models, but also for constructing the static aspects of systems through forward and reverse engineering.

Getting Started

If you are not used to the game, soccer looks like a terribly simple sport—an unruly mob of people madly running about a field chasing a white ball. Looking at the blurred image of bodies in motion, there hardly seems to be any subtlety or style to it.

Freeze the motion for a moment, then classify the individual players, and a very different picture of the game emerges. No longer just a mass of humanity, you'll be able to distinguish the forwards, halfbacks, and fullbacks. Dig a bit deeper and you'll understand how these players collaborate, following strategies for goal-tending, moving the ball, stealing the ball, and attacking. In a winning team, you won't find players placed randomly around the field.

Instead, at every moment of the game, you'll find their placement on the field and their relationship to other players well calculated.

Trying to visualize, specify, construct, or document a software-intensive system is similar. If you were to trace the control flow of a running system, you'd quickly lose sight of the bigger picture for how the system's parts are organized, especially if you have multiple threads of control. Similarly, if you have a complex data structure, just looking at the state of one object at a time doesn't help much. Rather, you need to study a snapshot of the object, its neighbors, and its relationships to these neighbors. In all but the simplest object-oriented systems, you'd find a multitude of objects present, each standing in precise relationship with others. In fact, when an object-oriented system breaks, it's typically not because of a failure in logic, but because of broken connections among objects or a mangled state in individual objects.

Class diagrams are discussed in Chapter 8; interactions are discussed in Chapter 15; interaction diagrams are discussed in Chapter 18.

With the UML, you use class diagrams to visualize the static aspects of your system's building blocks. You use interaction diagrams to visualize the dynamic aspects of your system, consisting of instances of these building blocks and messages dispatched among them. An object diagram covers a set of instances of the things found in a class diagram. An object diagram, therefore, expresses the static part of an interaction, consisting of the objects that collaborate, but without any of the messages passed among them. In both cases, an object diagram freezes a moment in time, as in Figure 14-1.

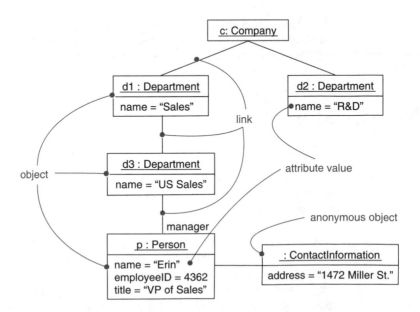

Figure 14-1: An Object Diagram

Terms and Concepts

An *object diagram* is a diagram that shows a set of objects and their relationships at a point in time. Graphically, an object diagram is a collection of vertices and arcs

Common Properties

The general properties of diagrams are discussed in Chapter 7.

An object diagram is a special kind of diagram and shares the same common properties as all other diagrams—that is, a name and graphical contents that are a projection into a model. What distinguishes an object diagram from all other kinds of diagrams is its particular content.

Contents

Objects are discussed in Chapter 13; links are discussed in Chapter 15; packages are discussed in Chapter 12; subsystems are discussed in Chapter 31.

Object diagrams commonly contain

- Objects
- Links

Like all other diagrams, object diagrams may contain notes and constraints.

Object diagrams may also contain packages or subsystems, both of which are used to group elements of your model into larger chunks. Sometimes, you'll want to place classes in your object diagrams, as well, especially when you want to visualize the classes behind each instance.

Class diagrams are discussed in Chapter 8; interaction diagrams are discussed in Chapter 18.

Note: An object diagram is essentially an instance of a class diagram or the static part of an interaction diagram. In either case, an object diagram contains primarily objects and links, and focuses on concrete or prototypical instances. Both component diagrams and deployment diagrams may contain instances, and if they contain only instances (and no messages), they too are considered to be special kinds of object diagrams.

Common Uses

Design views are discussed in Chapter 2.

You use object diagrams to model the static design view or static process view of a system just as you do with class diagrams, but from the perspective of real

or prototypical instances. This view primarily supports the functional requirements of a system—that is, the services the system should provide to its end
users. Object diagrams let you model static data structures.

When you model the static design view or static process view of a system, you
typically use object diagrams in one way:

■ To model object structures

*Interaction
diagrams are
discussed in
Chapter 18.*

Modeling object structures involves taking a snapshot of the objects in a system at a given moment in time. An object diagram represents one static frame
in the dynamic storyboard represented by an interaction diagram. You use
object diagrams to visualize, specify, construct, and document the existence of
certain instances in your system, together with their relationships to one
another.

Common Modeling Techniques

Modeling Object Structures

When you construct a class diagram, a component diagram, or a deployment
diagram, what you are really doing is capturing a set of abstractions that are
interesting to you as a group and, in that context, exposing their semantics and
their relationships to other abstractions in the group. These diagrams show
only potentiality. If class A has a one-to-many association to class B, then for
one instance of A there might be five instances of B; for another instance of A
there might be only one instance of B. Furthermore, at a given moment in time,
that instance of A, along with the related instances of B, will each have certain
values for their attributes and state machines.

If you freeze a running system or just imagine a moment of time in a modeled
system, you'll find a set of objects, each in a specific state, and each in a particular relationship to other objects. You can use object diagrams to visualize,
specify, construct, and document the structure of these objects. Object diagrams are especially useful for modeling complex data structures.

When you model your system's design view, a set of class diagrams can be
used to completely specify the semantics of your abstractions and their relationships. With object diagrams, however, you cannot completely specify the
object structure of your system. For an individual class, there may be a multitude of possible instances, and for a set of classes in relationship to one

another, there may be many times more possible configurations of these objects. Therefore, when you use object diagrams, you can only meaningfully expose interesting sets of concrete or prototypical objects. This is what it means to model an object structure—an object diagram shows one set of objects in relation to one another at one moment in time.

To model an object structure,

Mechanisms such as these are often coupled to use cases, as discussed in Chapters 16 and 28.

- Identify the mechanism you'd like to model. A mechanism represents some function or behavior of the part of the system you are modeling that results from the interaction of a society of classes, interfaces, and other things.
- For each mechanism, identify the classes, interfaces, and other elements that participate in this collaboration; identify the relationships among these things, as well.
- Consider one scenario that walks through this mechanism. Freeze that scenario at a moment in time, and render each object that participates in the mechanism.
- Expose the state and attribute values of each such object, as necessary, to understand the scenario.
- Similarly, expose the links among these objects, representing instances of associations among them.

For example, Figure 14-2 shows a set of objects drawn from the implementation of an autonomous robot. This figure focuses on some of the objects involved in the mechanism used by the robot to calculate a model of the world in which it moves. There are many more objects involved in a running system, but this diagram focuses on only those abstractions that are directly involved in creating this world view.

As this figure indicates, one object represents the robot itself (r, an instance of Robot), and r is currently in the state marked moving. This object has a link to w, an instance of World, which represents an abstraction of the robot's world model. This object has a link to a multiobject that consists of instances of Element, which represent entities that the robot has identified but not yet assigned in its world view. These elements are marked as part of the robot's global state.

At this moment in time, w is linked to two instances of Area. One of them (a2) is shown with its own links to three Wall and one Door object. Each of these walls is marked with its current width, and each is shown linked to its neighboring walls. As this object diagram suggests, the robot has recognized this enclosed area, which has walls on three sides and a door on the fourth.

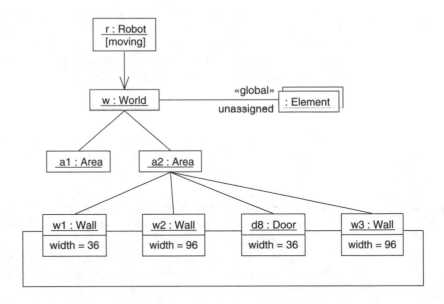

Figure 14-2: Modeling Object Structures

Forward and Reverse Engineering

Forward engineering (the creation of code from a model) an object diagram is theoretically possible but pragmatically of limited value. In an object-oriented system, instances are things that are created and destroyed by the application during run time. Therefore, you can't exactly instantiate these objects from the outside.

Component diagrams are discussed in Chapter 29; deployment diagrams are discussed in Chapter 30.

Although this is true of most typical object diagrams (which contain instances of classes), it's not true of object diagrams containing instances of components and of nodes. Both of these are special cases of component diagrams and deployment diagrams, respectively, and are discussed elsewhere. In these cases, component instances and node instances are things that live outside the running system and are amenable to some degree of forward engineering.

Reverse engineering (the creation of a model from code) an object diagram is a very different thing. In fact, while you are debugging your system, this is something that you or your tools will do all the time. For example, if you are chasing down a dangling link, you'll want to literally or mentally draw an object diagram of the affected objects to see where, at a given moment in time, an object's state or its relationship to other objects is broken.

To reverse engineer an object diagram,

- Chose the target you want to reverse engineer. Typically, you'll set your context inside an operation or relative to an instance of one particular class.
- Using a tool or simply walking through a scenario, stop execution at a certain moment in time.
- Identify the set of interesting objects that collaborate in that context and render them in an object diagram.
- As necessary to understand their semantics, expose these object's states.
- As necessary to understand their semantics, identify the links that exist among these objects.
- If your diagram ends up overly complicated, prune it by eliminating objects that are not germane to the questions about the scenario you need answered. If your diagram is too simplistic, expand the neighbors of certain interesting objects and expose each object's state more deeply.

Hints and Tips

When you create object diagrams in the UML, remember that every object diagram is just a graphical representation of the static design view or static process view of a system. This means that no single object diagram need capture everything about a system's design or process view. In fact, for all but trivial systems, you'll encounter hundreds if not thousands of objects, most of them anonymous. So it's impossible to completely specify all the objects of a system or all the ways in which these objects may be associated. Consequently, object diagrams reflect some of the concrete or prototypical objects that live in the running system.

A well-structured object diagram

- Is focused on communicating one aspect of a system's static design view or static process view.
- Represents one frame in the dynamic storyboard represented by an interaction diagram.
- Contains only those elements that are essential to understanding that aspect.

- Provides detail consistent with its level of abstraction; you should expose only those attribute values and other adornments that are essential to understanding.
- Is not so minimalist as to misinform the reader about semantics that are important.

When you draw an object diagram,

- Give it a name that communicates its purpose.
- Lay out its elements to minimize lines that cross.
- Organize its elements spatially so that things that are semantically close are laid out to be physically close.
- Use notes and color as visual cues to draw attention to important features of your diagram.
- Include the values, state, and role of each object as necessary to communicate your intent.

Section 4

BASIC BEHAVIORAL
MODELING

compression

tension

Chapter 15
INTERACTIONS

In this chapter

- Roles, links, messages, actions, and sequences
- Modeling flows of control
- Creating well-structured algorithms

In every interesting system, objects don't just sit idle; they interact with one another by passing messages. An interaction is a behavior that comprises a set of messages exchanged among a set of objects within a context to accomplish a purpose.

You use interactions to model the dynamic aspect of collaborations, representing societies of objects playing specific roles, all working together to carry out some behavior that's bigger than the sum of the elements. These roles represent prototypical instances of classes, interfaces, components, nodes, and use cases. Their dynamic aspects are visualized, specified, constructed, and documented as flows of control that may encompass simple, sequential threads through a system, as well as more-complex flows that involve branching, looping, recursion, and concurrency. You can model each interaction in two ways: by emphasizing its time ordering of messages, or by emphasizing its sequencing of messages in the context of some structural organization of objects.

Well-structured interactions are like well-structured algorithms—efficient, simple, adaptable, and understandable.

Getting Started

*The differ-
ences between
building a dog
house and
building a high
rise are
discussed in
Chapter 1.*

A building is a living thing. Although every building is constructed of static stuff, such as bricks, mortar, lumber, plastic, glass, and steel, those things work together dynamically to carry out behavior that is useful to those who use the building. Doors and windows open and close. Lights turn on and off. A building's furnace, air conditioner, thermostat, and ventilation ducts work together to regulate the building's temperature. In intelligent buildings, sensors detect the presence or absence of activity and adjust lighting, heating, cooling, and music as conditions change. Buildings are laid out to facilitate the flow of people and materials from place to place. More subtly, buildings are designed to adapt to changes in temperature, expanding and contracting during the day and night and across the seasons. All well-structured buildings are designed to react to dynamic forces, such as wind, earthquakes, and the movement of its occupants, in ways that keep the building in equilibrium.

Software-intensive systems are the same way. An airline system might manage many terabytes of information that sit untouched on some disk most of the time, only to be brought to life by outside events, such as the booking of a reservation, the movement of an aircraft, or the scheduling of a flight. In reactive systems, such as those found on the computer in a microwave oven, objects spring to life and work gets carried out when the system is stimulated by such events as a user pushing a button or by the passage of time.

*Modeling the
structural
aspects of a
system is
discussed in
Sections 2 and
3; you can also
model the
dynamic
aspects of a
system by
using state
machines, as
discussed in
Chapter 21;
object dia-
grams are
discussed in
Chapter 14;
interaction
diagrams are
discussed in
Chapter 18.*

In the UML, you model the static aspects of a system by using such elements as class diagrams and object diagrams. These diagrams let you visualize, specify, construct, and document the things that live in your system, including classes, interfaces, components, nodes, and use cases and their instances, together with the way those things sit in relationship to one another.

In the UML, you model the dynamic aspects of a system by using interactions. Like an object diagram, an interaction statically sets the stage for its behavior by introducing all the objects that work together to carry out some action. Going beyond object diagrams, however, interactions also introduce messages that are dispatched from object to object. Most often, messages involve the invocation of an operation or the sending of a signal; messages may also encompass the creation and destruction of other objects.

You use interactions to model the flow of control within an operation, a class, a component, a use case, or the system as a whole. Using interaction diagrams, you can reason about these flows in two ways. First, you can focus on how messages are dispatched across time. Second, you can focus on the structural relationships among the objects in an interaction and then consider how messages are passed within the context of that structure.

The UML provides a graphical representation of messages, as Figure 15-1 shows. This notation permits you to visualize a message in a way that lets you emphasize its most important parts: its name, parameters (if any), and sequence. Graphically, a message is rendered as a directed line and almost always includes the name of its operation.

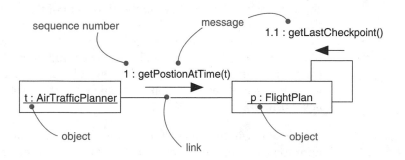

Figure 15-1: Messages, Links, and Sequencing

Terms and Concepts

An *interaction* is a behavior that comprises a set of messages exchanged among a set of objects within a context to accomplish a purpose. A *message* is a specification of a communication between objects that conveys information with the expectation that activity will ensue.

Context

Object diagrams show the structural connection among objects, as discussed in Chapter 14; systems and subsystems are discussed in Chapter 31; collaborations are discussed in Chapter 27.

You may find an interaction wherever objects are linked to one another. You'll find interactions in the collaboration of objects that exist in the context of your system or subsystem. You will also find interactions in the context of an operation. Finally, you'll find interactions in the context of a class.

Most often, you'll find interactions in the collaboration of objects that exist in the context of your system or subsystem as a whole. For example, in a system for Web commerce, you'll find objects on the client (such as instances of the classes `BookOrder` and `OrderForm`) interacting with one another. You'll also find objects on the client (again, such as instances of `BookOrder`) interacting with objects on the server (such as instances of `BackOrderManager`). These interactions therefore not only involve localized collaborations of objects (such as the interactions surrounding `OrderForm`), but they may also cut across many conceptual levels of your system (such as the interactions surrounding `BackOrderManager`).

Operations are discussed in Chapters 4 and 9; modeling an operation is discussed in Chapters 19 and 27.

You'll also find interactions among objects in the implementation of an operation. The parameters of an operation, any variables local to the operation, and any objects global to the operation (but still visible to the operation) may interact with one another to carry out the algorithm of that operation's implementation. For example, invoking the operation `moveToPosition(p : Position)` defined for a class in a mobile robot will involve the interaction of a parameter (`p`), an object global to the operation (such as the object `currentPosition`), and possibly several local objects (such as local variables used by the operation to calculate intermediate points in a path to the new position).

Classes are discussed in Chapters 4 and 9.

Finally, you will find interactions in the context of a class. You can use interactions to visualize, specify, construct, and document the semantics of a class. For example, to understand the meaning of a class `RayTraceAgent`, you might create interactions that show how the attributes of that class collaborate with one another (and with objects global to instances of the class and with parameters defined in the class's operations).

Components are discussed in Chapter 25; nodes are discussed in Chapter 26; use cases are discussed in Chapter 16; modeling the realization of a use case is discussed in Chapter 27; classifiers are discussed in Chapter 9.

Note: An interaction may also be found in the representation of a component, node, or use case, each of which, in the UML, is really a kind of classifier. In the context of a use case, an interaction represents a scenario that, in turn, represents one thread through the action of the use case.

Objects and Roles

The objects that participate in an interaction are either concrete things or prototypical things. As a concrete thing, an object represents something in the real world. For example, `p`, an instance of the class `Person`, might denote a particular human. Alternately, as a prototypical thing, `p` might represent any instance of `Person`.

Note: This is what distinguishes a collaboration. In a collaboration, the objects you find are prototypical things that play particular roles, not specific objects in the real world.

Abstract classes are discussed in Chapter 4; interfaces are discussed in Chapter 11.

In the context of an interaction, you may find instances of classes, components, nodes, and use cases. Although abstract classes and interfaces, by definition, may not have any direct instances, you may find instances of these things in an interaction. Such instances do not represent direct instances of the abstract class or of the interface, but may represent, respectively, indirect (or prototypical) instances of any concrete children of the abstract class of some concrete class that realizes that interface.

Instances are discussed in Chapter 13; object diagrams are discussed in Chapter 14.

You can think of an object diagram as a representation of the static aspect of an interaction, setting the stage for the interaction by specifying all the objects that work together. An interaction goes further by introducing a dynamic sequence of messages that may pass along the links that connect these objects.

Links

Associations are discussed in Chapters 5 and 10.

A link is a semantic connection among objects. In general, a link is an instance of an association. As Figure 15-2 shows, wherever a class has an association to another class, there may be a link between the instances of the two classes; wherever there is a link between two objects, one object can send a message to the other object.

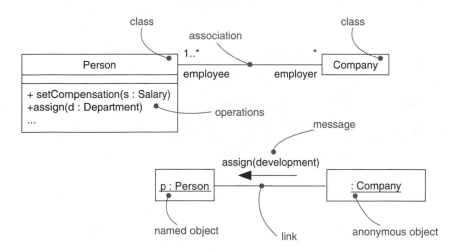

Figure 15-2: Links and Associations

Stereotypes
are discussed
in Chapter 6;
Appendix B
summarizes
the UML's
standard
elements;
examples of
these stereo-
types are
discussed in
Chapter 18.

A link specifies a path along which one object can dispatch a message to another (or the same) object. Most of the time, it is sufficient to specify that such a path exists. If you need to be more precise about how that path exists, you can adorn the appropriate end of the link with any of the following standard stereotypes.

- `association`   Specifies that the corresponding object is visible by association
- `self`   Specifies that the corresponding object is visible because it is the dispatcher of the operation
- `global`   Specifies that the corresponding object is visible because it is in an enclosing scope
- `local`   Specifies that the corresponding object is visible because it is in a local scope
- `parameter`   Specifies that the corresponding object is visible because it is a parameter

Note: As an instance of an association, a link may be rendered with most of the adornments appropriate to associations, such as a name, association role name, navigation, and aggregation. Multiplicity, however, does not apply to links, since they are instances of an association.

Messages

Object
diagrams are
discussed in
Chapter 14.

Suppose you have a set of objects and a set of links that connect those objects. If that's all you have, then you have a completely static model that can be represented by an object diagram. Object diagrams model the state of a society of objects at a given moment in time and are useful when you want to visualize, specify, construct, or document a static object structure.

Operations are
discussed in
Chapters 4
and 9; events
are discussed
in Chapter 20;
instances are
discussed in
Chapter 13.

Suppose you want to model the changing state of a society of objects over a period of time. Think of it as taking a motion picture of a set of objects, each frame representing a successive moment in time. If these objects are not totally idle, you'll see objects passing messages to other objects, sending events, and invoking operations. In addition, at each frame, you can explicitly visualize the current state and role of individual instances.

A message is the specification of a communication among objects that conveys information with the expectation that activity will ensue. The receipt of a message instance may be considered an instance of an event.

When you pass a message, the action that results is an executable statement that forms an abstraction of a computational procedure. An action may result in a change in state.

In the UML, you can model several kinds of actions.

Operations are discussed in Chapters 4 and 9; signals are discussed in Chapter 20.

- Call   Invokes an operation on an object; an object may send a message to itself, resulting in the local invocation of an operation
- Return   Returns a value to the caller
- Send   Sends a signal to an object
- Create   Creates an object
- Destroy   Destroys an object; an object may commit suicide by destroying itself

---

Note: You can model complex actions in the UML, as well. In addition to the five basic kinds of actions listed above, you can attach an arbitrary string to a message, in which you can write complex expressions. The UML does not specify the syntax or semantics of such strings.

Create and destroy are visualized as stereotypes, which are discussed in Chapter 6; the distinction between synchronous and asynchronous messages is most relevant in the context of concurrency, as discussed in Chapter 22.

The UML provides a visual distinction among these kinds of messages, as Figure 15-3 shows.

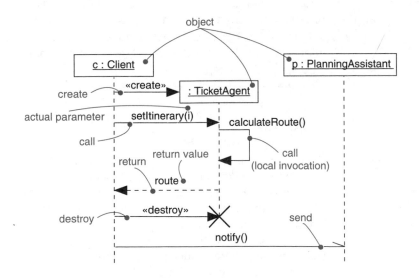

Figure 15-3: Messages

Classes are discussed in Chapters 4 and 9.

The most common kind of message you'll model is the call, in which one object invokes an operation of another (or the same) object. An object can't just call any random operation. If an object, such as c in the example above, calls the operation setItinerary on an instance of the class Ticket-Agent, the operation setItinerary must not only be defined for the class TicketAgent (that is, it must be declared in the class TicketAgent or one of its parents), it must also be visible to the caller c.

Note: Languages such as C++ are statically typed (although polymorphic), meaning that the legality of a call is checked at compilation time. Languages such as Smalltalk, however, are dynamically typed, meaning that you can't determine if an object can properly receive a message until execution time. In the UML, a well-formed model can in general be checked statically by a tool because, at modeling time, the developer typically knows the intent of the operation.

When an object calls an operation or sends a signal to another object, you can provide actual parameters to the message. Similarly, when an object returns control to another object, you can model the return value, as well.

Interfaces are discussed in Chapter 11.

Note: You can also qualify an operation by the class or interface in which it is declared. For example, invoking the operation register upon an instance of Student would polymorphically invoke whatever operation matches that name in the Student class hierarchy; invoking IMember::register would invoke the operation specified in the interface IMember (and realized by some suitable class, also in the Student class hierarchy).

Sequencing

Processes and threads are discussed in Chapter 22.

When an object passes a message to another object (in effect, delegating some action to the receiver), the receiving object might in turn send a message to another object, which might send a message to yet a different object, and so on. This stream of messages forms a sequence. Any sequence must have a beginning; the start of every sequence is rooted in some process or thread. Furthermore, any sequence will continue as long as the process or thread that owns it lives. A nonstop system, such as you might find in real time device control, will continue to execute as long as the node it runs on is up.

Systems are discussed in Chapter 31.

Each process and thread within a system defines a distinct flow of control, and within each flow, messages are ordered in sequence by time. To better visualize the sequence of a message, you can explicitly model the order of the message relative to the start of the sequence by prefixing the message with a sequence number set apart by a colon separator.

Most commonly, you can specify a procedural or nested flow of control, rendered using a filled solid arrowhead, as Figure 15-4 shows. In this case, the message findAt is specified as the first message nested in the second message of the sequence (2.1).

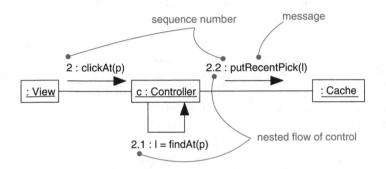

Figure 15-4: Procedural Sequence

Less common but also possible, as Figure 15-5 shows, you can specify a flat flow of control, rendered using a stick arrowhead, to model the nonprocedural progression of control from step to step. In this case, the message assert-Call is specified as the second message in the sequence.

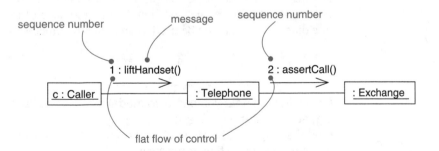

Figure 15-5: Flat Sequence

Note: The distinction between flat and procedural sequences is subtle and is really an advanced modeling issue. Typically, you'll use flat sequences only when modeling interactions in the context of use cases that involve the system as a whole, together with actors outside the system. Such sequences are often flat because control simply progresses from step to step, without any consideration for nested flows of control. In just about all other circumstances, you'll want to use procedural sequences, because they represent ordinary, nested operation calls of the type you find in most programming languages.

Processes and threads are discussed in Chapter 22; you can also specify asynchronous flow of control, rendered using a half stick arrowhead, as discussed in Chapter 22.

When you are modeling interactions that involve multiple flows of control, it's especially important to identify the process or thread that sent a particular message. In the UML, you can distinguish one flow of control from another by prefixing a message's sequence number with the name of the process or thread that sits at the root of the sequence. For example, the expression

        D5 : ejectHatch(3)

specifies that the operation ejectHatch is dispatched (with the actual argument 3) as the fifth message in the sequence rooted by the process or thread named D.

Not only can you show the actual arguments sent along with an operation or a signal in the context of an interaction, you can show the return values of a function as well. As the following expression shows, the value p is returned from the operation find, dispatched with the actual parameter "Rachelle". This is a nested sequence, dispatched as the second message nested in the third message nested in the first message of the sequence. In the same diagram, p can then be used as an actual parameter in other messages.

        1.3.2 : p := find("Rachelle")

Iteration, branching, and guarded messages are discussed in Chapter 18; timing marks are discussed in Chapter 23; stereotypes and constraints are discussed in Chapter 6.

Note: In the UML, you can also model more-complex forms of sequencing, such as iteration, branching, and guarded messages. In addition, to model timing constraints such as you might find in real time systems, you can associate timing marks with a sequence. Other, more exotic, forms of messaging, such as balking and time out, can be modeled by defining an appropriate message stereotype.

Creation, Modification, and Destruction

Constraints are discussed in Chapter 6.

Most of the time, the objects you show participating in an interaction exist for the entire duration of the interaction. However, in some interactions, objects may be created (specified by a `create` message) and destroyed (specified by a `destroy` message). The same is true of links: the relationships among objects may come and go. To specify if an object or link enters and/or leaves during an interaction, you can attach one of the following constraints to the element:

- `new`   Specifies that the instance or link is created during execution of the enclosing interaction
- `destroyed`   Specifies that the instance or link is destroyed prior to completion of execution of the enclosing interaction
- `transient`   Specifies that the instance or link is created during execution of the enclosing interaction but is destroyed before completion of execution

Lifelines are discussed in Chapter 18; the become *stereotype is discussed in Chapter 13.*

During an interaction, an object typically changes the values of its attributes, its state, or its roles. You can represent the modification of an object by replicating the object in the interaction (with possibly different attribute values, state, or roles). On a sequence diagram, you'd place each variant of the object on the same lifeline. In an interaction diagram, you'd connect each variant with a `become` message.

Representation

When you model an interaction, you typically include both objects (each one playing a specific role) and messages (each one representing the communication between objects, with some resulting action).

Interaction diagrams are discussed in Chapter 18.

You can visualize those objects and messages involved in an interaction in two ways: by emphasizing the time ordering of its messages, and by emphasizing the structural organization of the objects that send and receive messages. In the UML, the first kind of representation is called a sequence diagram; the second kind of representation is called a collaboration diagram. Both sequence diagrams and collaboration diagrams are kinds of interaction diagrams.

Sequence diagrams and collaboration diagrams are largely isomorphic, meaning that you can take one and transform it into the other without loss of information. There are some visual differences, however. First, sequence diagrams permit you to model the lifeline of an object. An object's lifeline represents the existence of the object at a particular time, possibly covering the object's creation and destruction. Second, collaboration diagrams permit you to model the structural links that may exist among the objects in an interaction.

Common Modeling Techniques

Modeling a Flow of Control

Use cases are discussed in Chapter 16; patterns and frameworks are discussed in Chapter 28; classes and operations are discussed in Chapters 4 and 9; interfaces are discussed in Chapter 11; components are discussed in Chapter 25; nodes are discussed in Chapter 26; you can also model the dynamic aspects of a system by using state machines, as discussed in Chapter 21.

The most common purpose for which you'll use interactions is to model the flow of control that characterizes the behavior of a system as a whole, including use cases, patterns, mechanisms, and frameworks, or the behavior of a class or an individual operation. Whereas classes, interfaces, components, nodes, and their relationships model the static aspects of your system, interactions model its dynamic aspects.

When you model an interaction, you essentially build a storyboard of the actions that take place among a set of objects. Techniques such as CRC cards are particularly useful in helping you to discover and think about such interactions.

To model a flow of control,

- Set the context for the interaction, whether it is the system as a whole, a class, or an individual operation.
- Set the stage for the interaction by identifying which objects play a role; set their initial properties, including their attribute values, state, and role.
- If your model emphasizes the structural organization of these objects, identify the links that connect them, relevant to the paths of communication that take place in this interaction. Specify the nature of the links using the UML's standard stereotypes and constraints, as necessary.
- In time order, specify the messages that pass from object to object. As necessary, distinguish the different kinds of messages; include parameters and return values to convey the necessary detail of this interaction.
- Also to convey the necessary detail of this interaction, adorn each object at every moment in time with its state and role.

Sequence diagrams are discussed in Chapter 18.

For example, Figure 15-6 shows a set of objects that interact in the context of a publish and subscribe mechanism (an instance of the observer design pattern). This figure includes three objects: p (a StockQuotePublisher), s1, and s2 (both instances of StockQuoteSubscriber). This figure is an example of a sequence diagram, which emphasizes the time order of messages.

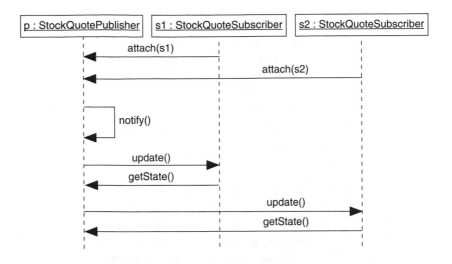

Figure 15-6: Flow of Control by Time

Collaboration diagrams are discussed in Chapter 18.

Figure 15-7 is semantically equivalent to the previous one, but it is drawn as a collaboration diagram, which emphasizes the structural organization of the objects. This figure shows the same flow of control, but it also provides a visualization of the links among these objects.

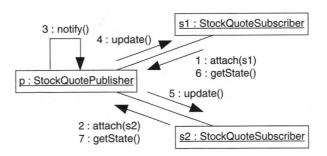

Figure 15-7: Flow of Control by Organization

Hints and Tips

When you model interactions in the UML, remember that every interaction represents the dynamic aspect of a society of objects. A well-structured interaction

- Is simple and should encompass only those objects that work together to carry out some behavior bigger than the sum of all these elements.
- Has a clear context and may represent the interaction of objects in the context of an operation, a class, or the system as a whole.
- Is efficient and should carry out its behavior with an optimal balance of time and resources.
- Is adaptable and elements of an interaction that are likely to change should be isolated so that they can be easily modified.
- Is understandable and should be straightforward, involving no hacks, hidden side effects, or obscure semantics.

When you draw an interaction in the UML

- Choose an emphasis for the interaction. You can emphasize either the ordering of messages over time or the sequencing of messages in the context of some structural organization of objects. You can't do both at the same time.
- Show only those properties of each object (such as attribute values, role, and state) that are important to understanding the interaction in its context.
- Show only those properties of each message (such as its parameters, concurrency semantics, and return value) that are important to understanding the interaction in its context.

UNIFIED MODELING LANGUAGE

Chapter 16

USE CASES

In this chapter box

In this chapter

- Use cases, actors, include, and extend
- Modeling the behavior of an element
- Realizing use cases with collaborations

No system exists in isolation. Every interesting system interacts with human or automated actors that use that system for some purpose, and those actors expect that system to behave in predictable ways. A use case specifies the behavior of a system or a part of a system and is a description of a set of sequences of actions, including variants, that a system performs to yield an observable result of value to an actor.

You apply use cases to capture the intended behavior of the system you are developing, without having to specify how that behavior is implemented. Use cases provide a way for your developers to come to a common understanding with your system's end users and domain experts. In addition, use cases serve to help validate your architecture and to verify your system as it evolves during development. As you implement your system, these use cases are realized by collaborations whose elements work together to carry out each use case.

Well-structured use cases denote essential system or subsystem behaviors only, and are neither overly general nor too specific.

Getting Started

A well-designed house is much more than a bunch of walls thrown together to hold up a roof that keeps out the weather. When you work with your architect to design your house, you'll give strong consideration to how you'll use that house. If you like entertaining, you'll want to think about the flow of people through your family room in a way that facilitates conversation and avoids dead ends that result in bunching. As you think about preparing meals for your family, you'll want to make sure your kitchen is designed for efficient placement of storage and appliances. Even plotting the path from your car to the kitchen in order to unload groceries will affect how you eventually connect rooms to one another. If you have a large family, you'll want to give thought to bathroom usage. Planning for the right number and right placement of bathrooms early on in the design will greatly reduce the risk of bottlenecks in the morning as your family heads to school and work. If you have teenagers, this issue has especially high risk, because the emotional cost of failure is high.

Reasoning about how you and your family will use your house is an example of use case–based analysis. You consider the various ways in which you'll use the house, and these use cases drive the architecture. Many families will have the same kinds of use cases—you use houses to eat, sleep, raise children, and hold memories. Every family will also have its own special use cases or variations of these basic ones. The needs of a large family, for example, are different from the needs of a single adult just out of college. It's these variations that have the greatest impact on the shape of your final home.

One key factor in creating use cases such as these is that you do so without specifying how the use cases are implemented. For example, you can specify how an ATM system should behave by stating in use cases how users interact with the system; you don't need to know anything about the inside of the ATM at all. Use cases specify desired behavior, they do not dictate how that behavior will be carried out. The great thing about this is that it lets you (as an end user and domain expert) communicate with your developers (who build systems that satisfy your requirements) without getting hung up on details. Those details will come, but use cases let you focus on the issues of highest risk to you.

In the UML, all such behaviors are modeled as use cases that may be specified independent of their realization. A use case is a description of a set of sequences of actions, including variants, that a system performs to yield an observable result of value to an actor. There are a number of important parts to this definition.

Interactions are discussed in Chapter 15; requirements are discussed in Chapter 6.
A use case describes a set of sequences, in which each sequence represents the interaction of the things outside the system (its actors) with the system itself (and its key abstractions). These behaviors are in effect system-level functions that you use to visualize, specify, construct, and document the intended behavior of your system during requirements capture and analysis. A use case represents a functional requirement of your system as a whole. For example, one central use case of a bank is to process loans.

A use case involves the interaction of actors and the system. An actor represents a coherent set of roles that users of use cases play when interacting with these use cases. Actors can be human or they can be automated systems. For example, in modeling a bank, processing a loan involves, among other things, the interaction between a customer and a loan officer.

A use case may have variants. In all interesting systems, you'll find use cases that are specialized versions of other use cases, use cases that are included as parts of other use cases, and use cases that extend the behavior of other core use cases. You can factor the common, reusable behavior of a set of use cases by organizing them according to these three kinds of relationships. For example, in modeling a bank, you'll find many variations among the basic use case of processing a loan, such as the difference in processing a jumbo mortgage versus a small business loan. In each case, however, these use cases share some degree of common behavior, such as the use case of qualifying the customer for the loan, a behavior that is part of processing every kind of loan.

A use case carries out some tangible amount of work. From the perspective of a given actor, a use case does something that's of value to an actor, such as calculate a result, generate a new object, or change the state of another object. For example, in modeling a bank, processing a loan results in the delivery of an approved loan, manifest in a pile of money handed to the customer.

Subsystems are discussed in Chapter 31; classes are discussed in Chapters 4 and 9; interfaces are discussed in Chapter 11.

You can apply use cases to your whole system. You can also apply use cases to part of your system, including subsystems and even individual classes and interfaces. In each case, these use cases not only represent the desired behavior of these elements, but they can also be used as the basis of test cases for these elements as they evolve during development. Use cases applied to subsystems are excellent sources of regression tests; use cases applied to the whole system are excellent sources of integration and system tests. The UML provides a graphical representation of a use case and an actor, as Figure 16-1 shows. This notation permits you to visualize a use case apart from its realization and in context with other use cases.

Figure 16-1: Actors and Use Cases

Terms and Concepts

The notation for use cases is similar to that for collaborations, as discussed in Chapter 27.

A *use case* is a description of a set of sequences of actions, including variants, that a system performs to yield an observable result of value to an actor. Graphically, a use case is rendered as an ellipse.

Names

A use case name must be unique within its enclosing package, as discussed in Chapter 12.

Every use case must have a name that distinguishes it from other use cases. A *name* is a textual string. That name alone is known as a *simple name*; a *path name* is the use case name prefixed by the name of the package in which that use case lives. A use case is typically drawn showing only its name, as in Figure 16-2.

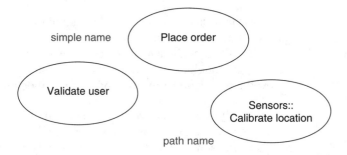

Figure 16-2: Simple and Path Names

Note: A use case name may be text consisting of any number of letters, numbers, and most punctuation marks (except for marks such as the colon, which is used to separate a class name and the name of its enclosing package) and may continue over several lines. In practice, use case names are short active verb phrases naming some behavior found in the vocabulary of the system you are modeling.

Use Cases and Actors

An actor represents a coherent set of roles that users of use cases play when interacting with these use cases. Typically, an actor represents a role that a human, a hardware device, or even another system plays with a system. For example, if you work for a bank, you might be a `LoanOfficer`. If you do your personal banking there, as well, you'll also play the role of Customer. An instance of an actor, therefore, represents an individual interacting with the system in a specific way. Although you'll use actors in your models, actors are not actually part of the system. They live outside the system.

Generalization is discussed in Chapters 5 and 10.

As Figure 16-3 indicates, actors are rendered as stick figures. You can define general kinds of actors (such as Customer) and specialize them (such as CommercialCustomer) using generalization relationships.

Stereotypes are discussed in Chapter 6.

Note: You can use the UML's extensibility mechanisms to stereotype an actor in order to provide a different icon that might offer a better visual cue for your purposes.

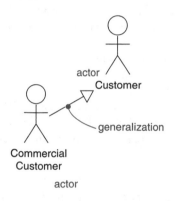

Figure 16-3: Actors

Association relationships are discussed in Chapters 5 and 10; messages are discussed in Chapter 15.

Actors may be connected to use cases only by association. An association between an actor and a use case indicates that the actor and the use case communicate with one another, each one possibly sending and receiving messages.

Use Cases and Flow of Events

A use case describes *what* a system (or a subsystem, class, or interface) does but it does not specify *how* it does it. When you model, it's important that you keep clear the separation of concerns between this outside and inside view.

You can specify the behavior of a use case by describing a flow of events in text clearly enough for an outsider to understand it easily. When you write this flow of events, you should include how and when the use case starts and ends, when the use case interacts with the actors and what objects are exchanged, and the basic flow and alternative flows of the behavior.

For example, in the context of an ATM system, you might describe the use case `ValidateUser` in the following way:

> *Main flow of events*: The use case starts when the system prompts the *Customer* for a PIN number. The *Customer* can now enter a PIN number via the keypad. The *Customer* commits the entry by pressing the Enter button. The system then checks this PIN number to see if it is valid. If the PIN number is valid, the system acknowledges the entry, thus ending the use case.

> *Exceptional flow of events*: The *Customer* can cancel a transaction at any time by pressing the Cancel button, thus restarting the use case. No changes are made to the *Customer*'s account.

> *Exceptional flow of events*: The *Customer* can clear a PIN number anytime before committing it and reenter a new PIN number.

> *Exceptional flow of events*: If the *Customer* enters an invalid PIN number, the use case restarts. If this happens three times in a row, the system cancels the entire transaction, preventing the *Customer* from interacting with the ATM for 60 seconds.

Note: You can specify a use case's flow of events in a number of ways, including informal structured text (as in the example above), formal structured text (with pre- and postconditions), and pseudocode.

Use Cases and Scenarios

Interaction diagrams, including sequence diagrams and collaboration diagrams, are discussed in Chapter 18.

Typically, you'll first describe the flow of events for a use case in text. As you refine your understanding of your system's requirements, however, you'll want to also use interaction diagrams to specify these flows graphically. Typically, you'll use one sequence diagram to specify a use case's main flow, and variations of that diagram to specify a use case's exceptional flows.

It is desirable to separate main versus alternative flows because a use case describes a set of sequences, not just a single sequence, and it would be impossible to express all the details of an interesting use case in just one sequence. For example, in a human resources system, you might find the use case `Hire employee`. This general business function might have many possible variations. You might hire a person from another company (the most common scenario); you might transfer a person from one division to another (common in international companies); or you might hire a foreign national (which involves its own special rules). Each of these variants can be expressed in a different sequence.

Instances are discussed in Chapter 13.

This one use case (`Hire employee`) actually describes a set of sequences in which each sequence in the set represents one possible flow through all these variations. Each sequence is called a scenario. A scenario is a specific sequence of actions that illustrates behavior. Scenarios are to use cases as instances are to classes, meaning that a scenario is basically one instance of a use case.

Note: There's an expansion factor from use cases to scenarios. A modestly complex system might have a few dozen use cases that capture its behavior, and each use case might expand out to several dozen scenarios. For each use case, you'll find primary scenarios (which define essential sequences) and secondary scenarios (which define alternative sequences).

Use Cases and Collaborations

Collaborations are discussed in Chapter 27.

A use case captures the intended behavior of the system (or subsystem, class, or interface) you are developing, without having to specify how that behavior is implemented. That's an important separation because the analysis of a system (which specifies behavior) should, as much as possible, not be influenced by implementation issues (which specify how that behavior is to be carried out). Ultimately, however, you have to implement your use cases, and you do so by creating a society of classes and other elements that work together to implement the behavior of this use case. This society of elements, including both its static and dynamic structure, is modeled in the UML as a collaboration.

Realization is discussed in Chapters 9 and 10.

As Figure 16-4 shows, you can explicitly specify the realization of a use case by a collaboration. Most of the time, though, a given use case is realized by exactly one collaboration, so you will not need to model this relationship explicitly.

Note: Although you may not visualize this relationship explicitly, the tools you use to manage your models will likely maintain this relationship.

Figure 16-4 Use Cases and Collaborations

Architecture is discussed in Chapter 2.

Note: Finding the minimal set of well-structured collaborations that satisfy the flow of events specified in all the use cases of a system is the focus of a system's architecture.

Organizing Use Cases

Packages are discussed in Chapter 12.

You can organize use cases by grouping them in packages in the same manner in which you can organize classes.

You can also organize use cases by specifying generalization, include, and extend relationships among them. You apply these relationships in order to factor common behavior (by pulling such behavior from other use cases that it includes) and in order to factor variants (by pushing such behavior into other use cases that extend it).

Generalization is discussed in Chapters 5 and 10.

Generalization among use cases is just like generalization among classes. Here it means that the child use case inherits the behavior and meaning of the parent use case; the child may add to or override the behavior of its parent; and the child may be substituted any place the parent appears (both the parent and the child may have concrete instances). For example, in a banking system, you might have the use case `Validate User`, which is responsible for verifying the identify of the user. You might then have two specialized children of this use case (`Check password` and `Retinal scan`), both of which behave just like `Validate User` and may be applied anywhere `Validate User` appears, yet both of which add their own behavior (the former by checking a textual password, the latter by checking the unique retina patterns of the user). As shown in Figure 16-5, generalization among use cases is rendered as a solid directed line with a large open arrowhead, just like generalization among classes.

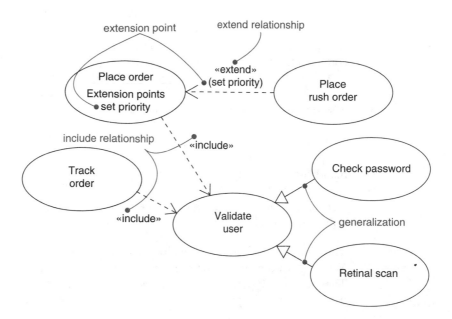

Figure 16-5: Generalization, Include, and Extend

An include relationship between use cases means that the base use case explicitly incorporates the behavior of another use case at a location specified in the base. The included use case never stands alone, but is only instantiated as part of some larger base that includes it. You can think of include as the base use case pulling behavior from the supplier use case.

You use an include relationship to avoid describing the same flow of events several times, by putting the common behavior in a use case of its own (the use case that is included by a base use case). The include relationship is essentially an example of delegation—you take a set of responsibilities of the system and capture it in one place (the included use case), then let all other parts of the system (other use cases) include the new aggregation of responsibilities whenever they need to use that functionality.

Dependency relationships are discussed in Chapters 5 and 10; stereotypes are discussed in Chapter 6.

You render an include relationship as a dependency, stereotyped as `include`. To specify the location in a flow of events in which the base use case includes the behavior of another, you simply write `include` followed by the name of the use case you want to include, as in the following flow for `Track order`.

> *Main flow of events*: Obtain and verify the order number. `include` (`Validate user`). For each part in the order, query its status, then report back to the user.

An extend relationship between use cases means that the base use case implicitly incorporates the behavior of another use case at a location specified indirectly by the extending use case. The base use case may stand alone, but under certain conditions, its behavior may be extended by the behavior of another use case. This base use case may be extended only at certain points called, not surprisingly, its extension points. You can think of extend as the extension use case pushing behavior to the base use case.

You use an extend relationship to model the part of a use case the user may see as optional system behavior. In this way, you separate optional behavior from mandatory behavior. You may also use an extend relationship to model a separate subflow that is executed only under given conditions. Finally, you may use an extend relationship to model several flows that may be inserted at a certain point, governed by explicit interaction with an actor.

Dependency relationships are discussed in Chapters 5 and 10; stereotypes and extra compartments are discussed in Chapter 6.

You render an extend relationship as a dependency, stereotyped as `extend`. You may list the extension points of the base use case in an extra compartment. These extension points are just labels that may appear in the flow of the base use case. For example, the flow for `Place order` might read as follows:

> *Main flow of events*: `include (Validate user)`. Collect the user's order items. `(set priority)`. Submit the order for processing.

In this example, `set priority` is an extension point. A use case may have more than one extension point (which may appear more than once), and these are always matched by name. Under normal circumstances, this base use case will execute without regard for the priority of the order. If, on the other hand, this is an instance of a priority order, the flow for this base case will carry out as above. But at the extension point `(set priority)`, the behavior of the extending use case `(Place rush order)` will be performed, then the flow will resume. If there are multiple extension points, the extending use case will simply fold in its flows in order.

Note: Organizing your use cases by extracting common behavior (through include relationships) and distinguishing variants (through extend relationships) is an important part of creating a simple, balanced, and understandable set of use cases for your system.

Other Features

Attributes and operations are discussed in Chapter 4.

Use cases are classifiers, so they may have attributes and operations that you may render just as for classes. You can think of these attributes as the objects inside the use case that you need to describe its outside behavior. Similarly, you can think of these operations as the actions of the system you need to describe a flow of events. These objects and operations may be used in your interaction diagrams to specify the behavior of the use case.

State machines are discussed in Chapter 21.

As classifiers, you can also attach state machines to use cases. You can use state machines as yet another way to describe the behavior represented by a use case.

Common Modeling Techniques

Modeling the Behavior of an Element

Systems and subsystems are discussed in Chapter 31; classes are discussed in Chapters 4 and 9.

The most common thing for which you'll apply use cases is to model the behavior of an element, whether it is the system as a whole, a subsystem, or a class. When you model the behavior of these things, it's important that you focus on what that element does, not how it does it.

Applying use cases to elements in this way is important for three reasons. First, by modeling the behavior of an element with use cases, you provide a way for domain experts to specify its outside view to a degree sufficient for developers to construct its inside view. Use cases provide a forum for your domain experts, end users, and developers to communicate to one another. Second, use cases provide a way for developers to approach an element and understand it. A system, subsystem, or class may be complex and full of operations and other parts. By specifying an element's use cases, you help users of these elements to approach them in a direct way, according to how they are likely to use them. In the absence of such use cases, users have to discover on their own how to use those elements. Use cases let the author of an element communicate his or her intent about how that element should be used. Third, use cases serve as the basis for testing each element as it evolves during development. By continuously testing each element against its use cases, you continuously validate its implementation. Not only do these use cases provide a source of regression tests, but every time you throw a new use case at an element, you are forced to reconsider your implementation to ensure that this element is resilient to change. If it is not, you must fix your architecture appropriately.

To model the behavior of an element,

- Identify the actors that interact with the element. Candidate actors include groups that require certain behavior to perform their tasks or that are needed directly or indirectly to perform the element's functions.
- Organize actors by identifying general and more specialized roles.
- For each actor, consider the primary ways in which that actor interacts with the element. Consider also interactions that change the state of the element or its environment or that involve a response to some event.
- Consider also the exceptional ways in which each actor interacts with the element.
- Organize these behaviors as use cases, applying include and extend relationships to factor common behavior and distinguish exceptional behavior.

For example, a retail system will interact with customers who place and track orders. In turn, the system will ship orders and bill the customer. As Figure 16-6 shows, you can model the behavior of such a system by declaring these behaviors as use cases (`Place order`, `Track order`, `Ship order`, and `Bill customer`). Common behavior can be factored out (`Validate customer`) and variants (`Ship partial order`) can be distinguished, as well. For each of these use cases, you would include a specification of the behavior, either by text, state machine, or interactions.

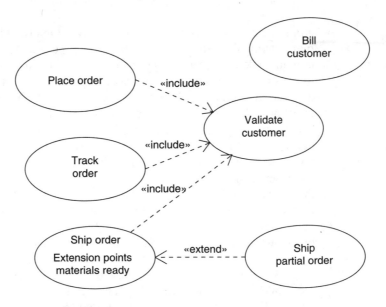

Figure 16-6: Modeling the Behavior of an Element

Packages are discussed in Chapter 12.

As your models get bigger, you will find that many use cases tend to cluster together in groups that are conceptually and semantically related. In the UML, you can use packages to model these clusters of classes.

Hints and Tips

When you model use cases in the UML, every use case should represent some distinct and identifiable behavior of the system or part of the system. A well-structured use case

- Names a single, identifiable, and reasonably atomic behavior of the system or part of the system.
- Factors common behavior by pulling such behavior from other use cases that it includes.
- Factors variants by pushing such behavior into other use cases that extend it.
- Describes the flow of events clearly enough for an outsider to easily understand it.
- Is described by a minimal set of scenarios that specify the normal and variant semantics of the use case.

When you draw a use case in the UML,

- Show only those use cases that are important to understand the behavior of the system or the part of the system in its context.
- Show only those actors that relate to these use cases.

UNIFIED
MODELING
LANGUAGE

Chapter 17

USE CASE DIAGRAMS

In this chapter

- Modeling the context of a system
- Modeling the requirements of a system
- Forward and reverse engineering

Activity diagrams are discussed in Chapter 19; statechart diagrams are discussed in Chapter 24; sequence and collaboration diagrams are discussed in Chapter 18.

Use case diagrams are one of the five diagrams in the UML for modeling the dynamic aspects of systems (activity diagrams, statechart diagrams, sequence diagrams, and collaboration diagrams are four other kinds of diagrams in the UML for modeling the dynamic aspects of systems). Use case diagrams are central to modeling the behavior of a system, a subsystem, or a class. Each one shows a set of use cases and actors and their relationships.

You apply use case diagrams to model the use case view of a system. For the most part, this involves modeling the context of a system, subsystem, or class, or modeling the requirements of the behavior of these elements.

Use case diagrams are important for visualizing, specifying, and documenting the behavior of an element. They make systems, subsystems, and classes approachable and understandable by presenting an outside view of how those elements may be used in context. Use case diagrams are also important for testing executable systems through forward engineering and for comprehending executable systems through reverse engineering.

Getting Started

Suppose someone hands you a box. On one side of that box, there are some buttons and a small LCD panel. Other than that, the box is nondescript; you aren't even given a hint about how to use it. You could randomly punch buttons and see what happens, but you'd be hard pressed to figure out what that box does or how to use it properly unless you spent a lot of trial-and-error time.

Software-intensive systems can be like that. If you are a user, you might be handed an application and told to use it. If the application follows normal conventions of the operating system you are used to, you might be able to get it to do something useful after a fashion, but you'd never come to understand its more complex and subtle behavior that way. Similarly, if you are a developer, you might be handed a legacy application or a set of components and told to use them. You'd be hard pressed to know how to use the elements until you formed a conceptual model for their use.

With the UML, you apply use case diagrams to visualize the behavior of a system, subsystem, or class so that users can comprehend how to use that element, and so that developers can implement that element. As Figure 17-1 shows, you can provide a use case diagram to model the behavior of that box—which most people would call a cellular phone.

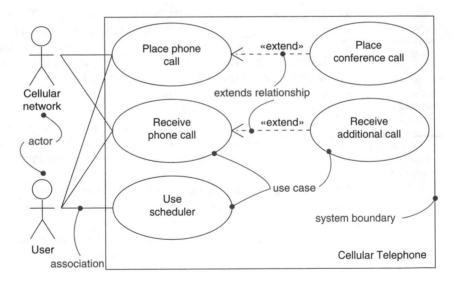

Figure 17-1: A Use Case Diagram

Terms and Concepts

A *use case diagram* is a diagram that shows a set of use cases and actors and their relationships.

Common Properties

The general
properties of
diagrams are
discussed in
Chapter 7.

A use case diagram is just a special kind of diagram and shares the same common properties as do all other diagrams—a name and graphical contents that are a projection into a model. What distinguishes a use case diagram from all other kinds of diagrams is its particular content.

Contents

Use cases and
actors are
discussed in
Chapter 16;
relationships
are discussed
in Chapters 5
and 10;
packages are
discussed in
Chapter 12;
instances are
discussed in
Chapter 13.

Use case diagrams commonly contain

- Use cases
- Actors
- Dependency, generalization, and association relationships

Like all other diagrams, use case diagrams may contain notes and constraints.

Use case diagrams may also contain packages, which are used to group elements of your model into larger chunks. Occasionally, you'll want to place instances of use cases in your diagrams, as well, especially when you want to visualize a specific executing system.

Common Uses

Use case
views are
discussed in
Chapter 2.

You apply use case diagrams to model the static use case view of a system. This view primarily supports the behavior of a system—the outwardly visible services that the system provides in the context of its environment.

When you model the static use case view of a system, you'll typically apply use case diagrams in one of two ways.

1. To model the context of a system

Modeling the context of a system involves drawing a line around the whole system and asserting which actors lie outside the system and interact with it. Here, you'll apply use case diagrams to specify the actors and the meaning of their roles.

Requirements
are discussed
in Chapters 4
and 6.

2. To model the requirements of a system

Modeling the requirements of a system involves specifying what that system should do (from a point of view of outside the system), independent of how that system should do it. Here, you'll apply use case diagrams to specify the desired behavior of the system. In this manner, a use case diagram lets you view the whole system as a black box; you can see what's outside the system and you can see how that system reacts to the things outside, but you can't see how that system works on the inside.

Common Modeling Techniques

Modeling the Context of a System

Given a system—any system—some things will live inside the system, some things will live outside it. For example, in a credit card validation system, you'll find such things as accounts, transactions, and fraud detection agents inside the system. Similarly, you'll find such things as credit card customers and retail institutions outside the system. The things that live inside the system are responsible for carrying out the behavior that those on the outside expect the system to provide. All those things on the outside that interact with the system constitute the system's context. This context defines the environment in which that system lives.

Systems are discussed in Chapter 31.

In the UML, you can model the context of a system with a use case diagram, emphasizing the actors that surround the system. Deciding what to include as an actor is important because in doing so you specify a class of things that interact with the system. Deciding what not to include as an actor is equally, if not more, important because that constrains the system's environment to include only those actors that are necessary in the life of the system.

To model the context of a system,

- Identify the actors that surround the system by considering which groups require help from the system to perform their tasks; which groups are needed to execute the system's functions; which groups interact with external hardware or other software systems; and which groups perform secondary functions for administration and maintenance.
- Organize actors that are similar to one another in a generalization/specialization hierarchy.
- Where it aids understandability, provide a stereotype for each such actor.
- Populate a use case diagram with these actors and specify the paths of communication from each actor to the system's use cases.

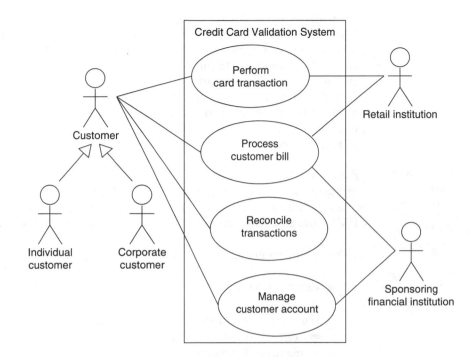

Figure 17-2: Modeling the Context of a System

For example, Figure 17-2 shows the context of a credit card validation system, with an emphasis on the actors that surround the system. You'll find Customers, of which there are two kinds (Individual customer and Corporate customer). These actors are the roles that humans play when interacting with the system. In this context, there are also actors that represent other institutions, such as Retail institution (with which a Customer performs a card transaction to buy an item or a service) and Sponsoring financial institution (which serves as the clearinghouse for the credit card account). In the real world, these latter two actors are likely software-intensive systems themselves.

Subsystems are discussed in Chapter 31. This same technique applies to modeling the context of a subsystem. A system at one level of abstraction is often a subsystem of a larger system at a higher level of abstraction. Modeling the context of a subsystem is therefore useful when you are building systems of interconnected systems.

Modeling the Requirements of a System

A requirement is a design feature, property, or behavior of a system. When you state a system's requirements, you are asserting a contract, established between those things that lie outside the system and the system itself, which declares what you expect that system to do. For the most part, you don't care how the system does it, you just care *that* it does it. A well-behaved system will carry out all its requirements faithfully, predictably, and reliably. When you build a system, it's important to start with agreement about what that system should do, although you will certainly evolve your understanding of those requirements as you iteratively and incrementally implement the system. Similarly, when you are handed a system to use, knowing how it behaves is essential to using it properly.

Notes can be used to state requirements, as discussed in Chapter 6.

Requirements can be expressed in various forms, from unstructured text to expressions in a formal language, and everything in between. Most, if not all, of a system's functional requirements can be expressed as use cases, and the UML's use case diagrams are essential for managing these requirements.

To model the requirements of a system,

- Establish the context of the system by identifying the actors that surround it.
- For each actor, consider the behavior that each expects or requires the system to provide.
- Name these common behaviors as use cases.
- Factor common behavior into new use cases that are used by others; factor variant behavior into new use cases that extend more main line flows.
- Model these use cases, actors, and their relationships in a use case diagram.
- Adorn these use cases with notes that assert nonfunctional requirements; you may have to attach some of these to the whole system.

Figure 17-3 expands on the previous use case diagram. Although it elides the relationships among the actors and the use cases, it adds additional use cases that are somewhat invisible to the average customer, yet are essential behaviors of the system. This diagram is valuable because it offers a common starting place for end users, domain experts, and developers to visualize, specify, construct, and document their decisions about the functional requirements of this system. For example, `Detect card fraud` is a behavior important to both the `Retail institution` and the `Sponsoring financial institution`. Similarly, `Report on account status` is another behavior required of the system by the various institutions in its context.

Modeling dynamics for load balancing and network reconfiguration are discussed in Chapter 23.

The requirement modeled by the use case `Manage network outage` is a bit different from all the others because it represents a secondary behavior of the system necessary for its reliable and continuous operation.

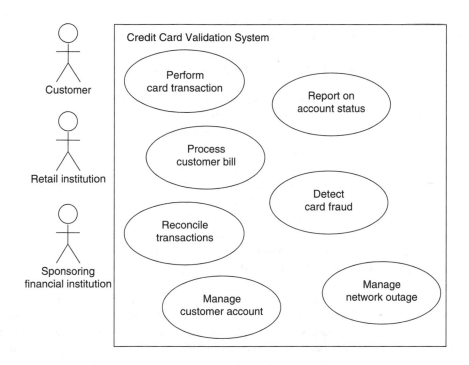

Figure 17-3: Modeling the Requirements of a System

*Subsystems
are discussed
in Chapter 31.*

This same technique applies to modeling the requirements of a subsystem.

Forward and Reverse Engineering

*Diagrams are
discussed in
Chapter 7; use
cases are
discussed in
Chapter 16.*

Most of the UML's other diagrams, including class, component, and statechart diagrams, are clear candidates for forward and reverse engineering because each has an analog in the executable system. Use case diagrams are a bit different in that they reflect rather than specify the implementation of a system, subsystem, or class. Use cases describe how an element behaves, not how that behavior is implemented, so it cannot be directly forward or reverse engineered.

Forward engineering is the process of transforming a model into code through a mapping to an implementation language. A use case diagram can be forward engineered to form tests for the element to which it applies. Each use case in a use case diagram specifies a flow of events (and variants of those flows), and these flows specify how the element is expected to behave—that's something worthy of testing. A well-structured use case will even specify pre- and post-conditions that can be used to define a test's initial state and its success criteria. For each use case in a use case diagram, you can create a test case that you can run every time you release a new version of that element, thereby confirming that it works as required before other elements rely on it.

To forward engineer a use case diagram,

- For each use case in the diagram, identify its flow of events and its exceptional flow of events.
- Depending on how deeply you choose to test, generate a test script for each flow, using the flow's preconditions as the test's initial state and its postconditions as its success criteria.
- As necessary, generate test scaffolding to represent each actor that interacts with the use case. Actors that push information to the element or are acted on by the element may either be simulated or substituted by its real-world equivalent.
- Use tools to run these tests each time you release the element to which the use case diagram applies.

Reverse engineering is the process of transforming code into a model through a mapping from a specific implementation language. Automatically reverse engineering a use case diagram is pretty much beyond the state of the art, simply because there is a loss of information when moving from a specification of how an element behaves to how it is implemented. However, you can study an existing system and discern its intended behavior by hand, which you can then put in the form of a use case diagram. Indeed, this is pretty much what you have to do anytime you are handed an undocumented body of software. The UML's use case diagrams simply give you a standard and expressive language in which to state what you discover.

To reverse engineer a use case diagram,

- Identify each actor that interacts with the system.
- For each actor, consider the manner in which that actor interacts with the system, changes the state of the system or its environment, or responds to some event.
- Trace the flow of events in the executable system relative to each actor. Start with primary flows and only later consider alternative paths.
- Cluster related flows by declaring a corresponding use case. Consider modeling variants using extend relationships, and consider modeling common flows by applying include relationships.
- Render these actors and use cases in a use case diagram, and establish their relationships.

Hints and Tips

When you create use case diagrams in the UML, remember that every use case diagram is just a graphical presentation of the static use case view of a system. This means that no single use case diagram need capture everything about a system's use case view. Collectively, all the use case diagrams of a system represent the system's complete static use case view; individually, each represents just one aspect.

A well-structured use case diagram

- Is focused on communicating one aspect of a system's static use case view.
- Contains only those use cases and actors that are essential to understanding that aspect.
- Provides detail consistent with its level of abstraction; you should expose only those adornments (such as extension points) that are essential to understanding.
- Is not so minimalist as to misinform the reader about semantics that are important.

When you draw a use case diagram,

- Give it a name that communicates its purpose.
- Lay out its elements to minimize lines that cross.
- Organize its elements spatially so that behaviors and roles that are semantically close are laid out physically close.
- Use notes and color as visual cues to draw attention to important features of your diagram.
- Try not to show too many kinds of relationships. In general, if you have complicated include and extend relationships, take these elements to another diagram.

Chapter 18

INTERACTION DIAGRAMS

In this chapter

- Modeling flows of control by time ordering
- Modeling flows of control by organization
- Forward and reverse engineering

Activity diagrams, statechart diagrams, and use case diagrams are three other kinds of diagrams used in the UML for modeling the dynamic aspects of systems; activity diagrams are discussed in Chapter 19; statechart diagrams are discussed in Chapter 24; use case diagrams are discussed in Chapter 17.

Sequence diagrams and collaboration diagrams—both of which are called interaction diagrams—are two of the five diagrams used in the UML for modeling the dynamic aspects of systems. An interaction diagram shows an interaction, consisting of a set of objects and their relationships, including the messages that may be dispatched among them. A sequence diagram is an interaction diagram that emphasizes the time ordering of messages; a collaboration diagram is an interaction diagram that emphasizes the structural organization of the objects that send and receive messages.

You use interaction diagrams to model the dynamic aspects of a system. For the most part, this involves modeling concrete or prototypical instances of classes, interfaces, components, and nodes, along with the messages that are dispatched among them, all in the context of a scenario that illustrates a behavior. Interaction diagrams may stand alone to visualize, specify, construct, and document the dynamics of a particular society of objects, or they may be used to model one particular flow of control of a use case.

Interaction diagrams are not only important for modeling the dynamic aspects of a system, but also for constructing executable systems through forward and reverse engineering.

Getting Started

When you watch a movie projected from film or broadcast on television, your mind actually plays tricks on you. Instead of seeing continuous motion as you would in live action, you really see a series of static images played back to you fast enough to give the illusion of continuous motion.

When directors and animators plan a film, they use the same technique but at lower fidelity. By storyboarding key frames, they build up a model of each scene, sufficient in detail to communicate the intent to all the stakeholders on the production team. In fact, creating this storyboard is a major activity in the production process, helping the team visualize, specify, construct, and document a model of the movie as it evolves from inception through construction and finally deployment.

Modeling the structural aspects of a system is discussed in Sections 2 and 3.

In modeling software-intensive systems, you have a similar problem: how do you model its dynamic aspects? Imagine, for a moment, how you might visualize a running system. If you have an interactive debugger attached to the system, you might be able to watch a section of memory and observe how it changes its contents over time. With a bit more focus, you might even monitor several objects of interest. Over time, you'd see the creation of some objects, changes in the value of their attributes, and then the destruction of some of them.

The value of visualizing the dynamic aspects of a system this way is quite limited, especially if you are talking about a distributed system with multiple concurrent flows of control. You might as well try to understand the human circulatory system by looking at the blood that passes through one point in one artery over time. A better way to model the dynamic aspects of a system is by building up storyboards of scenarios, involving the interaction of certain interesting objects and the messages that may be dispatched among them.

In the UML, you model these storyboards by using interaction diagrams. As Figure 18-1 shows, you can build up these storyboards in two ways: by emphasizing the time ordering of messages and by emphasizing the structural relationships among the objects that interact. Either way, the diagrams are semantically equivalent; you can convert one to the other without loss of information.

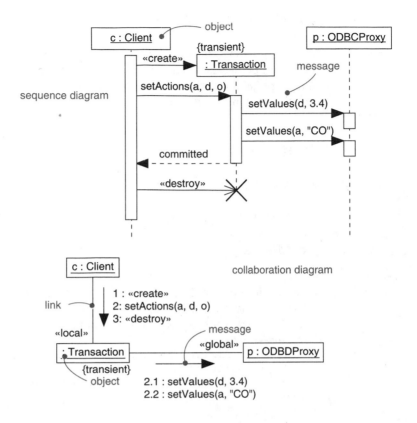

Figure 18-1: Interaction Diagrams

Terms and Concepts

An *interaction diagram* shows an interaction, consisting of a set of objects and their relationships, including the messages that may be dispatched among them. A *sequence diagram* is an interaction diagram that emphasizes the time ordering of messages. Graphically, a sequence diagram is a table that shows objects arranged along the X axis and messages, ordered in increasing time, along the Y axis. A *collaboration diagram* is an interaction diagram that emphasizes the structural organization of the objects that send and receive messages. Graphically, a collaboration diagram is a collection of vertices and arcs.

Common Properties

The general properties of diagrams are discussed in Chapter 7.

An interaction diagram is just a special kind of diagram and shares the same common properties as do all other diagrams—a name and graphical contents that are a projection into a model. What distinguishes an interaction diagram from all other kinds of diagrams is its particular content.

Contents

Objects are discussed in Chapter 13; links are discussed in Chapters 14 and 15; messages are discussed in Chapter 15; interactions are discussed in Chapter 15.

Interaction diagrams commonly contain

- Objects
- Links
- Messages

Note: An interaction diagram is basically a projection of the elements found in an interaction. The semantics of an interaction's context, objects and roles, links, messages, and sequencing apply to interaction diagrams.

Like all other diagrams, interaction diagrams may contain notes and constraints.

Sequence Diagrams

A sequence diagram emphasizes the time ordering of messages. As Figure 18-2 shows, you form a sequence diagram by first placing the objects that participate in the interaction at the top of your diagram, across the X axis. Typically, you place the object that initiates the interaction at the left, and increasingly more subordinate objects to the right. Next, you place the messages that these objects send and receive along the Y axis, in order of increasing time from top to bottom. This gives the reader a clear visual cue to the flow of control over time.

Sequence diagrams have two features that distinguish them from collaboration diagrams.

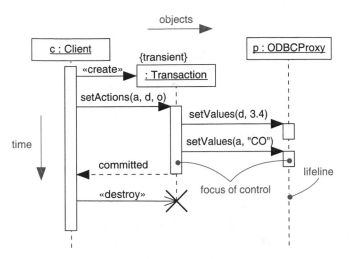

Figure 18-2: Sequence Diagram

*You can spec-
ify the vitality
of an object or
a link by
marking it with
a new,
destroyed,
or tran-
sient con-
straint, as
discussed in
Chapter 15;
representing
the changing
values, state,
and roles of an
object is
discussed in
Chapter 13.*

First, there is the object lifeline. An object lifeline is the vertical dashed line that represents the existence of an object over a period of time. Most objects that appear in an interaction diagram will be in existence for the duration of the interaction, so these objects are all aligned at the top of the diagram, with their lifelines drawn from the top of the diagram to the bottom. Objects may be created during the interaction. Their lifelines start with the receipt of the message stereotyped as `create`. Objects may be destroyed during the interaction. Their lifelines end with the receipt of the message stereotyped as `destroy` (and are given the visual cue of a large X, marking the end of their lives).

> **Note:** If an object changes the values of its attributes, its state, or its roles, you can place a copy of the object icon on its lifeline at the point the change occurs, showing those modifications.

Second, there is the focus of control. The focus of control is a tall, thin rectangle that shows the period of time during which an object is performing an action, either directly or through a subordinate procedure. The top of the rectangle is aligned with the start of the action; the bottom is aligned with its completion (and can be marked by a return message). You can show the nesting of a focus of control (caused by recursion, a call to a self-operation, or by a callback from another object) by stacking another focus of control slightly to the right of its parent (and can do so to an arbitrary depth). If you want to be especially precise about where the focus of control lies, you can also shade the region of the rectangle during which the object's method is actually computing (and control has not passed to another object).

Note: Unlike a sequence diagram, you don't show the lifeline of an object explicitly in a collaboration diagram, although you can show both `create` and `destroy` messages. In addition, you don't show the focus of control explicitly in a collaboration diagram, although each message's sequence number can indicate nesting.

Collaboration Diagrams

A collaboration diagram emphasizes the organization of the objects that participate in an interaction. As Figure 18-3 shows, you form a collaboration diagram by first placing the objects that participate in the interaction as the vertices in a graph. Next, you render the links that connect these objects as the arcs of this graph. Finally, you adorn these links with the messages that objects send and receive. This gives the reader a clear visual cue to the flow of control in the context of the structural organization of objects that collaborate.

Figure 18-3: Collaboration Diagram

Collaboration diagrams have two features that distinguish them from sequence diagrams.

First, there is the path. To indicate how one object is linked to another, you can attach a path stereotype to the far end of a link (such as «`local`», indicating that the designated object is local to the sender). Typically, you will only need to render the path of the link explicitly for `local`, `parameter`, `global`, and `self` (but not `association`) paths.

You can use an advanced form of sequence numbers to distinguish concurrent flows of control, as discussed in Chapter 22; path stereotypes are discussed in Chapter 17; complex branching and iteration can be more easily specified in activity diagrams, as discussed in Chapter 19.

Second, there is the sequence number. To indicate the time order of a message, you prefix the message with a number (starting with the message numbered 1), increasing monotonically for each new message in the flow of control (2, 3, and so on). To show nesting, you use Dewey decimal numbering (1 is the first message; 1.1 is the first message nested in message 1; 1.2 is the second message nested in message 1; and so on). You can show nesting to an arbitrary depth. Note also that, along the same link, you can show many messages (possibly being sent from different directions), and each will have a unique sequence number.

Most of the time, you'll model straight, sequential flows of control. However, you can also model more-complex flows, involving iteration and branching. An iteration represents a repeated sequence of messages. To model an iteration, you prefix the sequence number of a message with an iteration expression such as *[i := 1..n] (or just * if you want to indicate iteration but don't want to specify its details). An iteration indicates that the message (and any nested messages) will be repeated in accordance with the given expression. Similarly, a condition represents a message whose execution is contingent on the evaluation of a Boolean condition. To model a condition, you prefix the sequence number of a message with a condition clause, such as [x > 0]. The alternate paths of a branch will have the same sequence number, but each path must be uniquely distinguishable by a nonoverlapping condition.

For both iteration and branching, the UML does not prescribe the format of the expression inside the brackets; you can use pseudocode or the syntax of a specific programming language.

Note: You don't show the links among objects explicitly in a sequence diagram. You don't show the sequence number of a message in a sequence diagram explicitly either: it is implicit in the physical ordering of messages from top to bottom of the diagram. You can show iteration and branching, however. In a sequence diagram, the alternative paths of a branch are rendered by separate messages branching from the same point. Pragmatically, you can show only simple branching in sequence diagrams; you can show more complex branching in collaboration diagrams.

Semantic Equivalence

Because they both derive from the same information in the UML's metamodel, sequence diagrams and collaboration diagrams are semantically equivalent. As a result, you can take a diagram in one form and convert it to the other without any loss of information, as you can see in the previous two figures, which are semantically equivalent. However, this does not mean that both diagrams will explicitly visualize the same information. For example, in the previous two figures, the collaboration diagram shows how the objects are linked (note the «local» and «global» stereotypes), whereas the corresponding sequence diagram does not. Similarly, the sequence diagram shows message return (note the return value committed), but the corresponding collaboration diagram does not. In both cases, the two diagrams share the same underlying model, but each may render some things the other does not.

Common Uses

The five views of an architecture are discussed in Chapter 2; instances are discussed in Chapter 13; classes are discussed in Chapters 4 and 9; active classes are discussed in Chapter 22; interfaces are discussed in Chapter 11; components are discussed in Chapter 25; nodes are discussed in Chapter 26; systems and subsystems are discussed in Chapter 31; operations are discussed in Chapters 4 and 9; use cases are discussed in Chapter 16; collaborations are discussed in Chapter 27.

You use interaction diagrams to model the dynamic aspects of a system. These dynamic aspects may involve the interaction of any kind of instance in any view of a system's architecture, including instances of classes (including active classes), interfaces, components, and nodes.

When you use an interaction diagram to model some dynamic aspect of a system, you do so in the context of the system as a whole, a subsystem, an operation, or a class. You can also attach interaction diagrams to use cases (to model a scenario) and to collaborations (to model the dynamic aspects of a society of objects).

When you model the dynamic aspects of a system, you typically use interaction diagrams in two ways.

1. To model flows of control by time ordering

Here you'll use sequence diagrams. Modeling a flow of control by time ordering emphasizes the passing of messages as they unfold over time, which is a particularly useful way to visualize dynamic behavior in the context of a use case scenario. Sequence diagrams do a better job of visualizing simple iteration and branching than do collaboration diagrams.

2. To model flows of control by organization

Here you'll use collaboration diagrams. Modeling a flow of control by organization emphasizes the structural relationships among the instances in the interaction, along which messages may be passed. Collaboration diagrams do a better job of visualizing complex iteration and branching and of visualizing multiple concurrent flows of control than do sequence diagrams.

Common Modeling Techniques

Modeling Flows of Control by Time Ordering

Systems and subsystems are discussed in Chapter 31; operations and classes are discussed in Chapters 4 and 9; use cases are discussed in Chapter 16; collaborations are discussed in Chapter 27.

Consider the objects that live in the context of a system, subsystem, operation or class. Consider also the objects and roles that participate in a use case or collaboration. To model a flow of control that winds through these objects and roles, you use an interaction diagram; to emphasize the passing of messages as they unfold over time, you use a sequence diagram, a kind of interaction diagram.

To model a flow of control by time ordering,

- Set the context for the interaction, whether it is a system, subsystem, operation, or class, or one scenario of a use case or collaboration.
- Set the stage for the interaction by identifying which objects play a role in the interaction. Lay them out on the sequence diagram from left to right, placing the more important objects to the left and their neighboring objects to the right.
- Set the lifeline for each object. In most cases, objects will persist through the entire interaction. For those objects that are created and destroyed during the interaction, set their lifelines, as appropriate, and explicitly indicate their birth and death with appropriately stereotyped messages.
- Starting with the message that initiates this interaction, lay out each subsequent message from top to bottom between the lifelines, showing each message's properties (such as its parameters), as necessary to explain the semantics of the interaction.
- If you need to visualize the nesting of messages or the points in time when actual computation is taking place, adorn each object's lifeline with its focus of control.

Timing marks are discussed in Chapter 23; pre- and post-conditions are discussed in Chapter 4; packages are discussed in Chapter 12.

- If you need to specify time or space constraints, adorn each message with a timing mark and attach suitable time or space constraints.
- If you need to specify this flow of control more formally, attach pre- and postconditions to each message.

A single sequence diagram can show only one flow of control (although you can show simple variations by using the UML's notation for iteration and branching). Typically, you'll have a number of interaction diagrams, some of which are primary and others that show alternative paths or exceptional conditions. You can use packages to organize these collections of sequence diagrams, giving each diagram a suitable name to distinguish it from its siblings.

Signals are discussed in Chapter 20; timing marks are discussed in Chapter 23; constraints are discussed in Chapter 6; responsibilities are discussed in Chapter 4; notes are discussed in Chapter 6.

For example, Figure 18-4 shows a sequence diagram that specifies the flow of control involved in initiating a simple, two-party phone call. At this level of abstraction, there are four objects involved: two Callers (s and r), an unnamed telephone Switch, and c, the reification of the Conversation between the two parties. The sequence begins with one Caller (s) dispatching a signal (liftReceiver) to the Switch object. In turn, the Switch calls setDialTone on the Caller, and the Caller iterates on the message dialDigit. Note that this message has a timing mark (dialing) that is used in a timing constraint (its executionTime must be less than 30 seconds). This diagram does not indicate what happens if this time constraint is violated. For that you could include a branch or a completely separate sequence diagram. The Switch object then calls itself with the message routeCall. It then creates a Conversation object (c), to which it delegates the rest of the work. Although not shown in this interaction, c would have the additional responsibility of being a party in the switch's billing mechanism (which would be expressed in another interaction diagram). The Conversation object (c) rings the Caller (r), who asynchronously sends the message liftReceiver. The Conversation object then tells the Switch to connect the call, then tells both Caller objects to connect, after which they may exchange information, as indicated by the attached note.

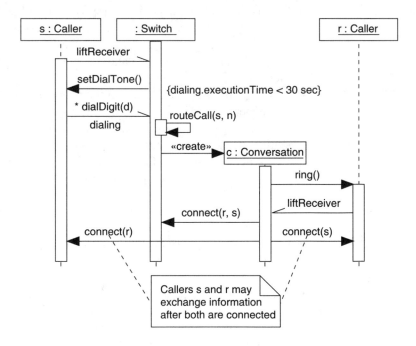

Figure 18-4: Modeling Flows of Control by Time Ordering

Note: In sequence diagrams, you may want to model the changing state, role, or attributes values of an object. There are two ways to do this. First, the object may appear multiple times in the diagram, each showing different state, role, or attribute values, and then you use a transition stereotyped as `become` to indicate its change. Second, for changing state, you can place a state icon directly on the object's lifeline.

An interaction diagram can begin or end at any point of a sequence. A complete trace of the flow of control would be incredibly complex, so it's reasonable to break up parts of a larger flow into separate diagrams.

Modeling Flows of Control by Organization

Systems and subsystems are discussed in Chapter 31; operations and classes are discussed in Chapters 4 and 9; use cases are discussed in Chapter 16; collaborations are discussed in Chapter 27.

Consider the objects that live in the context of a system, subsystem, operation, or class. Consider also the objects and roles that participate in a use case or collaboration. To model a flow of control that winds through these objects and roles, you use an interaction diagram; to show the passing of messages in the context of that structure, you use a collaboration diagram, a kind of interaction diagram.

To model a flow of control by organization,

Dependency relationships are discussed in Chapters 5 and 10; `become` and `copy` are discussed in Chapter 13; path stereotypes are discussed in Chapter 15.

- Set the context for the interaction, whether it is a system, subsystem, operation, or class, or one scenario of a use case or collaboration.
- Set the stage for the interaction by identifying which objects play a role in the interaction. Lay them out on the collaboration diagram as vertices in a graph, placing the more important objects in the center of the diagram and their neighboring objects to the outside.
- Set the initial properties of each of these objects. If the attribute values, tagged values, state, or role of any object changes in significant ways over the duration of the interaction, place a duplicate object on the diagram, update it with these new values, and connect them by a message stereotyped as `become` or `copy` (with a suitable sequence number).
- Specify the links among these objects, along which messages may pass.
  1. Lay out the association links first; these are the most important ones, because they represent structural connections.
  2. Lay out other links next, and adorn them with suitable path stereotypes (such as `global` and `local`) to explicitly specify how these objects are related to one another.
- Starting with the message that initiates this interaction, attach each subsequent message to the appropriate link, setting its sequence number, as appropriate. Show nesting by using Dewey decimal numbering.

Timing marks are discussed in Chapter 23; pre- and post-conditions are discussed in Chapter 4; packages are discussed in Chapter 12.

- If you need to specify time or space constraints, adorn each message with a timing mark and attach suitable time or space constraints.
- If you need to specify this flow of control more formally, attach pre- and postconditions to each message.

As with sequence diagrams, a single collaboration diagram can show only one flow of control (although you can show simple variations by using the UML's notation for interaction and branching). Typically, you'll have a number of such interaction diagrams, some of which are primary and others that show alternative paths or exceptional conditions. You can use packages to organize these collections of collaboration diagrams, giving each diagram a suitable name to distinguish it from its siblings.

For example, Figure 18-5 shows a collaboration diagram that specifies the flow of control involved in registering a new student at a school, with an emphasis on the structural relationships among these objects. You see five objects: a RegistrarAgent (r), a Student (s), two Course objects (c1 and c2), and an unnamed School object. The flow of control is numbered explicitly. Action begins with the RegistrarAgent creating a Student object, adding the student to the school (the message addStudent), then telling the Student object to register itself. The Student object then invokes getSchedule on itself, presumably obtaining the Course objects for which it must register. The Student object then adds itself to each Course object. The flow ends with s rendered again, showing that it has an updated value for its registered attribute.

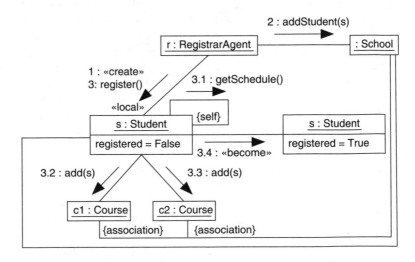

Figure 18-5: Modeling Flows of Control by Organization

Note that this diagram shows a link between the School object and the two Course objects, plus another link between the School object and the Student object, although no messages are shown along these paths. These links help explain how the Student object can see the two Course objects to which it adds itself. s, c1, and c2 are linked to the School via association, so s can find c1 and c2 during its call to getSchedule (which might return a collection of Course objects), indirectly through the School object.

Forward and Reverse Engineering

Forward engineering (the creation of code from a model) is possible for both sequence and collaboration diagrams, especially if the context of the diagram is an operation. For example, using the previous collaboration diagram, a reasonably clever forward engineering tool could generate the following Java code for the operation register, attached to the Student class.

```
public void register() {
  CourseCollection c = getSchedule();
  for (int i = 0; i < c.size(); i++)
    c.item(i).add(this);
  this.registered = true;
}
```

"Reasonably clever" means the tool would have to realize that getSchedule returns a CourseCollection object, which it could determine by looking at the operation's signature. By walking across the contents of this object using a standard iteration idiom (which the tool could know about implicitly), the code could then generalize to any number of course offerings.

Reverse engineering (the creation of a model from code) is also possible for both sequence and collaboration diagrams, especially if the context of the code is the body of an operation. Segments of the previous diagram could have been produced by a tool from a prototypical execution of the register operation.

Note: Forward engineering is straightforward; reverse engineering is hard. It's easy to get too much information from simple reverse engineering, and so the hard part is being clever about what details to keep.

However, more interesting than the reverse engineering of a model from code is the animation of a model against the execution of a deployed system. For example, given the previous diagram, a tool could animate the messages in the diagram as they were dispatched in a running system. Even better, with this tool under the control of a debugger, you could control the speed of execution, possibly setting breakpoints to stop the action at interesting points to examine the attribute values of individual objects.

Hints and Tips

When you create interaction diagrams in the UML, remember that sequence diagrams and collaboration diagrams are both projections on the same model of a system's dynamic aspects. No single interaction diagram can capture everything about a system's dynamic aspects. Rather, you'll want to use many interaction diagrams to model the dynamics of the system as a whole, as well as its subsystems, operations, classes, use cases, and collaborations.

A well-structured interaction diagram

- Is focused on communicating one aspect of a system's dynamics.
- Contains only those elements that are essential to understanding that aspect.
- Provides detail consistent with its level of abstraction and should expose only those adornments that are essential to understanding.
- Is not so minimalist that it misinforms the reader about semantics that are important.

When you draw an interaction diagram,

- Give it a name that communicates its purpose.
- Use a sequence diagram if you want to emphasize the time ordering of messages. Use a collaboration diagram if you want to emphasize the organization of the objects involved in the interaction.
- Lay out its elements to minimize lines that cross.
- Use notes and color as visual cues to draw attention to important features of your diagram.
- Use branching sparingly; you can represent complex branching much better using activity diagrams.

Chapter 19
ACTIVITY DIAGRAMS

In this chapter

- Modeling a workflow
- Modeling an operation
- Forward and reverse engineering

Sequence diagrams, collaboration diagrams, statechart diagrams, and use case diagrams also model the dynamic aspects of systems; sequence and collaboration diagrams are discussed in Chapter 18; statechart diagrams are discussed in Chapter 24; use case diagrams are discussed in Chapter 17; actions are discussed in Chapter 15.

Activity diagrams are one of the five diagrams in the UML for modeling the dynamic aspects of systems. An activity diagram is essentially a flowchart, showing flow of control from activity to activity.

You use activity diagrams to model the dynamic aspects of a system. For the most part, this involves modeling the sequential (and possibly concurrent) steps in a computational process. With an activity diagram, you can also model the flow of an object as it moves from state to state at different points in the flow of control. Activity diagrams may stand alone to visualize, specify, construct, and document the dynamics of a society of objects, or they may be used to model the flow of control of an operation. Whereas interaction diagrams emphasize the flow of control from object to object, activity diagrams emphasize the flow of control from activity to activity. An activity is an ongoing nonatomic execution within a state machine. Activities ultimately result in some action, which is made up of executable atomic computations that results in a change in state of the system or the return of a value.

Activity diagrams are not only important for modeling the dynamic aspects of a system, but also for constructing executable systems through forward and reverse engineering.

Getting Started

Consider the workflow associated with building a house. First, you select a site. Next, you commission an architect to design your house. After you've settled on the plan, your developer asks for bids to price the house. Once you agree on a price and a plan, construction can begin. Permits are secured, ground is broken, the foundation is poured, the framing is erected, and so on, until everything is done. You're then handed the keys and a certificate of occupancy, and you take possession of the house.

Although that's a tremendous simplification of what really goes on in a construction process, it does capture the critical path of the workflow. In a real project, there are lots of parallel activities among various trades. Electricians can be working at the same time as plumbers and carpenters, for example. You'll also encounter conditions and branches. For example, depending on the result of soils tests, you might have to blast, dig, or float. There might even be loops. For example, a building inspection might reveal code violations that result in scrap and rework.

In the construction industry, such techniques as Gantt charts and Pert charts are commonly used for visualizing, specifying, constructing, and documenting the workflow of the project.

Modeling the structural aspects of a system is discussed in Sections 2 and 3; interaction diagrams are discussed in Chapter 18.

In modeling software-intensive systems, you have a similar problem. How do you best model a workflow or an operation, both of which are aspects of the system's dynamics? The answer is that you have two basic choices, similar to the use of Gantt charts and Pert charts.

On the one hand, you can build up storyboards of scenarios, involving the interaction of certain interesting objects and the messages that may be dispatched among them. In the UML, you can model these storyboards in two ways: by emphasizing the time ordering of messages (using sequence diagrams) or by emphasizing the structural relationships among the objects that interact (using collaboration diagrams). Interaction diagrams such as these are akin to Gantt charts, which focus on the objects (resources) that carry out some activity over time.

Actions are discussed in Chapter 15.

On the other hand, you can model these dynamic aspects using activity diagrams, which focus first on the activities that take place among objects, as Figure 19-1 shows. In that regard, activity diagrams are akin to Pert charts. An activity diagram is essentially a <u>flowchart that emphasizes the activity that takes place over time</u>. You can think of an activity diagram as an interaction diagram turned inside out. An interaction diagram looks at the objects that pass messages; an activity diagram looks at the operations that are passed among objects. The semantic difference is subtle, but it results in a very different way of looking at the world.

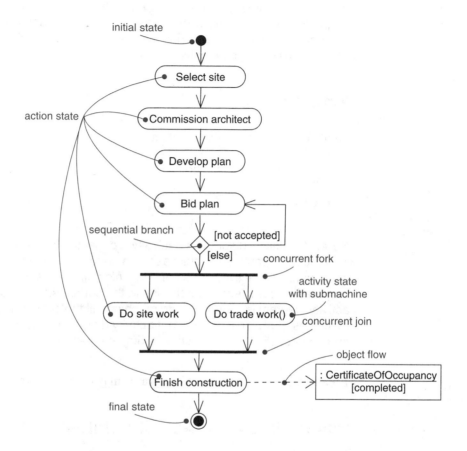

Figure 19-1: Activity Diagrams

Terms and Concepts

An *activity diagram* shows the flow from activity to activity. An *activity* is an ongoing nonatomic execution within a state machine. Activities ultimately result in some *action*, which is made up of executable atomic computations that result in a change in state of the system or the return of a value. Actions encompass calling another operation, sending a signal, creating or destroying an object, or some pure computation, such as evaluating an expression. Graphically, an activity diagram is a collection of vertices and arcs.

Common Properties

The general properties of diagrams are discussed in Chapter 7.

An activity diagram is just a special kind of diagram and shares the same common properties as do all other diagrams—a name and graphical contents that are a projection into a model. What distinguishes an interaction diagram from all other kinds of diagrams is its content.

Contents

States, transitions, and state machines are discussed in Chapter 21; objects are discussed in Chapter 13.

Activity diagrams commonly contain

- Activity states and action states
- Transitions
- Objects

Note: An activity diagram is basically a projection of the elements found in an activity graph, a special case of a state machine in which all or most states are activity states and in which all or most transitions are triggered by completion of activities in the source state. Because an activity diagram is a kind of state machine, all the characteristics of state machines apply. That means that activity diagrams may contain simple and composite states, branches, forks, and joins.

Like all other diagrams, activity diagrams may contain notes and constraints.

Action States and Activity States

Attributes and operations are discussed in Chapters 4 and 9; signals are discussed in Chapter 20; creation and destruction of objects are discussed in Chapter 15; states and state machines are discussed in Chapter 21.

In the flow of control modeled by an activity diagram, things happen. You might evaluate some expression that sets the value of an attribute or that returns some value. Alternately, you might call an operation on an object, send a signal to an object, or even create or destroy an object. These executable, atomic computations are called action states because they are states of the system, each representing the execution of an action. As Figure 19-2 shows, you represent an action state using a lozenge shape (a symbol with horizontal top and bottom and convex sides). Inside that shape, you may write any expression.

Note: The UML does not prescribe the language of these expressions. Abstractly, you might just use structured text; more concretely, you might use the syntax and semantics of a specific programming language.

Action states can't be decomposed. Furthermore, action states are atomic, meaning that events may occur, but the work of the action state is not interrupted. Finally, the work of an action state is generally considered to take insignificant execution time.

Figure 19-2: Action States

Modeling time and space is discussed in Chapter 23.

Note: In the real world, of course, every computation takes some amount of time and space. Especially for hard real time systems, it's important that you model these properties.

State machines, the parts of a state (including entry and exit actions) and submachines are discussed in Chapter 21.

In contrast, activity states can be further decomposed, their activity being represented by other activity diagrams. Furthermore, activity states are not atomic, meaning that they may be interrupted and, in general, are considered to take some duration to complete. You can think of an action state as a special case of an activity state. An action state is an activity state that cannot be further decomposed. Similarly, you can think of an activity state as a composite, whose flow of control is made up of other activity states and action states. Zoom into the details of an activity state, and you'll find another activity diagram. As Figure 19-3 shows, there's no notational distinction between action and activity states, except that an activity state may have additional parts, such as entry and exit actions (actions which are involved on entering and leaving the state, respectively) and submachine specifications.

Figure 19-3: Activity States

Note: Action states and activity states are just special kinds of states in a state machine. When you enter an action or activity state, you simply perform the action or the activity; when you finish, control passes to the next action or activity. Activity states are somewhat of a shorthand, therefore. An activity state is semantically equivalent to expanding its activity graph (and transitively so) in place until you only see actions. Nonetheless, activity states are important because they help you break complex computations into parts, in the same manner as you use operations to group and reuse expressions.

Transitions

Transitions are discussed in Chapter 21.

When the action or activity of a state completes, flow of control passes immediately to the next action or activity state. You specify this flow by using transitions to show the path from one action or activity state to the next action or activity state. In the UML, you represent a transition as a simple directed line, as Figure 19-4 shows.

Triggerless transitions may have guard conditions, meaning that such a transition will fire only if that condition is met; guard conditions are discussed in Chapter 21.

Note: Semantically, these are called triggerless, or completion, transitions because control passes immediately once the work of the source state is done. Once the action of a given source state completes, you execute that state's exit action (if any). Next, and without delay, control follows the transition and passes on to the next action or activity state. You execute that state's entry action (if any), then you perform the action or activity of the target state, again following the next transition once that state's work is done. This flow of control continues indefinitely (in the case of an infinite activity) or until you encounter a stop state.

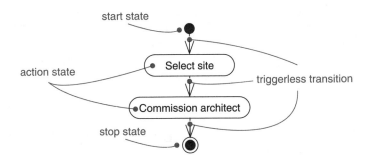

Figure 19-4: Triggerless Transitions

Indeed, a flow of control has to start and end someplace (unless, of course, it's an infinite flow, in which case it will have a beginning but no end). Therefore, as the figure shows, you may specify this initial state (a solid ball) and stop state (a solid ball inside a circle).

Branching

Branches are a notational convenience, semantically equivalent to multiple transitions with guards, as discussed in Chapter 21.

Simple, sequential transitions are common, but they aren't the only kind of path you'll need to model a flow of control. As in a flowchart, you can include a branch, which specifies alternate paths taken based on some Boolean expression. As Figure 19-5 shows, you represent a branch as a diamond. A branch may have one incoming transition and two or more outgoing ones. On each outgoing transition, you place a Boolean expression, which is evaluated only once on entering the branch. Across all these outgoing transitions, guards should not overlap (otherwise, the flow of control would be ambiguous), but they should cover all possibilities (otherwise, the flow of control would freeze).

As a convenience, you can use the keyword `else` to mark one outgoing transition, representing the path taken if no other guard expression evaluates to true.

Figure 19-5: Branching

Branching and iteration are possible in interaction diagrams, as discussed in Chapter 18.

You can achieve the effect of iteration by using one action state that sets the value of an iterator, another action state that increments the iterator, and a branch that evaluates if the iteration is finished.

Note: The UML does not prescribe the language of these expressions. Abstractly, you might just use structured text; more concretely, you might use the syntax and semantics of a specific programming language.

Forking and Joining

Each concurrent flow of control lives in the context of an independent active object, which is typically modeled as either a process or a thread, as discussed in Chapter 22; nodes are discussed in Chapter 26.

Simple and branching sequential transitions are the most common paths you'll find in activity diagrams. However—especially when you are modeling work-flows of business processes—you might encounter flows that are concurrent. In the UML, you use a synchronization bar to specify the forking and joining of these parallel flows of control. A synchronization bar is rendered as a thick horizontal or vertical line.

For example, consider the concurrent flows involved in controlling an audio-animatronic device that mimics human speech and gestures. As Figure 19-6 shows, a fork represents the splitting of a single flow of control into two or more concurrent flows of control. A fork may have one incoming transition and two or more outgoing transitions, each of which represents an independent flow of control. Below the fork, the activities associated with each of these paths continues in parallel. Conceptually, the activities of each of these flows are truly concurrent, although, in a running system, these flows may be either truly concurrent (in the case of a system deployed across multiple nodes) or sequential yet interleaved (in the case of a system deployed across one node), thus giving only the illusion of true concurrency.

As the figure also shows, a join represents the synchronization of two or more concurrent flows of control. A join may have two or more incoming transitions and one outgoing transition. Above the join, the activities associated with each of these paths continues in parallel. At the join, the concurrent flows synchro-nize, meaning that each waits until all incoming flows have reached the join, at which point one flow of control continues on below the join.

Active objects are discussed in Chapter 22; signals are discussed in Chapter 20.

Note: Joins and forks should balance, meaning that the number of flows that leave a fork should match the number of flows that enter its corre-sponding join. Also, activities that are in parallel flows of control may communicate with one another by sending signals. This style of commu-nicating sequential processes is called a coroutine. Most of the time, you model this style of communication using active objects. You can also model the sending of and response to these signals in the submachines associated with each communicating activity state. For example, sup-pose the activity `Stream audio` needed to tell the activity `Synch mouth` when important pauses and intonations occurred. In the state machine for `Stream audio`, you'd see signals sent to the state machine for `Synch mouth`. Similarly, in the state machine for `Synch mouth`, you'd see transitions triggered by these same signals, to which the `Synch mouth` state machine would respond.

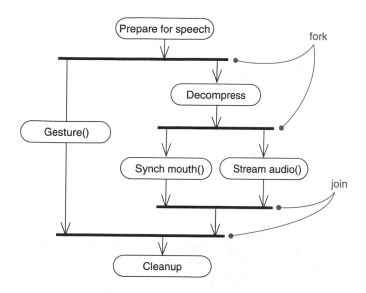

Figure 19-6: Forking and Joining

Swimlanes

You'll find it useful, especially when you are modeling workflows of business processes, to partition the activity states on an activity diagram into groups, each group representing the business organization responsible for those activities. In the UML, each group is called a swimlane because, visually, each group is divided from its neighbor by a vertical solid line, as shown in Figure 19-7. A swimlane specifies a locus of activities.

A swimlane is a kind of package; packages are discussed in Chapter 12; classes are discussed in Chapters 4 and 9; processes and threads are discussed in Chapter 22.

Each swimlane has a name unique within its diagram. A swimlane really has no deep semantics, except that it may represent some real-world entity. Each swimlane represents a high-level responsibility for part of the overall activity of an activity diagram, and each swimlane may eventually be implemented by one or more classes. In an activity diagram partitioned into swimlanes, every activity belongs to exactly one swimlane, but transitions may cross lanes.

Note: There's a loose connection between swimlanes and concurrent flows of control. Conceptually, the activities of each swimlane are generally—but not always—considered separate from the activities of neighboring swimlanes. That makes sense because, in the real world, the business organizations that generally map to these swimlanes are independent and concurrent.

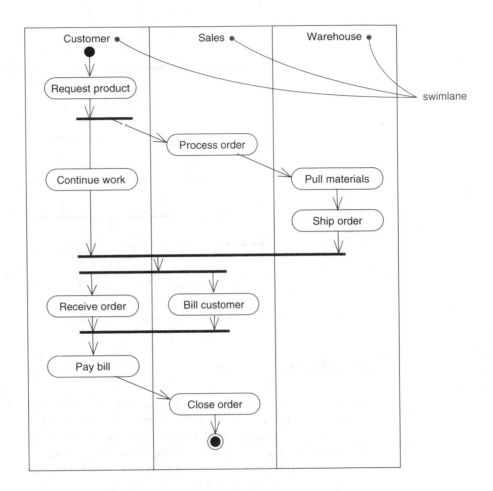

Figure 19-7: Swimlanes

Object Flow

Objects are discussed in Chapter 13; modeling the vocabulary of a system is discussed in Chapter 4.

Objects may be involved in the flow of control associated with an activity diagram. For example, in the workflow of processing an order as in the previous figure, the vocabulary of your problem space will also include such classes as `Order` and `Bill`. Instances of these two classes will be produced by certain activities (`Process order` will create an `Order` object, for example); other activities may modify these objects (for example, `Ship order` will change the state of the `Order` object to `filled`).

Dependency relationships are discussed in Chapters 5 and 10.

As Figure 19-8 shows, you can specify the things that are involved in an activity diagram by placing these objects in the diagram, connected using a dependency to the activity or transition that creates, destroys, or modifies them. This use of dependency relationships and objects is called an object flow because it represents the participation of an object in a flow of control.

The values and state of an object are discussed in Chapter 13; attributes are discussed in Chapters 4 and 9.

In addition to showing the flow of an object through an activity diagram, you can also show how its role, state and attribute values change. As shown in the figure, you represent the state of an object by naming its state in brackets below the object's name. Similarly, you can represent the value of an object's attributes by rendering them in a compartment below the object's name.

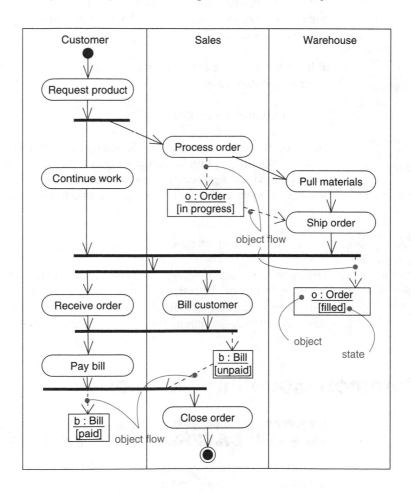

Figure 19-8: Object Flow

Common Uses

The five views of an architecture are discussed in Chapter 2; classes are discussed in Chapters 4 and 9; active classes are discussed in Chapter 22; interfaces are discussed in Chapter 11; components are discussed in Chapter 25; nodes are discussed in Chapter 26; systems and subsystems are discussed in Chapter 31; operations are discussed in Chapters 4 and 9; use cases and actors are discussed in Chapter 16.

You use activity diagrams to model the dynamic aspects of a system. These dynamic aspects may involve the activity of any kind of abstraction in any view of a system's architecture, including classes (which includes active classes), interfaces, components, and nodes.

When you use an activity diagram to model some dynamic aspect of a system, you can do so in the context of virtually any modeling element. Typically, however, you'll use activity diagrams in the context of the system as a whole, a subsystem, an operation, or a class. You can also attach activity diagrams to use cases (to model a scenario) and to collaborations (to model the dynamic aspects of a society of objects).

When you model the dynamic aspects of a system, you'll typically use activity diagrams in two ways.

1. To model a workflow

Here you'll focus on activities as viewed by the actors that collaborate with the system. Workflows often lie on the fringe of software-intensive systems and are used to visualize, specify, construct, and document business processes that involve the system you are developing. In this use of activity diagrams, modeling object flow is particularly important.

2. To model an operation

Here you'll use activity diagrams as flowcharts, to model the details of a computation. In this use of activity diagrams, the modeling of branch, fork, and join states is particularly important. The context of an activity diagram used in this way involves the parameters of the operation and its local objects.

Common Modeling Techniques

Modeling a Workflow

Modeling the context of a system is discussed in Chapter 17.

No software-intensive system exists in isolation; there's always some context in which a system lives, and that context always encompasses actors that interact with the system. Especially for mission critical, enterprise software, you'll find automated systems working in the context of higher-level business processes. These business processes are kinds of workflows because they represent the flow of work and objects through the business. For example, in a retail business, you'll have some automated systems (for example, point-of-sale systems that interact with marketing and warehouse systems), as well as human systems (the people that work at each retail outlet, as well as the tele-sales, marketing, buying, and shipping departments). You can model the business processes for the way these various automated and human systems collaborate by using activity diagrams.

To model a workflow,

Modeling the vocabulary of a system is discussed in Chapter 4; preconditions and postconditions are discussed in Chapter 9.

- Establish a focus for the workflow. For nontrivial systems, it's impossible to show all interesting workflows in one diagram.
- Select the business objects that have the high-level responsibilities for parts of the overall workflow. These may be real things from the vocabulary of the system, or they may be more abstract. In either case, create a swimlane for each important business object.
- Identify the preconditions of the workflow's initial state and the post-conditions of the workflow's final state. This is important in helping you model the boundaries of the workflow.
- Beginning at the workflow's initial state, specify the activities and actions that take place over time and render them in the activity diagram as either activity states or action states.
- For complicated actions, or for sets of actions that appear multiple times, collapse these into activity states, and provide a separate activity diagram that expands on each.
- Render the transitions that connect these activity and action states. Start with the sequential flows in the workflow first, next consider branching, and only then consider forking and joining.
- If there are important objects that are involved in the workflow, render them in the activity diagram, as well. Show their changing values and state as necessary to communicate the intent of the object flow.

For example, Figure 19-9 shows an activity diagram for a retail business, which specifies the workflow involved when a customer returns an item from a mail order. Work starts with the `Customer` action `Request return` and then flows through `Telesales` (`Get return number`), back to the `Customer` (`Ship item`), then to the `Warehouse` (`Receive item` then `Restock item`), finally ending in `Accounting` (`Credit account`). As the diagram indicates, one significant object (`i`, an instance of `Item`) also flows the process, changing from the `returned` to the `available` state.

> **Note:** Workflows are most often business processes, but not always.
> For example, you can also use activity diagrams to specify software
> development processes, such as your process for configuration man-
> agement. Furthermore, you can use activity diagrams to model nonsoft-
> ware systems, such as the flow of patients through a healthcare system.

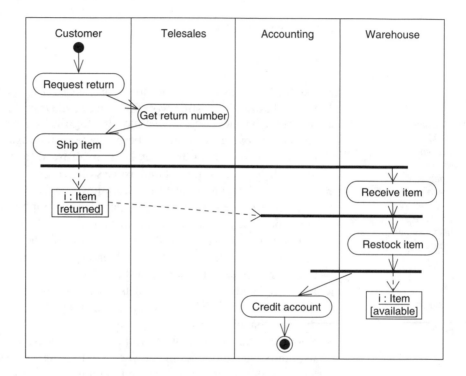

Figure 19-9: Modeling a Workflow

In this example, there are no branches, forks, or joins other than those associated with object flow.

Modeling an Operation

Classes and operations are discussed in Chapters 4 and 9; interfaces are discussed in Chapter 11.

An activity diagram can be attached to any modeling element for the purpose
of visualizing, specifying, constructing, and documenting that element's
behavior. You can attach activity diagrams to classes, interfaces, components,
nodes, use cases, and collaborations. The most common element to which
you'll attach an activity diagram is an operation.

Components are discussed in Chapter 25; nodes are discussed in Chapter 26; use cases are discussed in Chapter 16; collaborations are discussed in Chapter 27; preconditions, postconditions, and invariants are discussed in Chapter 9.

Used in this manner, an activity diagram is simply a flowchart of an operation's actions. An activity diagram's primary advantage is that all the elements in the diagram are semantically tied to a rich underlying model. For example, any other operation or signal that an action state references can be type checked against the class of the target object.

To model an operation,

- Collect the abstractions that are involved in this operation. This includes the operation's parameters (including its return type, if any), the attributes of the enclosing class, and certain neighboring classes.
- Identify the preconditions at the operation's initial state and the postconditions at the operation's final state. Also identify any invariants of the enclosing class that must hold during the execution of the operation.
- Beginning at the operation's initial state, specify the activities and actions that take place over time and render them in the activity diagram as either activity states or action states.
- Use branching as necessary to specify conditional paths and iteration.
- Only if this operation is owned by an active class, use forking and joining as necessary to specify parallel flows of control.

Active classes are discussed in Chapter 22.

For example, in the context of the class `Line`, Figure 19-10 shows an activity diagram that specifies the algorithm of the operation `intersection`, whose signature includes one parameter (`l`, an `in` parameter of the class `Line`) and one return value (of the class `Point`). The class `Line` has two attributes of interest: `slope` (which holds the slope of the line) and `delta` (which holds the offset of the line relative to the origin).

If an operation involves the interaction of a society of objects, you can also model the realization of that operation using collaborations, as discussed in Chapter 27.

The algorithm of this operation is simple, as shown in the following activity diagram. First, there's a guard that tests whether the `slope` of the current line is the same as the `slope` of parameter `l`. If so, the lines do not intersect, and a `Point` at (`0,0`) is returned. Otherwise, the operation first calculates an `x` value for the point of intersection, then a `y` value; `x` and `y` are both objects local to the operation. Finally, a `Point` at (`x,y`) is returned.

Note: Using activity diagrams to flowchart an operation lies on the edge of making the UML a visual programming language. You *can* flowchart every operation, but pragmatically, you won't want to. Writing the body of an operation in a specific programming language is usually more direct. You will want to use activity diagrams to model an operation when the behavior of that operation is complex and therefore difficult to understand just by staring at code. Looking at a flowchart will reveal things about the algorithm you could not have seen just by looking at the code.

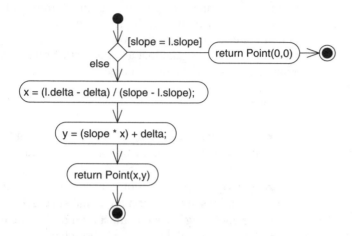

Figure 19-10: Modeling an Operation

Forward and Reverse Engineering

Forward engineering (the creation of code from a model) is possible for activity diagrams, especially if the context of the diagram is an operation. For example, using the previous activity diagram, a forward engineering tool could generate the following C++ code for the operation `intersection`.

```
Point Line::intersection (l : Line) {
  if (slope == l.slope) return Point(0,0);
  int x = (l.delta - delta) / (slope - l.slope);
  int y = (slope * x) + delta;
  return Point(x, y);
}
```

There's a bit of cleverness here, involving the declaration of the two local variables. A less-sophisticated tool might have first declared the two variables and then set their values.

Reverse engineering (the creation of a model from code) is also possible for activity diagrams, especially if the context of the code is the body of an operation. In particular, the previous diagram could have been generated from the implementation of the class `Line`.

More interesting than the reverse engineering of a model from code is the animation of a model against the execution of a deployed system. For example, given the previous diagram, a tool could animate the action states in the diagram as they were dispatched in a running system. Even better, with this tool also under the control of a debugger, you could control the speed of execution, possibly setting breakpoints to stop the action at interesting points in time to examine the attribute values of individual objects.

Hints and Tips

When you create activity diagrams in the UML, remember that activity diagrams are just projections on the same model of a system's dynamic aspects. No single activity diagram can capture everything about a system's dynamic aspects. Rather, you'll want to use many activity diagrams to model the dynamics of a workflow or an operation.

A well-structured activity diagram

- Is focused on communicating one aspect of a system's dynamics.
- Contains only those elements that are essential to understanding that aspect.
- Provides detail consistent with its level of abstraction; you expose only those adornments that are essential to understanding.
- Is not so minimalist that it misinforms the reader about important semantics.

When you draw an activity diagram,

- Give it a name that communicates its purpose.
- Start with modeling the primary flow. Address branching, concurrency, and object flow as secondary considerations, possibly in separate diagrams.
- Lay out its elements to minimize lines that cross.
- Use notes and color as visual cues to draw attention to important features of your diagram.

Section 5
ADVANCED BEHAVIORAL
MODELING

UNIFIED
MODELING
LANGUAGE

Chapter 20

EVENTS AND SIGNALS

In the real world, things happen. Not only do things happen, but lots of things may happen at the same time, and at the most unexpected times. "Things that happen" are called events, and each one represents the specification of a significant occurrence that has a location in time and space.

In the context of state machines, you use events to model the occurrence of a stimulus that can trigger a state transition. Events may include signals, calls, the passing of time, or a change in state.

Events may be synchronous or asynchronous, so modeling events is wrapped up in the modeling of processes and threads.

Getting Started

A perfectly static system is intensely uninteresting because nothing ever happens. All real systems have some dynamic dimension to them, and these dynamics are triggered by things that happen externally or internally. At an ATM machine, action is initiated by a user pressing a button to start a transaction. In an autonomous robot, action is initiated by the robot bumping into an object. In a network router, action is initiated by the detection of an overflow of message buffers. In a chemical plant, action is initiated by the passage of time sufficient for a chemical reaction.

In the UML, each thing that happens is modeled as an event. An event is the specification of a significant occurrence that has a location in time and space. A signal, the passing of time, and a change of state are asynchronous events, representing events that can happen at arbitrary times. Calls are generally synchronous events, representing the invocation of an operation.

The UML provides a graphical representation of an event, as Figure 20-1 shows. This notation permits you to visualize the declaration of events (such as the signal OffHook), as well as the use of events to trigger a state transition (such as the signal OffHook, which causes a transition from the Active to the Idle state of a telephone).

Figure 20-1: Events

Terms and Concepts

An *event* is the specification of a significant occurrence that has a location in time and space. In the context of state machines, an event is an occurrence of a stimulus that can trigger a state transition. A *signal* is a kind of event that represents the specification of an asynchronous stimulus communicated between instances.

Kinds of Events

Actors are discussed in Chapter 16; systems are discussed in Chapter 31.

Events may be external or internal. External events are those that pass between the system and its actors. For example, the pushing of a button and an interrupt from a collision sensor are both examples of external events. Internal events are those that pass among the objects that live inside the system. An overflow exception is an example of an internal event.

The creation and destruction of objects are also kinds of signals, as discussed in Chapter 15.

In the UML, you can model four kinds of events: signals, calls, the passing of time, and a change in state.

Signals

A signal represents a named object that is dispatched (thrown) asynchronously by one object and then received (caught) by another. Exceptions are supported by most contemporary programming languages and are the most common kind of internal signal that you will need to model.

Classes are discussed in Chapters 4 and 9; generalization is discussed in Chapters 5 and 10.

Signals have a lot in common with plain classes. For example, signals may have instances, although you don't generally need to model them explicitly. Signals may also be involved in generalization relationships, permitting you to model hierarchies of events, some of which are general (for example, the signal `NetworkFailure`) and some of which are specific (for example, a specialization of `NetworkFailure` called `WarehouseServerFailure`). Also as for classes, signals may have attributes and operations.

Note: The attributes of a signal serve as its parameters. For example, when you send a signal such as `Collision`, you can also specify a value for its attributes as parameters, such as `Collision(5.3)`.

State machines are discussed in Chapter 21; interactions are discussed in Chapter 15; interfaces are discussed in Chapter 11; dependencies are discussed in Chapter 5; stereotypes are discussed in Chapter 6.

A signal may be sent as the action of a state transition in a state machine or the sending of a message in an interaction. The execution of an operation can also send signals. In fact, when you model a class or an interface, an important part of specifying the behavior of that element is specifying the signals that its operations can send. In the UML, you model the relationship between an operation and the events that it can send by using a dependency relationship, stereotyped as `send`.

In the UML, as Figure 20-2 shows, you model signals (and exceptions) as stereotyped classes. You can use a dependency, stereotyped as `send`, to indicate that an operation sends a particular signal.

Figure 20-2: Signals

Call Events

State machines are discussed in Chapter 21.

Just as a signal event represents the occurrence of a signal, a call event represents the dispatch of an operation. In both cases, the event may trigger a state transition in a state machine.

Whereas a signal is an asynchronous event, a call event is, in general, synchronous. This means that when an object invokes an operation on another object that has a state machine, control passes from the sender to the receiver, the transition is triggered by the event, the operation is completed, the receiver transitions to a new state, and control returns to the sender.

As Figure 20-3 shows, modeling a call event is indistinguishable from modeling a signal event. In both cases, you show the event, along with its parameters, as the trigger for a state transition.

Figure 20-3: Call Events

Note: Although there are no visual cues to distinguish a signal event from a call event, the difference is clear in the backplane of your model. The receiver of an event will know the difference, of course (by declaring the operation in its operation list). Typically, a signal will be handled by its state machine, and a call event will be handled by a method. You can use your tools to navigate from the event to the signal or the operation.

Time and Change Events

A time event is an event that represents the passage of time. As Figure 20-4 shows, in the UML you model a time event by using the keyword `after` followed by some expression that evaluates to a period of time. Such expressions can be simple (for example, `after 2 seconds`) or complex (for example, `after 1 ms since exiting Idle`). Unless you specify it explicitly, the starting time of such an expression is the time since entering the current state.

A change event is an event that represents a change in state or the satisfaction of some condition. As Figure 20-4 shows, in the UML you model a change event by using the keyword `when` followed by some Boolean expression. You can use such expressions to mark an absolute time (such as `when time = 11:59`) or for the continuous test of an expression (for example, `when altitude < 1000`).

Figure 20-4: Time and Change Events

Note: Although a change event models a condition that is tested continuously, you can typically analyze the situation to see when to test the condition at discrete points in time.

Sending and Receiving Events

Processes and threads are discussed in Chapter 22.

Signal events and call events involve at least two objects: the object that sends the signal or invokes the operation, and the object to which the event is directed. Because signals are asynchronous, and because asynchronous calls are themselves signals, the semantics of events interact with the semantics of active objects and passive objects.

Instances are discussed in Chapter 13.

Any instance of any class can send a signal to or invoke an operation of a receiving object. When an object sends a signal, the sender dispatches the signal and then continues along its flow of control, not waiting for any return from the receiver. For example, if an actor interacting with an ATM system sends the signal `pushButton`, the actor may continue along its way independent of the system to which the signal was sent. In contrast, when an object calls an operation, the sender dispatches the operation and then waits for the receiver. For example, in a trading system, an instance of the class `Trader` might invoke the operation `confirmTransaction` on some instance of the class `Trade`, thereby affecting the state of the `Trade` object. If this is a synchronous call, the `Trader` object will wait until the operation is finished.

Note: In some situations, you may want to show one object sending a signal to a set of objects (multicasting) or to any object in the system that might be listening (broadcasting). To model multicasting, you'd show an object sending a signal to a collection containing a set of receivers. To model broadcasting, you'd show an object sending a signal to another object that represents the system as a whole.

State machines are discussed in Chapter 21; active objects are discussed in Chapter 22.

Any instance of any class can receive a call event or a signal. If this is a synchronous call event, then the sender and the receiver are in a rendezvous for the duration of the operation. This means that the flow of control of the sender is put in lock step with the flow of control of the receiver until the activity of the operation is carried out. If this is a signal, then the sender and receiver do not rendezvous: the sender dispatches the signal but does not wait for a response from the receiver. In either case, this event may be lost (if no response to the event is specified), it may trigger the receiver's state machine (if there is one), or it may just invoke a normal method call.

Operations are discussed in Chapter 4; extra class compartments are discussed in Chapter 4.

In the UML, you model the call events that an object may receive as operations on the class of the object. In the UML, you model the named signals that an object may receive by naming them in an extra compartment of the class, as shown in Figure 20-5.

Interfaces are discussed in Chapter 11; asynchronous operations are discussed in Chapter 22.

Note: You can also attach named signals to an interface in this same manner. In either case, the signals you list in this extra compartment are not the declarations of a signal, but only the use of a signal. Signals that are asynchronous operations are listed in the normal operation compartment of the class.

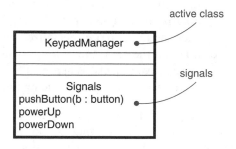

Figure 20-5: Signals and Active Classes.

Common Modeling Techniques

Modeling a Family of Signals

Generalization is discussed in Chapters 5 and 10.

In most event-driven systems, signal events are hierarchical. For example, an autonomous robot might distinguish between external signals, such as a `Collision`, and internal ones, such as a `HardwareFault`. External and internal signals need not be disjoint, however. Even within these two broad classifications, you might find specializations. For example, `HardwareFault` signals might be further specialized as `BatteryFault` and `MovementFault`. Even these might be further specialized, such as `MotorStall`, a kind of `MovementFault`.

State machines are discussed in Chapter 21.

By modeling hierarchies of signals in this manner, you can specify polymorphic events. For example, consider a state machine with a transition triggered only by the receipt of a `MotorStall`. As a leaf signal in this hierarchy, the transition can be triggered only by that signal, so it is not polymorphic. In contrast, suppose you modeled the state machine with a transition triggered by the receipt of a `HardwareFault`. In this case, the transition is polymorphic and can be triggered by a `HardwareFault` or any of its specializations, including `BatteryFault`, `MovementFault`, and `MotorStall`.

To model a family of signals,

- Consider all the different kinds of signals to which a given set of active objects may respond.

- Look for the common kinds of signals and place them in a generalization/specialization hierarchy using inheritance. Elevate more general ones and lower more specialized ones.
- Look for the opportunity for polymorphism in the state machines of these active objects. Where you find polymorphism, adjust the hierarchy as necessary by introducing intermediate abstract signals.

Abstract classes are discussed in Chapter 5.

Figure 20-6 models a family of signals that may be handled by an autonomous robot. Note that the root signal (`RobotSignal`) is abstract, which means that there may be no direct instances. This signal has two immediate concrete specializations (`Collision` and `HardwareFault`), one of which (`HardwareFault`) is further specialized. Note that the `Collision` signal has one parameter.

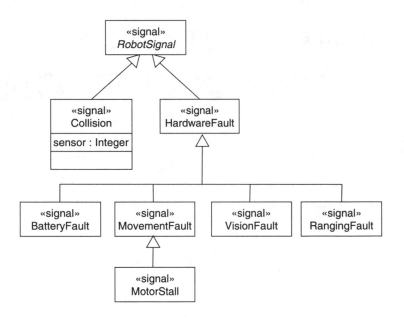

Figure 20-6: Modeling Families of Signals

Modeling Exceptions

Classes are discussed in Chapters 4 and 9; interfaces are discussed in Chapter 11.

An important part of visualizing, specifying, and documenting the behavior of a class or an interface is specifying the exceptions that its operations can raise. If you are handed a class or an interface, the operations you can invoke will be clear, but the exceptions that each operation may raise will not be clear unless you model them explicitly.

Stereotypes are discussed in Chapter 6.

In the UML, exceptions are kinds of signals, which you model as stereotyped classes. Exceptions may be attached to specification operations. Modeling exceptions is somewhat the inverse of modeling a general family of signals. You model a family of signals primarily to specify the kinds of signals an active object may receive; you model exceptions primarily to specify the kinds of exceptions that an object may throw through its operations.

To model exceptions,

- For each class and interface, and for each operation of such elements, consider the exceptional conditions that may be raised.
- Arrange these exceptions in a hierarchy. Elevate general ones, lower specialized ones, and introduce intermediate exceptions, as necessary.
- For each operation, specify the exceptions that it may raise. You can do so explicitly (by showing send dependencies from an operation to its exceptions) or you can put this in the operation's specification.

Template classes are discussed in Chapter 9.

Figure 20-7 models a hierarchy of exceptions that may be raised by a standard library of container classes, such as the template class Set. This hierarchy is headed by the abstract signal Exception and includes three specialized exceptions: Duplicate, Overflow, and Underflow. As shown, the add operation raises Duplicate and Overflow exceptions, and the remove operation raises only the Underflow exception. Alternatively, you could have put these dependencies in the background by naming them in each operation's specification. Either way, by knowing which exceptions each operation may send, you can create clients that use the Set class correctly.

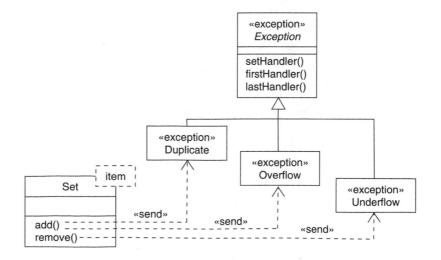

Figure 20-7: Modeling Exceptions

Hints and Tips

When you model an event,

- Build hierarchies of signals so that you exploit the common properties of related signals.
- Don't use sending signals, and especially sending exceptions, as a replacement for normal flow of control.
- Be sure you have a suitable state machine behind each element that may receive the event.
- Be sure to model not only those elements that may receive events, but also those elements that may send them.

When you draw an event in the UML,

- In general, model hierarchies of events explicitly, but model their use in the backplane of each class or operation that sends or receives such an event.

UNIFIED
MODELING
LANGUAGE

Chapter 21
STATE MACHINES

In this chapter

- States, transitions, and activities
- Modeling the lifetime of an object
- Creating well-structured algorithms

Interactions are discussed in Chapter 15; objects are discussed in Chapter 13.

Classes are discussed in Chapters 4 and 9; use cases are discussed in Chapter 16; systems are discussed in Chapter 31; activity diagrams are discussed in Chapter 19; statechart diagrams are discussed in Chapter 24.

Using an interaction, you can model the behavior of a society of objects that work together. Using a state machine, you can model the behavior of an individual object. A state machine is a behavior that specifies the sequences of states an object goes through during its lifetime in response to events, together with its responses to those events.

You use state machines to model the dynamic aspects of a system. For the most part, this involves specifying the lifetime of the instances of a class, a use case, or an entire system. These instances may respond to such events as signals, operations, or the passing of time. When an event occurs, some activity will take place, depending on the current state of the object. An activity is an ongoing nonatomic execution within a state machine. Activities ultimately result in some action, which is made up of executable atomic computations that result in a change in state of the model or a return of a value. The state of an object is a condition or situation during the life of an object during which it satisfies some condition, performs some activity, or waits for some event.

You can visualize a state machine in two ways: by emphasizing the flow of control from activity to activity (using activity diagrams), or by emphasizing the potential states of the objects and the transitions among those states (using statechart diagrams).

Well-structured state machines are like well-structured algorithms: They are efficient, simple, adaptable, and understandable.

Getting Started

Consider the life of your home's thermostat on one crisp fall day.

In the wee hours of the morning, things are pretty quiet for the humble thermostat. The temperature of the house is stable and, save for a rogue gust of wind or a passing storm, the temperature outside the house is stable, too. Toward dawn, however, things get more interesting. The sun starts to peek over the horizon, raising the ambient temperature slightly. Family members start to wake; someone might tumble out of bed and twist the thermostat's dial. Both of these events are significant to the home's heating and cooling system. The thermostat starts behaving like all good thermostats should, by commanding the home's heater (to raise the inside temperature) or air conditioner (to lower the inside temperature).

Once everyone has left for work or school, things get quiet, and the temperature of the house stabilizes once again. However, an automatic program might then cut in, commanding the thermostat to lower the temperature to save on electricity and gas. The thermostat goes back to work. Later in the day, the program comes alive again, this time commanding the thermostat to raise the temperature so that the family can come home to a cozy house.

In the evening, with the home filled with warm bodies and heat from cooking, the thermostat has a lot of work to do to keep the temperature even while it runs the heater and cooler efficiently.

Finally, at night, things return to a quiet state.

A number of software-intensive systems behave just like that thermostat. A pacemaker runs continuously but adapts to changes in blood pressure or activity. A network router runs continuously, as well, silently guiding asynchronous streams of bits, sometimes adapting its behavior in response to commands from the network administrator. A cell phone works on demand, responding to input from the user and to messages from the local cells.

Modeling the structural aspects of a system is discussed in Sections 2 and 3.

In the UML, you model the static aspects of a system by using such elements as class diagrams and object diagrams. These diagrams let you visualize, specify, construct, and document the things that live in your system, including classes, interfaces, components, nodes, and use cases and their instances, together with the way those things sit in relationship to one another.

You can also model the dynamic aspects of a system by using interactions, as discussed in Chapter 15; events are discussed in Chapter 20.

In the UML, you model the dynamic aspects of a system by using state machines. Whereas an interaction models a society of objects that work together to carry out some action, a state machine models the lifetime of a single object, whether it is an instance of a class, a use case, or even an entire system. In the life of an object, it may be exposed to a variety of events, such as a signal, the invocation of an operation, the creation or destruction of the object, the passing of time, or the change in some condition. In response to these events, the object reacts with some action, which represents an atomic computation that results in a change in state of the object or the return of a value. The behavior of such an object is therefore affected by the past. An object may receive an event, respond with an action, then change its state. An object may receive another event, and its response may be different, depending on its current state in response to the previous event.

Activity diagrams are discussed in Chapter 19; statechart diagrams are discussed in Chapter 24.

You use state machines to model the behavior of any modeling element, although, most commonly, that will be a class, a use case, or an entire system. State machines may be visualized in two ways. First, using activity diagrams, you can focus on the activities that take place within the object. Second, using statechart diagrams, you can focus on the event-ordered behavior of an object, which is especially useful in modeling reactive systems.

The UML provides a graphical representation of states, transitions, events, and actions, as Figure 21-1 shows. This notation permits you to visualize the behavior of an object in a way that lets you emphasize the important elements in the life of that object.

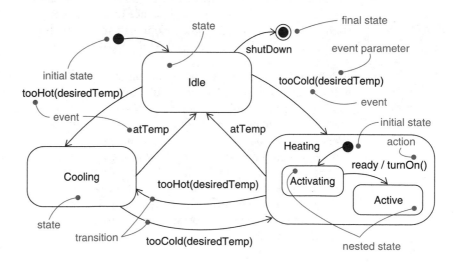

Figure 21-1: State Machines

Terms and Concepts

A *state machine* is a behavior that specifies the sequences of states an object goes through during its lifetime in response to events, together with its responses to those events. A *state* is a condition or situation during the life of an object during which it satisfies some condition, performs some activity, or waits for some event. An *event* is the specification of a significant occurrence that has a location in time and space. In the context of state machines, an event is an occurrence of a stimulus that can trigger a state transition. A *transition* is a relationship between two states indicating that an object in the first state will perform certain actions and enter the second state when a specified event occurs and specified conditions are satisfied. An *activity* is ongoing nonatomic execution within a state machine. An *action* is an executable atomic computation that results in a change in state of the model or the return of a value. Graphically, a state is rendered as a rectangle with rounded corners. A transition is rendered as a solid directed line.

Context

Objects are discussed in Chapter 13; messages are discussed in Chapter 15.

Every object has a lifetime. On creation, an object is born; on destruction, an object ceases to exist. In between, an object may act on other objects (by sending them messages), as well as be acted on (by being the target of a message). In many cases, these messages will be simple, synchronous operation calls. For example, an instance of the class `Customer` might invoke the operation `getAccountBalance` on an instance of the class `BankAccount`. Objects such as these don't need a state machine to specify their behavior because their current behavior does not depend on their past.

Signals are discussed in Chapter 20.

In other kinds of systems, you'll encounter objects that must respond to signals, which are asynchronous stimuli communicated between instances. For example, a cellular phone must respond to random phone calls (from other phones), keypad events (from the customer initiating a phone call), and to events from the network (when the phone moves from one call to another). Similarly, you'll encounter objects whose current behavior depends on their past behavior. For example, the behavior of an air-to-air missile guidance system will depend on its current state, such as `NotFlying` (it's not a good idea to launch a missile while it's attached to an aircraft that's still sitting on the ground) or `Searching` (you shouldn't arm the missile until you have a good idea what it's going to hit).

Active objects are discussed in Chapter 22; modeling reactive systems is discussed in Chapter 24; use cases and actors are discussed in Chapter 16; interactions are discussed in Chapter 15; interfaces are discussed in Chapter 11.

The behavior of objects that must respond to asynchronous stimulus or whose current behavior depends on their past is best specified by using a state machine. This encompasses instances of classes that can receive signals, including many active objects. In fact, an object that receives a signal but has no state machine will simply ignore that signal. You'll also use state machines to model the behavior of entire systems, especially reactive systems, which must respond to signals from actors outside the system.

Note: Most of the time, you'll use interactions to model the behavior of a use case, but you can also apply state machines for the same purpose. Similarly, you can apply state machines to model the behavior of an interface. Although an interface may not have any direct instances, a class that realizes such an interface may. Such a class must conform to the behavior specified by the state machine of this interface.

States

A state is a condition or situation during the life of an object during which it satisfies some condition, performs some activity, or waits for some event. An object remains in a state for a finite amount of time. For example, a `Heater` in a home might be in any of four states: `Idle` (waiting for a command to start heating the house), `Activating` (its gas is on, but it's waiting to come up to temperature), `Active` (its gas and blower are both on), and `ShuttingDown` (its gas is off but its blower is on, flushing residual heat from the system).

You can visualize the state of an object in an interaction, as discussed in Chapter 13; a state name must be unique within its enclosing state, in conformance with the rules discussed in Chapter 12; the last four parts of a state are discussed in later sections of this chapter.

When an object's state machine is in a given state, the object is said to be in that state. For example, an instance of `Heater` might be `Idle` or perhaps `ShuttingDown`.

A state has several parts.

1. Name	A textual string that distinguishes the state from other states; a state may be anonymous, meaning that it has no name
2. Entry/exit actions	Actions executed on entering and exiting the state, respectively
3. Internal transitions	Transitions that are handled without causing a change in state
4. Substates	The nested structure of a state, involving disjoint (sequentially active) or concurrent (concurrently active) substates

5. Deferred events   A list of events that are not handled in that state but, rather, are postponed and queued for handling by the object in another state

---

Note: A state name may be text consisting of any number of letters, numbers, and certain punctuation marks (except for marks such as the colon) and may continue over several lines. In practice, state names are short nouns or noun phrases drawn from the vocabulary of the system you are modeling. Typically, you capitalize the first letter of every word in a state name, as in `Idle` or `ShuttingDown`.

As Figure 21-2 shows, you represent a state as a rectangle with rounded corners.

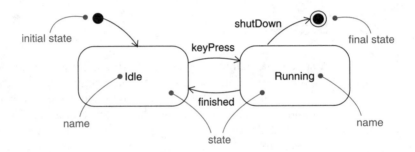

Figure 21-2: States

Initial and Final States As the figure shows, there are two special states that may be defined for an object's state machine. First, there's the initial state, which indicates the default starting place for the state machine or substate. An initial state is represented as a filled black circle. Second, there's the final state, which indicates that the execution of the state machine or the enclosing state has been completed. A final state is represented as a filled black circle surrounded by an unfilled circle.

Note: Initial and final states are really pseudostates. Neither may have the usual parts of a normal state, except for a name. A transition from an initial state to a final state may have the full complement of features, including a guard condition and action (but not a trigger event).

Transitions

A transition is a relationship between two states indicating that an object in the first state will perform certain actions and enter the second state when a specified event occurs and specified conditions are satisfied. On such a change of state, the transition is said to fire. Until the transition fires, the object is said to be in the source state; after it fires, it is said to be in the target state. For example, a Heater might transition from the Idle to the Activating state when an event such as tooCold (with the parameter desiredTemp) occurs.

A transition has five parts.

<table>
<tr><td>1. Source state</td><td>The state affected by the transition; if an object is in the source state, an outgoing transition may fire when the object receives the trigger event of the transition and if the guard condition, if any, is satisfied</td></tr>
<tr><td>2. Event trigger</td><td>The event whose reception by the object in the source state makes the transition eligible to fire, providing its guard condition is satisfied</td></tr>
<tr><td>3. Guard condition</td><td>A Boolean expression that is evaluated when the transition is triggered by the reception of the event trigger; if the expression evaluates True, the transition is eligible to fire; if the expression evaluates False, the transition does not fire and if there is no other transition that could be triggered by that same event, the event is lost</td></tr>
<tr><td>4. Action</td><td>An executable atomic computation that may directly act on the object that owns the state machine, and indirectly on other objects that are visible to the object</td></tr>
<tr><td>5. Target state</td><td>The state that is active after the completion of the transition</td></tr>
</table>

Events are discussed in Chapter 20.

As Figure 21-3 shows, a transition is rendered as a solid directed line from the source to the target state. A self-transition is a transition whose source and target states are the same.

Forking and joining are also discussed in Chapter 19.

Note: A transition may have multiple sources (in which case, it represents a join from multiple concurrent states) as well as multiple targets (in which case, it represents a fork to multiple concurrent states).

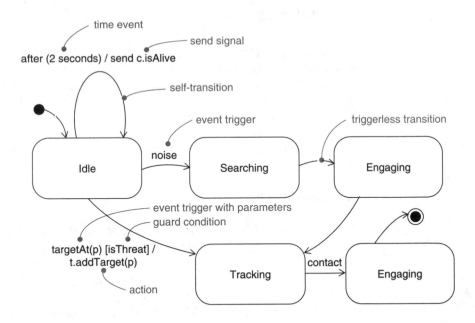

Figure 21-3: Transitions

Events are discussed in Chapter 20.

Event Trigger An event is the specification of a significant occurrence that has a location in time and space. In the context of state machines, an event is an occurrence of a stimulus that can trigger a state transition. As shown in the previous figure, events may include signals, calls, the passing of time, or a change in state. A signal or a call may have parameters whose values are available to the transition, including expressions for the guard condition and action.

It is also possible to have a triggerless transition, represented by a transition with no event trigger. A triggerless transition—also called a completion transition—is triggered implicitly when its source state has completed its activity.

Note: An event trigger may be polymorphic. For example, if you've specified a family of signals, then a transition whose trigger event is S can be triggered by S, as well as by any children of S.

Specifying a family of signals is discussed in Chapter 20; multiple, nonoverlapping guard conditions form a branch, as discussed in Chapter 19.

Guard Condition As the previous figure shows, a guard condition is rendered as a Boolean expression enclosed in square brackets and placed after the trigger event. A guard condition is evaluated only after the trigger event for its transition occurs. Therefore, it's possible to have multiple transitions from the same source state and with the same event trigger, as long as those conditions don't overlap.

A guard condition is evaluated just once for each transition at the time the event occurs, but it may be evaluated again if the transition is retriggered. Within the Boolean expression, you can include conditions about the state of an object (for example, the expression `aHeater in Idle`, which evaluates True if the `Heater` object is currently in the `Idle` state).

Change events are discussed in Chapter 20.

> **Note:** Although a guard condition is evaluated only once each time its transition triggers, a change event is potentially evaluated continuously.

Actions are discussed in Chapter 15.

Action An action is an executable atomic computation. Actions may include operation calls (to the object that owns the state machine, as well as to other visible objects), the creation or destruction of another object, or the sending of a signal to an object. As the previous figure shows, there's a special notation for sending a signal—the signal name is prefixed with the keyword `send` as a visual cue.

Activities are discussed in a later section of this chapter; dependencies are discussed in Chapters 5 and 10.

An action is atomic, meaning that it cannot be interrupted by an event and therefore runs to completion. This is in contrast to an activity, which may be interrupted by other events.

> **Note:** You can explicitly show the object to which a signal is sent by using a dependency stereotyped as `send`, whose source is the state and whose target is the object.

Advanced States and Transitions

You can model a wide variety of behavior using only the basic features of states and transitions in the UML. Using these features, you'll end up with flat state machines, which means that your behavioral models will consist of nothing more than arcs (transitions) and vertices (states).

However, the UML's state machines have a number of advanced features that help you to manage complex behavioral models. These features often reduce the number of states and transitions you'll need, and they codify a number of common and somewhat complex idioms you'd otherwise encounter using flat state machines. Some of these advanced features include entry and exit actions, internal transitions, activities, and deferred events.

Figure 21-4: Advanced States and Transitions

Entry and Exit Actions In a number of modeling situations, you'll want to dispatch the same action whenever you enter a state, no matter which transition led you there. Similarly, when you leave a state, you'll want to dispatch the same action no matter which transition led you away. For example, in a missile guidance system, you might want to explicitly announce the system is onTrack whenever it's in the Tracking state, and offTrack whenever it's out of the state. Using flat state machines, you can achieve this effect by putting those actions on every entering and exiting transition, as appropriate. However, that's somewhat error prone; you have to remember to add these actions every time you add a new transition. Furthermore, modifying this action means that you have to touch every neighboring transition.

As Figure 21-4 shows, the UML provides a shorthand for this idiom. In the symbol for the state, you can include an entry action (marked by the keyword event entry) and an exit action (marked by the keyword event exit), together with an appropriate action. Whenever you enter the state, its entry action is dispatched; whenever you leave the state, its exit action is dispatched.

Note: Entry and exit actions may not have arguments or guard conditions. However, the entry action at the top level of a state machine for a class may have parameters that represent the arguments that the machine receives when the object is created.

Internal Transitions Once inside a state, you'll encounter events you'll want to handle without leaving the state. These are called internal transitions, and they are subtly different from self-transitions. In a self-transition, such as you see in Figure 21-3, an event triggers the transition, you leave the state, an action (if any) is dispatched, and then you reenter the same state. Because this transition exits and then enters the state, a self-transition dispatches the state's exit action, then it dispatches the action of the self-transition, and finally, it dispatches the state's entry action. However, suppose you want to handle the event but don't want to fire the state's entry and exit actions. Using flat state machines, you can achieve that effect, but you have to be diligent about remembering which of a state's transitions have these entry and exit actions and which do not.

As Figure 21-4 shows, the UML provides a shorthand for this idiom, as well (for example, for the event `newTarget`). In the symbol for the state, you can include an internal transition (marked by an event). Whenever you are in the state and that event is triggered, the corresponding action is dispatched without leaving and then reentering the state. Therefore, the event is handled without dispatching the state's exit and then entry actions.

Note: Internal transitions may have events with parameters and guard conditions. As such, internal transitions are essentially interrupts.

Activities When an object is in a state, it generally sits idle, waiting for an event to occur. Sometimes, however, you may wish to model an ongoing activity. While in a state, the object does some work that will continue until it is interrupted by an event. For example, if an object is in the `Tracking` state, it might `followTarget` as long as it is in that state. As Figure 21-4 shows, in the UML, you use the special `do` transition to specify the work that's to be done inside a state after the entry action is dispatched. The activity of a `do` transition might name another state machine (such as `followTarget`). You can also specify a sequence of actions—for example, do / op1(a); op2(b); op3(c). Actions are never interruptible, but sequences of actions are. In between each action (separated by the semicolon), events may be handled by the enclosing state, which results in transitioning out of the state.

Events are discussed in Chapter 20.

Deferred Events Consider a state such as `Tracking`. As illustrated in Figure 21-3, suppose there's only one transition leading out of this state, triggered by the event `contact`. While in the state `Tracking`, any events other than `contact` and other than those handled by its substates will be lost. That means that the event may occur, but it will be postponed and no action will result because of the presence of that event.

In every modeling situation, you'll want to recognize some events and ignore others. You include those you want to recognize as the event triggers of transitions; those you want to ignore you just leave out. However, in some modeling situations, you'll want to recognize some events but postpone a response to them until later. For example, while in the `Tracking` state, you may want to postpone a response to signals such as `selfTest`, perhaps sent by some maintenance agent in the system.

In the UML, you can specify this behavior by using deferred events. A deferred event is a list of events whose occurrence in the state is postponed until a state in which the listed events are not deferred becomes active, at which time they occur and may trigger transitions as if they had just occurred. As you can see in the previous figure, you can specify a deferred event by listing the event with the special action `defer`. In this example, `selfTest` events may happen while in the `Tracking` state, but they are held until the object is in the `Engaging` state, at which time it appears as if they just occurred.

Note: The implementation of deferred events requires the presence of an internal queue of events. If an event happens but is listed as deferred, it is queued. Events are taken off this queue as soon as the object enters a state that does not defer these events.

Substates

These advanced features of states and transitions solve a number of common state machine modeling problems. However, there's one more feature of the UML's state machines—substates—that does even more to help you simplify the modeling of complex behaviors. A substate is a state that's nested inside another one. For example, a `Heater` might be in the `Heating` state, but also while in the `Heating` state, there might be a nested state called `Activating`. In this case, it's proper to say that the object is both `Heating` and `Activating`.

Composite states have a nested structure similar to composition, as discussed in Chapters 5 and 10.

A simple state is a state that has no substructure. A state that has substates—that is, nested states—is called a composite state. A composite state may contain either concurrent (orthogonal) or sequential (disjoint) substates. In the UML, you render a composite state just as you do a simple state, but with an optional graphic compartment that shows a nested state machine. Substates may be nested to any level.

Sequential Substates Consider the problem of modeling the behavior of an ATM. There are three basic states in which this system might be: `Idle` (waiting for customer interaction), `Active` (handling a customer's transaction), and `Maintenance` (perhaps having its cash store replenished). While `Active`, the behavior of the ATM follows a simple path: Validate the customer, select a transaction, process the transaction, and then print a receipt. After printing, the ATM returns to the `Idle` state. You might represent these stages of behavior as the states `Validating`, `Selecting`, `Processing`, and `Printing`. It would even be desirable to let the customer select and process multiple transactions after `Validating` the account and before `Printing` a final receipt.

The problem here is that, at any stage in this behavior, the customer might decide to cancel the transaction, returning the ATM to its Idle state. Using flat state machines, you can achieve that effect, but it's quite messy. Because the customer might cancel the transaction at any point, you'd have to include a suitable transition from every state in the Active sequence. That's messy because it's easy to forget to include these transitions in all the right places, and many such interrupting events means you end up with a multitude of transitions zeroing in on the same target state from various sources, but with the same event trigger, guard condition, and action.

Using sequential substates, there's a simpler way to model this problem, as Figure 21-5 shows. Here, the Active state has a substructure, containing the substates Validating, Selecting, Processing, and Printing. The state of the ATM changes from Idle to Active when the customer enters a credit card in the machine. On entering the Active state, the entry action readCard is performed. Starting with the initial state of the substructure, control passes to the Validating state, then to the Selecting state, and then to the Processing state. After Processing, control may return to Selecting (if the customer has selected another transaction) or it may move on to Printing. After Printing, there's a triggerless transition back to the Idle state. Notice that the Active state has an exit action, which ejects the customer's credit card.

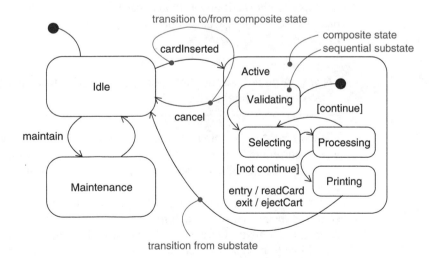

Figure 21-5: Sequential Substates

Notice also the transition from the Active state to the Idle state, triggered by the event cancel. In any substate of Active, the customer might cancel the transaction, and that returns the ATM to the `Idle` state (but only after ejecting the customer's credit card, which is the exit action dispatched on leaving the `Active` state, no matter what caused a transition out of that state). Without substates, you'd need a transition triggered by `cancel` on every substructure state.

Substates such as `Validating` and `Processing` are called sequential, or disjoint, substates. Given a set of disjoint substates in the context of an enclosing composite state, the object is said to be in the composite state and in only one of those substates (or the final state) at a time. Therefore, sequential substates partition the state space of the composite state into disjoint states.

From a source outside an enclosing composite state, a transition may target the composite state or it may target a substate. If its target is the composite state, the nested state machine must include an initial state, to which control passes after entering the composite state and after dispatching its entry action (if any). If its target is the nested state, control passes to the nested state, after dispatching the entry action (if any) of the composite state and then the entry action (if any) of the substate.

A transition leading out of a composite state may have as its source the composite state or a substate. In either case, control first leaves the nested state (and its exit action, if any, is dispatched), then it leaves the composite state (and its exit action, if any, is dispatched). A transition whose source is the composite state essentially cuts short (interrupts) the activity of the nested state machine.

Note: A nested sequential state machine may have at most one initial state and one final state.

History States A state machine describes the dynamic aspects of an object whose current behavior depends on its past. A state machine in effect specifies the legal ordering of states an object may go through during its lifetime.

Unless otherwise specified, when a transition enters a composite state, the action of the nested state machine starts over again at its initial state (unless, of course, the transition targets a substate directly). However, there are times you'd like to model an object so that it remembers the last substate that was active prior to leaving the composite state. For example, in modeling the behavior of an agent that does an unattended backup of computers across a network, you'd like it to remember where it was in the process if it ever gets interrupted by, for example, a query from the operator.

Using flat state machines, you can model this, but it's messy. For each sequential substate, you'd need to have its exit action post a value to some variable local to the composite state. Then the initial state to this composite state would need a transition to every substate with a guard condition, querying the variable. In this way, leaving the composite state would cause the last substate to be remembered; entering the composite state would transition to the proper substate. That's messy because it requires you to remember to touch every substate and to set an appropriate exit action. It leaves you with a multitude of transitions fanning out from the same initial state to different target substates with very similar (but different) guard conditions.

In the UML, a simpler way to model this idiom is by using history states. A history state allows a composite state that contains sequential substates to remember the last substate that was active in it prior to the transition from the composite state. As Figure 21-6 shows, you represent a shallow history state as a small circle containing the symbol H.

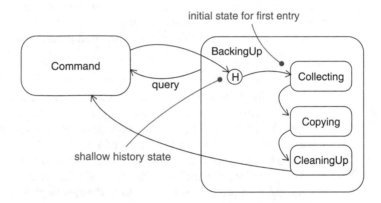

Figure 21-6: History State

If you want a transition to activate the last substate, you show a transition from outside the composite state directly to the history state. The first time you enter a composite state, it has no history. This is the meaning of the single transition from the history state to a sequential substate such as Collecting. The target of this transition specifies the initial state of the nested state machine the first time it is entered. Continuing, suppose that while in the BackingUp state and the Copying state, the query event is posted. Control leaves Copying and BackingUp (dispatching their exit actions as necessary) and returns to the Command state. When the action of Command completes, the triggerless transition returns to the history state of the composite state BackingUp. This time, because there is a history to the nested state machine, control passes back to the Copying state—thus bypassing the Collecting state—because

`Copying` was the last substate active prior to the transition from
`BackingUp`.

Note: the symbol `H` designates a shallow history, which remembers only
the history of the immediate nested state machine. You can also specify
deep history, shown as a small circle containing the symbol `H*`. Deep
history remembers down to the innermost nested state at any depth. If
you have only one level of nesting, shallow and deep history states are
semantically equivalent. If you have more than one level of nesting, shallow history remembers only the outermost nested state; deep history
remembers the innermost nested state at any depth.

In either case, if a nested state machine reaches a final state, it loses its stored
history and behaves as if it had not yet been entered for the first time.

Concurrent Substates Sequential substates are the most common kind of
nested state machine you'll encounter. In certain modeling situations, however,
you'll want to specify concurrent substates. These substates let you specify
two or more state machines that execute in parallel in the context of the enclosing object.

---

*Active objects
are discussed
in Chapter 22.*

Note: Another way to model concurrency is by using active objects.
Thus, rather than partitioning one object's state machine into two (or
more) concurrent substates, you could define two active objects, each of
which is responsible for the behavior of one of the concurrent substates.
If the behavior of one of these concurrent flows is affected by the state of
the other, you'll want to model this using concurrent substates. If the
behavior of one of these concurrent flows is affected by messages sent
to and from the other, you'll want to model this using active objects. If
there's little or no communication between the concurrent flows, then the
approach you choose is a matter of taste, although most of the time,
using active objects makes your design decisions more obvious.

---

*Forking and
joining are
discussed in
Chapter 19.*

For example, Figure 21-7 shows an expansion of the `Maintenance` state
from Figure 21-5. `Maintenance` is decomposed into two concurrent substates, `Testing` and `Commanding`, shown by nesting them in the `Mainte-
nance` state but separating them from one another with a dashed line. Each of
these concurrent substates is further decomposed into sequential substates.
When control passes from the `Idle` to the `Maintenance` state, control then
forks to two concurrent flows—the enclosing object will be in the `Testing`
state and the `Commanding` state. Furthermore, while in the `Commanding`
state, the enclosing object will be in the `Waiting` or the `Command` state.

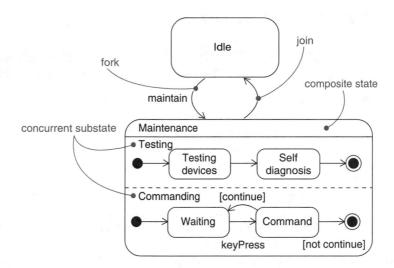

Figure 21-7: Concurrent Substates

Note: This is what distinguishes sequential substates and concurrent substates. Given two or more sequential substates at the same level, an object will be in one of those substates or the other. Given two or more concurrent substates at the same level, an object will be in a sequential state from each one of the concurrent substates.

Execution of these two concurrent substates continues in parallel. Eventually, each nested state machine reaches its final state. If one concurrent substate reaches its final state before the other, control in that substate waits at its final state. When both nested state machines reach their final state, control from the two concurrent substates joins back into one flow.

Whenever there's a transition to a composite state decomposed into concurrent substates, control forks into as many concurrent flows as there are concurrent substates. Similarly, whenever there's a transition from a composite substate decomposed into concurrent substates, control joins back into one flow. This holds true in all cases. If all concurrent substates reach their final state, or if there is an explicit transition out of the enclosing composite state, control joins back into one flow.

Note: A nested concurrent state machine does not have an initial, final, or history state. However, the sequential substates that compose a concurrent state may have these features.

Common Modeling Techniques

Modeling the Lifetime of an Object

Objects are discussed in Chapter 13; classes are discussed in Chapters 4 and 9; use cases are discussed in Chapter 16; systems are discussed in Chapter 31; interactions are discussed in Chapter 15.

The most common purpose for which you'll use state machines is to model the lifetime of an object, especially instances of classes, use cases, and the system as a whole. Whereas interactions model the behavior of a society of objects working together, a state machine models the behavior of a single object over its lifetime, such as you'll find with user interfaces, controllers, and devices.

When you model the lifetime of an object, you essentially specify three things: the events to which the object can respond, the response to those events, and the impact of the past on current behavior. Modeling the lifetime of an object also involves deciding on the order in which the object can meaningfully respond to events, starting at the time of the object's creation and continuing until its destruction.

To model the lifetime of an object,

Collaborations are discussed in Chapter 27.

Pre- and post-conditions are discussed in Chapter 10; interfaces are discussed in Chapter 11.

- Set the context for the state machine, whether it is a class, a use case, or the system as a whole.
  1. If the context is a class or a use case, collect the neighboring classes, including any parents of the class and any classes reachable by associations or dependences. These neighbors are candidate targets for actions and are candidates for including in guard conditions.
  2. If the context is the system as a whole, narrow your focus to one behavior of the system. Theoretically, every object in the system may be a participant in a model of the system's lifetime, and except for the most trivial systems, a complete model would be intractable.
- Establish the initial and final states for the object. To guide the rest of your model, possibly state the pre- and postconditions of the initial and final states, respectively.
- Decide on the events to which this object may respond. If already specified, you'll find these in the object's interfaces; if not already specified, you'll have to consider which objects may interact with the object in your context, and then which events they may possibly dispatch.
- Starting from the initial state to the final state, lay out the top-level states the object may be in. Connect these states with transitions triggered by the appropriate events. Continue by adding actions to these transitions.

- Identify any entry or exit actions (especially if you find that the idiom they cover is used in the state machine).
- Expand these states as necessary by using substates.
- Check that all events mentioned in the state machine match events expected by the interface of the object. Similarly, check that all events expected by the interface of the object are handled by the state machine. Finally, look to places where you explicitly want to ignore events.
- Check that all actions mentioned in the state machine are sustained by the relationships, methods, and operations of the enclosing object.
- Trace through the state machine, either manually or by using tools, to check it against expected sequences of events and their responses. Be especially diligent in looking for unreachable states and states in which the machine may get stuck.
- After rearranging your state machine, check it against expected sequences again to ensure that you have not changed the object's semantics.

For example, Figure 21-8 shows the state machine for the controller in a home security system, which is responsible for monitoring various sensors around the perimeter of the house.

In the lifetime of this controller class, there are four main states: Initializing (the controller is starting up), Idle (the controller is ready and waiting for alarms or commands from the user), Command (the controller is processing commands from the user), and Active (the controller is processing an alarm condition). When the controller object is first created, it moves first to the Initializing state and then unconditionally to the Idle state. The details of these two states are not shown, other than the self-transition with the time event in the Idle state. This kind of time event is common in embedded systems, which often have a heartbeat timer that causes a periodic check of the system's health.

Control passes from the Idle state to the Active state on receipt of an alarm event (which includes the parameter s, identifying the sensor that was tripped). On entering the Active state, setAlarm is dispatched as the entry action, and control then passes first to the Checking state (validating the alarm), then to the Calling state (calling the alarm company to register the alarm), and finally to the Waiting state. The Active and Waiting states are exited only upon clearing the alarm, or by the user signaling the controller for attention, presumably to issue a command.

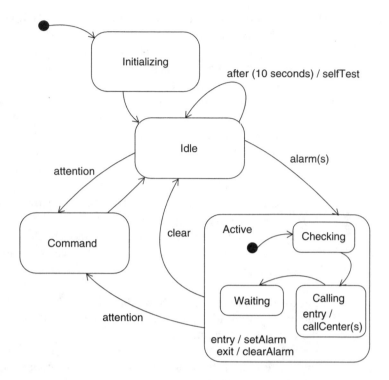

Figure 21-8: Modeling the Lifetime of An Object

Notice that there is no final state. That, too, is common in embedded systems, which are intended to run continuously.

Hints and Tips

When you model state machines in the UML, remember that every state machine represents the dynamic aspects of an individual object, typically representing an instance of a class, a use case, or the system as a whole. A well-structured state machine

- Is simple and therefore should not contain any superfluous states or transitions.
- Has a clear context and therefore may have access to all the objects visible to its enclosing object (these neighbors should be used only as necessary to carry out the behavior specified by the state machine).

■ Is efficient and therefore should carry out its behavior with an optimal balance of time and resources as required by the actions it dispatches.

Modeling the vocabulary of a system is discussed in Chapter 4.

■ Is understandable and therefore should name its states and transitions from the vocabulary of the system.

■ Is not nested too deeply (nesting substates at one or two levels will handle most complex behaviors).

■ Uses concurrent substates sparingly as using active classes is often a better alternative.

When you draw a state machine in the UML,

■ Avoid transitions that cross.

■ Expand composite states in place only as necessary to make the diagram understandable.

Chapter 22

PROCESSES AND THREADS

In this chapter

- Active objects, processes, and threads
- Modeling multiple flows of control
- Modeling interprocess communication
- Building thread-safe abstractions

Process views in the context of software architecture are discussed in Chapter 2.

Not only is the real world a harsh and unforgiving place, but it is a very busy place, as well. Events may happen and things may take place all at the same time. Therefore, when you model a system of the real world, you must take into account its process view, which encompasses the threads and processes that form the system's concurrency and synchronization mechanisms.

In the UML, you model each independent flow of control as an active object that represents a process or thread that can initiate control activity. A process is a heavyweight flow that can execute concurrently with other processes; a thread is a lightweight flow that can execute concurrently with other threads within the same process.

Building abstractions so that they work safely in the presence of multiple flows of control is hard. In particular, you have to consider approaches to communication and synchronization that are more complex than for sequential systems. You also have to be careful to neither over-engineer your process view (too many concurrent flows and your system ends up thrashing) nor under-engineer it (insufficient concurrency does not optimize the system's throughput.

Getting Started

Modeling dog-
houses and
high rises is
discussed in
Chapter 1.

In the life of a dog and his doghouse, the world is a pretty simple and sequential place. Eat. Sleep. Chase a cat. Eat some more. Dream about chasing cats.
Using the doghouse to sleep in or for shelter from the rain is never a problem
because the dog, and only the dog, needs to go in and out through the doghouse
door. There's never any contention for resources.

In the life of a family and its house, the world is not so simple. Without getting
too metaphysical, each family member lives his or her own life, yet still interacts with other members of the family (for dinner, watching television, playing
games, cleaning). Family members will share certain resources. Children
might share a bedroom; the whole family might share one phone or one computer. Family members will also share chores. Dad does the laundry and the
grocery shopping; mom does the bills and the yard work; the children help
with the cleaning and cooking. Contention among these shared resources and
coordination among these independent chores can be challenging. Sharing one
bathroom when everyone is getting ready to go to school or to work can be
problematic; dinner won't be served if dad didn't first get the groceries.

In the life of a high rise and its tenants, the world is really complex. Hundreds,
if not thousands, of people might work in the same building, each following his
or her own agenda. All must pass through a limited set of entrances. All must
jockey for the same bank of elevators. All must share the same heating, cooling, water, electrical, sanitation, and parking facilities. If they are to work
together optimally, they have to communicate and synchronize their interactions properly.

Objects are
discussed in
Chapter 13.

In the UML, each independent flow of control is modeled as an active object.
An active object is a process or thread that can initiate control activity. As for
every kind of object, an active object is an instance of a class. In this case, an
active object is an instance of an active class. Also as for every kind of object,
active objects can communicate with one another by passing messages,
although here, message passing must be extended with certain concurrency
semantics, to help you to synchronize the interactions among independent
flows.

In software, many programming languages directly support the concept of an
active object. Java, Smalltalk, and Ada all have concurrency built in. C++ supports concurrency through various libraries that build on a host operating system's concurrency mechanisms. Using the UML to visualize, specify,
construct, and document these abstractions is important because without doing
so, it's nearly impossible to reason about issues of concurrency, communication, and synchronization.

Classes are discussed in Chapters 4 and 9; signals are discussed in Chapter 20.

The UML provides a graphical representation of an active class, as Figure 22-1 shows. Active classes are kinds of classes, so have all the usual compartments for class name, attributes, and operations. Active classes often receive signals, which you typically enumerate in an extra compartment.

Figure 22-1: Active Class

Terms and Concepts

Interaction diagrams are discussed in Chapter 18.

An *active object* is an object that owns a process or thread and can initiate control activity. An *active class* is a class whose instances are active objects. A *process* is a heavyweight flow that can execute concurrently with other processes. A *thread* is a lightweight flow that can execute concurrently with other threads within the same process. Graphically, an active class is rendered as a rectangle with thick lines. Processes and threads are rendered as stereotyped active classes (and also appear as sequences in interaction diagrams).

Flow of Control

Actors are discussed in Chapter 16.

In a purely sequential system, there is one flow of control. This means that one thing, and one thing only, can take place at a time. When a sequential program starts, control is rooted at the beginning of the program and operations are dispatched one after another. Even if there are concurrent things happening among the actors outside the system, a sequential program will process only one event at a time, queuing or discarding any concurrent external events.

Actions are discussed in Chapter 15.

This is why it's called a flow of control. If you trace the execution of a sequential program, you'll see the locus of execution flow from one statement to another, in sequential order. You might see actions that branch, loop, and jump about, and if there is any recursion or iteration, you see the flow circle back on itself. Nonetheless, in a sequential system, there would be a single flow of execution.

In a concurrent system, there is more than one flow of control—that is, more than one thing can take place at a time. In a concurrent system, there are multiple simultaneous flows of control, each rooted at the head of an independent process or a thread. If you take a snapshot of a concurrent system while it's running, you'll logically see multiple loci of execution.

Nodes are discussed in Chapter 26.

In the UML, you use an active class to represent a process or thread that is the root of an independent flow of control and that is concurrent with all peer flows of control.

> **Note:** You can achieve true concurrency in one of three ways: first, by distributing active objects across multiple nodes; second, by placing active objects on nodes with multiple processors; and third, by a combination of both methods.

Classes and Events

Classes are discussed in Chapters 4 and 9.

Active classes are just classes, albeit ones with a very special property. An active class represents an independent flow of control, whereas a plain class embodies no such flow. In contrast to active classes, plain classes are implicitly called passive because they cannot independently initiate control activity.

Objects are discussed in Chapter 13; attributes and operations are discussed in Chapter 4; relationships are discussed in Chapters 4 and 10; extensibility mechanisms are discussed in Chapter 6; interfaces are discussed in Chapter 11.

You use active classes to model common families of processes or threads. In technical terms, this means that an active object—an instance of an active class—reifies (is a manifestation of) a process or thread. By modeling concurrent systems with active objects, you give a name to each independent flow of control. When an active object is created, the associated flow of control is started; when the active object is destroyed, the associated flow of control is terminated.

Active classes share the same properties as all other classes. Active classes may have instances. Active classes may have attributes and operations. Active classes may participate in dependency, generalization, and association (including aggregation) relationships. Active classes may use any of the UML's extensibility mechanisms, including stereotypes, tagged values, and constraints. Active classes may be the realization of interfaces. Active classes may be realized by collaborations, and the behavior of an active class may be specified by using state machines.

State machines are discussed in Chapter 21; events are discussed in Chapter 20.

In your diagrams, active objects may appear wherever passive objects appear. You can model the collaboration of active and passive objects by using interaction diagrams (including sequence and collaboration diagrams). An active object may appear as the target of an event in a state machine.

Speaking of state machines, both passive and active objects may send and receive signal events and call events.

Standard Elements

The UML's extensibility mechanisms are discussed in Chapter 6.

All of the UML's extensibility mechanisms apply to active classes. Most often, you'll use tagged values to extend active class properties, such as specifying the scheduling policy of the active class.

The UML's standard elements are summarized in Appendix B.

The UML defines two standard stereotypes that apply to active classes.

1. `process` Specifies a heavyweight flow that can execute concurrently with other processes
2. `thread`   Specifies a lightweight flow that can execute concurrently with other threads within the same process

Nodes are discussed in Chapter 26.

The distinction between a process and a thread arises from the two different ways a flow of control may be managed by the operating system of the node on which the object resides.

A process is heavyweight, which means that it is a thing known to the operating system itself and runs in an independent address space. Under most operating systems, such as Windows and Unix, each program runs as a process in its own address space. In general, all processes on a node are peers of one another, contending for all the same resources accessible on the node. Processes are never nested inside one another. If the node has multiple processors, then true concurrency on that node is possible. If the node has only one processor, there is only the illusion of true concurrency, carried out by the underlying operating system.

A thread is lightweight. It may be known to the operating system itself. More often, it is hidden inside a heavier-weight process and runs inside the address space of the enclosing process. In Java, for example, a thread is a child of the class `Thread`. All the threads that live in the context of a process are peers of one another, contending for the same resources accessible inside the process. Threads are never nested inside one another. In general, there is only the illusion of true concurrency among threads because it is processes, not threads, that are scheduled by a node's operating system.

Communication

*Interactions
are discussed
in Chapter 15.*

When objects collaborate with one another, they interact by passing messages from one to the other. In a system with both active and passive objects, there are four possible combinations of interaction that you must consider.

First, a message may be passed from one passive object to another. Assuming there is only one flow of control passing through these objects at a time, such an interaction is nothing more than the simple invocation of an operation.

*Signal events
and call events
are discussed
in Chapter 20.*

Second, a message may be passed from one active object to another. When that happens, you have interprocess communication, and there are two possible styles of communication. First, one active object might synchronously call an operation of another. That kind of communication has rendezvous semantics, which means that the caller calls the operation; the caller waits for the receiver to accept the call; the operation is invoked; a return object (if any) is passed back to the caller; and then the two continue on their independent paths. For the duration of the call, the two flows of controls are in lock step. Second, one active object might asynchronously send a signal or call an operation of another object. That kind of communication has mailbox semantics, which means that the caller sends the signal or calls the operation and then continues on its independent way. In the meantime, the receiver accepts the signal or call whenever it is ready (with intervening events or calls queued) and continues on its way after it is done. This is called a mailbox because the two objects are not synchronized; rather, one object drops off a message for the other.

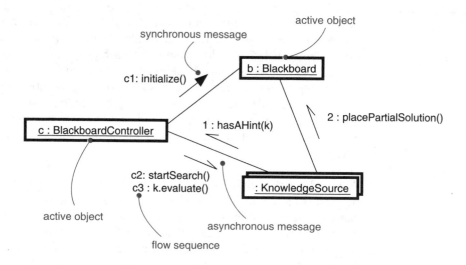

Figure 22-2: Communication

In the UML, you render a synchronous message as a full arrow and an asynchronous message as a half arrow, as in Figure 22-2.

Third, a message may be passed from an active object to a passive object. A difficulty arises if more than one active object at a time passes their flow of control through one passive object. In that situation, you have to model the synchronization of these two flows very carefully, as discussed in the next section.

Constraints are discussed in Chapter 6.

Fourth, a message may be passed from a passive object to an active one. At first glance, this may seem illegal, but if you remember that every flow of control is rooted in some active object, you'll understand that a passive object passing a message to an active object has the same semantics as an active object passing a message to an active object.

Note: It is possible to model variations of synchronous and asynchronous message passing by using constraints. For example, to model a balking rendezvous as found in Ada, you'd use a synchronous message with a constraint such as {wait = 0}, saying that the caller will not wait for the receiver. Similarly, you can model a time out by using a constraint such as {wait = 1 ms}, saying that the caller will wait no more than one millisecond for the receiver to accept the message.

Synchronization

Visualize for a moment the multiple flows of control that weave through a concurrent system. When a flow passes through an operation, we say that at a given moment, the locus of control is in the operation. If that operation is defined for some class, we can also say that at a given moment, the locus of control is in a specific instance of that class. You can have multiple flows of control in one operation (and therefore in one object), and you can have different flows of control in different operations (but still result in multiple flows of control in the one object).

The problem arises when more than one flow of control is in one object at the same time. If you are not careful, anything more than one flow will interfere with another, corrupting the state of the object. This is the classical problem of mutual exclusion. A failure to deal with it properly yields all sorts of race conditions and interference that cause concurrent systems to fail in mysterious and unrepeatable ways.

The key to solving this problem in object-oriented systems is by treating an object as a critical region. There are three alternatives to this approach, each of which involves attaching certain synchronization properties to the operations defined in a class. In the UML, you can model all three approaches.

1. Sequential   Callers must coordinate outside the object so that only one flow is in the object at a time. In the presence of multiple flows of control, the semantics and integrity of the object cannot be guaranteed.
2. Guarded   The semantics and integrity of the object is guaranteed in the presence of multiple flows of control by sequentializing all calls to all of the object's guarded operations. In effect, exactly one operation at a time can be invoked on the object, reducing this to sequential semantics.
3. Concurrent   The semantics and integrity of the object is guaranteed in the presence of multiple flows of control by treating the operation as atomic.

Some programming languages support these constructs directly. Java, for example, has the `synchronized` property, which is equivalent to the UML's `concurrent` property. In every language that supports concurrency, you can build support for all these properties by constructing them out of semaphores.

Constraints are discussed in Chapter 6.

As Figure 22-3 shows, you can attach these properties to an operation, which you can render in the UML by using constraint notation.

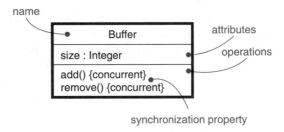

Figure 22-3: Synchronization

Note: It is possible to model variations of these synchronization primitives by using constraints. For example, you might modify the `concurrent` property by allowing multiple simultaneous readers but only a single writer.

Process Views

*Process views
in the context
of software
architecture
are discussed
in Chapter 2.*

Active objects play an important role in visualizing, specifying, constructing, and documenting a system's process view. The process view of a system encompasses the threads and processes that form the system's concurrency and synchronization mechanisms. This view primarily addresses the performance, scalability, and throughput of the system. With the UML, the static and dynamic aspects of this view are captured in the same kinds of diagrams as for the design view—that is, class diagrams, interaction diagrams, activity diagrams, and statechart diagrams, but with a focus on the active classes that represent these threads and processes.

Common Modeling Techniques

Modeling Multiple Flows of Control

*Mechanisms
are discussed
in Chapter 28;
class
diagrams are
discussed in
Chapter 8;
interaction
diagrams are
discussed in
Chapter 18.*

Building a system that encompasses multiple flows of control is hard. Not only do you have to decide how best to divide work across concurrent active objects, but once you've done that, you also have to devise the right mechanisms for communication and synchronization among your system's active and passive objects to ensure that they behave properly in the presence of these multiple flows. For that reason, it helps to visualize the way these flows interact with one another. You can do that in the UML by applying class diagrams (to capture their static semantics) and interaction diagrams (to capture their dynamic semantics) containing active classes and objects.

To model multiple flows of control,

*Process views
are discussed
in Chapter 2;
classes are
discussed in
Chapters 4
and 9; relation-
ships are
discussed in
Chapters 5
and 10.*

- Identify the opportunities for concurrent action and reify each flow as an active class. Generalize common sets of active objects into an active class. Be careful not to over-engineer the process view of your system by introducing too much concurrency.
- Consider a balanced distribution of responsibilities among these active classes, then examine the other active and passive classes with which each collaborates statically. Ensure that each active class is both tightly cohesive and loosely coupled relative to these neighboring classes and that each has the right set of attributes, operations, and signals.
- Capture these static decisions in class diagrams, explicitly highlighting each active class.
- Consider how each group of classes collaborates with one another dynamically. Capture those decisions in interaction diagrams. Explic-

itly show active objects as the root of such flows. Identify each related sequence by identifying it with the name of the active object.

■ Pay close attention to communication among active objects. Apply synchronous and asynchronous messaging, as appropriate.

■ Pay close attention to synchronization among these active objects and the passive objects with which they collaborate. Apply sequential, guarded, or concurrent operation semantics, as appropriate.

For example, Figure 22-4 shows part of the process view of a trading system. You'll find three objects that push information into the system concurrently: a StockTicker, an IndexWatcher, and a CNNNewsFeed (named s, i, and c, respectively). Two of these objects (s and i) communicate with their own Analyst instances (a1 and a2). At least as far as this model goes, the Analyst can be designed under the simplifying assumption that only one flow of control will be active in its instances at a time. Both Analyst instances, however, communicate simultaneously with an AlertManager (named m). Therefore, m must be designed to preserve its semantics in the presence of multiple flows. Both m and c communicate simultaneously with t, a TradingManager. Each flow is given a sequence number that is distinguished by the flow of control that owns it.

Note: Interaction diagrams such as these are useful in helping you to visualize where two flows of control might cross paths and, therefore, where you must pay particular attention to the problems of communication and synchronization. Tools are permitted to offer even more distinct visual cues, such as by coloring each flow in a distinct way.

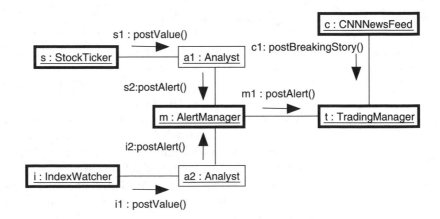

Figure 22-4: Modeling Flows of Control

State machines are discussed in Chapter 21.

In diagrams such as this, it's also common to attach corresponding state machines, with orthogonal states showing the detailed behavior of each active object.

Modeling Interprocess Communication

Signals and call events are discussed in Chapter 20.

As part of incorporating multiple flows of control in your system, you also have to consider the mechanisms by which objects that live in separate flows communicate with one another. Across threads (which live in the same address space), objects may communicate via signals or call events, the latter of which may exhibit either asynchronous or synchronous semantics. Across processes (which live in separate address spaces), you usually have to use different mechanisms.

Modeling location is discussed in Chapter 23.

The problem of interprocess communication is compounded by the fact that, in distributed systems, processes may live on separate nodes. Classically, there are two approaches to interprocess communication: message passing and remote procedure calls. In the UML, you still model these as asynchronous or synchronous events, respectively. But because these are no longer simple in-process calls, you need to adorn your designs with further information.

To model interprocess communication,

Stereotypes are discussed in Chapter 6; notes are discussed in Chapter 6; collaborations are discussed in Chapter 27; nodes are discussed in Chapter 26.

- Model the multiple flows of control.
- Consider which of these active objects represent processes and which represent threads. Distinguish them using the appropriate stereotype.
- Model messaging using asynchronous communication; model remote procedure calls using synchronous communication.
- Informally specify the underlying mechanism for communication by using notes, or more formally by using collaborations.

Figure 22-5 shows a distributed reservation system with processes spread across four nodes. Each object is marked using the `process` stereotype. Each object is also marked with a `location` tagged value, specifying its physical location. Communication among the `ReservationAgent`, `Ticketing-Manager`, and `HotelAgent` is asynchronous. Modeled with a note, communication is described as building on a Java Beans messaging service. Communication between the `TripPlanner` and the `ReservationSystem` is synchronous. The semantics of their interaction is found in the collaboration named `CORBA ORB`. The `TripPlanner` acts as a `client`, and the `ReservationAgent` acts as a `server`. By zooming into the collaboration, you'll find the details of how this server and client collaborate.

Figure 22-5: Modeling Interprocess Communication

Hints and Tips

A well-structured active class and active object

- Represents an independent flow of control that maximizes the potential for true concurrency in the system.
- Is not so fine-grained that it requires a multitude of other active elements that might result in an over-engineered and fragile process architecture.
- Carefully manages communication among peer active elements, choosing between asynchronous and synchronous messaging.
- Carefully treats each object as a critical region, using suitable synchronization properties to preserve its semantics in the presence of multiple flows of control.
- Explicitly distinguishes between process and thread semantics.

When you draw an active class or an active object in the UML,

- Show only those attributes, operations, and signals that are important in understanding the abstraction in its context.
- Explicitly show all operation synchronization properties.

UNIFIED
MODELING
LANGUAGE

Chapter 23
TIME AND SPACE

In this chapter

- Time, duration, and location
- Modeling timing constraints
- Modeling the distribution of objects
- Modeling objects that migrate
- Dealing with real time and distributed systems

The real world is a harsh and unforgiving place. Events may happen at unpredictable times, yet demand a specific response at a specific time. A system's resources may have to be distributed around the world—some of those resources might even move about—raising issues of latency, synchronization, security, and quality of service.

Modeling time and space is an essential element of any real time and/or distributed system. You use a number of the UML's features, including timing marks, time expressions, constraints, and tagged values, to visualize, specify, construct, and document these systems.

Dealing with real time and distributed systems is hard. Good models reveal the necessary and sufficient properties of a system's time and space characteristics.

Getting Started

When you start to model most software systems, you can usually assume a frictionless environment—messages are sent in zero time, networks never go down, workstations never fail, the load across your network is always evenly balanced. Unfortunately, the real world does not work that way—messages do take time to deliver (and, sometimes, never get delivered), networks do go

down, workstations do fail, and a network's load is often unbalanced. Therefore, when you encounter systems that must operate in the real world, you have
to take into account the issues of time and space.

A real time system is one in which certain behavior must be carried out at a
precise absolute or relative time and within a predictable, often constrained,
duration. At one extreme, such systems may be hard real time and require complete and repeatable behavior within nanoseconds or milliseconds. At the other
extreme, models may be near real time and also require predictable behavior,
but on the order of seconds or longer.

*Components
are discussed
in Chapter 25;
nodes are
discussed in
Chapter 26.*

A distributed system is one in which components may be physically distributed
across nodes. These nodes may represent different processors physically
located in the same box, or they may even represent computers that are located
half a world away from one another.

To represent the modeling needs of real time and distributed systems, the UML
provides a graphic representation for timing marks, time expressions, timing
constraints, and location, as Figure 23-1 shows.

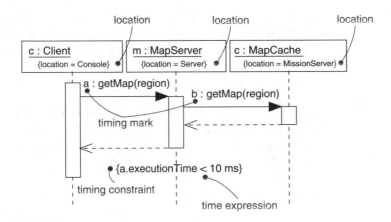

Figure 23-1: Timing Constraints and Location

Terms and Concepts

A *timing mark* is a denotation for the time at which an event occurs. Graphically, a timing mark is formed as an expression from the name given to the
message (which is typically different from the name of the action dispatched

by the message). A *time expression* is an expression that evaluates to an absolute or relative value of time. A *timing constraint* is a semantic statement about the relative or absolute value of time. Graphically, a timing constraint is rendered as for any constraint—that is, a string enclosed by brackets and generally connected to an element by a dependency relationship. *Location* is the placement of a component on a node. Graphically, location is rendered as a tagged value—that is, a string enclosed by brackets and placed below an element's name, or as the nesting of components inside nodes.

Time

Events, including time events, are discussed in Chapter 20; messages and interactions are discussed in Chapter 15; constraints are discussed in Chapter 6.

Real time systems are, by their very name, time-critical systems. Events may happen at regular or irregular times; the response to an event must happen at predictable absolute times or at predictable times relative to the event itself.

The passing of messages represents the dynamic aspect of any system, so when you model the time-critical nature of a system with the UML, you can give a name to each message in an interaction to be used as a timing mark. Messages in an interaction are usually not given names. They are mainly rendered with the name of an event, such as a signal or a call. As a result, you can't use the event name to write an expression because the same event may trigger different messages. If the designated message is ambiguous, use the explicit name of the message in a timing mark to designate the message you want to mention in a time expression. A timing mark is nothing more than an expression formed from the name of a message in an interaction. Given a message name, you can refer to any of three functions of that message—that is, `startTime`, `stopTime`, and `executionTime`. You can then use these functions to specify arbitrarily complex time expressions, perhaps even using weights or offsets that are either constants or variables (as long as those variables can be bound at execution time). Finally, as shown in Figure 23-2, you can place these time expressions in a timing constraint to specify the timing behavior of the system. As constraints, you can render them by placing them adjacent to the appropriate message, or you can explicitly attach them using dependency relationships.

Note: Especially for complex systems, it's a good idea to write expressions with named constants instead of writing explicit times. You can define those constants in one part of your model and then refer to those constants in multiple places. In that way, it's easier to update your model if the timing requirements of your system change.

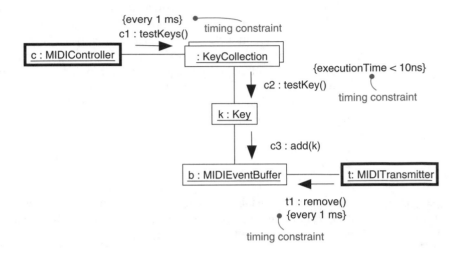

Figure 23-2: Time

The semantics tagged value is discussed in Chapter 9.

Note: You can also apply time expressions to operations. The standard tagged value called `semantics` can be attached to any operation, and by using a time expression there, you can specify the operation's time complexity. Time complexity typically models the minimum, maximum, and/or average time in which you expect that operation to complete. Specifying an operation's time complexity in effect specifies a time budget for the operation, which you can use in two ways. First, by asserting your time budgets during development and then by measuring the running system, you can make intelligent comparisons about the as-designed versus the as-built behavior of your system. Second, by adding up the results (designed or actual) of the time expression for all the operations in an interaction, you can calculate the time complexity of an entire transaction.

Location

Components are discussed in Chapter 25; nodes are discussed in Chapter 26.

Distributed systems, by their nature, encompass components that are physically scattered among the nodes of a system. For many systems, components are fixed in place at the time they are loaded on the system; in other systems, components may migrate from node to node.

Deployment diagrams are discussed in Chapter 30; the class/ object dichot- omy is dis- cussed in Chapters 2 and 13.

In the UML, you model the deployment view of a system by using deployment diagrams that represent the topology of the processors and devices on which your system executes. Components such as executables, libraries, and tables reside on these nodes. Each instance of a node will own instances of certain components, and each instance of a component will be owned by exactly one instance of a node (although instances of the same kind of component may be spread across different nodes). For example, as Figure 23-3 shows, the executable component `vision.exe` may reside on the node named `KioskServer`.

Classes are discussed in Chapters 4 and 9.

Instances of plain classes may reside on a node, as well. For example, as Fig- ure 23-3 shows, an instance of the class `LoadAgent` lives on the node named `Router`.

Tagged values and extra com- partments are discussed in Chapter 6.

As the figure illustrates, you can model the location of an element in two ways in the UML. First, as shown for the `KioskServer`, you can physically nest the element (textually or graphically) in a extra compartment in its enclosing node. Second, as shown for the `LoadAgent`, you can use the defined tagged value `location` to designate the node on which the class instance resides. You'll typically use the first form when it's important for you to give a visual cue in your diagrams about the spatial separation and grouping of components. Similarly, you'll use the second form when modeling the location of an ele- ment is important, but secondary, to the diagram at hand, such as when you want to visualize the passing of messages among instances.

The become and copy stereotypes are discussed in Chapter 13.

Note: The second form for modeling the location of an element is espe- cially useful when you want to show the redistribution of a component over time. For example, you can use a become message to model an object currently residing at one location and moving to another location. Similarly, you can use a copy message to show the semantic relation- ship between distant objects.

Figure 23-3: Location

Common Modeling Techniques

Modeling Timing Constraints

Constraints, one of the UML's extensibility mechanisms, are discussed in Chapter 6.

Modeling the absolute time of an event, modeling the relative time between events, and modeling the time it takes to carry out an action are the three primary time-critical properties of real time systems for which you'll use timing constraints.

To model timing constraints,

- For each event in an interaction, consider whether it must start at some absolute time. Model that real time property as a timing constraint on the message.
- For each interesting sequence of messages in an interaction, consider whether there is an associated maximum relative time for that sequence. Model that real time property as a timing constraint on the sequence.
- For each time critical operation in each class, consider its time complexity. Model those semantics as timing constraints on the operation.

For example, as shown in Figure 23-4, the left-most constraint specifies the repeating start time the call event `refresh`. Similarly, the center timing constraint specifies the maximum duration for calls to `getImage`. Finally, the right-most constraint specifies the time complexity of the call event `getImage`.

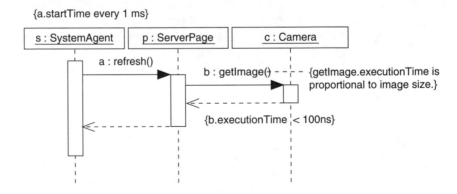

Figure 23-4: Modeling Timing Constraint

Note: Observe that `executionTime` may be applied to actions such as `getImage`, as well as to timing marks such as `a` and `b`. Also, timing constraints such as these may be written as free-form text. If you want to specify your semantics more precisely, you can use the UML's Object Constraint Language (OCL), described further in *The Unified Modeling Language Reference Manual.*

Often, you'll choose short names for messages, so that you don't confuse them with operation names.

Modeling the Distribution of Objects

Modeling the distribution of a component is discussed in Chapter 25.

When you model the topology of a distributed system, you'll want to consider the physical placement of both components and class instances. If your focus is the configuration management of the deployed system, modeling the distribution of components is especially important in order to visualize, specify, construct, and document the placement of physical things such as executables, libraries, and tables. If your focus is the functionality, scalability, and throughput of the system, modeling the distribution of objects is what's important.

Modeling processes and threads is discussed in Chapter 22.

Deciding how to distribute the objects in a system is a wicked problem, and not just because the problems of distribution interact with the problems of concurrency. Naive solutions tend to yield profoundly poor performance, and over-engineering solutions aren't much better. In fact, they are probably worse because they usually end up being brittle.

To model the distribution of objects,

- For each interesting class of objects in your system, consider its locality of reference. In other words, consider all its neighbors and their locations. A tightly coupled locality will have neighboring objects close by; a loosely coupled one will have distant objects (and thus, there will be latency in communicating with them). Tentatively allocate objects closest to the actors that manipulate them.
- Next consider patterns of interaction among related sets of objects. Co-locate sets of objects that have high degrees of interaction, to reduce the cost of communication. Partition sets of objects that have low degrees of interaction.
- Next consider the distribution of responsibilities across the system. Redistribute your objects to balance the load of each node.
- Consider also issues of security, volatility, and quality of service, and redistribute your objects as appropriate.

■ Render this allocation in one of two ways:
1. By nesting objects in the nodes of a deployment diagram
2. By explicitly indicating the location of the object as a tagged value

Object diagrams are discussed in Chapter 14.

Figure 23-5 provides an object diagram that models the distribution of certain objects in a retail system. The value of this diagram is that it lets you visualize the physical distribution of certain key objects. As the diagram shows, two objects reside on a `Workstation` (the `Order` and `Sales` objects), two objects reside on a `Server` (the `ObserverAgent` and the `Product` objects), and one object resides on a `DataWarehouse` (the `ProductTable` object).

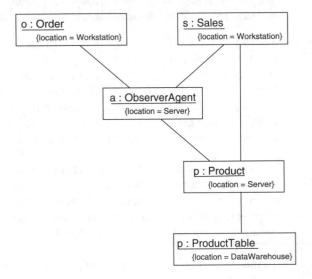

Figure 23-5: Modeling the Distribution of Objects

Modeling Objects that Migrate

For many distributed systems, components and objects, once loaded on the system, stay put. For their lifetime, from creation to destruction, they never leave the node on which they were born. There are certain classes of distributed systems, however, for which things move about, usually for one of two reasons.

First, you'll find objects migrating in order to move closer to actors and other objects they need to work with to do their job better. For example, in a global shipping system, you'd see objects that represent ships, containers, and manifests moving from node to node to track their physical counterpart. If you have a ship in Hong Kong, it makes for better locality of reference to put the object representing the ship, its containers, and its manifest on a node in Hong Kong. When that ship sails to San Diego, you'd want to move the associated objects, as well.

Second, you'll find objects migrating in response to the failure of a node or connection or to balance the load across multiple nodes. For example, in an air traffic control system, the failure of one node cannot be allowed to stall a nation's entire operations. Rather, a failure-tolerant system such as this will migrate elements to other nodes. Performance and throughput may be reduced, but safe functionality will be preserved. Similarly, and especially in Web-based systems that must deal with unpredictable peaks in demand, you'll often want to build mechanisms to automatically balance the processing load, perhaps by migrating components and objects to underused nodes.

Deciding how to migrate the objects in a system is an even more wicked problem than simple static distribution because migration raises difficult problems of synchronization and preservation of identity.

To model the migration of objects,

Mechanisms are discussed in Chapter 28.

The become *and* copy *stereotypes are discussed in Chapter 13.*

- Select an underlying mechanism for physically transporting objects across nodes.
- Render the allocation of an object to a node by explicitly indicating its location as a tagged value.
- Using the become and copy stereotyped messages, render the allocation of an object to a new node.
- Consider the issues of synchronization (keeping the state of cloned objects consistent) and identity (preserving the name of the object as it moves).

Collaboration diagrams are discussed in Chapter 18.

Figure 23-6 provides a collaboration diagram that models the migration of a Web agent that moves from node to node, collecting information and bidding on resources in order to automatically deliver a lowest-cost travel ticket. Specifically, this diagram shows an instance (named t) of the class TravelAgent migrating from one server to another. Along the way, the object interacts with anonymous Auctioneer instances at each node, eventually delivering a bid for the Itinerary object, located on the client server.

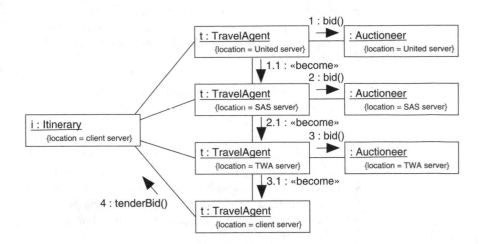

Figure 23-6: Modeling Objects that Migrate

Hints and Tips

A well-structured model with time and space properties

- Exposes only those time and space properties that are necessary and sufficient to capture the desired behavior of the system.
- Centralizes the use of those properties so that they are easy to find and easy to modify.

When you draw a time or space property in the UML,

- Give your timing marks (the names of messages) meaningful names.
- Clearly distinguish between relative and absolute time expressions.
- Show space properties primarily by tagged value. Use the nested form only when it's important to visualize the placement of elements across a deployed system.

UNIFIED
MODELING
LANGUAGE

Chapter 24
STATECHART DIAGRAMS

In this chapter

- Modeling reactive objects
- Forward and reverse engineering

Sequence diagrams, collaboration diagrams, activity diagrams, and use case diagrams also model the dynamic aspects of systems; sequence diagrams and collaboration diagrams are discussed in Chapter 18; activity diagrams are discussed in Chapter 19; use case diagrams are discussed in Chapter 17.

Statechart diagrams are one of the five diagrams in the UML for modeling the dynamic aspects of systems. A statechart diagram shows a state machine. An activity diagram is a special case of a statechart diagram in which all or most of the states are activity states and all or most of the transitions are triggered by completion of activities in the source state. Thus, both activity and statechart diagrams are useful in modeling the lifetime of an object. However, whereas an activity diagram shows flow of control from activity to activity, a statechart diagram shows flow of control from state to state.

You use statechart diagrams to model the dynamic aspects of a system. For the most part, this involves modeling the behavior of reactive objects. A reactive object is one whose behavior is best characterized by its response to events dispatched from outside its context. A reactive object has a clear lifetime whose current behavior is affected by its past. Statechart diagrams may be attached to classes, use cases, or entire systems in order to visualize, specify, construct, and document the dynamics of an individual object.

Statechart diagrams are not only important for modeling the dynamic aspects of a system, but also for constructing executable systems through forward and reverse engineering.

Getting Started

The differences between building a dog house and building a high rise are discussed in Chapter 1.

Consider the investor who finances the building of a new high rise. She is unlikely to be interested in the details of the building process. The selection of materials, the scheduling of the trades, and the many meetings about engineering details and activities are important to the builder, but far less so to the person bankrolling the project.

The investor is interested in getting a good return on the investment, and that also means protecting the investment against risk. A really trusting investor will give a builder a pile of money, walk away for a while, and return only when the builder is ready to hand over the keys to the building. Such an investor is really interested in the final state of the building.

A more pragmatic investor will still trust the builder, but will also want to verify that the project is on track before releasing money. So, rather than give the builder an unattended pile of money to dip into, the prudent investor will set up clear milestones for the project, each of which is tied to the completion of certain activities, and only after which money is released to the builder for the next phase of the project. For example, a modest amount of funds might be released at the project's inception, to fund the architectural work. After the architectural vision has been approved, then more funds may be released to pay for the engineering work. After that work is completed to the project stakeholders' satisfaction, a larger pile of money may be released so that the builder can proceed with breaking ground. Along the way, from ground breaking to issuance of the certificate of occupancy, there are other milestones.

Gantt charts and Pert charts are discussed in Chapter 19.

Each of these milestones names a stable state of the project: architecture complete, engineering done, ground broken, infrastructure completed, building sealed, and so on. For the investor, following the changing state of the building is more important than following the flow of activities, which is what the builder might be doing by using Pert charts to model the workflow of the project.

Activity diagrams as flowcharts are discussed in Chapter 19; state machines are discussed in Chapter 21.

In modeling software-intensive systems, as well, you'll find the most natural way to visualize, specify, construct, and document the behavior of certain kinds of objects is by focusing on the flow of control from state to state rather than from activity to activity. You would do the latter with a flowchart (and in the UML, with an activity diagram). Imagine, for a moment, modeling the behavior of an embedded home security system. Such a system runs continuously, reacting to events from the outside, such as a window break. In addition, the order of events changes the way the system behaves. For example, the detection of a window break will only trigger an alarm if the system is first armed. The behavior of such a system is best specified by modeling its stable states (for example, `Idle`, `Armed`, `Active`, `Checking`, and so on), the events that trigger a change from state to state, and the actions that occur on each state change.

In the UML, you model the event-ordered behavior of an object by using statechart diagrams. As Figure 24-1 shows, a statechart diagram is simply a presentation of a state machine, emphasizing the flow of control from state to state.

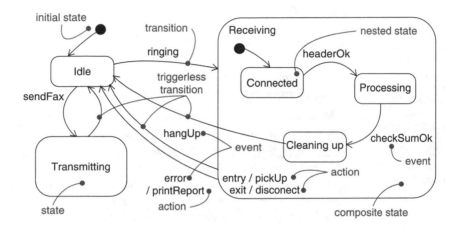

Figure 24-1: Statechart Diagram

Terms and Concepts

A *statechart diagram* shows a state machine, emphasizing the flow of control from state to state. A *state machine* is a behavior that specifies the sequences of states an object goes through during its lifetime in response to events, together with its responses to those events. A *state* is a condition or situation in the life of an object during which it satisfies some condition, performs some activity, or waits for some event. An *event* is the specification of a significant occurrence that has a location in time and space. In the context of state machines, an event is an occurrence of a stimulus that can trigger a state transition. A *transition* is a relationship between two states indicating that an object in the first state will perform certain actions and enter the second state when a specified event occurs and specified conditions are satisfied. An *activity* is ongoing nonatomic execution within a state machine. An *action* is an executable atomic computation that results in a change in state of the model or the return of a value. Graphically, a statechart diagram is a collection of vertices and arcs.

Common Properties

The general properties of diagrams are discussed in Chapter 7.

A statechart diagram is just a special kind of diagram and shares the same common properties as do all other diagrams—that is, a name and graphical contents that are a projection into a model. What distinguishes a statechart diagram from all other kinds of diagrams is its content.

Contents

Simple states, composite states, transitions, events, and actions are discussed in Chapter 21; activity diagrams are discussed in Chapter 19.

Statechart diagrams commonly contain

- Simple states and composite states
- Transitions, including events and actions

Note: A statechart diagram is basically a projection of the elements found in a state machine. This means that statechart diagrams may contain branches, forks, joins, action states, activity states, objects, initial states, final states, history states, and so on. Indeed, a statechart diagram may contain any and all features of a state machine. What distinguishes an activity diagram from a statechart diagram is that an activity diagram is basically a projection of the elements found in an activity graph, a special case of a state machine in which all or most states are activity states and in which all or most transitions are triggered by completion of activities in the source state.

Notes and constraints are discussed in Chapter 6.

Like all other diagrams, statechart diagrams may contain notes and constraints.

Common Uses

The five views of an architecture are discussed in Chapter 2; instances are discussed in Chapter 13; classes are discussed in Chapters 4 and 9.

You use statechart diagrams to model the dynamic aspects of a system. These dynamic aspects may involve the event-ordered behavior of any kind of object in any view of a system's architecture, including classes (which includes active classes), interfaces, components, and nodes.

When you use a statechart diagram to model some dynamic aspect of a system, you do so in the context of virtually any modeling element. Typically, however, you'll use statechart diagrams in the context of the system as a whole, a subsystem, or a class. You can also attach statechart diagrams to use cases (to model a scenario).

Active classes
are discussed
in Chapter 22;
interfaces are
discussed in
Chapter 11;
components
are discussed
in Chapter 25;
nodes are
discussed in
Chapter 26;
use cases are
discussed in
Chapter 16;
systems are
discussed in
Chapter 31.

When you model the dynamic aspects of a system, a class, or a use case, you'll typically use statechart diagrams in one way.

- To model reactive objects

A reactive – or event-driven – object is one whose behavior is best characterized by its response to events dispatched from outside its context. A reactive object is typically idle until it receives an event. When it receives an event, its response usually depends on previous events. After the object responds to an event, it becomes idle again, waiting for the next event. For these kinds of objects, you'll focus on the stable states of that object, the events that trigger a transition from state to state, and the actions that occur on each state change.

Note: In contrast, you'll use activity diagrams to model a workflow or to model an operation. Activity diagrams are better suited to modeling the flow of activities over time, such as you would represent in a flowchart.

Common Modeling Techniques

Modeling Reactive Objects

Interactions
are discussed
in Chapter 15;
activity
diagrams are
discussed in
Chapter 19.

The most common purpose for which you'll use statechart diagrams is to model the behavior of reactive objects, especially instances of classes, use cases, and the system as a whole. Whereas interactions model the behavior of a society of objects working together, a statechart diagram models the behavior of a single object over its lifetime. Whereas an activity diagram models the flow of control from activity to activity, a statechart diagram models the flow of control from event to event.

Modeling the
lifetime of an
object is
discussed in
Chapter 21.

When you model the behavior of a reactive object, you essentially specify three things: the stable states in which that object may live, the events that trigger a transition from state to state, and the actions that occur on each state change. Modeling the behavior of a reactive object also involves modeling the lifetime of an object, starting at the time of the object's creation and continuing until its destruction, highlighting the stable states in which the object may be found.

Time and
space are
discussed in
Chapter 23.

A stable state represents a condition in which an object may exist for some identifiable period of time. When an event occurs, the object may transition from state to state. These events may also trigger self- and internal transitions, in which the source and the target of the transition are the same state. In reaction to an event or a state change, the object may respond by dispatching an action.

Note: When you model the behavior of a reactive object, you can specify its action by tying it to a transition or to a state change. In technical terms, a state machine whose actions are all attached to transitions is called a Mealy machine; a state machine whose actions are all attached to states is called a Moore machine. Mathematically, the two styles have equivalent power. In practice, you'll typically develop statechart diagrams that use a combination of Mealy and Moore machines.

To model a reactive object,

Pre- and post-conditions are discussed in Chapter 10; interfaces are discussed in Chapter 11.

- Choose the context for the state machine, whether it is a class, a use case, or the system as a whole.
- Choose the initial and final states for the object. To guide the rest of your model, possibly state the pre- and postconditions of the initial and final states, respectively.
- Decide on the stable states of the object by considering the conditions in which the object may exist for some identifiable period of time. Start with the high-level states of the object and only then consider its possible substates.
- Decide on the meaningful partial ordering of stable states over the lifetime of the object.
- Decide on the events that may trigger a transition from state to state. Model these events as triggers to transitions that move from one legal ordering of states to another.
- Attach actions to these transitions (as in a Mealy machine) and/or to these states (as in a Moore machine).
- Consider ways to simplify your machine by using substates, branches, forks, joins, and history states.
- Check that all states are reachable under some combination of events.
- Check that no state is a dead end from which no combination of events will transition the object out of that state.
- Trace through the state machine, either manually or by using tools, to check it against expected sequences of events and their responses.

For example, Figure 24-2 shows the statechart diagram for parsing a simple context-free language, such as you might find in systems that stream in or stream out messages to XML. In this case, the machine is designed to parse a stream of characters that match the syntax

```
message : '<' string '>' string ';'
```

The first string represents a tag; the second string represents the body of the message. Given a stream of characters, only well-formed messages that follow this syntax may be accepted.

Events are discussed in Chapter 20.

As the figure shows, there are only three stable states for this state machine: Waiting, GettingToken, and GettingBody. This statechart is designed as a Mealy machine, with actions tied to transitions. In fact, there is only one event of interest in this state machine, the invocation of put with the actual parameter c (a character). While Waiting, this machine throws away any character that does not designate the start of a token (as specified by the guard condition). When the start of a token is received, the state of the object changes to GettingToken. While in that state, the machine saves any character that does not designate the end of a token (as specified by the guard condition). When the end of a token is received, the state of the object changes to GettingBody. While in that state, the machine saves any character that does not designate the end of a message body (as specified by the guard condition). When the end of a message is received, the state of the object changes to Waiting, and a value is returned indicating that the message has been parsed (and the machine is ready to receive another message).

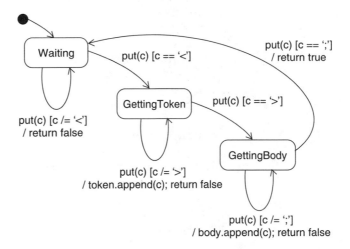

Figure 24-2: Modeling Reactive Objects

Note that this statechart specifies a machine that runs continuously; there is no final state.

Forward and Reverse Engineering

Forward engineering (the creation of code from a model) is possible for state-chart diagrams, especially if the context of the diagram is a class. For example, using the previous statechart diagram, a forward engineering tool could generate the following Java code for the class `MessageParser`.

```java
class MessageParser {
public boolean put(char c) {
   switch (state) {
     case Waiting:
       if (c == '<') {
         state = GettingToken;
         token = new StringBuffer();
         body = new StringBuffer();
       }
       break;
     case GettingToken :
       if (c == '>')
         state = GettingBody;
       else
         token.append(c);
       break;
     case GettingBody :
       if (c == ';') {
         state = Waiting;
         return true; }
       else
         body.append(c);
   }
   return false;
 }
public StringBuffer getToken() {
   return token;
 }
public StringBuffer getBody() {
   return body;
 }
private final static int Waiting = 0;
private final static int GettingToken = 1;
private final static int GettingBody = 2;
private int state = Waiting;
private StringBuffer token, body;
}
```

This requires a little cleverness. The forward engineering tool must generate the necessary private attributes and final static constants.

Reverse engineering (the creation of a model from code) is theoretically possible, but practically not very useful. The choice of what constitutes a meaningful state is in the eye of the designer. Reverse engineering tools have no capacity for abstraction and therefore cannot automatically produce meaningful statechart diagrams. More interesting than the reverse engineering of a model from code is the animation of a model against the execution of a deployed system. For example, given the previous diagram, a tool could animate the states in the diagram as they were reached in the running system. Similarly, the firing of transitions could be animated, showing the receipt of events and the resulting dispatch of actions. Under the control of a debugger, you could control the speed of execution, setting breakpoints to stop the action at interesting states to examine the attribute values of individual objects.

Hints and Tips

When you create statechart diagrams in the UML, remember that every statechart diagram is just a projection on the same model of a system's dynamic aspects. A single statechart diagram can capture the semantics of a single reactive object, but no one statechart diagram can capture the semantics of an entire nontrivial system.

A well-structured statechart diagram

- Is focused on communicating one aspect of a system's dynamics.
- Contains only those elements that are essential to understanding that aspect.
- Provides detail consistent with its level of abstraction (expose only those features that are essential to understanding).
- Uses a balance between the styles of Mealy and Moore machines.

When you draw a statechart diagram,

- Give it a name that communicates its purpose.
- Start with modeling the stable states of the object, then follow with modeling the legal transitions from state to state. Address branching, concurrency, and object flow as secondary considerations, possibly in separate diagrams.
- Lay out its elements to minimize lines that cross.

UNIFIED
MODELING
LANGUAGE

Section 6
ARCHITECTURAL
MODELING

superstructure
The vertical extension of a building or other construction above the foundation.

• roof

shell
The exterior framework or walls and roof of a building.

• ceiling
• room
• wall
• window
• door
• floor
• mechanical systems

• structure

• foundation

substructure
The underlying structure forming the foundation of a building or other construction.

• building site

system
A group of interacting, interrelated, or interdependent things or parts forming a complex or unified whole, esp. to serve a common purpose.

UNIFIED
MODELING
LANGUAGE

Chapter 25
COMPONENTS

Components live in the material world of bits and therefore are an important building block in modeling the physical aspects of a system. A component is a physical and replaceable part of a system that conforms to and provides the realization of a set of interfaces.

You use components to model the physical things that may reside on a node, such as executables, libraries, tables, files, and documents. A component typically represents the physical packaging of otherwise logical elements, such as classes, interfaces, and collaborations.

Good components define crisp abstractions with well-defined interfaces, making it possible to easily replace older components with newer, compatible ones.

Getting Started

The end product of a construction company is a physical building that exists in the real world. You build logical models to visualize, specify, and document your decisions about the building envelope; the placement of walls, doors, and

343

windows; the routing of electrical and plumbing systems; and the overall architectural style. When you actually construct the building, these walls, doors, windows, and other conceptual things get turned into real, physical things.

The differences between building a dog house and building a high rise are discussed in Chapter 1.

These logical and physical views are both necessary. If you are building a disposable building for which the cost of scrap and rework is essentially zero (for example, if you are building a doghouse), you can probably go straight to the physical building without doing any logical modeling. If, on the other hand, you are building something enduring for which the cost of change or failure is high, then building both logical and physical models is the pragmatic thing to do to manage risk.

It's the same thing when building a software-intensive system. You do logical modeling to visualize, specify, and document your decisions about the vocabulary of your domain and the structural and behavioral way those things collaborate. You do physical modeling to construct the executable system. Whereas these logical things live in the conceptual world, the physical things live in the world of bits—that is, they ultimately reside on physical nodes and can be executed directly or can, in some indirect manner, participate in an executing system.

Interfaces are discussed in Chapter 11.

In the UML, all these physical things are modeled as components. A component is a physical thing that conforms to and realizes a set of interfaces. Interfaces therefore bridge your logical and physical models. For example, you may specify an interface for a class in a logical model, and that same interface will carry over to some physical component that realizes it.

In software, many operating systems and programming languages directly support the concept of a component. Object libraries, executables, COM+ components, and Enterprise Java Beans are all examples of components that may be represented directly in the UML by using components. Not only can components be used to model these kinds of things, they can also be used to represent other things that participate in an executing system, such as tables, files, and documents.

Stereotypes are discussed in Chapter 6.

The UML provides a graphical representation of a component, as Figure 25-1 shows. This canonical notation permits you to visualize a component apart from any operating system or programming language. Using stereotypes, one of the UML's extensibility mechanisms, you can tailor this notation to represent specific kinds of components.

Figure 25-1: Components

Terms and Concepts

A *component* is a physical and replaceable part of a system that conforms to and provides the realization of a set of interfaces. Graphically, a component is rendered as a rectangle with tabs.

Names

A component name must be unique within its enclosing package, as discussed in Chapter 12; tagged values and compartments are discussed in Chapter 6.

Every component must have a name that distinguishes it from other components. A *name* is a textual string. That name alone is known as a *simple name*; a *path name* is the component name prefixed by the name of the package in which that component lives. A component is typically drawn showing only its name, as in Figure 25-2. Just as with classes, you may draw components adorned with tagged values or with additional compartments to expose their details, as you see in the figure.

Figure 25-2: Simple and Extended Components

Note: A component name may be text consisting of any number of letters, numbers, and certain punctuation marks (except for marks such as the colon, which is used to separate a component name and the name of its enclosing package) and may continue over several lines. In practice, component names are short nouns or noun phrases drawn from the vocabulary of the implementation and, depending on your target operating system, include extensions (such as `java` and `dll`).

Components and Classes

Classes are discussed in Chapters 4 and 9; interactions are discussed in Chapter 15.

In many ways, components are like classes: Both have names; both may realize a set of interfaces; both may participate in dependency, generalization, and association relationships; both may be nested; both may have instances; both may be participants in interactions. However, there are some significant differences between components and classes.

- Classes represent logical abstractions; components represent physical things that live in the world of bits. In short, components may live on nodes, classes may not.
- Components represent the physical packaging of otherwise logical components and are at a different level of abstraction.
- Classes may have attributes and operations directly. In general, components only have operations that are reachable only through their interfaces.

Nodes are discussed in Chapter 26.

The first difference is the most important. When modeling a system, deciding if you should use a class or a component involves a simple decision—if the thing you are modeling lives directly on a node, use a component; otherwise, use a class.

Dependency relationships are discussed in Chapters 5 and 10; collaborations are discussed in Chapter 27.

The second difference suggests a relationship between classes and components. In particular, a component is the physical implementation of a set of other logical elements, such as classes and collaborations. As Figure 25-3 shows, the relationship between a component and the classes it implements can be shown explicitly by using a dependency relationship. Most of the time, you'll never need to visualize these relationships graphically. Rather, you will keep them as a part of the component's specification.

Interfaces are discussed in Chapter 11.

The third difference points out how interfaces bridge components and classes. As described in more detail in the next section, components and classes may both realize an interface, but a component's services are usually available only through its interfaces.

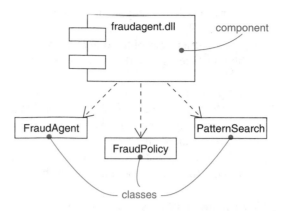

Figure 25-3: Components and Classes

Note: Components are also class-like in that you can (but rarely do) specify attributes and operations for them. You will need to do so only if you're modeling a reflective system that can manipulate its own components.

Components and Interfaces

Interfaces are discussed in Chapter 11.

An interface is a collection of operations that are used to specify a service of a class or a component. The relationship between component and interface is important. All the most common component-based operating system facilities (such as COM+, CORBA, and Enterprise Java Beans) use interfaces as the glue that binds components together.

Modeling distributed systems is discussed in Chapter 23.

Using one of these facilities, you decompose your physical implementation by specifying interfaces that represent the major seams in the system. You then provide components that realize the interfaces, along with other components that access the services through their interfaces. This mechanism permits you to deploy a system whose services are somewhat location-independent and, as discussed in the next section, replaceable.

Realization is discussed in Chapter 10.

As Figure 25-4 indicates, you can show the relationship between a component and its interfaces in one of two ways. The first (and most common) style renders the interface in its elided, iconic form. The component that realizes the interface is connected to the interface using an elided realization relationship. The second style renders the interface in its expanded form, perhaps revealing its operations. The component that realizes the interface is connected to the interface using a full realization relationship. In both cases, the component that accesses the services of the other component through the interface is connected to the interface using a dependency relationship.

An interface that a component realizes is called an *export interface*, meaning an interface that the component provides as a service to other components. A component may provide many export interfaces. The interface that a component uses is called an *import interface*, meaning an interface that the component conforms to and so builds on. A component may conform to many import interfaces. Also, a component may both import and export interfaces.

A given interface may be exported by one component and imported by another. The fact that this interface lies between the two components breaks the direct dependency between the components. A component that uses a given interface will function properly no matter what component realizes that interface. Of course, a component can be used in a context if and only if all its import interfaces are provided by the export interfaces of other components.

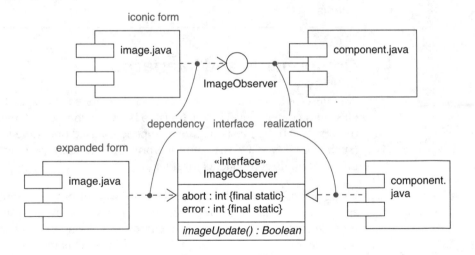

Figure 25-4: Components and Interfaces

Note: Interfaces span logical and physical boundaries. The same interface you find used or realized by a component will be found used or realized by the classes that the component implements.

Binary Replaceability

The basic intent of every component-based operating system facility is to permit the assembly of systems from binary replaceable parts. This means that you can create a system out of components and then evolve that system by adding new components and replacing old ones, without rebuilding the system. Interfaces are the key to making this happen. When you specify an interface, you can drop into the executable system any component that conforms to or provides that interface. You can extend the system by making the components provide new services through other interfaces, which, in turn, other components can discover and use. These semantics explain the intent behind the definition of components in the UML. A component is a physical and replaceable part of a system that conforms to and provides the realization of a set of interfaces.

First, a component is *physical*. It lives in the world of bits, not concepts.

Second, a component is *replaceable*. A component is substitutable—it is possible to replace a component with another that conforms to the same interfaces. Typically, the mechanism of inserting or replacing a component to form a run time system is transparent to the component user and is enabled by object models (such as COM+ and Enterprise Java Beans) that require little or no intervening transformation or by tools that automate the mechanism.

Systems and subsystems are discussed in Chapter 31.

Third, a component is *part of a system*. A component rarely stands alone. Rather, a given component collaborates with other components and in so doing exists in the architectural or technology context in which it is intended to be used. A component is logically and physically cohesive and thus denotes a meaningful structural and/or behavioral chunk of a larger system. A component may be reused across many systems. Therefore, a component represents a fundamental building block on which systems can be designed and composed. This definition is recursive—a system at one level of abstraction may simply be a component at a higher level of abstraction.

Fourth, as discussed in the previous section, a component *conforms to and provides the realization of a set of interfaces*.

Kinds of Components

Three kinds of components may be distinguished.

First, there are *deployment components*. These are the components necessary and sufficient to form an executable system, such as dynamic libraries (DLLs) and executables (EXEs). The UML's definition of component is broad enough to address classic object models, such as COM+, CORBA, and Enterprise Java Beans, as well as alternative object models, perhaps involving dynamic Web pages, database tables, and executables using proprietary communication mechanisms.

Second, there are *work product components*. These components are essentially the residue of the development process, consisting of things such as source code files and data files from which deployment components are created. These components do not directly participate in an executable system but are the work products of development that are used to create the executable system.

Third are *execution components*. These components are created as a consequence of an executing system, such as a COM+ object, which is instantiated from a DLL.

Organizing Components

Packages are discussed in Chapter 12.

You can organize components by grouping them in packages in the same manner in which you organize classes.

Relationships are discussed in Chapters 5 and 10.

You can also organize components by specifying dependency, generalization, association (including aggregation), and realization relationships among them.

Standard Elements

The UML's extensibility mechanisms are discussed in Chapter 6.

All the UML's extensibility mechanisms apply to components. Most often, you'll use tagged values to extend component properties (such as specifying the version of a development component) and stereotypes to specify new kinds of components (such as operating system-specific components).

The UML's standard elements are summarized in Appendix B.

The UML defines five standard stereotypes that apply to components:

1. `executable`   Specifies a component that may be executed on a node
2. `library`   Specifies a static or dynamic object library
3. `table`   Specifies a component that represents a database table
4. `file`   Specifies a component that represents a document containing source code or data
5. `document`   Specifies a component that represents a document

Note: The UML does not specify defined icons for any of these stereotypes, although Appendix B offers some notation from common practice.

Common Modeling Techniques

Modeling Executables and Libraries

The most common purpose for which you'll use components is to model the deployment components that make up your implementation. If you are deploying a trivial system whose implementation consists of exactly one executable file, you will not need to do any component modeling. If, on the other hand, the system you are deploying is made up of several executables and associated object libraries, doing component modeling will help you to visualize, specify, construct, and document the decisions you've made about the physical system. Component modeling is even more important if you want to control the versioning and configuration management of these parts as your system evolves.

These decisions are also affected by the topology of your target system, as discussed in Chapter 26.

For most systems, these deployment components are drawn from the decisions you make about how to segment the physical implementation of your system. These decisions will be affected by a number of technical issues (such as your choice of component-based operating system facilities), configuration management issues (such as your decisions about which parts will likely change over time), and reuse issues (that is, deciding which components you can reuse in or from other systems).

To model executables and libraries,

- Identify the partitioning of your physical system. Consider the impact of technical, configuration management, and reuse issues.
- Model any executables and libraries as components, using the appropriate standard elements. If your implementation introduces new kinds of components, introduce a new appropriate stereotype.
- If it's important for you to manage the seams in your system, model the significant interfaces that some components use and others realize.
- As necessary to communicate your intent, model the relationships among these executables, libraries, and interfaces. Most often, you'll want to model the dependencies among these parts in order to visualize the impact of change.

The UML's standard elements are summarized in Appendix B.

For example, Figure 25-5 shows a set of components drawn from a personal productivity tool that runs on a single personal computer. This figure includes one executable (`animator.exe`, with a tagged value noting its version number) and four libraries (`dlog.dll`, `wrfrme.dll`, `render.dll`, and `raytrce.dll`), all of which use the UML's standard elements for executables and libraries, respectively. This diagram also presents the dependencies among these components.

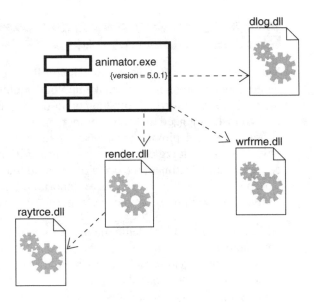

Figure 25-5: Modeling Executables and Libraries

Note: Directly showing a dependency between two components is actually an elided view of the real intercomponent relationships. A component rarely depends on another component directly but, rather, imports one or more interfaces exported by another. For example, you could have rewritten the figure above by indicating explicitly the interfaces that `render.dll` realizes (exports) and that `animator.exe` uses (imports). For simplicity, you can elide these details simply by showing a dependency between the two components.

Packages are discussed in Chapter 12.

As your models get bigger, you will find that many components tend to cluster together in groups that are conceptually and semantically related. In the UML, you can use packages to model these clusters of components.

Modeling deployment is discussed in Chapter 26.

For larger systems that are deployed across several computers, you'll want to model the way your components are distributed by asserting the nodes on which they are located.

Modeling Tables, Files, and Documents

Modeling the executables and libraries that make up the physical implementation of your system is useful, but often you'll find there are a host of ancillary deployment components that are neither executables nor libraries and yet are critical to the physical deployment of your system. For example, your implementation might include data files, help documents, scripts, log files, initialization files, and installation/removal files. Modeling these components is an important part of controlling the configuration of your system. Fortunately, you can use UML components to model all of these artifacts.

To model tables, files, and documents,

- Identify the ancillary components that are part of the physical implementation of your system.
- Model these things as components. If your implementation introduces new kinds of artifacts, introduce a new appropriate stereotype.
- As necessary to communicate your intent, model the relationships among these ancillary components and the other executables, libraries, and interfaces in your system. Most often, you'll want to model the dependencies among these parts in order to visualize the impact of change.

For example, Figure 25-6 builds on the previous figure and shows the tables, files, and documents that are part of the deployed system surrounding the executable `animator.exe`. This figure includes one document (`animator.hlp`), one simple file (`animator.ini`), and one database table (`shapes.tbl`), all of which use the UML's standard elements for documents, files, and tables, respectively.

Modeling logical and physical databases are discussed in Chapters 8 and 29, respectively.

Modeling databases can get complicated when you start dealing with multiple tables, triggers, and stored procedures. To visualize, specify, construct, and document these features, you'll need to model the logical schema, as well as the physical databases.

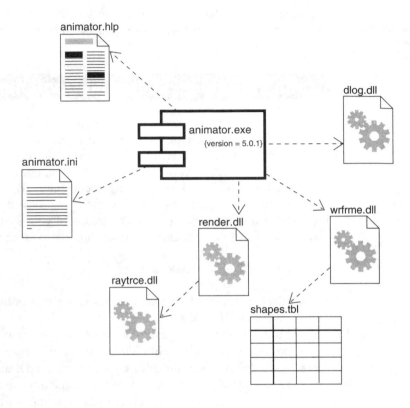

Figure 25-6: Modeling Tables, Files, and Documents

Modeling an API

If you are a developer who's assembling a system from component parts, you'll often want to see the application programming interfaces (APIs) that you can use to glue these parts together. APIs represent the programmatic seams in your system, which you can model using interfaces and components.

An API is essentially an interface that is realized by one or more components. As a developer, you'll really care only about the interface itself; which component realizes an interface's operations is not relevant as long as *some* component realizes it. From a system configuration management perspective, though, these realizations are important because you need to ensure that, when you publish an API, there's some realization available that carries out the API's obligations. Fortunately, with the UML, you can model both perspectives.

Interfaces are discussed in Chapter 11; use cases are discussed in Chapter 16.

The operations associated with any semantically rich API will be fairly extensive, so most of the time you won't need to visualize all these operations at once. Instead, you'll tend to keep the operations in the backplane of your models and use interfaces as handles with which you can find these sets of operations. If you want to construct executable systems against these APIs, you will need to add enough detail so that your development tools can compile against the properties of your interfaces. Along with the signatures of each operation, you'll probably also want to include uses cases that explain how to use each interface.

To model an API,

- Identify the programmatic seams in your system and model each seam as an interface, collecting the attributes and operations that form this edge.
- Expose only those properties of the interface that are important to visualize in the given context; otherwise, hide these properties, keeping them in the interface's specification for reference, as necessary.
- Model the realization of each API only insofar as it is important to show the configuration of a specific implementation.

Figure 25-7 exposes the APIs of the executable in the previous two figures. You'll see four interfaces that form the API of the executable: `IApplication`, `IModels`, `IRendering`, and `IScripts`.

Figure 25-7: Modeling an API

Modeling Source Code

The most common purpose for which you'll use components is to model the physical parts that make up your implementation. This also includes the modeling of all the ancillary parts of your deployed system, including tables, files, documents, and APIs. The second most common purpose for which you'll use components is to model the configuration of all the source code files that your development tools use to create these components. These represent the work product components of your development process.

Modeling source code graphically is particularly useful for visualizing the compilation dependencies among your source code files and for managing the splitting and merging of groups of these files when you fork and join development paths. In this manner, UML components can be the graphical interface to your configuration management and version control tools.

For most systems, source code files are drawn from the decisions you make about how to segment the files your development environment needs. These files are used to store the details of your classes, interfaces, collaborations, and other logical elements as an intermediate step to creating the physical, binary components that are derived from these elements by your tools. Most of the time, these tools will impose a style of organization (one or two files per class is common), but you'll still want to visualize the relationships among these files. How you organize groups of these files using packages and how you manage versions of these files is driven by your decisions about how to manage change.

To model source code,

- Depending on the constraints imposed by your development tools, model the files used to store the details of all your logical elements, along with their compilation dependencies.
- If it's important for you to bolt these models to your configuration management and version control tools, you'll want to include tagged values, such as version, author, and check in/check out information, for each file that's under configuration management.
- As far as possible, let your development tools manage the relationships among these files, and use the UML only to visualize and document these relationships.

For example, Figure 25-8 shows some source code files that are used to build the library `render.dll` from the previous examples. This figure includes four header files (`render.h`, `rengine.h`, `poly.h`, and `colortab.h`) that represent the source code for the specification of certain classes. There is also one implementation file (`render.cpp`) that represents the implementation of one of these headers.

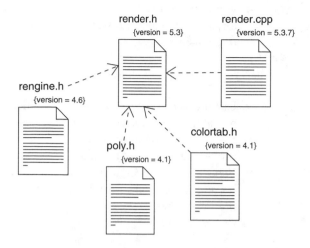

Figure 25-8: Modeling Source Code

Packages are discussed in Chapter 12.

As your models get bigger, you will find that many source code files tend to cluster together in groups that are conceptually and semantically related. Most of the time, your development tools will place these groups in separate directories. In the UML, you can use packages to model these clusters of source code files.

Trace relationships, a kind of dependency, are discussed in Chapters 5 and 10.

In the UML, it is possible to visualize the relationship of a class to its source code file and, in turn, the relationship of a source code file to its executable or library by using trace relationships. However, you'll rarely need to go to this detail of modeling.

Hints and Tips

When you model components in the UML, remember that you are modeling in the physical dimension. A well-structured component

- Provides a crisp abstraction of something drawn from the physical aspect of the system.
- Provides the realization of a small, well-defined set of interfaces.
- Directly implements a set of classes that work together to carry out the semantics of these interfaces with economy and elegance.

■ Is loosely coupled relative to other components; most often, you'll model components only in connection with dependency and realization relationships.

When you draw a component in the UML,

■ Use the iconic form of an interface unless it's necessary to explicitly reveal the operations offered by that interface.
■ Show only those interfaces that are necessary to understand the meaning of that component in the given context.
■ Especially if you are using components to model things such as libraries and source code, reveal the values of tags associated with versioning.

Chapter 26
DEPLOYMENT

Nodes, just like components, live in the material world and are an important building block in modeling the physical aspects of a system. A node is a physical element that exists at run time and represents a computational resource, generally having at least some memory and, often, processing capability.

You use nodes to model the topology of the hardware on which your system executes. A node typically represents a processor or a device on which components may be deployed.

Good nodes crisply represent the vocabulary of the hardware in your solution domain.

Getting Started

Modeling non-software things is discussed in Chapter 4.

The components you develop or reuse as part of a software-intensive system must be deployed on some set of hardware in order to execute. This is in effect what a software-intensive *system* is all about—such a system encompasses both software and hardware.

*The five
views of an
architecture
are discussed
in Chapter 2.*

When you architect a software-intensive system, you have to consider both its logical and physical dimensions. On the logical side, you'll find things such as classes, interfaces, collaborations, interactions, and state machines. On the physical side, you'll find components (which represent the physical packaging of these logical things) and nodes (which represent the hardware on which these components are deployed and execute).

*Stereotypes
are discussed
in Chapter 6.*

The UML provides a graphical representation of node, as Figure 26-1 shows. This canonical notation permits you to visualize a node apart from any specific hardware. Using stereotypes—one of the UML's extensibility mechanisms— you can (and often will) tailor this notation to represent specific kinds of processors and devices.

Figure 26-1: Nodes

Note: The UML is mainly intended for modeling software-intensive systems, although the UML, in conjunction with textual hardware modeling languages, such as VHDL, can be quite expressive for modeling hardware systems. The UML is also sufficiently expressive for modeling the topologies of stand-alone, embedded, client/server, and distributed systems.

Terms and Concepts

A *node* is a physical element that exists at run time and represents a computational resource, generally having at least some memory and, often, processing capability. Graphically, a node is rendered as a cube.

Names

A node name must be unique within its enclosing package, as discussed in Chapter 12.

Every node must have a name that distinguishes it from other nodes. A *name* is a textual string. That name alone is known as a *simple name*; a *path name* is the node name prefixed by the name of the package in which that node lives. A node is typically drawn showing only its name, as in Figure 26-2. Just as with classes, you may draw nodes adorned with tagged values or with additional compartments to expose their details.

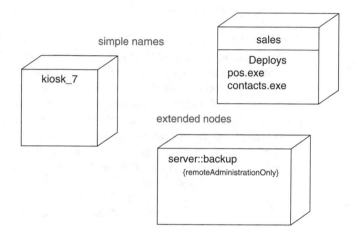

Figure 26-2: Simple and Extended Nodes

Note: A node name may be text consisting of any number of letters, numbers, and certain punctuation marks (except for marks such as the colon, which is used to separate a node name and the name of its enclosing package) and may continue over several lines. In practice, node names are short nouns or noun phrases drawn from the vocabulary of the implementation.

Nodes and Components

Components are discussed in Chapter 25.

In many ways, nodes are a lot like components: Both have names; both may participate in dependency, generalization, and association relationships; both may be nested; both may have instances; both may be participants in interactions. However, there are some significant differences between nodes and components.

- Components are things that participate in the execution of a system; nodes are things that execute components.
- Components represent the physical packaging of otherwise logical elements; nodes represent the physical deployment of components.

This first difference is the most important. Simply put, nodes execute components; components are things that are executed by nodes.

Dependency relationships are discussed in Chapters 5 and 10.

The second difference suggests a relationship among classes, components, and nodes. In particular, a component is the materialization of a set of other logical elements, such as classes and collaborations, and a node is the location upon which components are deployed. A class may be implemented by one or more components, and, in turn, a component may be deployed on one or more nodes. As Figure 26-3 shows, the relationship between a node and the components it deploys can be shown explicitly by using a dependency relationship. Most of the time, you won't need to visualize these relationships graphically but will keep them as a part of the node's specification.

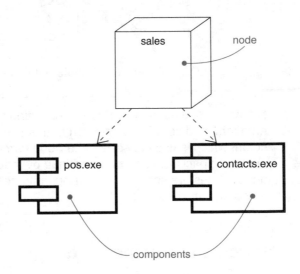

Figure 26-3: Nodes and Components

A set of objects or components that are allocated to a node as a group is called a *distribution unit*.

that you can specify attributes and
might specify that a node pro-
and `memory`, as well as the
suspend.

grouping them in packages in the same manner in
classes and components.

ze nodes by specifying dependency, generalization, and
(including aggregation) relationships among them.

tions

mon kind of relationship you'll use among nodes is an associa-
ontext, an association represents a physical connection among
an Ethernet connection, a serial line, or a shared bus, as Figure
ou can even use associations to model indirect connections, such
nk between distant processors.

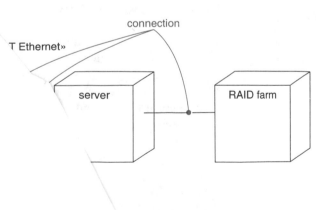

nections

associations at your
ity, and constraints.
ciations if you want
guish between a 10-

alone,
of

will
repre-
at has
ice is a
d at this
ces to the

oyment view

es, then stereo-
evices that are
appropriate ste-

erations that

tereotypes each
cessor; the `kiosk`
of processors; and
of device.

Because nodes are class-like, you have the full power of
disposal. This means that you can include roles, multiplic
As in the previous figure, you should stereotype these asso
to model new kinds of connections—for example, to distin
T Ethernet connection and an RS-232 serial connection.

Common Modeling Techniques

Modeling Processors and Devices

Modeling the processors and devices that form the topology of a stand-
embedded, client/server, or distributed system is the most common use o
nodes.

*The UML's
extensibility
mechanisms
are discussed
in Chapter 6.*

Because all of the UML's extensibility mechanisms apply to nodes, you
often use stereotypes to specify new kinds of nodes that you can use to
sent specific kinds of processors and devices. A *processor* is a node th
processing capability, meaning that it can execute a component. A *de*
node that has no processing capability (at least, none that are modele
level of abstraction) and, in general, represents something that interf
real world.

To model processors and devices,

- Identify the computational elements of your system's dep
  and model each as a node.
- If these elements represent generic processors and devic
  type them as such. If they are kinds of processors and d
  part of the vocabulary of your domain, then specify an
  reotype with an icon for each.
- As with class modeling, consider the attributes and o
  might apply to each node.

For example, Figure 26-5 takes the previous diagram and
node. The server is a node stereotyped as a generic pro
and the console are nodes stereotyped as special kind
the RAID farm is a node stereotyped as a special kind

Note: Nodes are probably the most stereotyped building block in the UML. When, as part of systems engineering, you model the deployment view of a software-intensive system, there's great value in providing visual cues that speak to your intended audience. If you are modeling a processor that's a common kind of computer, render it with an icon that looks like that computer. If you are modeling a common device, such as a cellular phone, fax, modem, or camera, render it with an icon that looks like that device.

Figure 26-5: Processors and Devices

Modeling the Distribution of Components

The semantics of location are discussed in Chapter 23.

When you model the topology of a system, it's often useful to visualize or specify the physical distribution of its components across the processors and devices that make up the system.

To model the distribution of components,

- For each significant component in your system, allocate it to a given node.
- Consider duplicate locations for components. It's not uncommon for the same kind of component (such as specific executables and libraries) to reside on multiple nodes simultaneously.

■ Render this allocation in one of three ways.
1. Don't make the allocation visible, but leave it as part of the back-plane of your model—that is, in each node's specification.
2. Using dependency relationships, connect each node with the components it deploys.
3. List the components deployed on a node in an additional compart-ment.

Instances are discussed in Chapter 11; object diagrams are discussed in Chapter 14.

Using the third approach, Figure 26-6 takes the earlier diagrams and specifies the executable components that reside on each node. This diagram is a bit dif-ferent from the previous ones in that it is an object diagram, visualizing spe-cific instances of each node. In this case, the RAID farm and kiosk instances are both anonymous and the other two instances are named (c for the console and s for the server). Each processor in this figure is rendered with an additional compartment showing the component it deploys. The server object is also rendered with its attributes (processorSpeed and memory) and their values visible.

Figure 26-6: Modeling the Distribution of Components.

The migration of compo-nents across nodes is discussed in Chapter 30.

Components need not be statically distributed across the nodes in a system. In the UML, it is possible to model the dynamic migration of components from node to node, as in an agent-based system or a high-reliability system that involves clustered servers and replicated databases.

Hints and Tips

A well-structured node

- Provides a crisp abstraction of something drawn from the vocabulary of the hardware in your solution domain.
- Is decomposed only to the level necessary to communicate your intent to the reader.
- Exposes only those attributes and operations that are relevant to the domain you are modeling.
- Directly deploys a set of components that reside on the node.
- Is connected to other nodes in a manner that reflects the topology of the real world system.

When you draw a node in the UML,

- For your project or organization as a whole, define a set of stereotypes with appropriate icons to provide meaningful visual cues to your readers.
- Show only the attributes and operations (if any) that are necessary to understand the meaning of that node in the given context.

UNIFIED
MODELING
LANGUAGE

Chapter 27
COLLABORATIONS

In the context of a system's architecture, a collaboration allows you to name a conceptual chunk that encompasses both static and dynamic aspects. A collaboration names a society of classes, interfaces, and other elements that work together to provide some cooperative behavior that's bigger than the sum of all its parts.

You use collaborations to specify the realization of use cases and operations, and to model the architecturally significant mechanisms of your system.

Getting Started

Think about the most beautiful building you've even seen—perhaps the Taj Mahal or Notre Dame. Both structures exhibit a quality that's hard to name. In many ways, both structures are architecturally simple, yet they are also profoundly deep. In each, you can immediately recognize a consistent symmetry. Look harder, and you'll see details that are themselves beautiful and that work together to produce a beauty and functionality that's greater than the individual parts.

Now think about the ugliest building you've even seen—perhaps your local fast food outlet. You'll find a visual cacophony of architectural styles—a touch of modernism combined with a Georgian roof line, all decorated in a jarring fashion, with bold colors that assault the eye. Usually, these buildings are pure manipulation, with narrow function and hardly any form.

What's the difference between these two kinds of civil architecture? First, in buildings of quality, you'll find a harmony of design that's lacking in the others. Quality architecture uses a small set of architectural styles applied in a consistent fashion. For example, the Taj Mahal uses complex, symmetrical, and balanced geometric elements throughout. Second, in buildings of quality, you'll find common patterns that transcend the building's individual elements. For example, in Notre Dame, certain walls are load bearing and serve to support the cathedral's dome. Yet some of these same walls, along with other architectural details, serve as part of the building's system for diverting water and waste.

The five views of an architecture are discussed in Chapter 2.

So it is with software. A quality software-intensive system is not only functionally sound, but it also exhibits a harmony and balance of design that makes it resilient to change. This harmony and balance most often come from the fact that all well-structured object-oriented systems are full of patterns. Look at any quality object-oriented system, and you'll see elements that work together in common ways to provide some cooperative behavior that's bigger than the sum of all its parts. In a well-structured system, many of the elements, in various combinations, will participate in different mechanisms.

Patterns and frameworks are discussed in Chapter 28.

Note: A pattern provides a common solution to a common problem in some context. In any well-structured system, you'll find a spectrum of patterns, including idioms (representing common ways of programming), mechanisms (design patterns that represent conceptual chunks of a system's architecture), and frameworks (architectural patterns that provide extensible templates for applications within a domain).

Structural modeling is discussed in Sections 2 and 3; behavioral modeling is discussed in Sections 4 and 5; interactions are discussed in Chapter 15.

In the UML, you model mechanisms using collaborations. A collaboration gives a name to the conceptual building blocks of your system, encompassing both structural and behavioral elements. For example, you might have a distributed management information system whose databases are spread across several nodes. From the user's perspective, updating information looks atomic; from the inside perspective, it's not so simple, because such an action has to touch multiple machines. To give the illusion of simplicity, you'd want to devise a transaction mechanism with which a client could name what looks like a single, atomic transaction, even across various databases. Such a mechanism would span multiple classes working together to carry out a transaction. Many of these classes would be involved in other mechanisms as well, such as mechanisms for making information persistent. This collection of classes (the structural part), together with their interactions (the behavioral part), forms a mechanism, which, in the UML, you can represent as a collaboration.

Use cases are discussed in Chapter 16; operations are discussed in Chapters 4 and 9.

Collaborations not only name a system's mechanisms, they also serve as the realization of use cases and operations.

The UML provides a graphical representation for collaborations, as Figure 27-1 shows. This notation permits you to visualize the structural and behavioral building blocks of a system, especially as they may overlap the classes, interfaces, and other elements of the system.

Figure 27-1: Collaborations

Class diagrams are discussed in Chapter 8; interaction diagrams are discussed in Chapter 18.

Note: This notation lets you visualize a collaboration from the outside as one chunk. What's often more interesting is what's inside this notation. Zoom into a collaboration, and you'll be led to other diagrams—most notably, class diagrams (for the collaboration's structural part) and interaction diagrams (for the collaboration's behavioral part).

Terms and Concepts

The notation for collaborations is intentionally similar to that for use cases, as discussed in Chapter 16.

A *collaboration* is a society of classes, interfaces, and other elements that work together to provide some cooperative behavior that's bigger than the sum of all its parts. A collaboration is also the specification of how an element, such as a classifier (including a class, interface, component, node, or use case) or an operation, is realized by a set of classifiers and associations playing specific roles used in a specific way. Graphically, a collaboration is rendered as an ellipse with dashed lines.

Names

A collaboration name must be unique within its enclosing package, as discussed in Chapter 12.

Every collaboration must have a name that distinguishes it from other collaborations. A *name* is a textual string. That name alone is known as a *simple name*; a *path name* is the collaboration name prefixed by the name of the package in which that collaboration lives. Typically, a collaboration is drawn showing only its name, as in the previous figure.

Note: A collaboration name may be text consisting of any number of letters, numbers, and certain punctuation marks (except for marks such as the colon, which is used to separate a collaboration name and the name of its enclosing package) and may continue over several lines. In practice, collaboration names are short nouns or noun phrases drawn from the vocabulary of the system you are modeling. Typically, you capitalize the first letter of a collaboration name, as in `Transaction` or `Chain of responsibility`.

Structure

Structural elements are discussed in Sections 2 and 3.

Collaborations have two aspects: a structural part that specifies the classes, interfaces, and other elements that work together to carry out the named collaboration, and a behavioral part that specifies the dynamics of how those elements interact.

Classifiers are discussed in Chapter 9; relationships are discussed in Chapters 5 and 10.

The structural part of a collaboration may include any combination of classifiers, such as classes, interfaces, components, and nodes. Within a collaboration, these classifiers may be organized using all the usual UML relationships, including associations, generalizations, and dependencies. In fact, the structural aspects of a collaboration may use the full range of the UML's structural modeling facilities.

Packages are discussed in Chapter 12; subsystems are discussed in Chapter 31; use cases are discussed in Chapter 16.

However, unlike packages or subsystems, a collaboration does not own any of its structural elements. Rather, a collaboration simply references or uses the classes, interfaces, components, nodes, and other structural elements that are declared elsewhere. That's why a collaboration names a conceptual chunk—not a physical chunk—of a system's architecture. Therefore, a collaboration may cut across many levels of a system. Furthermore, the same element may appear in more than one collaboration (and some elements will not be named as part of any collaboration at all).

For example, given a Web-based retail system described by a dozen or so use cases (such as `Purchase Items`, `Return Items`, and `Query Order`), each use case will be realized by a single collaboration. In addition, each of these collaborations will share some of the same structural elements (such as the classes Customer and Order), but they will be organized in different ways. You'll also find collaborations deeper inside the system, which represent architecturally significant mechanisms. For example, in this same retail system, you might have a collaboration called Internode messaging that specifies the details of secure messaging among nodes.

Class diagrams are discussed in Chapter 8.

Given a collaboration that names a conceptual chunk of a system, you can zoom inside that collaboration to expose the structural details of its parts. For example, Figure 27-2 illustrates how zooming inside the collaboration Internode messaging might reveal the following set of classes, rendered in a class diagram.

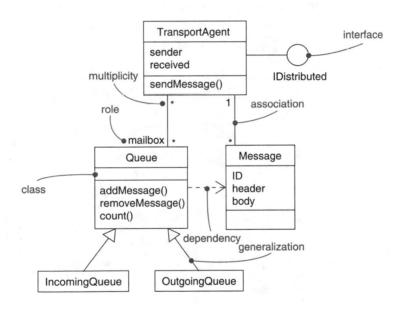

Figure 27-2: Structural Aspects of a Collaboration

Behavior

Interaction diagrams are discussed in Chapter 18; instances are discussed in Chapter 13.

Whereas the structural part of a collaboration is typically rendered using a class diagram, the behavioral part of a collaboration is typically rendered using an interaction diagram. An interaction diagram specifies an interaction that represents a behavior comprised of a set of messages that are exchanged among a set of objects within a context to accomplish a specific purpose. An interaction's context is provided by its enclosing collaboration, which establishes the classes, interfaces, components, nodes, and other structural elements whose instances may participate in that interaction.

The behavioral part of a collaboration may be specified by one or more interaction diagrams. If you want to emphasize the time ordering of messages, use a sequence diagram. If you want to emphasize the structural relationships among these objects as they collaborate, use a collaboration diagram. Either diagram is appropriate because, for most purposes, they are semantically equivalent.

This means that when you model a society of classes by naming their interaction as a collaboration, you can zoom inside that collaboration to expose the details of their behavior. For example, zooming inside the collaboration named `Internode messaging` might reveal the interaction diagram shown in Figure 27-3.

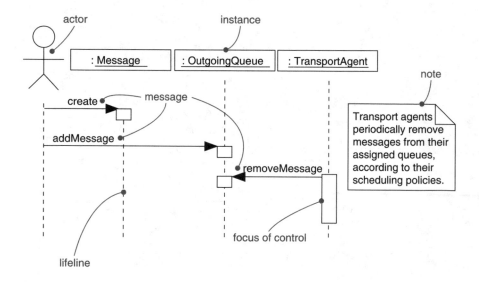

Figure 27-3: Behavioral Aspects of a Collaboration

Note: The behavioral parts of a collaboration must be consistent with its structural parts. This means that the objects found in a collaboration's interactions must be instances of classes found in its structural part. Similarly, the messages named in an interaction must relate to operations visible in the collaboration's structural part. You can have more than one interaction associated with a collaboration, each of which may show a different—but consistent—aspect of its behavior.

Organizing Collaborations

The heart of a system's architecture is found in its collaborations, because the mechanisms that shape a system represent significant design decisions. All well-structured object-oriented systems are composed of a modestly sized and regular set of such collaborations, so it's important for you to organize your collaborations well. There are two kinds of relationships concerning collaborations that you'll need to consider.

Use cases are discussed in Chapter 16; operations are discussed in Chapters 4 and 9; realization relationships are discussed in Chapter 10.

First, there is the relationship between a collaboration and the thing it realizes. A collaboration may realize either a classifier or an operation, which means that the collaboration specifies the structural and behavioral realization of that classifier or operation. For example, a use case (which names a set of sequences of actions that a system performs) may be realized by a collaboration. That use case, including its associated actors and neighboring use cases, provides a context for the collaboration. Similarly, an operation (which names the implementation of a service) may be realized by a collaboration. That operation, including its parameters and possible return value, also provides a context for the collaboration. The relationship between a use case or an operation and the collaboration that realizes it is modeled as a realization relationship.

Classifiers are discussed in Chapter 9.

Note: A collaboration may realize any kind of classifier, including classes, use cases, interfaces, components, and nodes. A collaboration that models a mechanism of the system may also stand alone, therefore its context is the system as a whole.

Second, there is the relationship among collaborations. Collaborations may refine other collaborations, and you also model this relationship as a refinement. The refinement relationships among collaborations typically mirror the refinement relationships among the use cases they represent.

Figure 27-4 illustrates these two kinds of relationships.

Packages are discussed in Chapter 12.

Note: Collaborations, like any other modeling element in the UML, may be grouped into larger packages. Typically, you'll only need to do this for very large systems.

Figure 27-4: Organizing Collaborations

Common Modeling Techniques

Modeling the Realization of a Use Case

Use cases are discussed in Chapter 16.

One of the purposes for which you'll use collaborations is to model the realization of a use case. You'll typically drive the analysis of your system by identifying your system's use cases, but when you finally turn to implementation, you'll need to realize these use cases with concrete structures and behaviors. In general, every use case should be realized by one or more collaborations. For the system as a whole, the classifiers involved in a given collaboration that is linked to a use case will participate in other collaborations, as well. In this way, the structural contents of collaborations tend to overlap one another.

To model the realization of a use case,

- Identify those structural elements necessary and sufficient to carry out the semantics of the use case.
- Capture the organization of these structural elements in class diagrams.
- Consider the individual scenarios that represent this use case. Each scenario represents a specific path through the use case.

- Capture the dynamics of these scenarios in interaction diagrams. Use sequence diagrams if you want to emphasize the time ordering of messages. Use collaboration diagrams if you want to emphasize the structural relationships among these objects as they collaborate.
- Organize these structural and behavioral elements as a collaboration that you can connect to the use case via realization.

For example, Figure 27-5 shows a set of use cases drawn from a credit card validation system, including the primary use cases `Place order` and `Generate bill`, together with two other subordinate use cases, `Detect card fraud` and `Validate transaction`. Although most of the time you won't need to model this relationship explicitly (but will leave it up to your tools), this figure explicitly models the realization of `Place order` by the collaboration `Order management`. In turn, this collaboration can be further expanded into its structural and behavioral aspects, leading you to class diagrams and interaction diagrams. It is through the realization relationship that you connect a use case to its scenarios.

In most cases, you won't need to model the relationship between a use case and the collaboration that realizes it explicitly. Instead, you'll tend to leave that

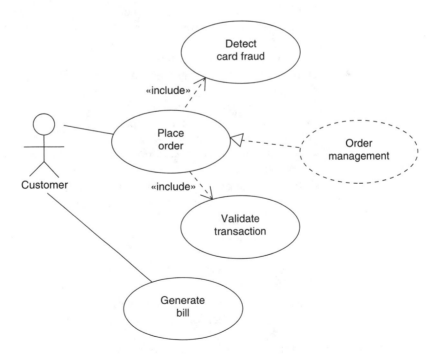

Figure 27-5: Modeling the Realization of a Use Case

in the backplane of your model. Then let tools use that connection to help you navigate between a use case and its realization.

Modeling the Realization of an Operation

Operations are discussed in Chapters 4 and 9.

Another purpose for which you'll use collaborations is to model the realization of an operation. In many cases, you can specify the realization of an operation by going straight to code. However, for those operations that require the collaboration of a number of objects, it's better to model their implementation via collaborations before you dive into code.

Activity diagrams are discussed in Chapter 19.

Note: You can also model an operation using activity diagrams. Activity diagrams are essentially flowcharts. So for those algorithmically intensive operations that you want to model explicitly, activity diagrams are usually the best choice. However, if your operation requires the participation of many objects, you'll want to use collaborations, because they let you model the structural, as well as behavioral, aspects of an operation.

The parameters, return value, and objects local to an operation provide the context for its realization. Therefore, these elements are visible to the structural aspect of the collaboration that realizes the operation, just as actors are visible to the structural aspect of a collaboration that realizes a use case. You can model the relationship among these parts using class diagrams that specify the structural part of a collaboration

To model the implementation of an operation,

Notes are discussed in Chapter 6.

- Identify the parameters, return value, and other objects visible to the operation.
- If the operation is trivial, represent its implementation directly in code, which you can keep in the backplane of your model, or explicitly visualize it in a note.
- If the operation is algorithmically intensive, model its realization using an activity diagram.
- If the operation is complex or otherwise requires some detailed design work, represent its implementation as a collaboration. You can further expand the structural and behavioral parts of this collaboration using class and interaction diagrams, respectively.

Active classes are discussed in Chapter 22.

For example, Figure 27-6 shows the active class RenderFrame with three of its operations exposed. The function progress is simple enough to be implemented directly in code, as specified in the attached note. However, the operation render is much more complicated, so its implementation is realized by the collaboration Ray trace. Although not shown here, you could zoom inside the collaboration to see its structural and behavioral aspects.

Figure 27-6: Modeling the Realization of an Operation

Modeling a Mechanism

Patterns and frameworks are discussed in Chapter 28; an example of modeling a mechanism is discussed in the same chapter.

In all well-structured object-oriented systems, you'll find a spectrum of patterns. At one end, you'll find idioms that represent patterns of use of the implementation language. At the other end, you'll find architectural patterns and frameworks that shape the system as a whole and impose a particular style. In the middle, you'll find mechanisms that represent common design patterns by which the things in the system interact with one another in common ways. You can represent a mechanism in the UML as a collaboration.

Mechanisms are collaborations that stand alone; their context is not a single use case or an operation but, rather, the system as a whole. Any element visible in that part of the system is a candidate for participation in a mechanism.

Mechanisms such as these represent architecturally significant design decisions and should not be treated lightly. Typically, your system's architect will devise its mechanisms, and you'll evolve these mechanisms with each new release. At the end, you'll find your system simple (because these mechanisms reify common interactions), understandable (because you can approach the system from its mechanisms), and resilient (by tuning each mechanism, you tune the system as a whole).

To model a mechanism,

- Identify the major mechanisms that shape your system's architecture. These mechanisms are driven by the overall architectural style you choose to impose on your implementation, along with the style appropriate to your problem domain.

- Represent each of these mechanisms as a collaboration.
- Expand on the structural and behavioral part of each collaboration. Look for sharing, where possible.
- Validate these mechanisms early in the development lifecycle (they are of strategic importance), but evolve them with each new release, as you learn more about the details of your implementation.

Hints and Tips

When you model collaborations in the UML, remember that every collaboration should represent either the realization of a use case or operation or should stand alone as a mechanism of the system. A well-structured collaboration

- Consists of both structural and behavioral aspects.
- Provides a crisp abstraction of some identifiable interaction in the system.
- Is rarely completely independent, but will overlap with the structural elements of other collaborations.
- Is understandable and simple.

When you draw a collaboration in the UML,

- Explicitly render a collaboration only when it's necessary to understand its relationship to other collaborations, classifiers, operations, or the system as a whole. Otherwise, use collaborations, but keep them in the backplane.
- Organize collaborations according to the classifier or operation they represent, or in packages associated with the system as a whole.

Chapter 28
PATTERNS AND FRAMEWORKS

In this chapter

- Patterns and frameworks
- Modeling design patterns
- Modeling architectural patterns
- Making patterns approachable

All well-structured systems are full of patterns. A pattern provides a common solution to a common problem in a given context. A mechanism is a design pattern that applies to a society of classes; a framework is typically an architectural pattern that provides an extensible template for applications within a domain.

You use patterns to specify mechanisms and frameworks that shape the architecture of your system. You make a pattern approachable by clearly identifying the slots, tabs, knobs, and dials that a user of that pattern may adjust in order to apply the pattern in a particular context.

Getting Started

It's amazing to think of the various ways you can assemble a pile of lumber to build a house. In the hands of a master builder in San Francisco, you might see that pile transformed into a Victorian-style house, complete with a gabled roof line and brightly colored, storybook siding. In the hands of a master builder in Maine, you might see that same pile transformed into saltbox house, with clapboard siding and rectangular shapes throughout.

From the outside, these two houses represent clearly different architectural styles. Every builder, drawing from experience, must choose a style that best meets the needs of his or her customer, and then adapt that style to the customer's wishes and the constraints of the building site and local covenants.

For the inside, each builder must also design the house to solve some common problems. There are only so many proven ways to engineer trusses to support a roof; there are only so many proven ways to design a load-bearing wall that must also handle openings for doors and windows. Every builder must select the appropriate mechanisms that solve these common problems, adapted to an overall architectural style and the constraints of local building codes.

Building a software-intensive system is just like that. Every time you raise your eyes above individual lines of code, you'll find common mechanisms that shape the way you organize your classes and other abstractions. For example, in an event-driven system, using the chain of responsibility design pattern is a common way to organize event handlers. Raise your eyes above the level of these mechanisms, and you'll find common frameworks that shape your system's entire architecture. For example, in information systems, using a three-tier architecture is a common way to achieve a clear separation of concerns among the system's user interface, its persistent information, and its business objects and rules.

Collaborations are discussed in Chapter 27; packages are discussed in Chapter 12.

In the UML, you will typically model design patterns—also called mechanisms—which you can represent as collaborations. Similarly, you will typically model architectural patterns as frameworks, which you can represent as stereotyped packages.

The UML provides a graphical representation for both kinds of patterns, as Figure 28-1 shows.

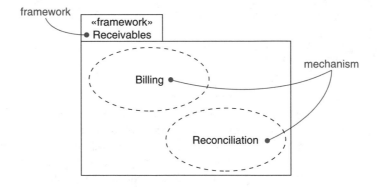

Figure 28-1: Mechanisms and Frameworks

Terms and Concepts

A *pattern* is a common solution to a common problem in a given context. A *mechanism* is a design pattern that applies to a society of classes. A *framework* is an architectural pattern that provides an extensible template for applications within a domain.

Patterns and Architecture

Software architecture is discussed in Chapter 2.

Whether you're architecting a new system or evolving an existing one, you never really start from scratch. Rather, experience and convention will lead you to apply common ways to solve common problems. For example, if you are building a user-intensive system, one proven way to organize your abstractions is to use a model-view-controller pattern, in which you clearly separate objects (the model) from their presentation (the view) and the agents that keep the two in sync (the controller). Similarly, if you are building a system for solving cryptograms, one proven way to organize your system is to use a blackboard architecture, which is well-suited to attacking intractable problems in opportunistic ways.

Both of these are examples of patterns—common solutions to common problems in a given context. In all well-structured systems, you'll find lots of patterns at various levels of abstraction. Design patterns specify the structure and behavior of a society of classes; architectural patterns specify the structure and behavior of an entire system.

Patterns are part of the UML simply because patterns are important parts of a developer's vocabulary. By making the patterns in your system explicit, you make your system far more understandable and easier to evolve and maintain. For example, if you are handed a new, raw body of code to extend, you'll struggle for a while trying to figure out how it all fits together. On the other hand, if you are handed that same body of code and told, "These classes collaborate using a publish-and-subscribe mechanism," you will be a lot further down the path of understanding how it works. The same idea applies to a system as a whole. Saying "This system is organized as a set of pipes and filters" explains a great deal about the system's architecture that would otherwise be difficult to comprehend just by starting at individual classes.

Patterns help you to visualize, specify, construct, and document the artifacts of a software-intensive system. You can forward engineer a system by selecting an appropriate set of patterns and applying them to the abstractions specific to your domain. You can also reverse engineer a system by discovering the patterns it embodies, although that's hardly a perfect process. Even better, when you deliver a system, you can specify the patterns it embodies so that when someone later tries to reuse or adapt that system, its patterns will be clearly manifest.

In practice, there are two kinds of patterns of interest—design patterns and frameworks—and the UML provides a means of modeling both. When you model either pattern, you'll find that it typically stands alone in the context of some larger package, except for dependency relationships bind them to other parts of your system.

Mechanisms

A mechanism is just another name for a design pattern that applies to a society of classes. For example, one common design problem you'll encounter in Java is adapting a class that knows how to respond to a certain set of events so that it responds to a slightly different set, without altering the original class. A common solution to this problem is the adaptor pattern, a structural design pattern that converts one interface to another. This pattern is so common that it makes sense to name it and then model it so that you can use it anytime you encounter a similar problem.

In modeling, these mechanisms show up in two ways.

Collaborations are discussed in Chapter 27.

First, as shown in the previous figure, a mechanism simply names a set of abstractions that work together to carry out some common and interesting behavior. You model these mechanisms as plain collaborations because they just name a society of classes. Zoom into that collaboration, and you'll see its structural aspects (typically rendered as class diagrams), as well as its behavioral aspects (typically rendered as interaction diagrams). Collaborations such as these cut across individual abstractions in the system; a given class will likely be a member of many collaborations.

Template classes are discussed in Chapter 9.

Second, as shown in Figure 28-2, a mechanism names a template for a set of abstractions that work together to carry out some common and interesting behavior. You model these mechanisms as parameterized collaborations, which are rendered in the UML similar to the way template classes are rendered. Zoom into that collaboration, and you'll see its structural and behavioral aspects. Zoom out of the collaboration, and you'll see how that pattern applies to your system by binding the template parts of the collaboration to existing abstractions in your system. When you model a mechanism as a parameterized collaboration, you identify the slots, tabs, knobs, and dials you use to adapt that pattern by means of its template parameters. Collaborations such as these may appear repeatedly in your system, bound to different sets of abstractions. In this example, the `Subject` and the `Observer` of the pattern are bound to the concrete classes `TaskQueue` and `SliderBar`, respectively.

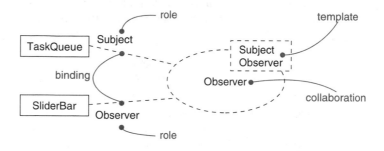

Figure 28-2: Mechanisms

Note: Deciding to model a mechanism as a plain collaboration versus a parameterized one is straightforward. Use a plain collaboration if all you are doing is naming a specific society of classes in your system that work together; use a template collaboration if you can abstract the essential structural and behavioral aspects of the mechanism in a completely domain-independent way, which you can then bind to your abstractions in a given context.

Frameworks

A framework is an architectural pattern that provides an extensible template for applications within a domain. For example, one common architectural pattern you'll encounter in real time systems is a cyclic executive, which divides time into frames and subframes, during which processing takes place under strict deadlines. Choosing this pattern versus its alternative (an event-driven architecture) colors your entire system. Because this pattern (and its alternative) is so common, it makes sense to name it as a framework.

The five views of an architecture are discussed in Chapter 2.

A framework is bigger than a mechanism. In fact, you can think of a framework as a kind of micro-architecture that encompasses a set of mechanisms that work together to solve a common problem for a common domain. When you specify a framework, you specify the skeleton of an architecture, together with the slots, tabs, knobs, and dials that you expose to users who want to adapt that framework to their own context.

Packages are discussed in Chapter 12; stereotypes are discussed in Chapter 6.

In the UML, you model a framework as a stereotyped package. Zoom inside that package, and you'll see mechanisms that live in any of various views of a system's architecture. For example, not only might you find parameterized collaborations, you might also find use cases (which explain how to use the framework), as well as plain collaborations (which provide sets of abstractions that you can build upon—for instance, by subclassing).

Events are discussed in Chapter 20.

Figure 28-3 illustrates such a framework, named `CyclicExecutive`. Among other things, this framework includes a collaboration (`Common-Events`) encompassing a set of event classes, along with a mechanism (`EventHandler`) for processing these events in a cyclic fashion. A client that builds on this framework (such as `Pacemaker`) could build on the abstractions in `CommonEvents` via subclassing and could also apply an instance of the `EventHandler` mechanism.

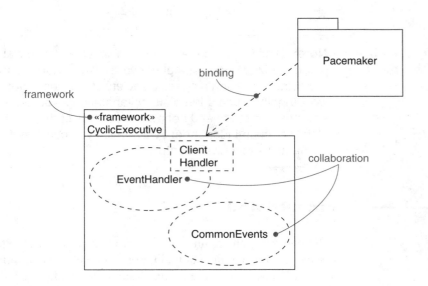

Figure 28-3: Frameworks

Note: Frameworks can be distinguished from plain class libraries. A class library contains abstractions that your abstractions instantiate or invoke; a framework contains abstractions that may instantiate or invoke your abstractions. Both of these kinds of connections constitute the framework's slots, tabs, knobs, and dials that you must adjust in order to adapt the framework to your context.

Common Modeling Techniques

Modeling Design Patterns

One thing for which you'll use patterns is to model a design pattern. When you model a mechanism such as this, you have to take into account its inside, as well as its outside, view.

When viewed from the outside, a design pattern is rendered as a parameterized collaboration. As a collaboration, a pattern provides a set of abstractions whose structure and behavior work together to carry out some useful function. The collaboration's parameters name the elements that a user of this pattern must bind. This makes the design pattern a template that you use in a particular context by supplying elements that match the template parameters.

When viewed from the inside, a design pattern is simply a collaboration and is rendered with its structural and behavioral parts. Typically, you'll model the inside of this collaboration with a set of class diagrams (for the structural aspect) and a set of interactions (for the behavioral aspect). The collaboration's parameters name certain of these structural elements, which, when the design pattern is bound in a particular context, are instantiated using abstractions from that context.

To model a design pattern,

Using collaborations to model a mechanism is discussed in Chapter 27.

- Identify the common solution to the common problem and reify it as a mechanism.
- Model the mechanism as a collaboration, providing its structural, as well as its behavioral, aspects.
- Identify the elements of the design pattern that must be bound to elements in a specific context and render them as parameters to the collaboration.

For example, Figure 28-4 shows a use of the `Command` design pattern (as discussed in Gamma, et al., *Design Patterns*, Reading, Massachusetts: Addison-Wesley, 1995). As its documentation states, this pattern "encapsulates a request as an object, thereby letting you parameterize clients with different requests, queue or log requests, and support undoable operations." As the model indicates, this design pattern has four parameters that, when you apply the pattern, must be bound to elements in a given context. This model shows such a binding, in which `Application`, `PasteCommand`, `OpenCommand`, `MenuItem`, and `Document` are bound to the design pattern's parameters.

Note that `PasteCommand` and `OpenCommand` are bound a little differently than the others. Both are subclasses of the `Command` class, provided by the design pattern itself. If you understand how the design pattern works, then by seeing this model, you'll know exactly how these five classes work together in context. Very likely, your system will use this pattern a number of times, perhaps with different bindings. The ability to reuse a design pattern like this as a first-class modeling element is what makes developing with patterns so powerful.

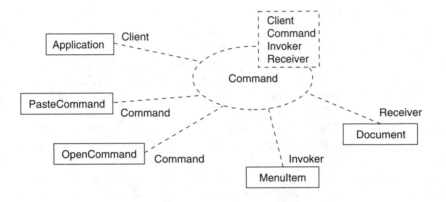

Figure 28-4: Modeling a Design Pattern

Note: Although not shown here, the classifiers that concretely manifest this design pattern (`Application`, `PasteCommand`, `OpenCommand`, `MenuItem`, and `Document`) are structured to be isomorphic with the generic design pattern itself, as shown in Figure 28-5. Therefore, where there is an association from `Client` to `Receiver` in the generic design pattern, for example, there also exists an association from `Application` to `Document`. Applying a pattern applies both the things and the relationships of the pattern.

Collaborations are discussed in Chapter 27; class diagrams are discussed in Chapter 8; interaction diagrams are discussed in Chapter 18.

To complete your model of a design pattern, you must specify its structural, as well as its behavioral, parts, which represent the inside of the collaboration.

For example, Figure 28-5 shows a class diagram that represents the structure of this design pattern. Notice how this diagram uses classes that are named as parameters to the pattern.

Figure 28-6 shows a sequence diagram that represents the behavior of this design pattern.

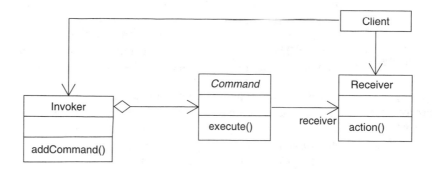

Figure 28-5: Modeling the Structural Aspect of a Design Pattern

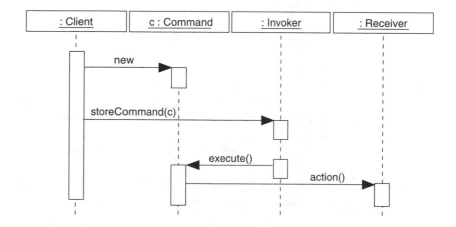

Figure 28-6: Modeling the Behavioral Aspect of a Design Pattern

Modeling Architectural Patterns

The other thing for which you'll use patterns is to model architectural patterns. When you model such a framework, you are, in effect, modeling the infrastructure of an entire architecture that you plan to reuse and adapt to some context.

Packages are discussed in Chapter 12.

A framework is rendered as a stereotyped package. As a package, a framework provides a set of elements, including—but certainly not limited to—classes, interfaces, use cases, components, nodes, collaborations, and even other frameworks. In fact, you'll place in a framework all the abstractions that work together to provide an extensible template for applications within a domain. Some of these elements will be public and represent resources that clients can build on. These are the "tabs" of the framework that you can connect to the abstractions in your context. Some of these public elements will be design patterns and represent resources to which clients bind. These are the "slots" of the framework that you fill in when you bind to the design pattern. Finally, some of these elements will be protected or private and represent encapsulated elements of the framework that are hidden from the outside view.

Software architecture Is discussed in Chapter 2.

When you model an architectural pattern, remember that a framework is, in fact, a description of an architecture, albeit one that is incomplete and possibly parameterized. As such, everything you know about modeling a well-structured architecture applies to modeling well-structured frameworks. The best frameworks are not designed in isolation; to do so is a guaranteed way to fail. Rather, the best frameworks are harvested from existing architectures that are proven to work, and the frameworks evolve to find the slots, tabs, knobs, and dials that are necessary and sufficient to make that framework adaptable to other domains.

To model an architectural pattern,

- Harvest the framework from an existing, proven architecture.
- Model the framework as a stereotyped package, containing all the elements (and especially the design patterns) that are necessary and sufficient to describe the various views of that framework.
- Expose the slots, tabs, knobs, and dials necessary to adapt the framework in the form of design patterns and collaborations. For the most part, this means making it clear to the user of the pattern which classes must be extended, which operations must be implemented, and which signals must be handled.

For example, Figure 28-7 shows a specification of the `Blackboard` architectural pattern (as discussed in Buschmann, et al., *Pattern-Oriented Software Architecture*, New York, New York: Wiley, 1996). As its documentation states, this pattern "tackles problems that do not have a feasible deterministic solution for the transformation of raw data into high-level data structures." The heart of this architecture is the `Blackboard` design pattern, which dictates how `KnowledgeSources`, a `Blackboard`, and a `Controller` collaborate. This framework also includes the design pattern `Reasoning engine`, which specifies a general mechanism for how each `KnowledgeSource` is driven. Finally, as the figure shows, this framework exposes one use case, `Apply new knowledge sources`, which explains to a client how to adapt the framework itself.

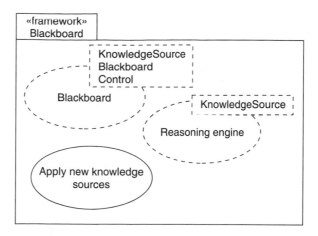

Figure 28-7: Modeling an Architectural Pattern

Note: In practice, modeling a framework completely is no less a task than modeling a system's architecture completely. In some ways, the task is even harder because to make the framework approachable, you must also expose the slots, tabs, knobs, and dials of the framework, and perhaps even provide meta-use cases (such as `Apply new knowledge sources`) that explain how to adapt the framework, as well as plain use cases that explain how the framework behaves.

Hints and Tips

When you model patterns in the UML, remember that they work at many levels of abstraction, from individual classes to the shape of the system as a whole. The most interesting kinds of patterns are mechanisms and frameworks. A well-structured pattern

- Solves a common problem in a common way.
- Consists of both structural and behavioral aspects.
- Exposes the slots, tabs, knobs, and dials by which you adapt those aspects to apply them to some context.
- Is atomic, meaning that it is not easily broken into smaller patterns.
- Tends to cut across individual abstractions in the system.

When you draw a pattern in the UML,

- Expose the elements of the pattern that you must adapt to apply it in context.
- Make the pattern approachable by supplying use cases for using, as well as adapting, the pattern.

Chapter 29

COMPONENT DIAGRAMS

> **In this chapter**
>
> - Modeling source code
> - Modeling executable releases
> - Modeling physical databases
> - Modeling adaptable systems
> - Forward and reverse engineering

Deployment diagrams, the second kind of diagram used in modeling he physical aspects of an object-oriented system, are discussed in Chapter 30.

Component diagrams are one of the two kinds of diagrams found in modeling the physical aspects of object-oriented systems. A component diagram shows the organization and dependencies among a set of components.

You use component diagrams to model the static implementation view of a system. This involves modeling the physical things that reside on a node, such as executables, libraries, tables, files, and documents. Component diagrams are essentially class diagrams that focus on a system's components.

Component diagrams are not only important for visualizing, specifying, and documenting component-based systems, but also for constructing executable systems through forward and reverse engineering.

Getting Started

When you build a house, you must do more than create blueprints. Mind you, blueprints are important because they help you visualize, specify, and document the kind of house you want to build so that you'll build the right house at the right time at the right price. Eventually, however, you've got to turn your floor plans and elevation drawings into real walls, floors, and ceilings made of wood, stone, or metal. Not only will you build your house out of these raw materials, you'll also incorporate pre-built components, such as cabinets, windows, doors, and vents. If you are renovating a house, you'll reuse even larger components, such as whole rooms and frameworks.

It's the same with software. You create use case diagrams to reason about the desired behavior of your system. You specify the vocabulary of your domain with class diagrams. You create sequence diagrams, collaboration diagrams, statechart diagrams, and activity diagrams to specify the way the things in your vocabulary work together to carry out this behavior. Eventually, you will turn these logical blueprints into things that live in the world of bits, such as executables, libraries, tables, files, and documents. You'll find that you must build some of these components from scratch, but you'll also end up reusing older components in new ways.

With the UML, you use component diagrams to visualize the static aspect of these physical components and their relationships and to specify their details for construction, as in Figure 29-1.

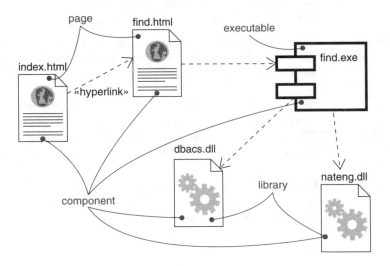

Figure 29-1: A Component Diagram

Terms and Concepts

A *component diagram* shows a set of components and their relationships. Graphically, a component diagram is a collection of vertices and arcs.

Common Properties

The general properties of diagrams are discussed in Chapter 7.

A component diagram is just a special kind of diagram and shares the same common properties as do all other diagrams—a name and graphical contents that are a projection into a model. What distinguishes a component diagram from all other kinds of diagrams is its particular content.

Contents

Components are discussed in Chapter 25; interfaces are discussed in Chapter 11; relationships are discussed in Chapters 5 and 10; packages are discussed in Chapter 12; subsystems are discussed in Chapter 31; instances are discussed in Chapter 13; class diagrams are discussed in Chapter 8.

Component diagrams commonly contain

- Components
- Interfaces
- Dependency, generalization, association, and realization relationships

Like all other diagrams, component diagrams may contain notes and constraints.

Component diagrams may also contain packages or subsystems, both of which are used to group elements of your model into larger chunks. Sometimes, you'll want to place instances in your component diagrams, as well, especially when you want to visualize one instance of a family of component-based systems.

Note: In many ways, a component diagram is just a special kind of class diagram that focuses on a system's components.

Common Uses

Implementation views, in the context of software architecture, are discussed in Chapter 2.

You use component diagrams to model the static implementation view of a system. This view primarily supports the configuration management of a system's parts, made up of components that can be assembled in various ways to produce a running system.

When you model the static implementation view of a system, you'll typically use component diagrams in one of four ways.

1. To model source code

With most contemporary object-oriented programming languages, you'll cut code using integrated development environments that store your source code in files. You can use component diagrams to model the configuration management of these files, which represent work-product components.

2. To model executable releases

A release is a relatively complete and consistent set of artifacts delivered to an internal or external user. In the context of components, a release focuses on the parts necessary to deliver a running system. When you model a release using component diagrams, you are visualizing, specifying, and documenting the decisions about the physical parts that constitute your software—that is, its deployment components.

3. To model physical databases

Persistence is discussed in Chapter 23; modeling logical database schemas is discussed in Chapter 8.

Think of a physical database as the concrete realization of a schema, living in the world of bits. Schemas, in effect, offer an API to persistent information; the model of a physical database represents the storage of that information in the tables of a relational database or the pages of an object-oriented database. You use component diagrams to represent these and other kinds of physical databases.

4. To model adaptable systems

Some systems are quite static; their components enter the scene, participate in an execution, and then depart. Other systems are more dynamic, involving mobile agents or components that migrate for purposes of load balancing and failure recovery. You use component diagrams in conjunction with some of the UML's diagrams for modeling behavior to represent these kinds of systems.

Common Modeling Techniques

Modeling Source Code

If you develop software in Java, you'll usually save your source code in .java files. If you develop software using C++, you'll typically store your source code in header files (.h files) and bodies (.cpp files). If you use IDL to develop COM+ or CORBA applications, one interface from your design view will often expand into four source code files: the interface itself, the client proxy, the server stub, and a bridge class. As your application grows, no matter which language you use, you'll find yourself organizing these files into larger groups. Furthermore, during the construction phase of development, you'll probably end up creating new versions of some of these files for each new incremental release you produce, and you'll want to place these versions under the control of a configuration management system.

The *file* stereotype for components is discussed in Chapter 25.

Much of the time, you will not need to model this aspect of a system directly. Instead, you'll let your development environment keep track of these files and their relationships. Sometimes, however, it's helpful to visualize these source code files and their relationships using component diagrams. Component diagrams used in this way typically contain only work-product components stereotyped as files, together with dependency relationships. For example, you might reverse engineer a set of source code files to visualize their web of compilation dependencies. You can go in the other direction by specifying the relationships among your source code files and then using those models as input to compilation tools, such as `make` on Unix. Similarly, you might want to use component diagrams to visualize the history of a set of source code files that are under configuration management. By extracting information from your configuration management system, such as the number of times a source code file has been checked out over a period of time, you can use that information to color component diagrams, showing "hot spots" of change among your source code files and areas of architectural churn.

To model a system's source code,

- Either by forward or reverse engineering, identify the set of source code files of interest and model them as components stereotyped as files.
- For larger systems, use packages to show groups of source code files.
- Consider exposing a tagged value indicating such information as the version number of the source code file, its author, and the date it was last changed. Use tools to manage the value of this tag.
- Model the compilation dependencies among these files using dependencies. Again, use tools to help generate and manage these dependencies.

The *trace* dependency stereotype is discussed in Chapter 10.

For example, Figure 29-2 shows five source code files. `signal.h` is a header file. Three of its versions are shown, tracing from new versions back to their older ancestors. Each variant of this source code file is rendered with a tagged value exposing its version number.

This header file (`signal.h`) is used by two other files (`interp.cpp` and `signal.cpp`), both of which are bodies. One of these files (`interp.cpp`) has a compilation dependency to another header (`irq.h`); in turn, `device.cpp` has a compilation dependency to `interp.cpp`. Given this component diagram, it's easy to trace the impact of changes. For example, changing the source code file `signal.h` will require the recompilation of three other files: `signal.cpp`, `interp.cpp`, and transitively, `device.cpp`. As this diagram also shows, the file `irq.h` is not affected.

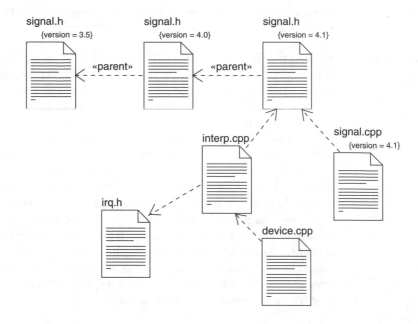

Figure 29-2: Modeling Source Code

Diagrams such as this can easily be generated by reverse engineering from the information held by your development environment's configuration management tools.

Modeling an Executable Release

Releasing a simple application is easy: You throw the bits of a single executable file on a disk, and your users just run that executable. For these kinds of applications, you don't need component diagrams because there's nothing difficult to visualize, specify, construct, or document.

Releasing anything other than a simple application is not so easy. You need the main executable (usually, a .exe file), but you also need all its ancillary parts, such as libraries (commonly .dll files if you are working in the context of COM+, or .class and .jar files if you are working in the context of Java), databases, help files, and resource files. For distributed systems, you'll likely have multiple executables and other parts scattered across various nodes. If you are working with a system of applications, you'll find that some of these components are unique to each application but that many are shared among applications. As you evolve your system, controlling the configuration of these many components becomes an important activity—and a more difficult one because changes in the components associated with one application may affect the operation of other applications.

For this reason, you use component diagrams to visualize, specify, construct, and document the configuration of your executable releases, encompassing the deployment components that form each release and the relationships among those components. You can use component diagrams to forward engineer a new system and to reverse engineer an existing one.

When you create component diagrams such as these, you actually just model a part of the things and relationships that make up your system's implementation view. For this reason, each component diagram should focus on one set of components at a time.

To model an executable release,

The UML's extensibility mechanisms are discussed in Chapter 6; interfaces are discussed in Chapter 11.

- Identify the set of components you'd like to model. Typically, this will involve some or all the components that live on one node, or the distribution of these sets of components across all the nodes in the system.
- Consider the stereotype of each component in this set. For most systems, you'll find a small number of different kinds of components (such as executables, libraries, tables, files, and documents). You can use the UML's extensibility mechanisms to provide visual cues for these stereotypes.
- For each component in this set, consider its relationship to its neighbors. Most often, this will involve interfaces that are exported (realized) by certain components and then imported (used) by others. If you want to expose the seams in your system, model these interfaces explicitly. If you want your model at a higher level of abstraction, elide these relationships by showing only dependencies among the components.

For example, Figure 29-3 models part of the executable release for an autonomous robot. This figure focuses on the deployment components associated with the robot's driving and calculation functions. You'll find one component (`driver.dll`) that exports an interface (`IDrive`) that is, in turn, imported by another component (`path.dll`). `driver.dll` exports one other interface (`ISelfTest`) that is probably used by other components in the system, although they are not shown here. There's one other component shown in this diagram (`collision.dll`), and it, too, exports a set of interfaces, although these details are elided: `path.dll` is shown with a dependency directly to `collision.dll`.

There are many more components involved in this system. However, this diagram only focuses on those deployment components that are directly involved in moving the robot. Note that in this component-based architecture, you could replace a specific version of `driver.dll` with another that realized the same (and perhaps additional) interfaces, and `path.dll` would still function properly. If you want to be explicit about the operations that `driver.dll` realizes, you could always render its interface using class notation, stereotyped as «interface».

Figure 29-3: Modeling an Executable Release

Modeling a Physical Database

Modeling a logical database schema is discussed in Chapter 8.

A logical database schema captures the vocabulary of a system's persistent data, along with the semantics of their relationships. Physically, these things are stored in a database for later retrieval, either a relational database, an object-oriented one, or a hybrid object/relational database. The UML is well suited to modeling physical databases, as well as logical database schemas.

Physical database design is beyond the scope of this book; the focus here is simply to show you how you can model databases and tables using the UML.

Mapping a logical database schema to an object-oriented database is straightforward because even complex inheritance lattices can be made persistent directly. Mapping a logical database schema to a relational database is not so simple, however. In the presence of inheritance, you have to make decisions about how to map classes to tables. Typically, you can apply one or a combination of three strategies.

1. Define a separate table for each class. This is a simple but naive approach because it introduces maintenance headaches when you add new child classes or modify your parent classes.
2. Collapse your inheritance lattices so that all instances of any class in a hierarchy has the same state. The downside with this approach is that you end up storing superfluous information for many instances.

3. Separate parent and child states into different tables. This approach best mirrors your inheritance lattice, but the downside is that traversing your data will require many cross-table joins.

When designing a physical database, you also have to make decisions about how to map operations defined in your logical database schema. Object-oriented databases make the mapping fairly transparent. But, with relational databases, you have to make some decisions about how these logical operations are implemented. Again, you have some choices.

1. For simple CRUD (create, read, update, delete) operations, implement them with standard SQL or ODBC calls.
2. For more-complex behavior (such as business rules), map them to triggers or stored procedures.

Given these general guidelines, to model a physical database,

- Identify the classes in your model that represent your logical database schema.
- Select a strategy for mapping these classes to tables. You will also want to consider the physical distribution of your databases. Your mapping strategy will be affected by the location in which you want your data to live on your deployed system.
- To visualize, specify, construct, and document your mapping, create a component diagram that contains components stereotyped as tables.
- Where possible, use tools to help you transform your logical design into a physical design.

The UML's standard elements are summarized in Appendix B.

Figure 29-4 shows a set of database tables drawn from an information system for a school. You will find one database (`school.db`, rendered as a component stereotyped as `database`) that's composed of five tables: `student`, `class`, `instructor`, `department`, and `course` (rendered as a component stereotyped as `table`, one of the UML's standard elements). In the corresponding logical database schema, there was no inheritance, so mapping to this physical database design is straightforward.

Although not shown in this example, you can specify the contents of each table. Components can have attributes, so a common idiom when modeling physical databases is to use these attributes to specify the columns of each table. Similarly, components can have operations, and these can be used to denote stored procedures.

Figure 29-4: Modeling a Physical Database

Modeling Adaptable Systems

All the component diagrams shown thus far have been used to model static views. Their components spend their entire lives on one node. This is the most common situation you'll encounter, but especially in the domain of complex, distributed systems, you'll need to model dynamic views. For example, you might have a system that replicates its databases across several nodes, switching the one that is the primary database when a server goes down. Similarly, if you are modeling a globally distributed 24x7 operation (that is, a system that's up 24 hours a day, 7 days a week), you will likely encounter mobile agents, components that migrate from node to node to carry out some transaction. To model these dynamic views, you'll need to use a combination of component diagrams, object diagrams, and interaction diagrams.

To model an adaptable system,

The location tagged value is discussed in Chapter 23; object diagrams are discussed in Chapter 15.

- Consider the physical distribution of the components that may migrate from node to node. You can specify the location of a component instance by marking it with a location tagged value, which you can then render in a component diagram (although, technically speaking, a diagram that contains only instances is an object diagram).
- If you want to model the actions that cause a component to migrate, create a corresponding interaction diagram that contains component instances. You can illustrate a change of location by drawing the same instance more than once, but with different values for its location tagged value.

For example, Figure 29-5 models the replication of the database from the previous figure. We show two instances of the component `school.db`. Both instances are anonymous, and both have a different value for their location tagged value. There's also a note, which explicitly specifies which instance replicates the other.

Figure 29-5: Modeling Adaptable Systems

If you want to show the details of each database, you can render them in their canonical form—a component stereotyped as a `database`.

Interaction diagrams are discussed in Chapter 18.

Although not shown here, you could use an interaction diagram to model the dynamics of switching from one primary database to another.

Forward and Reverse Engineering

Forward engineering and reverse engineering components are pretty direct, because components are themselves physical things (executables, libraries, tables, files, and documents) that are therefore close to the running system. When you forward engineer a class or a collaboration, you really forward engineer to a component that represents the source code, binary library, or executable for that class or collaboration. Similarly, when you reverse engineer source code, binary libraries, or executables, you really reverse engineer to a component or set of components that, in turn, trace to classes or collaborations.

Choosing to forward engineer (the creation of code from a model) a class or collaboration to source code, a binary library, or an executable is a mapping decision you have to make. You'll want to take your logical models to source code if you are interested in controlling the configuration management of files that are then manipulated by a development environment. You'll want to take your logical models directly to binary libraries or executables if you are interested in managing the components that you'll actually deploy on a running system. In some cases, you'll want to do both. A class or collaboration may be denoted by source code, as well as by a binary library or executable.

To forward engineer a component diagram,

- For each component, identify the classes or collaborations that the component implements.
- Choose the target for each component. Your choice is basically between source code (a form that can be manipulated by development tools) or a binary library or executable (a form that can be dropped into a running system).
- Use tools to forward engineer your models.

Reverse engineering class diagrams is discussed in Chapter 8.

Reverse engineering (the creation of a model from code) a component diagram is not a perfect process because there is always a loss of information. From source code, you can reverse engineer back to classes; this is the most common thing you'll do. Reverse engineering source code to components will uncover compilation dependencies among those files. For binary libraries, the best you can hope for is to denote the library as a component and then discover its interfaces by reverse engineering. This is the second most common thing you'll do with component diagrams. In fact, this is a useful way to approach a set of new libraries that may be otherwise poorly documented. For executables, the best you can hope for is to denote the executable as a component and then disassemble its code—something you'll rarely need to do unless you work in assembly language.

To reverse engineer a component diagram,

- Choose the target you want to reverse engineer. Source code can be reverse engineered to components and then classes. Binary libraries can be reverse engineered to uncover their interfaces. Executables can be reverse engineered the least.
- Using a tool, point to the code you'd like to reverse engineer. Use your tool to generate a new model or to modify an existing one that was previously forward engineered.
- Using your tool, create a component diagram by querying the model. For example, you might start with one or more components, then expand the diagram by following relationships or neighboring components. Expose or hide the details of the contents of this component diagram as necessary to communicate your intent.

For example, Figure 29-6 provides a component diagram that represents the reverse engineering of the ActiveX component `vbrun.dll`. As the figure shows, the component realizes 11 interfaces. Given this diagram, you can begin to understand the semantics of the component by next exploring the details of its interfaces.

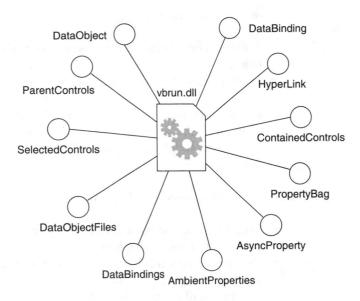

Figure 29-6: Reverse Engineering

Especially when you reverse engineer from source code, and sometimes when you reverse engineer from binary libraries and executables, you'll do so in the context of a configuration management system. This means that you'll often be working with specific versions of files or libraries, with all versions of a configuration compatible with one another. In these cases, you'll want to include a tagged value that represents the component version, which you can derive from your configuration management system. In this manner, you can use the UML to visualize the history of a component across various releases.

Hints and Tips

When you create component diagrams in the UML, remember that every component diagram is just a graphical presentation of the static implementation view of a system. This means that no single component diagram need capture everything about a system's implementation view. Collectively, all the component diagrams of a system represent the system's complete static implementation view; individually, each represents just one aspect.

A well-structured component diagram

- Is focused on communicating one aspect of a system's static implementation view.
- Contains only those elements that are essential to understanding that aspect.
- Provides detail consistent with its level of abstraction, with only those adornments that are essential to understanding exposed.
- Is not so minimalist that it misinforms the reader about important semantics.

When you draw a component diagram,

- Give it a name that communicates its purpose.
- Lay out its elements to minimize lines that cross.
- Organize its elements spatially so that things that are semantically close are laid out physically close.
- Use notes and color as visual cues to draw attention to important features of your diagram.
- Use stereotyped elements carefully. Choose a small set of common icons for your project or organization and use them consistently.

UNIFIED
MODELING
LANGUAGE

Chapter 30

DEPLOYMENT DIAGRAMS

In this chapter

- Modeling an embedded system
- Modeling a client/server system
- Modeling a fully distributed system
- Forward and reverse engineering

Component diagrams, the second kind of diagram used in modeling the physical aspects of an object-oriented system, are discussed in Chapter 29.

Deployment diagrams are one of the two kinds of diagrams used in modeling the physical aspects of an object-oriented system. A deployment diagram shows the configuration of run time processing nodes and the components that live on them.

You use deployment diagrams to model the static deployment view of a system. For the most part, this involves modeling the topology of the hardware on which your system executes. Deployment diagrams are essentially class diagrams that focus on a system's nodes.

Deployment diagrams are not only important for visualizing, specifying, and documenting embedded, client/server, and distributed systems, but also for managing executable systems through forward and reverse engineering.

Getting Started

When you create a software-intensive system, your main focus as a software developer is on architecting and deploying its software. However, as a systems engineer, your main focus is on the system's hardware *and* software and in managing the trade-offs between the two. Whereas software developers work with somewhat intangible artifacts, such as models and code, system developers work with quite tangible hardware, as well.

The UML is primarily focused on facilities for visualizing, specifying, constructing, and documenting software artifacts, but it's also designed to address hardware artifacts. This is not to say that the UML is a general-purpose hardware description language like VHDL. Rather, the UML is designed to model many of the hardware aspects of a system sufficient for a software engineer to specify the platform on which the system's software executes and for a systems engineer to manage the system's hardware/software boundary. In the UML, you use class diagrams and component diagrams to reason about the structure of your software. You use sequence diagrams, collaboration diagrams, statechart diagrams, and activity diagrams to specify the behavior of your software. At the edge of your system's software and hardware, you use deployment diagrams to reason about the topology of processors and devices on which your software executes.

With the UML, you use deployment diagrams to visualize the static aspect of these physical nodes and their relationships and to specify their details for construction, as in Figure 30-1.

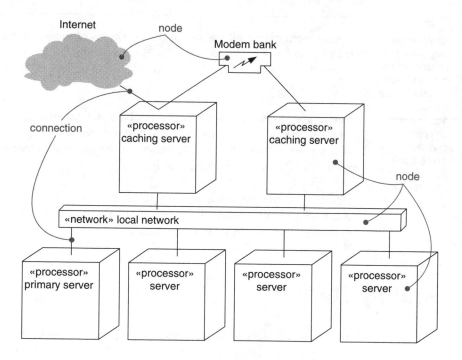

Figure 30-1: A Deployment Diagram

Terms and Concepts

A *deployment diagram* is a diagram that shows the configuration of run time processing nodes and the components that live on them. Graphically, a deployment diagram is a collection of vertices and arcs.

Common Properties

The general properties of diagrams are discussed in Chapter 7.

A deployment diagram is just a special kind of diagram and shares the same common properties as all other diagrams—a name and graphical contents that are a projection into a model. What distinguishes a deployment diagram from all other kinds of diagrams is its particular content.

Contents

Nodes are discussed in Chapter 26; relationships are discussed in Chapters 5 and 10; components are discussed in Chapter 25; packages are discussed in Chapter 12; subsystems are discussed in Chapter 31; instances are discussed in Chapter 13; class diagrams are discussed in Chapter 8.

Deployment diagrams commonly contain

- Nodes
- Dependency and association relationships

Like all other diagrams, deployment diagrams may contain notes and constraints.

Deployment diagrams may also contain components, each of which must live on some node. Deployment diagrams may also contain packages or subsystems, both of which are used to group elements of your model into larger chunks. Sometimes, you'll want to place instances in your deployment diagrams, as well, especially when you want to visualize one instance of a family of hardware topologies.

Note: In many ways, a deployment diagram is just a special kind of class diagram, which focuses on a system's nodes.

Common Uses

Deployment views in the context of software architecture are discussed in Chapter 2.

You use deployment diagrams to model the static deployment view of a system. This view primarily addresses the distribution, delivery, and installation of the parts that make up the physical system.

There are some kinds of systems for which deployment diagrams are unnecessary. If you are developing a piece of software that lives on one machine and interfaces only with standard devices on that machine that are already managed by the host operating system (for example, a personal computer's keyboard, display, and modem), you can ignore deployment diagrams. On the other hand, if you are developing a piece of software that interacts with devices that the host operating system does not typically manage or that is physically distributed across multiple processors, then using deployment diagrams will help you reason about your system's software-to-hardware mapping.

When you model the static deployment view of a system, you'll typically use deployment diagrams in one of three ways.

1. To model embedded systems

An embedded system is a software-intensive collection of hardware that interfaces with the physical world. Embedded systems involve software that controls devices such as motors, actuators, and displays and that, in turn, is controlled by external stimuli such as sensor input, movement, and temperature changes. You can use deployment diagrams to model the devices and processors that comprise an embedded system.

2. To model client/server systems

Modeling the distribution of components is discussed in Chapter 26.

A client/server system is a common architecture focused on making a clear separation of concerns between the system's user interface (which lives on the client) and the system's persistent data (which lives on the server). Client/server systems are one end of the continuum of distributed systems and require you to make decisions about the network connectivity of clients to servers and about the physical distribution of your system's software components across the nodes. You can model the topology of such systems by using deployment diagrams.

3. To model fully distributed systems

At the other end of the continuum of distributed systems are those that are widely, if not globally, distributed, typically encompassing multiple levels of servers. Such systems are often hosts to multiple versions of software components, some of which may even migrate from node to node. Crafting such systems requires you to make decisions that enable the continuous change in the system's topology. You can use deployment diagrams to visualize the system's current topology and distribution of components to reason about the impact of changes on that topology.

Common Modeling Techniques

Modeling an Embedded System

Nodes and devices are discussed in Chapter 26.

Developing an embedded system is far more than a software problem. You have to manage the physical world in which there are moving parts that break and in which signals are noisy and behavior is nonlinear. When you model such a system, you have to take into account its interface with the real world, and that means reasoning about unusual devices, as well as nodes.

The UML's extensibility mechanisms are discussed in Chapter 6.

Deployment diagrams are useful in facilitating the communication between your project's hardware engineers and software developers. By using nodes that are stereotyped to look like familiar devices, you can create diagrams that are understandable by both groups. Deployment diagrams are also helpful in reasoning about hardware/software trade-offs. You'll use deployment diagrams to visualize, specify, construct, and document your system engineering decisions.

To model an embedded system,

- Identify the devices and nodes that are unique to your system.
- Provide visual cues, especially for unusual devices, by using the UML's extensibility mechanisms to define system-specific stereotypes with appropriate icons. At the very least, you'll want to distinguish processors (which contain software components) and devices (which, at that level of abstraction, don't directly contain software).
- Model the relationships among these processors and devices in a deployment diagram. Similarly, specify the relationship between the components in your system's implementation view and the nodes in your system's deployment view.
- As necessary, expand on any intelligent devices by modeling their structure with a more detailed deployment diagram.

For example, Figure 30-2 shows the hardware for a simple autonomous robot. You'll find one node (`Pentium motherboard`) stereotyped as a processor.

Surrounding this node are eight devices, each stereotyped as a device and rendered with an icon that offers a clear visual cue to its real-world equivalent.

Figure 30-2: Modeling an Embedded System

Modeling a Client/Server System

The moment you start developing a system whose software no longer resides on a single processor, you are faced with a host of decisions: How do you best distribute your software components across these nodes? How do they communicate? How do you deal with failure and noise? At one end of the spectrum of distributed systems, you'll encounter client/server systems, in which there's a clear separation of concerns between the system's user interface (typically managed by the client) and its data (typically managed by the server).

There are many variations on this theme. For example, you might choose to have a thin client, meaning that it has a limited amount of computational capacity and does little more than manage the user interface and visualization of information. Thin clients may not even host a lot of components but, rather, may be designed to load components from the server, as needed, as with Enterprise Java Beans. On the other hand, you might chose to have a thick client, meaning that it has a goodly amount of computational capacity and does more than just visualization. A thick client typically carries out some of the system's logic and business rules. The choice between thin and thick clients is an architectural decision that's influenced by a number of technical, economic, and political factors.

Either way, partitioning a system into its client and server parts involves making some hard decisions about where to physically place its software components and how to impose a balanced distribution of responsibilities among those components. For example, most management information systems are essentially three-tier architectures, which means that the system's GUI, business logic, and database are physically distributed. Deciding where to place the system's GUI and database are usually fairly obvious, so the hard part lies in deciding where the business logic lives.

You can use the UML's deployment diagrams to visualize, specify, and document your decisions about the topology of your client/server system and how its software components are distributed across the client and server. Typically, you'll want to create one deployment diagram for the system as a whole, along with other, more detailed, diagrams that drill down to individual segments of the system.

To model a client/server system,

- Identify the nodes that represent your system's client and server processors.
- Highlight those devices that are germane to the behavior of your system. For example, you'll want to model special devices, such as credit card readers, badge readers, and display devices other than monitors, because their placement in the system's hardware topology are likely to be architecturally significant.
- Provide visual cues for these processors and devices via stereotyping.
- Model the topology of these nodes in a deployment diagram. Similarly, specify the relationship between the components in your system's implementation view and the nodes in your system's deployment view.

Packages are discussed in Chapter 12; multiplicity is discussed in Chapter 10.

For example, Figure 30-3 shows the topology of a human resources system, which follows a classical client/server architecture. This figure illustrates the client/server split explicitly by using the packages named `client` and `server`. The client package contains two nodes (`console` and `kiosk`), both of which are stereotyped and are visually distinguishable. The server package contains two kinds of nodes (`caching server` and `server`), and both of these have been adorned with some of the components that reside on each. Note also that `caching server` and `server` are marked with explicit multiplicities, specifying how many instances of each are expected in a particular deployed configuration. For example, this diagram indicates that there may be two or more `caching servers` in any deployed instance of the system.

Figure 30-3: Modeling a Client/Server System

Modeling a Fully Distributed System

Distributed systems come in many forms, from simple two-processor systems to those that span many geographically dispersed nodes. The latter are typically never static. Nodes are added and removed as network traffic changes and processors fail; new and faster communication paths may be established in parallel with older, slower channels that are eventually decommissioned. Not only may the topology of these systems change, but the distribution of their software components may change, as well. For example, database tables may be replicated across servers, only to be moved, as traffic dictates. For some global systems, components may follow the sun, migrating from server to server as the business day begins in one part of the world and ends in another.

Visualizing, specifying, and documenting the topology of fully distributed systems such as these are valuable activities for the systems administrator, who must keep tabs on an enterprise's computing assets. You can use the UML's deployment diagrams to reason about the topology of such systems. When you document fully distributed systems using deployment diagrams, you'll want to expand on the details of the system's networking devices, each of which you can represent as a stereotyped node.

To model a fully distributed system,

- Identify the system's devices and processors as for simpler client/server systems.
- If you need to reason about the performance of the system's network or the impact of changes to the network, be sure to model these communi-

Packages are
discussed in
Chapter 12.

Use cases are
discussed in
Chapter 16;
interaction
diagrams are
described in
Chapter 20;
instances are
discussed in
Chapter 13.

cation devices to the level of detail sufficient to make these assessments.

- Pay close attention to logical groupings of nodes, which you can specify by using packages.
- Model these devices and processors using deployment diagrams. Where possible, use tools that discover the topology of your system by walking your system's network.
- If you need to focus on the dynamics of your system, introduce use case diagrams to specify the kinds of behavior you are interested in, and expand on these use cases with interaction diagrams.

Note: When modeling a fully distributed system, it's common to reify the network itself as an node. For example, the Internet might be represented as a node (as in Figure 30-1, shown a stereotyped node). You can also reify a local area network (LAN) or wide-area network (WAN) in the same way (as in Figure 30-1). In each case, you can use the node's attributes and operations to capture properties about the network.

Figure 30-4 shows the topology of a fully distributed system. This particular deployment diagram is also an object diagram, for it contains only instances. You can see three consoles (anonymous instances of the stereotyped node `console`), which are linked to the `Internet` (clearly a singleton node). In turn, there are three instances of `regional servers`, which serve as front ends of `country servers`, only one of which is shown. As the note indicates, country servers are connected to one another, but their relationships are not shown in this diagram.

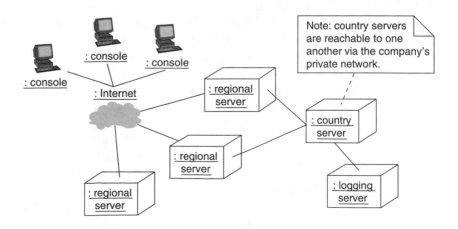

Figure 30-4: Modeling a Fully Distributed System

In this diagram, the Internet has been reified as a stereotyped node.

Forward and Reverse Engineering

There's only a modest amount of forward engineering (the creation of code from models) that you can do with deployment diagrams. For example, after specifying the physical distribution of components across the nodes in a deployment diagram, it is possible to use tools that then push these components out to the real world. For system administrators, using the UML in this way helps you visualize what can be a very complicated task.

Reverse engineering (the creation of models from code) from the real world back to deployment diagrams is of tremendous value, especially for fully distributed systems that are under constant change. You'll want to supply a set of stereotyped nodes that speak the language of your system's network administrators, in order to tailor the UML to their domain. The advantage of using the UML is that it offers a standard language that addresses not only their needs, but the needs of your project's software developers, as well.

To reverse engineer a deployment diagram,

- Choose the target that you want to reverse engineer. In some cases, you'll want to sweep across your entire network; in others, you can limit your search.
- Choose also the fidelity of your reverse engineering. In some cases, it's sufficient to reverse engineer just to the level of all the system's processors; in others, you'll want to reverse engineer the system's networking peripherals, as well.
- Use a tool that walks across your system, discovering its hardware topology. Record that topology in a deployment model.
- Along the way, you can use similar tools to discover the components that live on each node, which you can also record in a deployment model. You'll want to use an intelligent search, for even a basic personal computer can contain gigabytes of components, many of which may not be relevant to your system.
- Using your modeling tools, create a deployment diagram by querying the model. For example, you might start with visualizing the basic client/server topology, then expand on the diagram by populating certain nodes with components of interest that live on them. Expose or hide the details of the contents of this deployment diagram as necessary to communicate your intent.

Hints and Tips

When you create deployment diagrams in the UML, remember that every deployment diagram is just a graphical presentation of the static deployment view of a system. This means that no single deployment diagram need capture everything about a system's deployment view. Collectively, all the deployment diagrams of a system represent the system's complete static deployment view; individually, each represents just one aspect.

A well-structured deployment diagram

- Focuses on communicating one aspect of a system's static deployment view.
- Contains only those elements that are essential to understanding that aspect.
- Provides detail consistent with its level of abstraction; expose only those adornments that are essential to understanding.
- Is not so minimalist that it misinforms the reader about important semantics.

When you draw a deployment diagram,

- Give it a name that communicates its purpose.
- Lay out its elements to minimize lines that cross.
- Organize its elements spatially so that things that are semantically close are laid out physically close.
- Use notes and color as visual cues to draw attention to important features of your diagram.
- Use stereotyped elements carefully. Choose a small set of common icons for your project or organization, and use them consistently.

Chapter 31

SYSTEMS AND MODELS

The UML is a graphical language for visualizing, specifying, constructing, and documenting the artifacts of a software-intensive system. You use the UML to model systems. A model is a simplification of reality—an abstraction of a system—created in order to better understand the system. A system, possibly decomposed into a collection of subsystems, is a set of elements organized to accomplish a purpose and described by a set of models, possibly from different viewpoints. Things like classes, interfaces, components, and nodes are important parts of a system's model. In the UML, you use models to organize these and all the other abstractions of a system. As you move to more-complex domains, you'll find that a system at one level of abstraction looks like a subsystem at another, higher, level. In the UML, you can model systems and subsystems as a whole so that you can seamlessly move up to problems of scale.

Well-structured models help you visualize, specify, construct, and document a complex system from different, yet interrelated, aspects. Well-structured systems are functionally, logically, and physically cohesive, formed of loosely coupled subsystems.

Getting Started

Building a dog house doesn't take a lot of thought. The needs of a dog are simple, so to satisfy all but the most demanding dog, you can just do it.

The differences between building a dog house and building a high rise are discussed in Chapter 1.

Building a house or a high rise takes a lot more thought. The needs of a family or a building's tenants are not so simple, so to satisfy even the least demanding client, you can't just do it. Rather, you have to do some modeling. Different stakeholders will look at the problem from different angles and with different concerns. That's why, for complex buildings, you'll end up creating floor plans, elevation plans, heating/cooling plans, electrical plans, plumbing plans, and perhaps even networking plans. There's no one model that can adequately capture all the interesting aspects of a complex building.

Diagrams are discussed in Chapter 7; the five views of a software architecture are discussed in Chapter 2.

In the UML, you organize all the abstractions of a software-intensive system into models, each of which represents some relatively independent, yet important, aspect of the system under development. You then use diagrams to visualize interesting collections of these abstractions. Looking at the five views of an architecture is a particularly useful way to channel the attention of a software system's different stakeholders. Collectively, these models work together to provide a complete statement of a system's structure and behavior.

For larger systems, you'll find that the elements of such systems can be meaningfully decomposed into separate subsystems, each of which looks just like a smaller system when viewed from a lower level of abstraction.

The UML's extensibility mechanisms are discussed in Chapter 6; packages are discussed in Chapter 12.

The UML provides a graphical representation for systems and subsystems, as Figure 31-1 shows. This notation permits you to visualize the decomposition of a system into smaller subsystems. Graphically, a system and a subsystem are rendered as a stereotyped package icon. Models and views don't have a special graphical representation (other than rendering them as stereotyped packages) because they are primarily things that are manipulated by tools that you use to organize the different aspects of a system.

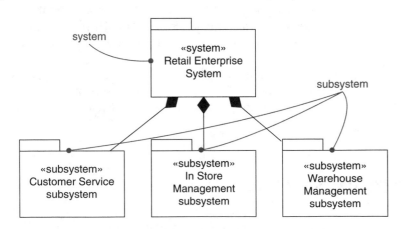

Figure 31-1: Systems and Subsystems

Terms and Concepts

A *system*, possibly decomposed into a collection of subsystems, is a set of elements organized to accomplish a purpose and described by a set of models, possibly from different viewpoints. A *subsystem* is a grouping of elements of which some constitute a specification of the behavior offered by other contained elements. Graphically, a system and a subsystem are rendered as a stereotyped package icon. A *model* is a simplification of reality, an abstraction of a system, created in order to better understand the system. A *view* is a projection of a model, which is seen from one perspective or vantage point and omits entities that are not relevant to this perspective.

Systems and Subsystems

A system is the thing itself that you are developing and for which you build models. A system encompasses all the artifacts that constitute that thing, including all its models and modeling elements, such as classes, interfaces, components, nodes, and their relationships. Everything you need to visualize, specify, construct, and document a system is part of that system, and everything you don't need to visualize, specify, construct, and document a system lies outside that system.

Stereotypes are discussed in Chapter 6; packages are discussed in Chapter 12; classes are discussed in Chapters 4 and 9; use cases are discussed in Chapter 16; state machines are discussed in Chapter 21; collaborations are discussed in Chapter 27.

In the UML, a system is rendered as a stereotyped package, as shown in the previous figure. As a stereotyped package, a system owns elements. If you zoom inside a system, you'll see all its models and individual modeling elements (including diagrams), perhaps further decomposed into subsystems. As a classifier, a system may have instances (a system may be deployed in multiple instances in the real world), attributes and operations (actors outside the system may act on the system as a whole), use cases, state machines, and collaborations, all of which may specify the behavior of the system. A system may even realize interfaces, which is important when you are constructing systems of systems.

A subsystem is simply a part of a system, and is used to decompose a complex system into nearly independent parts. A system at one level of abstraction may be a subsystem of a system at a higher level of abstraction.

In the UML, a subsystem is rendered as a stereotyped package icon, also shown in the previous figure. Semantically, a subsystem is both a kind of package, as well as a kind of classifier.

Aggregation and generalization are discussed in Chapters 5 and 10.

The primary relationship among systems and subsystems is aggregation. A system (the whole) may contain zero or more subsystems (the parts). You can also have generalization relationships among systems and subsystems. Using generalization, you can model families of systems and subsystems, some of which represent general kinds of systems and others of which represent specific tailorings of those systems.

Note: A system represents the highest-level thing in a given context; the subsystems that make up a system provide a complete and nonoverlapping partitioning of the system as a whole.

Models and Views

A model is a simplification of reality, in which reality is defined in the context of the system being modeled. In short, a model is an abstraction of a system. A subsystem represents a partitioning of the elements of a larger system into independent parts; a model is a partitioning of the abstractions that visualize, specify, construct, and document that system. The difference is subtle but important. You decompose a system into subsystems so that you can develop and deploy these parts somewhat independently; you partition the abstractions of a system or a subsystem into models so that you can better understand the thing you are developing and deploying. Just as a complex system such as an aircraft may have many parts (for example, the airframe, propulsion, avionics, and passenger subsystems), those subsystems and the system as a whole may be modeled from a number of different points of view (such as from the perspective of structural, dynamic, electrical, and heating/cooling models, for example).

Packages are discussed in Chapter 12.

A model is a special kind of package. Because you'll rarely need to model models explicitly, there's no special graphical rendering defined for models in the UML. Tools need to manipulate models, however, so a tool will typically use package notation to represent a model as seen by the tool.

The five views of a software architecture are discussed in Chapter 2.

As a package, a model owns elements. The models associated with a system or subsystem completely partition the elements of that system or subsystem, meaning that every element is owned by exactly one package. Typically, you'll organize the artifacts of a system or subsystem into a set of nonoverlapping models, covered by the five views of software architecture that are described elsewhere.

Diagrams are discussed in Chapter 7.

A model (for example, a process model) may contain so many artifacts (such as active classes, relationships, and interactions) that in systems of scale, you simply cannot embrace all those artifacts at once. Think of a view as a projection into a model. For each model, you'll have a number of diagrams that exist to give you a peek into the things owned by the model. A view encompasses a subset of the things owned by a model; a view typically may not cross model boundaries. As described in the next section, there are no direct relationships among models, although you'll find trace relationships among the elements contained in different models.

Note: The UML does not dictate which models you should use to visualize, specify, construct, and document a system, although the Rational Unified Process does suggest a proven set of models.

Trace

Relationships are discussed in Chapters 5 and 10.

Specifying relationships among elements such as classes, interfaces, components, and nodes is an important structural part of any model. Specifying the relationships among elements such as documents, diagrams, and packages that live in different models is an important part of managing the development artifacts of complex systems, many of which may exist in multiple versions.

Dependencies are discussed in Chapter 5; stereotypes are discussed in Chapter 6.

In the UML, you can model the conceptual relationship among elements that live in different models by using a trace relationship; a trace may not be applied among elements in the same model. A trace is represented as a stereotyped dependency. You can often ignore the direction of this dependency, although you'll typically direct it to the older or more-specific element, as in Figure 31-2. The two most common uses for the trace relationship are to trace from requirements to implementation (and all the artifacts in between) and to trace from version to version.

Figure 31-2: Trace Relationships

Note: Most of the time, you will not want to render trace relationships explicitly but, rather, will treat them as hyperlinks.

Common Modeling Techniques

Modeling the Architecture of a System

Architecture and modeling are discussed in Chapter 1.

The most common use for which you'll apply systems and models is to organize the elements you use to visualize, specify, construct, and document a system's architecture. Ultimately, this touches virtually all the artifacts you'll find in a software development project. When you model a system's architecture, you capture decisions about the system's requirements, its logical elements, and its physical elements. You'll also model both structural and behavioral aspects of the systems and the patterns that shape these views. Finally, you'll want to focus on the seams between subsystems and the tracing from requirements to deployment.

To model the architecture of a system,

The five views of a software architecture are discussed in Chapter 2; diagrams are discussed in Chapter 7.

- Identify the views that you'll use to represent your architecture. Most often, you'll want to include a use case view, a design view, a process view, an implementation view, and a deployment view, as shown in Figure 31-3.
- Specify the context for this system, including the actors that surround it.
- As necessary, decompose the system into its elementary subsystems.

Figure 31-3: Modeling a System's Architecture

The following activities apply to the system, as well as to its subsystems.

- Specify a use case view of the system, encompassing the use cases that describe the behavior of the system as seen by its end users, analysts, and testers. Apply use case diagrams to model static aspects, and interaction diagrams, statechart diagrams, and activity diagrams to model the dynamic aspects.
- Specify a design view of the system, encompassing the classes, interfaces, and collaborations that form the vocabulary of the problem and its solution. Apply class diagrams and object diagrams to model static aspects, and interaction diagrams, statechart diagrams, and activity diagrams to model the dynamic aspects.
- Specify a process view of the system, encompassing the threads and processes that form the system's concurrency and synchronization mechanisms. Apply the same diagrams as for the design view, but with a focus on active classes and objects that represent threads and processes.
- Specify an implementation view of the system, encompassing the components that are used to assemble and release the physical system. Apply component diagrams to model static aspects, and interaction diagrams, statechart diagrams, and activity diagrams to model the dynamic aspects.
- Specify a deployment view of the system, encompassing the nodes that form the system's hardware topology on which the system executes. Apply deployment diagrams to model static aspects, and interaction diagrams, statechart diagrams, and activity diagrams to model the dynamic aspects.
- Model the architectural patterns and design patterns that shape each of these models using collaborations.

The Rational Unified Process is discussed in Chapter 2.

Understand that you don't ever create a system's architecture in one big-bang event. Rather, a well-structured process for the UML involves the successive refinement of a system's architecture in a manner that is use case–driven, architecture-centric, and iterative and incremental.

The UML's extensibility mechanisms are discussed in Chapter 6.

For all but the most trivial systems, you'll have to manage versions of your system's artifacts. You can use the UML's extensibility mechanisms—and tagged values, in particular—to capture your decisions about the version of each element.

Modeling Systems of Systems

A system at one level of abstraction will look like a subsystem of a higher level of abstraction. Similarly, a subsystem at one level of abstraction will look like a full-fledged system from the perspective of the team responsible for creating it.

All complex systems exhibit this kind of hierarchy. As you move to systems of greater and greater complexity, you'll find it necessary to decompose your effort into subsystems, each of which can be developed somewhat separately, and iteratively and incrementally grown into the whole system. The development of a subsystem looks just like the development of a system.

To model a system or a subsystem,

- Identify major functional parts of the system that may be developed, released, and deployed somewhat independently. Technical, political, legacy, and legal issues will often shape how you draw the lines around each subsystem.
- For each subsystem, specify its context, just as you do for the system as a whole; the actors that surround a subsystem encompass all its neighboring subsystems, so they must all be designed to collaborate.
- For each subsystem, model its architecture just as you do for the system as a whole.

Hints and Tips

It's important to choose the right set of models to visualize, specify, construct, and document a system. A well-structured model

- Provides a simplification of reality from a distinct and relatively independent point of view.
- Is self-contained in that it requires no other content to understand its semantics.
- Is loosely coupled to other models via trace relationships.
- Collectively (with other neighboring models) provides a complete statement of a system's artifacts.

nt to decompose complex systems into well-structured
ructured system

, logically, and physically cohesive.
posed into nearly independent subsystems that them-
.ems at a lower level of abstraction.
ized, specified, constructed, and documented via a set of
ionoverlapping models.

cial graphical representation in the UML (other than ren-
otyped package icons), although you'll typically find them
as packages, each of which represents a partitioning of the
i from a particular point of view.

stem or a subsystem in the UML,

starting point for all the artifacts associated with that sys-
m.
asic aggregation among the system and its subsystems;
leave the details of their connections to lower-level

UNIFIED
MODELING
LANGUAGE

Section 7
WRAPPING UP

UNIFIED
MODELING
LANGUAGE

Chapter 32
APPLYING THE UML

Simple problems are easy to model with the UML. Hard problems are easy to model, too, especially after you've become fluent in the language.

Reading about using the UML is one thing, but it's only through *using* the language that you will come to master it. Depending on your background, there are different ways to approach using the UML for the first time. As you gain more experience, you will come to understand and appreciate its more subtle parts.

If you can think it, the UML can model it.

Transitioning to the UML

You can model 80 percent of most problems by using about 20 percent of the UML. Basic structural things, such as classes, attributes, operations, use cases, components, and packages, together with basic structural relationships, such as dependency, generalization, and association, are sufficient to create static models for many kinds of problem domains. Add to that list basic behavioral things, such as simple state machines and interactions, and you can model many useful aspects of a system's dynamics. You'll need to use only the more advanced features of the UML once you start modeling the things you encounter in more-complex situations, such as modeling concurrency and distribution.

A conceptual model for the UML is discussed in Chapter 2.

A good starting place for using the UML is to model some of the basic abstractions or behavior that already exist in one of your systems. Develop a conceptual model of the UML so that you'll have a framework around which you can grow your understanding of the language. Later on, you'll better understand how the more advanced parts of the UML fit together. As you attack more-complex problems, drill down into specific features of the UML by studying the common modeling techniques in this book.

If you are new to object-orientation,

- Start by getting comfortable with the idea of abstraction. Team exercises with CRC cards and use case analysis are excellent ways to develop your skills of identifying crisp abstractions.
- Model a simple static part of your problem using classes, dependency, generalization, and association to get familiar with visualizing societies of abstractions.
- Use simple sequence or collaboration diagrams to model a dynamic part of your problem. Building a model of user interaction with the system is a good starting place and will give you an immediate payback by helping you reason through some of the system's more important use cases.

If you are new to modeling,

- Start by taking a part of some system you've already built—preferably implemented in some object-oriented programming language, such as Java or C++—and build a UML model of these classes and their relationships.
- Using the UML, try to capture some details of programming idioms or mechanisms you used in that system, which are in your head but you can't put down directly in the code.
- Especially if you have a nontrivial application, try to reconstruct a model of its architecture by using UML packages to represent its major structural elements.
- After you become comfortable with the vocabulary of the UML and before you start cutting code on your next project, build a UML model of that part of the system first. Think about the structure or behavior you've specified, and only then, when you are happy with its size, shape, and semantics, use that model as a framework for your implementation.

If you are already experienced with another object-oriented method,

- Take a look at your current modeling language and construct a mapping from its elements to the elements of the UML. In most cases—especially if you are currently using the Booch, OOSE, or OMT methods — you'll find a one-to-one mapping and that most of the changes are cosmetic.
- Consider some wicked modeling problem that you found clumsy or impossible to model with your current modeling language. Look at some of the advanced features of the UML that might address that problem with greater clarity or simplicity.

If you are a power user,

- Be sure you first develop a conceptual model of the UML. You may miss its harmony of concepts if you dive into the most sophisticated parts of the language without first understanding its basic vocabulary.
- Pay particular attention to the UML's features for modeling components, concurrency, distribution, and patterns—issues that often involve complex and subtle semantics.
- Look also at the UML's extensibility mechanisms and see how you might tailor the UML to directly speak the vocabulary of your domain. Take care to resist the temptation to go to extremes that yield a UML model that no one but other power users will recognize.

Where to Go Next

This user guide is part of a larger set of books that, collectively, can help you learn how to apply the UML. In addition to the user guide, there is *The Unified Modeling Language Reference Manual*, which provides a comprehensive reference to the syntax and semantics of the UML, and *The Unified Software Development Process*, which presents a recommended development process for use with the UML.

To learn more about modeling from the principal authors of the UML, take a look at the following references:

- Booch, G. *Object-Oriented Analysis and Design with Applications*, 2nd ed. Redwood City, California, Addison-Wesley Publishing Company, 1993.

- Jacobson, I., Christerson, M., Jonsson, P., and Overgaard, G. *Object-Oriented Software Engineering: A Use Case Driven Approach*. Wokingham, England, Addison-Wesley Publishing Company, 1992.
- Rumbaugh, J., Blaha, M., Premerlani, W., Eddy, F., and Lorensen, W. *Object-Oriented Modeling and Design*. Englewood Cliffs, New Jersey, Prentice-Hall, 1991.

You can read more about statecharts in

- Harel, D. "Statecharts: A Visual Formalism for Complex Systems," Science of Computer Programming 8 (1987), pp. 231-274 (Also, Technical Report, The Weizman Institute, 1984).

The latest information about the UML can be found on the Web at `www.rational.com`. At that location and also at `www.omg.org`, you'll find the latest version of the UML standard.

UML NOTATION

A overview of the UML is discussed in Chapter 2.

The UML is a language for visualizing, specifying, constructing, and documenting the artifacts of a software-intensive system. As a language, the UML has a well-defined syntax and semantics. The most visible part of the UML's syntax is its graphical notation.

This appendix summarizes the elements of the UML notation.

Things

Structural Things

Structural things are the nouns of UML models. These include classes, interfaces, collaborations, use cases, active classes, components, and nodes.

Behavioral Things

Behavioral things are the dynamic parts of UML models. These include interactions and state machines.

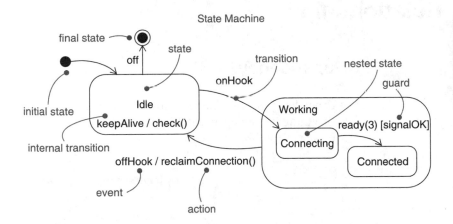

Grouping Things

Grouping things are the organizational parts of UML models. This includes packages.

Annotational Things

Annotational things are the explanatory parts of UML models. This includes notes.

Relationships

Dependency

A dependency is a semantic relationship between two things in which a change to one thing (the independent thing) may affect the semantics of the other thing (the dependent thing).

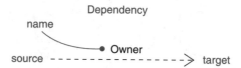

Association

An association is a structural relationship that describes a set of links; a link is a connection among objects.

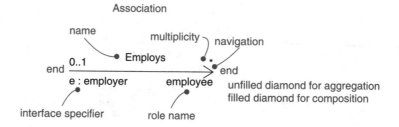

Generalization

Generalization is a specialization/generalization relationship in which objects of the specialized element (the child) are substitutable for objects of the generalized element (the parent).

Extensibility

The UML provides three mechanisms for extending the language's syntax and semantics: stereotypes (which represent new modeling elements), tagged values (which represent new modeling attributes), and constraints (which represent new modeling semantics).

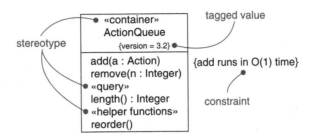

Diagrams

A diagram is the graphical presentation of a set of elements, most often rendered as a connected graph of vertices (things) and arcs (relationships). A diagram is a projection into a system. The UML includes nine such diagrams.

1. Class diagram	A structural diagram that shows a set of classes, interfaces, collaborations, and their relationships
2. Object diagram	A structural diagram that shows a set of objects and their relationships
3. Use case diagram	A behavioral diagram that shows a set of use cases and actors and their relationships
4. Sequence diagram	A behavioral diagram that shows an interaction, emphasizing the time ordering of messages
5. Collaboration diagram	A behavioral diagram that shows an interaction, emphasizing the structural organization of the objects that send and receive messages
6. Statechart diagram	A behavioral diagram that shows a state machine, emphasizing the event-ordered behavior of an object
7. Activity diagram	A behavioral diagram that shows a state machine, emphasizing the flow from activity to activity

8. Component diagram   A structural diagram that shows a set of components and their relationships

9. Deployment diagram   A structural diagram that shows a set of nodes and their relationships

Appendix B
UML STANDARD ELEMENTS

*The UML's
extensibility
mechanisms
are discussed
in Chapter 6.*

The UML provides a standard language for writing software blueprints. However, no language could ever be sufficient to express all nuances of all models across all domains for all time. The UML is therefore designed to be open-ended, making it possible for you to extend the language in controlled ways. The UML's extensibility mechanisms include

- Stereotypes
- Tagged values
- Constraints

A *stereotype* extends the vocabulary of the UML, allowing you to create new kinds of building blocks that are derived from existing ones but are specific to your problem. A *tagged value* extends the properties of a UML building block, allowing you to create new information in that element's specification. A *constraint* extends the semantics of a UML building block, allowing you to add new rules or modify existing ones.

Collectively, these three extensibility mechanisms allow you to shape and to grow the UML to your project's needs. These mechanisms also let the UML adapt to new software technology, such as the likely emergence of more-powerful distributed programming languages and the impact of fusion with hardware modeling languages for modeling systems. You can add new building blocks, modify the specification of existing ones, and even change their semantics. Naturally, it's important that you do so in controlled ways so that through these extensions, you remain true to the UML's purpose, namely, the communication of information.

You can use the UML without ever needing these extensibility mechanisms. In fact, by treating variants of the UML's building blocks as extensions, the core of the UML is made smaller and simpler.

However, as you build more-complex models and need to visualize or specify certain subtle, yet important, semantics, you'll find yourself using a few stereotypes, tagged values, and constraints over and over again. Some extensions are so common that they have been defined in the UML as standard elements.

This appendix describes these standard elements.

Stereotypes

The following stereotypes are defined as standard elements of the UML. For each stereotype, the following table gives its name, the symbol of the UML to which it applies, and its meaning.

Note: Some items in this table are technically not stereotypes; they are standard keywords. The distinction is subtle. In the UML's metamodel, items such as `trace` are manifest, meaning that they are an explicit part of the metamodel and so are not really stereotypes. From the perspective of the developer, however, you still render them by using stereotype notation. These items are specified as standard keywords in order to reserve the use of their name in a manner that is consistent with the UML's metamodel. In the following table, keywords are highlighted in italics.

Typically, a stereotyped element is rendered by placing the stereotype name above the element's name and enclosing the stereotype name in guillemets, as in «trace». Each stereotype may have an associated icon that may be used as an alternative form for visualizing the element. Although the UML does not specify such icons for any of the standard stereotypes, the following table offers a few suggested notations drawn from common practice.

Stereotype/ *Keyword*	Applies to symbol	Meaning
actor	class	Specifies a coherent set of roles that users of use cases play when interacting with these use cases
access	dependency	Specifies that the public contents of the target package are accessible to the namespace of the source package
association	link end	Specifies that the corresponding object is visible by association

Stereotype/ *Keyword*	Applies to symbol	Meaning
become	message	Specifies that the target is the same object as the source but at a later point in time and with possibly different values, state, or roles
bind	dependency	Specifies that the source instantiates the target template using the given actual parameters
call	dependency	Specifies that the source operation invokes the target operation
copy	message	Specifies that the target object is an exact but independent copy of the source
create	event message	Specifies that the target object is created by the event or the message
derive	dependency	Specifies that the source may be computed from the target
destroy	event message	Specifies that the target object is destroyed by the event or the message
document	component	Specifies a component that represents a document
enumeration	class	Specifies an enumerated type, including its possible values as a set of identifiers
exception	class	Specifies an event that may be thrown or caught by an operation
executable	component	Specifies a component that may be executed on a node
extend	dependency	Specifies that the target use case extends the behavior of the source use case at the given extension point

Appendix B

Stereotype/ *Keyword*	Applies to symbol	Meaning
facade	package	Specifies a package that is only a view on some other package
file	component	Specifies a component that represents a document containing source code or data
framework	package	Specifies a package consisting mainly of patterns
friend	dependency	Specifies that the source is given special visibility into the target
global	link end	Specifies that the corresponding object is visible because it is in an enclosing scope
import	dependency	Specifies that the public contents of the target package enter the flat namespace of the source, as if they had been declared in the source
implementation	generalization	Specifies that the child inherits the implementation of the parent but does not make public nor support its interfaces, thereby violating substitutability
implementa-tionClass	class	Specifies the implementation of a class in some programming language
include	dependency	Specifies that the source use case explicitly incorporates the behavior of another use case at a location specified by the source
instanceOf	dependency	Specifies that the source object is an instance of the target classifier
instantiate	dependency	Specifies that operations on the source class create instances of the target class
interface	class	Specifies a collection of operations that are used to specify a service of a class or a component

Stereotype/ *Keyword*	Applies to symbol	Meaning
invariant	constraint	Specifies a constraint that must always hold for the associated element
library	component	Specifies a static or dynamic object library
local	link end	Specifies that the corresponding object is visible because it is in a local scope
metaclass	classifier	Specifies a classifier whose objects are all classes
model	package	Specifies a semantically closed abstraction of a system
parameter	link end	Specifies that the corresponding object is visible because it is a parameter
postcondition	constraint	Specifies a constraint that must hold after the invocation of an operation
powertype	class dependency	Specifies a classifier whose objects are all the children of a given parent; specifies that the target is a power-type of the source
precondition	constraint	Specifies a constraint that must hold before the invocation of an operation
process	class	Specifies a classifier whose instances represent a heavyweight flow
refine	dependency	Specifies that the source is at a finer degree of abstraction than the target
requirement	comment	Specifies a desired feature, property, or behavior of a system
responsibility	comment	Specifies a contract by or an obligation of the class
self	link end	Specifies that the corresponding object is visible because it is the dispatcher of the message

Appendix B

Stereotype/ *Keyword*	Applies to symbol	Meaning
send	dependency	Specifies that the source operation sends the target event
signal	class	Specifies an asynchronous stimulus communicated among instances
stereotype	class	Specifies that the classifier is a stereotype that may be applied to other elements
stub	package	Specifies a package that serves as a proxy for the public contents of another package
subsystem	package	Specifies a grouping of elements of which some constitute a specification of the behavior offered by the other contained elements
system	package	Specifies a package representing the entire system being modeled
table	component	Specifies a component that represents a database table
thread	class	Specifies a classifier whose instances represent a lightweight flow of control
trace	dependency	Specifies that the target is an historical ancestor of the source
type	class	Specifies an abstract class that is used only to specify the structure and behavior (but not the implementation) of a set of objects
use	dependency	Specifies that the semantics of the source element depends on the semantics of the public part of the target
utility	class	Specifies a class whose attributes and operations are all class-scoped

Tagged Values

The following tagged values are defined as standard elements of the UML. For each tagged value, this table gives its name, the element of the UML to which it applies, and its meaning.

In most cases, a tagged value is rendered by placing the tag name and its value below the name of the element to which it is attached and enclosing the tagged value in braces, as in `{location = client}`. Tags with long text values may be rendered in a separate compartment at the bottom of the classifier's icon.

Tagged value	Applies to symbol	Meaning
documentation	all elements	Specifies a comment, description, or explanation of the element to which it is attached
location	most elements	Specifies the node or component on which the element resides
persistence	class association attribute	Specifies if the state of the instance is preserved after the process that created the instance terminates; values are persistent (preserve the value) and transient (do not preserve the value)
semantics	class operation	Specifies the meaning of the class or operation

Constraints

The following constraints are defined as standard elements of the UML. For each constraint, this table gives its name, the element of the UML to which it applies, and its meaning.

In most cases, a constraint is rendered by placing it adjacent to an element and enclosing the constraint in braces, as in `{complete}`. You can also render a constraint by placing it in a note connected to its element by a dependency.

Constraint	Applies to symbol	Meaning
complete	generalization	Specifies that all children in the generalization have been specified in the model (although some may be elided in the diagram) and that no additional children are permitted
destroyed	instance link	Specifies that the instance or link is destroyed prior to completion of execution of the enclosing interaction
disjoint	generalization	Specifies that objects of the given parent may have no more than one of the given children as a type
implicit	association	Specifies that the relationship is not manifest but is only conceptual
incomplete	generalization	Specifies that not all children in the generalization have been specified (even if some are elided) and that additional children are permitted
new	instance link	Specifies that the instance or link is created during execution of the enclosing interaction
overlapping	generalization	Specifies that objects of the given parent may have more than one of the given children as a type
transient	instance link	Specifies that the instance or link is created during execution of the enclosing interaction but is destroyed before completion of execution
xor	association	Specifies that, over a set of associations, exactly one is manifest for each associated object

Appendix C
RATIONAL UNIFIED PROCESS

A process is a set of partially ordered steps intended to reach a goal. In software engineering, your goal is to efficiently and predictably deliver a software product that meets the needs of your business.

The UML is largely process-independent, meaning that you can use it with a number of software engineering processes. The Rational Unified Process is one such life cycle approach that is especially well-suited to the UML. The goal of the Rational Unified Process is to enable the production of highest quality software that meets end-user needs within predictable schedules and budgets. The Rational Unified Process captures some of the best current software development practices in a form that is tailorable for a wide range of projects and organizations. On the management side, the Rational Unified Process provides a disciplined approach on how to assign tasks and responsibilities within a software development organization.

This appendix summarizes the elements of the Rational Unified Process.

Characteristics of the Process

The Rational Unified Process is an *iterative* process. For simple systems, it would seem perfectly feasible to sequentially define the whole problem, design the entire solution, build the software, and then test the end product. However, given the complexity and sophistication demanded of current systems, this linear approach to system development is unrealistic. An iterative approach advocates an increasing understanding of the problem through successive refinements and an incremental growth of an effective solution over multiple cycles. Built into the iterative approach is the flexibility to accommodate new requirements or tactical changes in business objectives. It also allows the project to identify and resolve risks sooner rather than later.

The Rational Unified Process's activities emphasize the creation and maintenance of *models* rather than paper documents. Models—especially those specified using the UML—provide semantically rich representations of the software system under development. They can be viewed in multiple ways, and the information represented can be instantaneously captured and controlled electronically. The rationale behind the Rational Unified Process's focus on models rather than paper documents is to minimize the overhead associated with generating and maintaining documents and to maximize the relevant information content.

Development under the Rational Unified Process is *architecture-centric*. The process focuses on the early development and baselining of a software architecture. Having a robust architecture in place facilitates parallel development, minimizes rework, and increases the probability of component reuse and eventual system maintainability. This architectural blueprint serves as a solid basis against which to plan and manage software component-based development.

Development activities under the Rational Unified Process are *use case–driven*. The Rational Unified Process places strong emphasis on building systems based on a thorough understanding of how the delivered system will be used. The notions of use cases and scenarios are used to align the process flow from requirements capture through testing and to provide traceable threads through development to the delivered system.

The Rational Unified Process supports *object-oriented techniques*. Each model is object-oriented. Rational Unified Process models are based on the concepts of objects and classes and the relationships among them, and they use the UML as its common notation.

The Rational Unified Process is a *configurable* process. Although no single process is suitable for all software development organizations, the Rational Unified Process is tailorable and can be scaled to fit the needs of projects ranging from small software development teams to large development organizations. The Rational Unified Process is founded on a simple and clear process architecture that provides commonality across a family of processes, and yet can be varied to accommodate various situations. Contained in the Rational Unified Process is guidance about how to configure the process to suit the needs of an organization.

The Rational Unified Process encourages objective ongoing *quality control* and *risk management*. Quality assessment is built into the process, in all activities and involving all participants, using objective measurements and criteria. It is not treated as an afterthought or as a separate activity. Risk management is built into the process, so that risks to the success of the project are identified and attacked early in the development process, when there is time to react.

Phases and Iterations

A *phase* is the span of time between two major milestones of the process in which a well-defined set of objectives are met, artifacts are completed, and decisions are made whether to move into the next phase. As Figure C-1 illustrates, the Rational Unified Process consists of the following four phases:

1. Inception   Establish the business case for the project
2. Elaboration   Establish a project plan and a sound architecture
3. Construction Grow the system
4. Transition   Supply the system to its end users

Inception and elaboration encompass the engineering activities of the development life cycle; construction and transition constitute its production.

Within each phase are a number of iterations. An *iteration* represents a complete development cycle, from requirements capture in analysis to implementation and testing, that results in the release of an executable project.

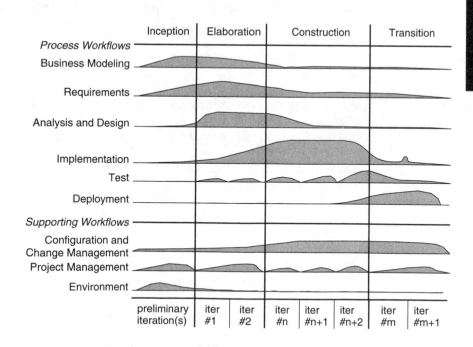

Figure C-1: The Software Development Life Cycle

Each phase and iteration has some risk mitigation focus and concludes with a well-defined milestone. The milestone review provides a point in time to assess how well key goals have been met and whether the project needs to be restructured in any way to proceed.

Phases

Inception During the inception phase, you establish the business case for the system and delimit the project's scope. The business case includes success criteria, risk assessment, estimates of the resources needed, and a phase plan showing a schedule of major milestones. During inception, it's common to create an executable prototype that serves as a proof of concept.

At the end of the inception phase, you examine the life cycle objectives of the project and decide whether to proceed with full-scale development.

Elaboration The goals of the elaboration phase are to analyze the problem domain, establish a sound architectural foundation, develop the project plan, and eliminate the highest risk elements of the project. Architectural decisions must be made with an understanding of the whole system. This implies that you describe most of the system's requirements. To verify the architecture, you implement a system that demonstrates the architectural choices and executes significant use cases.

At the end of the elaboration phase, you examine the detailed system objectives and scope, the choice of architecture, and the resolution of major risks, and decide whether to proceed with construction.

Construction During the construction phase, you iteratively and incrementally develop a complete product that is ready to transition to its user community. This implies describing the remaining requirements and acceptance criteria, fleshing out the design, and completing the implementation and test of the software.

At the end of the construction phase, you decide if the software, sites, and users are all ready to go operational.

Transition During the transition phase, you deploy the software to the user community. Once the system has been put into the hands of its end users, issues often arise that require additional development in order to adjust the system, correct some undetected problems, or finish some features that have been postponed. This phase typically starts with a beta release of the system, which is then replaced with the production system.

At the end of the transition phase, you decide whether the life cycle objectives of the project have been met and determine if you should start another development cycle. This is also a point at which you wrap up the lessons learned on the project in order to improve your development process, which will be applied to the next project.

Iterations

Each phase in the Rational Unified Process can be further broken down into iterations. An iteration is a complete development loop resulting in a release (internal or external) of an executable product constituting a subset of the final product under development, which then is grown incrementally from iteration to iteration to become the final system. Each iteration goes through the various process workflows, although with a different emphasis on each process workflow, depending on the phase. During inception, the focus is on requirements capture. During elaboration, the focus turns toward analysis and design. In construction, implementation is the central activity, and transition centers on deployment.

Development Cycles

Going through the four major phases is called a development cycle, and it results in one software generation. The first pass through the four phases is called the initial development cycle. Unless the life of the product stops, an existing product will evolve into its next generation by repeating the same sequence of inception, elaboration, construction, and transition phases. This is the evolution of the system, so the development cycles after the initial development cycles are its evolution cycles.

Process Workflows

The Rational Unified Process consists of nine process workflows.

1. Business modeling   Describes the structure and dynamics of the organization
2. Requirements   Describes the use case–based method for eliciting requirements
3. Analysis and design   Describes the multiple architectural views

Appendix C

4.	Implementation	Takes into account software development, unit test, and integration
5.	Test	Describes test cases, procedures, and defect-tracking metrics
6.	Deployment	Covers the deliverable system configuration
7.	Configuration management	Controls changes to and maintains the integrity of a project's artifacts
8.	Project Management	Describes various strategies of working with an iterative process
9.	Environment	Covers the necessary infrastructure required to develop a system

Captured within each process workflow is a set of correlated artifacts and activities. An *artifact* is some document, report, or executable that is produced, manipulated, or consumed. An *activity* describes the tasks—thinking steps, performing steps, and reviewing steps—performed by workers to create or modify artifacts, together with the techniques and guidelines to perform the tasks, possibly including the use of tools to help automate some of the tasks.

Important connections among the artifacts are associated with certain of these process workflows. For example, the use case model generated during requirements capture is *realized by* the design model from the analysis and design process, *implemented by* the implementation model from the implementation process, and *verified by* the test model from the test process.

Artifacts

Each Rational Unified Process activity has associated artifacts, either required as an input or generated as an output. Some artifacts are used to direct input to subsequent activities, kept as reference resources on the project, or generated in a format as contractual deliverables.

Models

Modeling is discussed in Chapter 1.

Models are the most important kind of artifact in the Rational Unified Process. A model is a simplification of reality, created to better understand the system being created. In the Rational Unified Process, there are nine models that collectively cover all the important decisions that go into visualizing, specifying, constructing, and documenting a software-intensive system.

1. Business model   Establishes an abstraction of the organization
2. Domain model   Establishes the context of the system
3. Use case model   Establishes the system's functional requirements
4. Analysis model (optional)   Establishes an idea design
5. Design model   Establishes the vocabulary of the problem and its solution
6. Process model (optional)   Establishes the system's concurrency and synchronization mechanisms
7. Deployment model   Establishes the hardware topology on which the system is executed
8. Implementation model   Establishes the parts used to assemble and release the physical system
9. Test model   Establishes the paths by which the system is validated and verified

Architecture is discussed in Chapter 2.

A view is a projection into a model. In the Rational Unified Process, the architecture of a system is captured in five interlocking views: the design view, process view, deployment view, implementation view, and use case view.

Other Artifacts

The Rational Unified Process's artifacts are categorized as either management artifacts or technical artifacts. The Rational Unified Process's technical artifacts may be divided into four main sets.

1. Requirements set   Describes what the system must do
2. Design set   Describes how the system is to be constructed
3. Implementation set   Describes the assembly of developed software components
4. Deployment set   Provides all the data for the deliverable configuration

Requirements Set This set groups all information describing what the system must do. This may comprise a use case model, a nonfunctional requirements model, a domain model, an analysis model, and other forms of expression of the user's needs, including but not limited to mock-ups, interface prototypes, regulatory constraints, and so on.

Design Set This set groups information describing how the system is to be constructed and captures decisions about how the system is to be built, taking into account all the constraints of time, budget, legacy, reuse, quality objec-

Appendix C

tives, and so forth. This may comprise a design model, a test model, and other forms of expression of the system's nature, including but not limited to prototypes and executable architectures.

Implementation Set This set groups all information about the elements of the software that comprises the system, including but not limited to source code in various programming languages, configuration files, data files, software components, and so on, together with the information describing how to assemble the system.

Deployment Set This set groups all information about the way the software is actually packaged, shipped, installed, and run on the target environment.

GLOSSARY

abstract class A class that cannot be directly instantiated.

abstraction The essential characteristics of an entity that distinguish it from all other kinds of entities. An abstraction defines a boundary relative to the perspective of the viewer.

action An executable atomic computation that results in a change in state of the system or the return of a value.

action expression An expression that evaluates to a collection of actions.

action state A state that represents the execution of an atomic action, typically the invocation of an operation.

activation The execution of an operation.

active class A class whose instances are active objects.

active object An object that owns a process or thread and can initiate control activity.

activity Ongoing nonatomic execution within a state machine.

activity diagram A diagram that shows the flow from activity to activity; activity diagrams address the dynamic view of a system. A special case of a state diagram in which all or most of the states are activity states and in which all or most of the transitions are triggered by completion of activities in the source states.

actor A coherent set of roles that users of use cases play when interacting with the use cases.

actual parameter A function or procedure argument.

adornment Detail from an element's specification added to its basic graphical notation.

aggregate A class that represents the "whole" in an aggregation relationship.

aggregation A special form of association that specifies a whole-part relationship between the aggregate (the whole) and a component (the part).

architecture The set of significant decisions about the organization of a software system, the selection of the structural elements and their interfaces by which the system is composed, together with their behavior as specified in the collaborations among those elements, the composition of these structural and behavioral elements into progressively larger subsystems, and the architectural style that guides this organization—these elements and their interfaces, their collaborations, and their composition. Software architecture is not only concerned with structure and behavior, but also with usage, functionality, performance, resilience, reuse, comprehensibility, economic and technology constraints and trade-offs, and aesthetic concerns.

architecture-centric In the context of the software development life cycle, a process that focuses on the early development and baselining of a software architecture, then uses the system's architecture as a primary artifact for conceptualizing, constructing, managing, and evolving the system under development.

argument A specific value corresponding to a parameter.

artifact A piece of information that is used or produced by a software development process.

association A structural relationship that describes a set of links, in which a link is a connection among objects; the semantic relationship between two or more classifiers that involves the connections among their instances.

association class A modeling element that has both association and class properties. An association class can be seen as an association that also has class properties, or as a class that also has association properties.

association end The endpoint of an association, which connects that association to a classifier.

asynchronous action A request in which the sending object does not pause to wait for results.

attribute A named property of a classifier that describes a range of values that instances of the property may hold.

behavior The observable effects of an event, including its results.

behavioral feature A dynamic feature of an element such as an operation or method.

binary association An association between two classes.

binding The creation of an element from a template by supplying arguments for the parameters of the template.

Boolean An enumeration whose values are true and false.

Boolean expression An expression that evaluates to a Boolean value.

cardinality The number of elements in a set.

child A subclass.

class A description of a set of objects that share the same attributes, operations, relationships, and semantics.

class diagram A diagram that shows a set of classes, interfaces, and collaborations and their relationships; class diagrams address the static design view of a system; a diagram that shows a collection of declarative (static) elements.

classifier A mechanism that describes structural and behavioral features. Classifiers include classes, interfaces, datatypes, signals, components, nodes, use cases, and subsystems.

client A classifier that requests service from another classifier.

collaboration A society of roles and other elements that work together to provide some cooperative behavior that's bigger than the sum of all its parts; the specification of how an element, such as a use case or an operation, is realized by a set of classifiers and associations playing specific roles and used in a specific way.

collaboration diagram An interaction diagram that emphasizes the structural organization of the objects that send and receive messages; a diagram that shows interactions organized around instances and their links to each other.

comment An annotation attached to an element or a collection of elements.

component A physical and replaceable part of a system that conforms to and provides the realization of a set of interfaces.

component diagram A diagram that shows the organization of and dependencies among a set of components; component diagrams address the static implementation view of a system.

composite A class that is related to one or more classes by a composition relationship.

composite state A state that consists of either concurrent substates or disjoint substates.

composition A form of aggregation with strong ownership and coincident lifetime of the parts by the whole; parts with nonfixed multiplicity may

Glossary

be created after the composite itself, but once created they live and die with it; such parts can also be explicitly removed before the death of the composite.

concrete class A class that can be directly instantiated.

concurrency The occurrence of two or more activities during the same time interval. Concurrency can be achieved by interleaving or simultaneously executing two or more threads.

concurrent substate An orthogonal substate that can be held simultaneously with other substates contained in the same composite state.

constraint An extension of the semantics of a UML element, allowing you to add new rules or modify existing ones.

container An object that exists to contain other objects and that provides operations to access or iterate over its contents.

containment hierarchy A namespace hierarchy consisting of elements and the aggregation relationships that exist between them.

context A set of related elements for a particular purpose, such as to specify an operation.

construction The third phase of the software development life cycle, in which the software is brought from an executable architectural baseline to the point at which it is ready to be transitioned to the user community.

datatype A type whose values have no identity. Datatypes include primitive built-in types (such as numbers and strings), as well as enumeration types (such as Boolean).

delegation The ability of an object to issue a message to another object in response to a message.

dependency A semantic relationship between two things in which a change to one thing (the independent thing) may affect the semantics of the other thing (the dependent thing).

deployment diagram A diagram that shows the configuration of run time processing nodes and the components that live on them; a deployment diagram addresses the static deployment view of a system.

deployment view The view of a system's architecture that encompasses the nodes that form the system's hardware topology on which the system executes; a deployment view addresses the distribution, delivery, and installation of the parts that make up the physical system.

derived element A model element that can be computed from another element, but that is shown for clarity or that is included for design purposes even though it adds no semantic information.

design view The view of a system's architecture that encompasses the classes, interfaces, and collaborations that form the vocabulary of the problem and its solution; a design view addresses the functional requirements of a system.

diagram The graphical presentation of a set of elements, most often rendered as a connected graph of vertices (things) and arcs (relationships).

disjoint substate A substate that cannot be held simultaneously with other substates contained in the same composite state.

distribution unit A set of objects or components that are allocated to a node as a group.

domain An area of knowledge or activity characterized by a set of concepts and terminology understood by practitioners in that area.

dynamic classification A semantic variation of generalization in which an object may change type or role.

dynamic view An aspect of a system that emphasizes its behavior.

elaboration The second phase of the software development life cycle, in which the product vision and its architecture are defined.

element An atomic constituent of a model.

elision Modeling an element with certain of its parts hidden to simplify the view.

enumeration A list of named values used as the range of a particular attribute type.

event The specification of a significant occurrence that has a location in time and space; in the context of state machines, an event is an occurrence of a stimulus that can trigger a state transition.

execution The running of a dynamic model.

export In the context of packages, to make an element visible outside its enclosing namespace.

expression A string that evaluates to a value of a particular type.

extensibility mechanism One of three mechanisms (stereotypes, tagged values, and constraints) that permit you to extend the UML in controlled ways.

feature A property, such as an operation or an attribute, that is encapsulated within another entity, such as an interface, a class, or a datatype.

fire To execute a state transition.

Glossary

focus of control A symbol on a sequence diagram that shows the period of time during which an object is performing an action directly or through a subordinate operation.

formal parameter A parameter.

forward engineering The process of transforming a model into code through a mapping to a specific implementation language.

framework An architectural pattern that provides an extensible template for applications within a domain.

generalization A specialization/generalization relationship, in which objects of the specialized element (the child) are substitutable for objects of the generalized element (the parent).

guard condition A condition that must be satisfied in order to enable an associated transition to fire.

implementation A concrete realization of the contract declared by an interface; a definition of how something is constructed or computed.

implementation inheritance The inheritance of the implementation of a more specific element; also includes inheritance of the interface.

implementation view The view of a system's architecture that encompasses the components used to assemble and release the physical system; an implementation view addresses the configuration management of the system's releases, made up of somewhat independent components that can be assembled in various ways to produce a running system.

import In the context of packages, a dependency that shows the package whose classes may be referenced within a given package (including packages recursively embedded within it).

inception The first phase of the software development life cycle, in which the seed idea for the development is brought to the point of being sufficiently well-founded to warrant entering into the elaboration phase.

incomplete Modeling an element with certain of its parts missing.

inconsistent Modeling an element for which the integrity of the model is not guaranteed.

incremental In the context of the software development life cycle, a process that involves the continuous integration of the system's architecture to produce releases, with each new release embodying incremental improvements over the other.

inheritance The mechanism by which more-specific elements incorporate the structure and behavior or more-general elements.

instance A concrete manifestation of an abstraction; an entity to which a set of operations can be applied and that has a state that stores the effects of the operations.

integrity How things properly and consistently relate to one another.

interaction A behavior that comprises a set of messages that are exchanged among a set of objects within a particular context to accomplish a purpose.

interaction diagram A diagram that shows an interaction, consisting of a set of objects and their relationships, including the messages that may be dispatched among them; interaction diagrams address the dynamic view of a system; a generic term that applies to several types of diagrams that emphasize object interactions, including collaboration diagrams, sequence diagrams, and activity diagrams.

iteration A distinct set of activities with a baseline plan and evaluation criteria that results in a release, either internal or external.

iterative In the context of the software development life cycle, a process that involves managing a stream of executable releases.

interface A collection of operations that are used to specify a service of a class or a component.

interface inheritance The inheritance of the interface of a more specific element; does not include inheritance of the implementation.

level of abstraction One place in a hierarchy of abstractions ranging from high levels of abstraction (very abstract) to low levels of abstraction (very concrete).

link A semantic connection among objects; an instance of an association.

link end An instance of an association end.

location The placement of a component on a node.

mechanism A design pattern that applies to a society of classes.

message A specification of a communication between objects that conveys information with the expectation that activity will ensue; the receipt of a message instance is normally considered an instance of an event.

metaclass A class whose instances are classes.

method The implementation of an operation.

model A simplification of reality, created in order to better understand the system being created; a semantically closed abstraction of a system.

multiple classification A semantic variation of generalization in which an object may belong directly to more than one class.

multiple inheritance A semantic variation of generalization in which a child may have more than one parent.

multiplicity A specification of the range of allowable cardinalities that a set may assume.

n-ary association An association among three or more classes.

name What you call a thing, relationship, or diagram; a string used to identify an element.

namespace A scope in which names may be defined and used; within a namespace, each name denotes a unique element.

node A physical element that exists at run time and that represents a computational resource, generally having at least some memory and, often times, processing capability.

note A graphic symbol for rendering constraints or comments attached to an element or a collection of elements.

object A concrete manifestation of an abstraction; an entity with a well-defined boundary and identity that encapsulates state and behavior; an instance of a class.

Object Constraint Language (OCL) A formal language used to express side effect–free constraints.

object diagram A diagram that shows a set of objects and their relationships at a point in time; object diagrams address the static design view or static process view of a system.

object lifeline A line in a sequence diagram that represents the existence of an object over a period of time.

operation The implementation of a service that can be requested from any object of the class in order to affect behavior.

package A general-purpose mechanism for organizing elements into groups.

parameter The specification of a variable that can be changed, passed, or returned.

parameterized element The descriptor for an element with one or more unbound parameters.

parent A superclass.

persistent object An object that exists after the process or thread that created it has ceased to exist.

pattern A common solution to a common problem in a given context.

phase The span of time between two major milestones of the development process during which a well-defined set of objectives are met, artifacts are completed, and decisions are made whether to move into the next phase.

postcondition A constraint that must be true at the completion of an operation.

precondition A constraint that must be true when an operation is invoked.

primitive type A basic type, such as an integer or a string.

process A heavyweight flow of control that can execute concurrently with other processes.

process view The view of a system's architecture that encompasses the threads and processes that form the system's concurrency and synchronization mechanisms; a process view addresses the performance, scalability, and throughput of the system.

product The artifacts of development, such as models, code, documentation, and work plans.

projection A mapping from a set to a subset of it.

property A named value denoting a characteristic of an element.

pseudostate A vertex in a state machine that has the form of a state but doesn't behave as a state; pseudostates include initial, final, and history vertices.

qualifier An association attribute whose values partition the set of objects related to an object across an association.

realization A semantic relationships between classifiers, in which one classifier specifies a contract that another classifier guarantees to carry out.

receive The handling of a message instance passed from a sender object.

receiver The object handling a message instance passed from a sender object.

refinement A relationship that represents a fuller specification of something that has already been specified at a certain level of detail.

relationship A semantic connection among elements.

release A relatively complete and consistent set of artifacts delivered to an internal or external user; the delivery of such a set.

request The specification of a stimulus sent to an object.

requirement A desired feature, property, or behavior of a system.

Glossary

responsibility A contract or obligation of a type or class.

reverse engineering The process of transforming code into a model through a mapping from a specific implementation language.

risk-driven In the context of the software development life cycle, a process in which each new release is focused on attacking and reducing the most significant risks to the success of the project.

role The behavior of an entity participating in a particular context.

scenario A specific sequence of actions that illustrates behavior.

scope The context that gives meaning to a name.

send The passing of a message instance from a sender object to a receiver object.

sender The object passing a message instance to a receiver object.

sequence diagram An interaction diagram that emphasizes the time ordering of messages.

signal The specification of an asynchronous stimulus communicated between instances.

signature The name and parameters of an operation.

single inheritance A semantic variation of generalization in which a child may have only one parent.

specification A textual statement of the syntax and semantics of a specific building block; a declarative description of what something is or does.

state A condition or situation during the life of an object during which it satisfies some condition, performs some activity, or waits for some event.

statechart diagram A diagram that shows a state machine; statechart diagrams address the dynamic view of a system

state machine A behavior that specifies the sequences of states an object goes through during its lifetime in response to events, together with its responses to those events.

static classification A semantic variation of generalization in which an object may not change type and may not change role.

static view An aspect of a system that emphasizes its structure.

stereotype An extension of the vocabulary of the UML, which allows you to create new kinds of building blocks that are derived from existing ones but that are specific to your problem.

stimulus An operation or a signal.

string A sequence of text characters.

structural feature A static feature of an element.

subclass In a generalization relationship, the specialization of another class, the parent.

substate A state that is part of a composite state.

subsystem A grouping of elements of which some constitute a specification of the behavior offered by the other contained elements.

superclass In a generalization relationship, the generalization of another class, the child.

supplier A type, class, or component that provides services that can be invoked by others.

swimlane A partition on an interaction diagram for organizing responsibilities for actions.

synchronous action A request in which the sending object pauses to wait for results.

system Possibly decomposed into a collection of subsystems, a set of elements organized to accomplish a specific purpose and described by a set of models, possibly from different viewpoints.

tagged value An extension of the properties of a UML element, which allows you to create new information in that element's specification.

template A parameterized element.

task A single path of execution through a program, a dynamic model, or some other representation of control flow; a thread or a process.

thread A lightweight flow of control that can execute concurrently with other threads in the same process.

time A value representing an absolute or relative moment.

time event An event that denotes the time elapsed since the current state was entered.

time expression An expression that evaluates to an absolute or relative value of time.

timing constraint A semantic statement about the relative or absolute value of time or duration.

timing mark A denotation for the time at which an event occurs.

trace A dependency that indicates an historical or process relationship between two elements that represent the same concept, without rules for deriving one from the other.

transient object An object that exists only during the execution of the thread or process that created it.

transition The fourth phase of the software development life cycle, in which the software is turned into the hands of the user community; a relationship between two states indicating that an object in the first state will perform certain actions and enter the second state when a specified event occurs and conditions are satisfied.

type A stereotype of class used to specify a domain of objects, together with the operations (but not methods) applicable to the objects.

type expression An expression that evaluates to a reference to one or more types.

UML The Unified Modeling Language, a language for visualizing, specifying, constructing, and documenting the artifacts of a software-intensive system.

usage A dependency in which one element (the client) requires the presence of another element (the supplier) for its correct functioning or implementation.

use case A description of a set of sequences of actions, including variants, that a system performs that yields an observable result of value to an actor.

use case diagram A diagram that shows a set of use cases and actors and their relationships; use case diagrams address the static use case view of a system.

use case–driven In the context of the software development life cycle, a process in which use cases are used as a primary artifact for establishing the desired behavior of the system, for verifying and validating the system's architecture, for testing, and for communicating among the stakeholders of the project.

use case view The view of a system's architecture that encompasses the use cases that describe the behavior of the system as seen by its end users, analysts, and testers.

value An element of a type domain.

view A projection into a model, which is seen from a given perspective or vantage point and omits entities that are not relevant to this perspective.

visibility How a name can be seen and used by others.

INDEX

Index

Index

This book is published as part of ACM Press Books—a collaboration between the Association for Computing (ACM) and Addison Wesley Longman. ACM is the oldest and largest educational and scientific society in the information technology field. Through its high-quality publications and services, ACM is a major force in advancing the skills and knowledge of IT professionals throughout the world. For further information about ACM, contact:

ACM Member Services
1515 Broadway, 17th Floor
New York, NY 10036-5701
Phone: 1-212-626-0500
Fax: 1-212-944-1318
E-mail: ACMHELP@ACM.org

ACM European Service Center
108 Cowley Road
Oxford OX41JF
United Kingdom
Phone: +44-1865-382338
Fax: +44-1865-381338
E-mail: acm_europe@acm.org
URL: http://www.acm.org

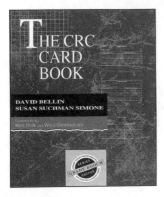

The CRC Card Book

David Bellin and Susan Suchman Simone
Forewords by Kent Beck and Ward Cunningham
Addison-Wesley Object Technology Series

CRC Cards help project teams "act out" the various parts of a problem domain. The application developer can use these cards to define the Classes, the Relationships between classes, and the Collaboration between these classes (CRC) prior to beginning the object-oriented design of the application program. The case studies in this book are presented in the engaging style of a novella to demonstrate how personalities and organizational culture come into play when using the CRC technique. C++, Java, and Smalltalk experts provide implementation examples in each language.

0-201-89535-8 • Paperback • 320 Pages • ©1997

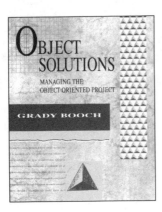

Object Solutions

Managing the Object-Oriented Project
Grady Booch
Addison-Wesley Object Technology Series

Object Solutions is a direct outgrowth of Grady Booch's experience with object-oriented projects in development around the world. This book focuses on the development process, and is the perfect resource for developers and managers who want to implement object technologies for the first time or refine their existing object-oriented development practice. Drawing upon his knowledge of strategies used in both successful and unsuccessful projects, the author offers pragmatic advice for applying object technologies and controlling projects effectively.

0-8053-0594-7 • Paperback • 336 pages • ©1996

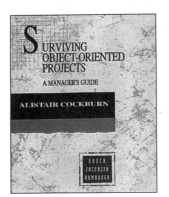

Surviving Object-Oriented Projects

A Manager's Guide
Alistair Cockburn
Addison-Wesley Object Technology Series

This book allows you to survive, and ultimately succeed with, an object-oriented project. Alistair Cockburn draws on his personal experience and extensive knowledge to provide the information that managers need to combat the unforeseen challenges that await them during project implementation. *Surviving Object-Oriented Projects* supports its key points through short case studies taken from real object-oriented projects. An appendix collects these guidelines and solutions into brief "crib sheets"—ideal for handy reference.

0-201-49834-0 • Paperback • 272 pages • ©1998

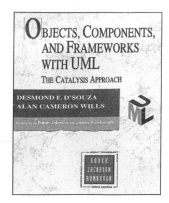

Objects, Components, and Frameworks with UML
The Catalysis Approach
Desmond F. D'Souza and Alan Cameron Wills
Addison-Wesley Object Technology Series

Catalysis is a rapidly emerging UML-based method for component and framework-based development with objects. The authors describe a unique UML-based approach to precise specification of component interfaces using a type model, enabling precise external description of behavior without constraining implementations. This approach provides application developers and system architects with well-defined and reusable techniques that help them build open distributed object systems from components and frameworks.

0-201-31012-0 • Paperback • 800 pages • ©1999

Real-Time UML
Developing Efficient Objects for Embedded Systems
Bruce Powel Douglass
Addison-Wesley Object Technology Series

The Unified Modeling Language is particularly suited to modeling real-time and embedded systems. *Real-Time UML* is the introduction that developers of real-time systems need to make the transition to object-oriented analysis and design with UML. The book covers the important features of the UML, and shows how to effectively use these features to model real-time systems. Special in-depth discussions of finite state machines, object identification strategies, and real-time design patterns to help beginning and experienced developers alike are also included.

0-201-32579-9 • Paperback • 400 pages • ©1998

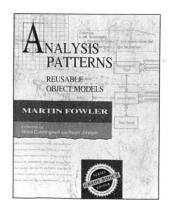

Analysis Patterns
Reusable Object Models
Martin Fowler
Addison-Wesley Object Technology Series

Martin Fowler shares with you his wealth of object modeling experience and his keen eye for solving repeating problems and transforming the solutions into reusable models. *Analysis Patterns* provides a catalog of patterns that have emerged in a wide range of domains, including trading, measurement, accounting, and organizational relationships.

0-201-89542-0 • Hardcover • 672 pages • ©1997

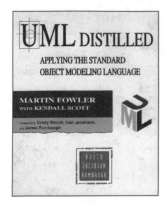

UML Distilled

Applying the Standard Object Modeling Language
Martin Fowler with Kendall Scott
Foreword by Grady Booch, Ivar Jacobson, and James Rumbaugh
Addison-Wesley Object Technology Series

Recipient of *Software Development* magazine's 1997 Productivity Award, this concise overview introduces you to the Unified Modeling Language, highlighting the key elements of its notation, semantics, and processes. Included is a brief explanation of UML's history, development, and rationale, as well as discussions on how UML can be integrated into the object-oriented development process. The book also profiles various modeling techniques associated with UML—use cases, CRC cards, design by contract, dynamic classification, interfaces, and abstract classes.

0-201-32563-2 • Paperback • 208 pages • ©1997

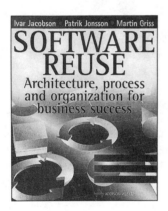

Software Reuse

Architecture, Process, and Organization for Business Success
Ivar Jacobson, Martin Griss, and Patrik Jonsson
Addison-Wesley Object Technology Series

This book brings software engineers, designers, programmers, and their managers a giant step closer to a future in which object-oriented component-based software engineering is the norm. Jacobson, Griss, and Jonsson develop a coherent model and set of guidelines for ensuring success with large-scale, systematic, object-oriented reuse. Their framework, referred to as "Reuse-Driven Software Engineering Business" (Reuse Business) deals systematically with the key business process, architecture, and organization issues that hinder success with reuse.

0-201-92476-5 • Hardcover • 560 pages • ©1997

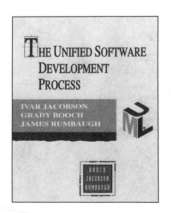

The Unified Software Development Process

Ivar Jacobson, Grady Booch, and James Rumbaugh
Addison-Wesley Object Technology Series

The Unified Software Development Process goes beyond other object-oriented analysis and design methods by detailing a family of processes that incorporate the complete lifecycle of software development. This new book, representing the collaboration of Ivar Jacobson, Grady Booch, and James Rumbaugh, clearly describes the different higher-level constructs—notation as well as semantics—used in the models. Thus stereotypes such as use cases and actors, packages, classes, interfaces, active classes, processes and threads, nodes, and most relations are described intuitively in the context of a model.

0-201-57169-2 • Hardcover • 512 pages • ©1999

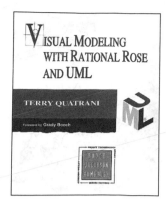

Visual Modeling with Rational Rose and UML

Terry Quatrani
Addison-Wesley Object Technology Series

Terry Quatrani, the Rose Evangelist for Rational Software Corporation, teaches you visual modeling and the UML, enabling you to apply an iterative and incremental process to analysis and design. With the practical direction offered in this book, you will be able to specify, visualize, document, and create software solutions. Highlights of this book include an examination of system behavior from a use case approach; a discussion of the concepts and notations used for finding objects and classes; an introduction to the notation needed to create and document a system's architecture; and a review of the iteration planning process.

0-201-31016-3 • Paperback • 240 pages • ©1998

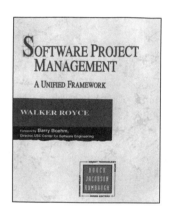

Software Project Management

A Unified Framework
Walker Royce
Foreword by Barry Boehm
Addison-Wesley Object Technology Series

This book presents a new management framework uniquely suited to the complexities of modern software development. Walker Royce's pragmatic perspective exposes the shortcomings of many well-accepted management priorities and equips software professionals with state-of-the-art knowledge derived from his twenty years of successful from-the-trenches management experience. In short, the book provides the software industry with field-proven benchmarks for making tactical decisions and strategic choices that will enhance an organization's probability of success.

0-201-30958-0 • Hardcover • 448 pages • ©1998

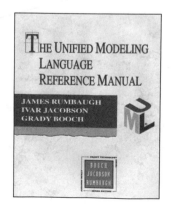

The Unified Modeling Language Reference Manual

James Rumbaugh, Ivar Jacobson, and Grady Booch
Addison-Wesley Object Technology Series

James Rumbaugh, Ivar Jacobson, and Grady Booch have created the definitive reference to the UML. This two-color book covers every aspect and detail of the UML and presents the modeling language in a useful reference format that serious software architects or programmers should have on their bookshelf. The book is organized by topic and designed for quick access. The authors also provide the necessary information to enable existing OMT, Booch, and OOSE notation users to make the transition to UML. The book provides an overview of the semantic foundation of the UML through a concise appendix.

0-201-30998-X • Hardcover with CD-ROM • 480 pages • ©1999

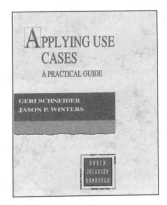

Applying Use Cases
A Practical Guide
Geri Schneider and Jason P. Winters
Addison-Wesley Object Technology Series

Applying Use Cases provides a practical and clear introduction to developing use cases, demonstrating their use via a continuing case study. Using the Unified Software Development Process as a framework and the Unified Modeling Language as a notation, the authors step the reader through applying use cases in the different phases of the process, focusing on where and how use cases are best applied. The book also offers insight into the common mistakes and pitfalls that can plague an object-oriented project.

0-201-30981-5 • Paperback • 208 pages • ©1998

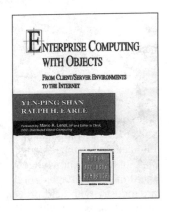

Enterprise Computing with Objects
From Client/Server Environments to the Internet
Yen-Ping Shan and Ralph H. Earle
Addison-Wesley Object Technology Series

This book helps you place rapidly evolving technologies—such as the Internet, the World Wide Web, distributed computing, object technology, and client/server systems—in their appropriate contexts when preparing for the development, deployment, and maintenance of information systems. The authors distinguish what is essential from what is incidental, while imparting a clear understanding of how the underlying technologies fit together. The book examines essential topics, including data persistence, security, performance, scalability, and development tools.

0-201-32566-7 • Paperback • 448 pages • ©1998

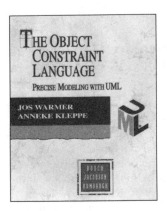

The Object Constraint Language
Precise Modeling with UML
Jos Warmer and Anneke Kleppe
Addison-Wesley Object Technology Series

The Object Constraint Language is a new notational language, a subset of the Unified Modeling Language, that allows software developers to express a set of rules that govern very specific aspects of an object in object-oriented applications. With the OCL, developers are able to more easily express unique limitations and write the fine print that is often necessary in complex software designs. The authors' pragmatic approach and illustrative use of examples will help application developers to quickly get up to speed.

0-201-37940-6 • Paperback • 144 pages • ©1999

Addison-Wesley Computer and Engineering Publishing Group

Free
Object Technology Poster

Register this Book

Visit: **http://www.awl.com/cseng/register**

Register your book by entering this code: **alih-lcce-htnz-jpiv**, and we will mail you a copy of this useful poster, highlighting key elements of UML Notation and key figures from this book a handsome display to be referred to again and again. Offer available while poster supplies last.

Contact Us via Email

cepubprof@awl.com
Ask general questions about our books.
Sign up for our electronic mailing lists.
Submit corrections for our web site.

bexpress@awl.com
Request an Addison-Wesley catalog.
Get answers to questions regarding
your order or our products.

innovations@awl.com
Request a current Innovations Newsletter.

webmaster@awl.com
Send comments about our web site.

jcs@awl.com
Submit a book proposal.
Send errata for an Addison-Wesley book.

cepubpublicity@awl.com
Request a review copy for a member of the media
interested in reviewing new Addison-Wesley titles.

We encourage you to patronize the many fine retailers who stock Addison-Wesley titles. Visit our online directory to find stores near you or visit our online store: **http://store.awl.com/** or call **800-824-7799**.

Addison Wesley Longman
Computer and Engineering Publishing Group
One Jacob Way, Reading, Massachusetts 01867 USA
TEL 781-944-3700 ¥ FAX 781-942-3076

BIRKBECK COLLEGE

1911685927

BIRKBECK COLLEGE
Malet Street, London WC1E 7HX
020 7631 6239
If not previously recalled for another reader,
this book should be returned or renewed
before the latest date stamped below.

9/8/00

1 7 MAY 2002   2 7 JUN 2005

- 8 FEB 2001   0 8 AUG 2002   1 2 APR 2007

1 3 MAR 2001   1 3 SEP 2002

2 6 MAR 2001   - 2 JAN 2003   1 7 MAY 2009

18/4/01
9/5/01   0 6 FEB 2003
30/5/01   3 0 SEP 2003
27/6/01   - 1 MAR 2010

                2 9 NOV 2003

3 1 OCT 2001   2 2 DEC 2003
2 0 MAR 2002   2 2 JUL 2004

2 8 APR 2002   1 7 FEB 2005